T0390732

Anti-Veiling Campaigns in the Muslim World

In recent years bitter controversies have erupted across Europe and the Middle East about women's veiling, and especially their wearing of the face-veil or niqab. Yet the deeper issues contained within these controversies—secularism versus religious belief, individual freedom versus social or family coercion, identity versus integration—are not new but are strikingly prefigured by earlier conflicts. This book examines the state-sponsored anti-veiling campaigns that swept across wide swathes of the Muslim world in the inter-war period, especially in Turkey and the Balkans, Iran, Afghanistan, and the Soviet republics of the Caucasus and Central Asia. It shows how veiling was officially discouraged and ridiculed as backward and, although it was rarely banned, veiling was politicized and turned into a rallying-point for a wider opposition. Asking a number of questions about this earlier anti-veiling discourse and the policies flowing from it, and the reactions that it provoked, the book illuminates and contextualizes contemporary debates about gender, Islam and modernism.

Stephanie Cronin is a Lecturer in Iranian History at the University of Oxford, UK.

Durham Modern Middle East and Islamic World Series

Series Editor: Anoushiravan Ehteshami
University of Durham

1. **Economic Development in Saudi Arabia**
   *Rodney Wilson, with
   Abdullah Al-Salamah,
   Monica Malik and
   Ahmed Al-Rajhi*

2. **Islam Encountering Globalisation**
   Edited by Ali Mohammadi

3. **China's Relations with Arabia and the Gulf, 1949–99**
   Mohamed Bin Huwaidin

4. **Good Governance in the Middle East Oil Monarchies**
   *Edited by Tom Pierre Najem
   and Martin Hetherington*

5. **The Middle East's Relations with Asia and Russia**
   *Edited by Hannah Carter and
   Anoushiravan Ehteshami*

6. **Israeli Politics and the Middle East Peace Process, 1988–2002**
   Hassan A. Barari

7. **The Communist Movement in the Arab World**
   Tareq Y. Ismael

8. **Oman – The Islamic Democratic Tradition**
   Hussein Ghubash

9. **The Secret Israeli-Palestinian Negotiations in Oslo**
   Their success and why
   the process ultimately failed
   Sven Behrendt

10. **Globalization and Geopolitics in the Middle East**
    Old games, new rules
    Anoushiravan Ehteshami

11. **Iran-Europe Relations**
    Challenges and opportunities
    Seyyed Hossein Mousavian

12. **Islands and International Politics in the Persian Gulf**
    The Abu Musa and Tunbs in
    strategic perspective
    Kourosh Ahmadi

13. **Monetary Union in the Gulf**
    Prospects for a single currency
    in the Arabian Peninsula
    Emilie Rutledge

14. **Contested Sudan**
    The political economy of war
    and reconstruction
    Ibrahim Elnur

15. **Palestinian Politics and the Middle East Peace Process**
    Consensus and competition in
    the Palestinian negotiation team
    Ghassan Khatib

16. **Islam in the Eyes of the West**
Images and realities in an age
of terror
*Edited by Tareq Y. Ismael and
Andrew Rippin*

17. **Islamic Extremism in Kuwait**
From the Muslim Brotherhood
to Al-Qaeda and other Islamic
political groups
Falah Abdullah al-Mdaires

18. **Iraq, Democracy and the Future
of the Muslim World**
*Edited by Ali Paya and
John Esposito*

19. **Islamic Entrepreneurship**
*Rasem N. Kayed and
M. Kabir Hassan*

20. **Iran and the International
System**
*Edited by Anoushiravan
Ehteshami and Reza Molavi*

21. **The International Politics of the
Red Sea**
*Anoushiravan Ehteshami and
Emma C. Murphy*

22. **Palestinian Christians in Israel**
State attitudes towards
non-Muslims in a Jewish State
Una McGahern

23. **Iran–Turkey Relations,
1979–2011**
Conceptualising the dynamics
of politics, religion and security
in middle-power states
Suleyman Elik

24. **The Sudanese Communist Party**
Ideology and party politics
Tareq Y. Ismael

25. **The Muslim Brotherhood in
Contemporary Egypt**
Democracy defined or confined?
Mariz Tadros

26. **Social and Gender Inequality in
Oman**
The power of religious and
political tradition
Khalid M. Al-Azri

27. **American Democracy
Promotion in the Changing
Middle East**
From Bush to Obama
*Edited by Shahram Akbarzadeh,
James Piscatori,
Benjamin MacQueen and
Amin Saikal*

28. **China-Saudi Arabia Relations,
1990–2012**
Marriage of convenience or
strategic alliance?
Naser M. Al-Tamimi

29. **Adjudicating Family Law in
Muslim Courts**
Cases from the contemporary
Muslim world
Edited by Elisa Giunchi

30. **Muslim Family Law in Western
Courts**
Edited by Elisa Giunchi

31. **Anti-Veiling Campaigns in the
Muslim World**
Gender, modernism and the
politics of dress
Edited by Stephanie Cronin

32. **Russia-Iran Relations Since the
End of the Cold War**
Eric D. Moore

Anti-Veiling Campaigns in the Muslim World

Gender, modernism and the politics of dress

**Edited by
Stephanie Cronin**

LONDON AND NEW YORK

First published 2014
by Routledge
2 Park Square, Milton Park, Abingdon, Oxon, OX14 4RN

and by Routledge
711 Third Avenue, New York, NY 10017

Routledge is an imprint of the Taylor & Francis Group, an informa business

© 2014 selection and editorial material, Stephanie Cronin; individual
chapters, the contributors

The right of Stephanie Cronin to be identified as author of the editorial
material, and of the individual authors as authors of their contributions, has
been asserted by her in accordance with sections 77 and 78 of the
Copyright, Designs and Patents Act 1988.

All rights reserved. No part of this book may be reprinted or reproduced or
utilised in any form or by any electronic, mechanical, or other means, now
known or hereafter invented, including photocopying and recording, or in
any information storage or retrieval system, without permission in writing
from the publishers.

Trademark notice: Product or corporate names may be trademarks or
registered trademarks, and are used only for identification and explanation
without intent to infringe.

British Library Cataloguing in Publication Data
A catalogue record for this book is available from the British Library

Library of Congress Cataloging in Publication Data
  Anti-veiling campaigns in the Muslim world : gender, modernism and the
politics of dress / [edited by] Stephanie Cronin.
    pages cm – (Durham modern Middle East and Islamic world series)
  Includes bibliographical references and index.
  1. Hijab (Islamic clothing) 2. Veils–Religious aspects–Islam. 3. Hijab
(Islamic clothing)–Government policy. 4. Clothing and dress–Political
aspects–Islamic countries. 5. Muslim women–Social conditions. I. Cronin,
Stephanie.
  BP190.5.H44A58 2014
  305.48'697–dc23
                2013040891

ISBN: 978-0-415-71138-8 (hbk)
ISBN: 978-1-315-88455-4 (ebk)

Typeset in Times New Roman
by Taylor & Francis Books

Contents

List of Figures	ix
List of Contributors	x
Acknowledgments	xiv
Note on transliteration	xv

Introduction: Coercion or empowerment?
Anti-veiling campaigns: a comparative perspective   1
STEPHANIE CRONIN

PART I
Turkey   37

1   From face veil to cloche hat: the backward Ottoman versus new
Turkish woman in urban public discourse   39
KATHRYN LIBAL

2   Anti-veiling campaigns and local elites in Turkey of the 1930s:
a view from the periphery   59
SEVGI ADAK

3   Everyday resistance to unveiling and flexible secularism in early
republican Turkey   86
MURAT METİNSOY

PART II
Iran and Afghanistan   119

4   Unveiling ambiguities: revisiting 1930s Iran's *kashf-i hijab*
campaign   121
JASAMIN ROSTAM-KOLAYI AND AFSHIN MATIN-ASGARI

viii   *Contents*

5   Dressing up (or down): veils, hats, and consumer fashions in
    interwar Iran   149
    FIROOZEH KASHANI-SABET

6   Astrakhan, borqa', chadari, dreshi: the economy of dress in
    early-twentieth-century Afghanistan   163
    THOMAS WIDE

PART III
Soviet Central Asia and the Caucasus   203

7   Women-initiated unveiling: state-led campaigns in Uzbekistan
    and Azerbaijan   205
    MARIANNE KAMP

PART IV
The Balkans   229

8   Behind the veil: the reform of Islam in interwar Albania or the
    search for a "modern" and "European" Islam   231
    NATHALIE CLAYER

9   Difference unveiled: Bulgarian national imperatives and the
    re-dressing of Muslim women, 1878–1989   252
    MARY NEUBURGER

    Bibliography   267
    Index   279

List of Figures

1	Women of Kokand, Uzbekistan, wearing *paranji* and *chachvon*, early twentieth century	140
2	Man in traditional clothing accompanied by two women with their face veils drawn aside, Iran, late nineteenth / early twentieth century	141
3	Egyptian woman on a donkey	142
4	Two Egyptian women heavily veiled	142
5	Veiled African Muslim women, presumably ex-slaves, photographed in Constanta, Romania, *c.* 1910s / 1920s	143
6	Turkish woman from Smyrna (Izmir), 1907, wearing the newly fashionable transparent white chiffon yashmak	144
7	Three veiled Turkish women showing their ankles and with semi-transparent veils, early 1920s	145
8	Schoolgirls wearing *chadors*, but without face-veils, over fashionable Western clothing	146
9	Veiled Muslim women at Sarajevo market, Bosnia, 1930s	147
10	Veiled Muslim women, Bulgaria, 1930s	147
11	Some leading figures and army commanders with their wives in an official ceremony held in Iran on the anniversary of removal of veils	148
12	Women athletes parading, Turkey, 1936	148

List of Contributors

Sevgi Adak is a PhD Researcher at Leiden University, School of Middle Eastern Studies, and a Research Fellow at the International Institute for Social History, Amsterdam. After graduating from Bilkent University, Department of Political Science, she enrolled at Sabanci University in Istanbul and completed her MA degree at the Graduate Program in History with her thesis, "Formation of Authoritarian Secularism in Turkey: Ramadans in the Early Republican Era, 1923–38." In addition, she holds another MA degree in political science from York University, Toronto, and an MPhil degree in political science from Central European University, Budapest. Her PhD dissertation project is on state-society relations in early republican Turkey, with a focus on anti-veiling campaigns. Sevgi Adak's latest publications include an article in Turkish entitled "Ramadans and the Formation of Kemalist Secularism (1923–38)," published in *Tarih ve Toplum*, Autumn 2011, and a co-authored book chapter, "Is 'Dialogue among Civilizations' a True Remedy for 'Clash of Civilizations'? Rethinking Civilizationist Categories with Reference to Turkey-EU Relations," published in Mojtaba Mahdavi and W. Andy Knight (eds.), *Dialogue and "Dignity of Difference": Building Capacity for Otherness* (Ashgate, 2012). Her academic interests include modern Turkish history, state-society relations in the Middle East, women's history and contemporary feminisms in the Middle East.

Nathalie Clayer is Professor at the EHESS (Paris), a Senior Research Fellow at the CNRS (Paris) in the CETOBAC department (Centre d'études turques, ottomanes, balkaniques et centrasiatiques, CNRS-EHESS-Collège de France), and head of this department. Her main research interests are religion, nationalism, and state-building processes in the Ottoman Empire and in the Balkans, especially among the Albanians. Among her recent publications are *Aux origines du nationalisme albanais. La naissance d'une nation majoritairement musulmane en Europe* (Karthala, 2007), *Islam in Inter-War Europe* (Hurst, 2008) co-edited with Eric Germain, *Conflicting Loyalties in the Balkans. The Great Powers, the Ottoman Empire and Nation-Building* (Tauris, 2011) co-edited with Hannes Grandits and Robert

Pichler, *L'autorité religieuse et ses limites en terres d'islam* (Brill, 2013) co-edited with Alexandre Papas and Benoît Fliche, and *Les musulmans de l'Europe du Sud-Est* with Xavier Bougarel (Karthala, 2013).

Stephanie Cronin received her PhD from SOAS (London) in 1992. She has taught at SOAS and at Cambridge University and was an Iran Heritage Foundation Fellow at Northampton University for many years. She is now Lecturer in Iranian History at the Faculty of Oriental Studies, University of Oxford, and a member of St Antony's College. She is a member of the Editorial Boards of *Middle Eastern Studies* and *Iranian Studies*, of the Advisory Council for *Qajar Studies*, and of the Editorial Advisory Board of *Iran* (Journal of the British Institute of Persian Studies). She is the author of *Armies and State-building in the Modern Middle East: Politics, Nationalism and Military Reform* (I. B. Tauris, 2014); *Shahs, Soldiers and Subalterns* (Palgrave Macmillan, 2010); *Tribal Politics in Iran* (Routledge, 2006); and *The Army and the Creation of the Pahlavi State in Iran, 1910–26* (I. B. Tauris, 1997); and editor of *Iranian-Russian Encounters: Empires and Revolutions since 1800* (Routledge, 2012); *Subalterns and Social Protest* (Routledge, 2007); *Reformers and Revolutionaries in Modern Iran* (Routledge, 2004); and *The Making of Modern Iran* (Routledge, 2003).

Marianne Kamp is Associate Professor of History at the University of Wyoming. She earned her PhD in Near Eastern Languages and Civilizations from the University of Chicago. Her research concerns twentieth-century social history of Uzbekistan, gender studies of Central Asia, and oral history. She is the author of *The New Woman in Uzbekistan: Islam, Modernity and Unveiling under Communism* (University of Washington Press, 2006) and numerous articles. Her current research involves oral histories about collectivization of agriculture.

Firoozeh Kashani-Sabet is the Robert I. Williams Term Professor of History at the University of Pennsylvania. She is the author of *Frontier Fictions: Shaping the Iranian Nation, 1804–1946* (Princeton University Press, 1999) and *Conceiving Citizens: Women and the Politics of Motherhood in Iran* (Oxford University Press, 2011), which received the 2012 book award from the *Journal of Middle East Women's Studies* for outstanding scholarship in the field of Middle East gender studies. She is also the author of a novel, entitled *Martyrdom Street* (Syracuse University Press, 2010). Currently, she is working on several book projects. Building on the research in her first book on frontiers and identity formation in the Middle East, Professor Kashani-Sabet is completing a forthcoming work, *Tales of Trespassing: Borderland Histories of Iran and the Middle East* (under contract to Cambridge University Press), in which she expands on her arguments about nature, ethnicity, and border communities in Middle Eastern modernity. She is also preparing a book on America's historical relationship with Iran and the Islamic world, entitled *American Divines, Persian Diplomats: A*

xii *Contributors*

History of US-Iranian Relations, 1833–1979 (under contract to Princeton University Press). In her spare time, she enjoys playing the piano, listening to music, and taking long walks.

Kathryn Libal, PhD, is Associate Professor of Social Work and Associate Director of the Human Rights Institute at the University of Connecticut. She earned her doctorate in anthropology at the University of Washington. She specializes in human rights, social welfare, and the state and has published journal and book articles on women's and children's rights movements in Turkey; advocacy efforts of international non-governmental organizations on behalf of Iraqi refugees; and social work in the Middle East. In addition to this body of work focusing on Turkey and the Middle East, Libal examines the localization of human rights norms and practices in the United States. She has co-edited the volume, *Human Rights in the United States: Beyond Exceptionalism* (Cambridge) with Dr. Shareen Hertel and a new project on the politics of food security and food policy in the United States as a human rights concern. She has also co-authored, with Dr. Scott Harding, a short text on *Human Rights Based Approaches to Community Practice in the United States* (Springer, forthcoming).

Afshin Matin-asgari is Professor of Middle East History at California State University, Los Angeles and author of *Iranian Student Opposition to the Shah* (Mazda, 2001) and several articles and book chapters on twentieth-century Iranian political, religious, and intellectual history.

Murat Metinsoy is Assistant Professor at Istanbul University, Faculty of Economics, Political Science and International Relations Department, and Turkish Academy of Sciences Fellow at Middle East Technical University, Department of History. He received his PhD degree from Bogazici University in 2010 with a dissertation titled "Everyday Politics of Ordinary People: Public Opinion, Dissent, and Resistance in Early Republican Turkey, 1925–39." He studies particularly social history of early Republican Turkey, labor history, peasant movements, everyday and informal forms of popular resistance and the social impact of the wars in Turkey during the twentieth century. His first book, *Turkey in World War II: War and Everyday Life* (Homer, 2007) published in Turkish, deals with the survival strategies of the peasants and working class in the face of authoritarian policies and was awarded the Best Young Social Scientist Award by The Turkish Social Science Association and the Best Book Award by the Ottoman Bank Archives and Research Center. One of this recent international articles is "Fragile Hegenony, Flexible Authoritarianism, and Governing from Below: Politicans' Reports in Early Republican Turkey", published in International Journal of Middle East Studies, November 2011. He carried out doctoral research at Ohio State University in 2007–08 and received several post-doctoral research fellowships from the American Research Institute in Turkey in 2011, The Scientific and Technological

Research Council of Turkey in 2011–12, and The Turkish Academy of Science in 2012–14. He is now preparing his second book on the everyday politics of peasants and rural unrest in interwar Turkey.

Mary Neuburger received her PhD in history at the University of Washington in 1997, with a speciality in south eastern Europe. She is currently a Professor in the Department of History at the University of Texas, as well as Director of the Center for Russian, East European and Eurasian Studies. She is the author of two books, *The Orient Within: Muslim Minorities and the Negotiation of Nationhood in Modern Bulgaria* (Cornell University Press, 2004) and *Balkan Smoke: Tobacco and the Making of Modern Bulgaria 1856–1989* (Cornell University Press, 2012). She is co-editor, with Paulina Bren, of *Communism Unwrapped: Consumption in Cold War Eastern Europe* (Oxford University Press, 2013).

Jasamin Rostam-Kolayi is an Associate Professor in the Department of History at California State University, Fullerton. She received her PhD from the University of California, Los Angeles and has published articles on themes in early-twentieth-century Iranian history, including women's education, religious minorities, and US-Iran relations. Her articles have appeared in the *Journal of Middle East Women's Studies*, *Middle East Women's Studies*, *Iranian Studies*, *Middle East Critique*, and several edited collections.

Thomas Wide is a DPhil candidate in Oriental Studies at Balliol College, Oxford University. He holds a BA in Classics and Oriental Studies from Oxford, and an MA in Middle Eastern Studies from Harvard University, where he was also a Kennedy Scholar. He currently lives in Kabul where he is Country Director of the cultural heritage NGO Turquoise Mountain.

Acknowledgments

This volume is the result of a conference held at St Antony's College, University of Oxford, in September 2011. I would like to thank St Antony's for allowing the conference the use of its facilities, and the Faculty of Oriental Studies, Oxford and the Iran Heritage Foundation for providing financial support.

I am grateful to Mohammad Awadzadeh of the Institute for Iranian Contemporary Historical Studies, Andrew Hale at the Anahita Gallery, Gina Martin at National Geographic, and Tess Hines at the Mary Evans Picture Library for their help with obtaining the images contained in this volume.

Anoushirvan Ehteshami, the general editor of the Durham Modern Middle East and Islamic World series, and Helena Hurd, the editorial assistant at Routledge, were both indispensable. Lubica Pollakova did sterling work on the bibliography and index.

Two chapters were previously published. "Behind the veil: The reform of Islam in inter-war Albania or the search for a 'modern' and 'European' Islam" by Nathalie Clayer first appeared in *Islam in Inter-War Europe* (Hurst, 2008), eds. Nathalie Clayer and Eric Germain. "Difference unveiled: Bulgarian national imperatives and the re-dressing of Muslim women in the Communist period 1945–89" by Mary Neuburger was first published in *Nationalities Papers*, vol. 25 (1997), copyright © Association for the Study of Nationalities, reprinted by permission of Taylor & Francis Ltd, www.tandf online.com, on behalf of the Association for the Study of Nationalities. I am grateful to the editors and publishers of both publications, Nathalie Clayer and Eric Germain, and Florian Bieber of *Nationalities Papers*, Michael Dwyer of Hurst and Co, and Routledge.

Note on transliteration

There has been no attempt to impose a uniform system of transliteration on the chapters in this volume. Decisions about transliteration have been left to individual contributors.

Introduction: coercion or empowerment?

Anti-veiling campaigns: a comparative perspective

Stephanie Cronin

The decision by the French National Assembly in 2010 to ban the wearing of the *niqab* (Muslim face-veil) in public was the culmination of an intense controversy.[1] It was calculated that only a tiny minority of Muslim women in France wore the face-veil. Yet, for both supporters and opponents of the ban, the issue appeared to raise fundamental existential questions. Supporters of the ban were accused of Islamophobic racism; its opponents of endangering the secular character of the French republic. Polemics about the *niqab*, furthermore, transcended the usual fault lines of French politics, with support for the ban able to draw on a long tradition of secularism and anti-clericalism on the French Left, the usual first line of defence for immigrant rights. The controversy in France over the face-veil, which followed a long, similarly articulated dispute over the wearing of the headscarf in French schools, was particularly sharp, but found echoes across Western Europe. In the broad contours of their arguments, the opposing voices reproduced debates in Europe which had already developed in majority Muslim countries, most notably Turkey and Tunisia.[2] Both sides claimed to speak for women's empowerment and agency, but were divided by issues of secularism versus religious belief, individual freedom versus social and family coercion and identity versus integration.

The eruption in Europe of the controversy over the *niqab*, and indeed over Islamic clothing, *hijab*, in general, followed and was partly fuelled by the US invasion and occupation of Afghanistan, and the placing of Afghan women's emancipation at the centre of a new Western interventionist discourse. Their brutal enforcement of full veiling and seclusion on Afghan women was a key trope in the depiction of the Taliban as incorrigibly backward, indeed medieval, and barbaric. This in turn took place against a backdrop of growing hostility to the Islamic Republic of Iran, where, again, the imposition of compulsory *hijab* was identified in the West as a sharp manifestation of Iran's disregard for individual human rights. The political and historical realities of these two countries, and the widely differing forms of veiling practiced in each, were disregarded, the veiled woman in both Afghanistan and Iran mobilized to represent for the West the self-imposed exclusion of these societies from the modern world.

2   *Stephanie Cronin*

More recently, as a result of the empowerment of Islamist trends after the 'Arab Spring', the question of veiling across the Arab world, and of women's right to veil or not, has also acquired a new salience. Indeed, in general, over the last decades of the twentieth century, with the weakening and collapse of secular nationalism and the emergence and re-emergence of discourses based on Islamic tenets, veiling, voluntary and enforced, has moved to the top of the political agenda.[3] It is, furthermore, no longer an issue which affects only the world beyond Europe's borders, wherever those borders may be imagined to be. As the case of France shows, owing to the presence in Europe of substantial immigrant Muslim communities, often possessing a new level of confidence and articulating a new opposition to Western foreign policy, and the rise of an Islamophobic far-Right, debates over veiling have taken on an unprecedented significance within European domestic politics. Both within the Muslim world and in Europe, polarized debates about the meaning of veiling may again be heard, these debates signifying, as in earlier periods, a much wider political and cultural clash. Once again, voices may be heard defining veiling as a symbol of the backwardness of the non-European 'Other' and counterposing Islam to the very essence of European identity.

Yet neither the French campaign against the *niqab* nor the Turkish secular elite's horror at the spread of *hijab* is new, but are strikingly prefigured by earlier conflicts. Across the Muslim world by the late nineteenth century the question of female dress in general, and the face-veil in particular, had come to occupy an important place in a developing indigenous critique of existing gender relations. This critique of gender relations, in turn, was a key trope in a wider discourse of modernism which sought to explain and also, crucially, to remedy the perceived backwardness of Muslim societies. According to this discourse, the entire social organism suffered from the debilitating effects of the veiling and seclusion of half the population, and the half responsible for raising the next generation at that. It laid particular emphasis on education for women and the reform of family law, especially as it related to polygyny, child marriage and the male right of repudiation, as routes to the creation of good wives and mothers, happy companiate marriages and healthy and stable families. A sine qua non of this agenda was opposition to seclusion, with veiling as the symbol, and sometimes even the cause, of the degradation of both women and therefore also of men. The modernist gender discourse generated intense controversies. These controversies reached a crescendo in the early twentieth century, becoming subsumed into broader debates about Middle Eastern self-defence, on the intellectual, cultural and ideological, and also political and economic levels, from a relentlessly expanding European hegemony.

The modernist gender discourse, and the opposition to veiling and female seclusion which was embedded within it, appeared and took shape between the late nineteenth century and the First World War. From the early 1920s, this discourse was empowered across much of the Muslim world as a result of the seizure of state control by a variety of modernist regimes. During the 1920s

Introduction: coercion or empowerment? 3

and 1930s, in Turkey, Iran, Afghanistan, Central Asia, the Caucasus and the Balkans, veiling became a target of government disapprobation, was publicly ridiculed as backward and officially discouraged in a variety of ways. Although these countries were ruled by very different regimes – in Turkey, a republic led by a charismatic war hero; modernizing monarchs, Reza Shah and King Amanullah, in Iran and Afghanistan; Communist parties in Central Asia and the Caucasus – their anti-veiling campaigns bore, at least at first sight, certain broad similarities. For the nationalist, modernizing and secularizing elites, who identified profoundly with European mores, unveiling became a key signifier of modernity and a central element in an emerging national character. In interwar Central Asia and the Caucasus, the infant Soviet state launched anti-veiling drives as part of its wider struggle for a revolutionary transformation, social and cultural as well as economic. Although very different political formations, these regimes, whether elite nationalist or communist, were all opposed to what they viewed as the reactionary forces of Islam and tradition, forces which they equated and conflated, and all wished to create a new and modern woman, unveiled, educated and integrated into the workforce.

These anti-veiling campaigns were everywhere presented as emancipatory. Yet everywhere the state's sponsorship of authoritarian anti-veiling campaigns led to an intense politicization of the issue. Unveiling became a battleground on which enemies of the sponsoring regimes might mobilize a more general opposition. For the secular elites, unveiling remained a signifier of modernity. For their opponents, unveiling became symptomatic of a loss of cultural integrity and a weakening of religious feeling, the last means by which European power might be resisted.

Each anti-veiling campaign of the interwar period has received its share of attention, but analysis has always remained largely within the confines of a national framework. Despite their extraordinary synchronicity, there has as yet been little or no attempt to view these movements from a comparative perspective, to try to determine precisely which features they shared and what was specific, even unique, to each country's experience.[4] Many questions remain to be clarified. What was actually meant by unveiling? What did the anti-veiling discourse envisage as the ideal appearance of the newly-unveiled woman? Is it accurate to speak of the emergence of a modernist pan-Islamic gender discourse and counter-discourse within which a critique of veiling was embedded? Did the emergence of nationalism fracture these pan-Islamic conceptualizations of veiling? What role was played in the construction of these discourses by tropes drawn from European Orientalism? How important was the circulation of ideas within the Muslim world itself? To what extent and through what mechanisms was each individual country influenced by processes of change underway among its neighbours? What was the impact of changes in fashion, in the ordinary sense of taste in dress, but also in the wider sense of major trends in social attitudes and official policies? What was the connection between anti-veiling campaigns and reforms in male clothing?

4   *Stephanie Cronin*

How did the empowered nationalist and communist regimes of the interwar period enforce unveiling? What role did legal change play? What was the role of coercion versus education and propaganda? Who was in favour of unveiling and who against? What was the role of women's organizations? What meaning does the concept of women's agency have in the context of the still prevailing patriarchal social structures and the authoritarian modernization characterizing the anti-veiling regimes? What strategies did women employ to manage the new expectations placed on them? What types of opposition did unveiling provoke? What was the reaction of men? How can the shocking levels of violence accompanying unveiling in Central Asia be explained? Was the conceptualization of veiling as a social evil unique or can it be better understood by placing it within a more generalized modernist preoccupation with eradicating local practices relating to women's bodies such as Chinese foot binding or female circumcision in Africa? What did the anti-veiling campaigns achieve? To what extent was the re-emergence of veiling since the 1970s a reaction to these campaigns or the product of entirely different and new circumstances?

The immense symbolic significance which the *niqab* or face-veil acquired, both for its supporters and its opponents, was a marked feature of the recent controversy in France. In fact, contemporary debates demonstrate considerable semantic and conceptual confusion regarding the veil, a confusion which is a reflection of an actually diverse reality. This actual diversity has, however, been largely ignored in the debates, as each side has struggled to impose its own interpretation of veiling. The more commonly used word *hijab* possesses a range of possible meanings. It might imply a general demeanour of modesty in public, and might also refer to any variety of headscarf worn by Muslim women, perhaps also to loose robes enveloping the body, sometimes but not necessarily including the face-veil. Complementing the vagueness of the term, a wide variety of interpretations may be observed among veiling women, depending on background. For the contemporary well-educated Islamist woman who asserts her decision to veil as one informed by choice and agency and a rejection of tradition, and for whom *hijab* is a public declaration of identity and piety, the most common form of dress is an international style of loose coat and headscarf, emphasizing her membership of the transnational *umma*. The face-veil is rarely seen in this milieu. Yet, even among those women who wish to assert the primacy of their Islamic identity, there are significant differences. Quite separately to the fashion common among the younger generation of modern female Islamists, heavily influenced by the sartorial innovations which women devised in Iran after the 1979 revolution, there has also been a reversion to, or perhaps novel adoption of, older forms of dress, including the face-veil, under the influence of Saudi and Gulf norms and practices. Interestingly, the types of *hijab* adopted by the woman usually reflect and are reflected by the type of clothing, in particular the type of beard, trimmed or untrimmed, and robe or Western trousers, worn by her husband, indicating the continuing importance of gender complementarity

Introduction: coercion or empowerment? 5

and a significance of forms of male dress often submerged beneath the paradoxical visibility of the veil. This political and psychological need for gender complementarity in dress, indicating a supposed similiarity of identity and outlook, has been of some significance in the historical struggle over veiling.

A similar lack of clarity and precision about what was meant by the veil, and perhaps also an ideologically charged indifference to actual social realities, was also evident among the earliest advocates of change in the Muslim world. In the nineteenth century, as in the twenty-first, forms of dress, and the presence or absence of face-veiling, varied widely depending on class, geography and social context. The face-veil was usually worn by women of the better-off classes, or those who aspired to these classes, and was primarily an urban phenomenon. It was in fact a way of demonstrating that a family possessed enough wealth to keep its female members secluded and economically inactive and therefore entitled to claim a superior social status. Face-veil and body robes might be worn by poorer urban women but in such a way as to permit interaction with the wider society.[5] The full face-veil was rarely found among peasants or nomads, by far the numerically largest element of the population, except perhaps in a modified form on the occasion of their rare visits to towns. On the other hand, some form of hair covering was universal, and rural women or working women in towns might adopt the habit of pulling their scarves across part of their faces on the appearance of strangers. In the pre-modern Muslim world, therefore, the vast majority of women rarely or never wore the face-veil and dressed in local 'folk' costume, appropriate to their lives of agricultural or pastoral labour and including culturally specific types of body, head and hair covering. Nonetheless, by the late nineteenth century, the type of clothing, including and especially the face-veil, typically worn only by better-off urban women whose families had the wealth and status to sustain a lifestyle of female seclusion, had come to be identified by an emerging modernist intelligentsia as a key signifier and cause of the backwardness of Muslim societies in general.

Why then, it may be asked, did the form of clothing worn only by a small minority of the female population acquire such immense symbolic significance? It was of course the urban elites who incubated the modernists of the late nineteenth and early twentieth centuries and it was therefore primarily urban women, especially those from the same elites, who were most present in the modernist vision. It was precisely such women who were subject to the most rigid requirements of covering in public. It was also women from such families who first began to demand, in imitation of their male relatives, access to education, to a life beyond the confines of domesticity, and to an amelioration of the disabilities placed on them by existing family codes and practices. The character of emerging critiques of gender practices and veiling itself may therefore best be comprehended if modernism itself is understood as essentially an elite project. In general, the elite character of gender modernism may perhaps be best illustrated by its prioritizing of female education as a panacea, in societies where the vast majority of men were illiterate, no more educated than their sisters, mothers and daughters. The class dimension of the modernist critique of veiling also begins to explain the very varied receptions which it received. Whereas the first women to unveil, and the most ardent advocates of unveiling, were from the socially, culturally and economically secure elites, the middling classes, the aspiring, the upwardly mobile and the nouveau riche were among the staunchest defenders of an imagined 'tradition' in clothing practices and were even eager to adopt anew these traditions as markers of their social advance.

The role of Europe in the construction of the modernist gender discourse, and specifically the attitude to veiling embedded within it, has given rise to considerable controversy. The new intelligentsia, originating from within elite families where veiling and seclusion was most closely maintained and reproduced, consisted precisely of those men who were most in contact with Europe and European ideas and who were becoming most sharply aware of the differences in gender relations prevailing in the West and the East. Certainly Europeans themselves, having quickly identified Islam as the fount and source of general backwardness and every particular social evil, especially the allegedly degraded position of Muslim women, were vocal critics of veiling. The prurient gender obsessions of European travellers and officials in the Muslim world and their fascination with the exoticism of the harem and the provocative concealment represented to them by the veil have been well-documented.[6]

It has been argued that the modernist gender discourse, and especially its critique of veiling, was, as might be expected from its elite character, directly derived from European Orientalism. The notion that elite critiques of existing gender relations were the result of the internalization of European prejudices and a conscious or unconscious capitulation to imperial hegemony has been most cogently argued by Leila Ahmed and has shaped much subsequent scholarship.[7] She asserts, for example, that Qasim Amin's seminal 1899 text, *Tahrir al-Mar'a* (The Liberation of Women), with its call for an end to veiling and gender segregation, marked not the beginning of feminism but rather the importing of the colonial narrative of women and Islam into mainstream indigenous discourse.[8] She describes the unhealthy psychological reaction of the upper-class Qasim Amin, 'smarting under the humiliation of being described as uncivilized' by Europeans because Egyptian women were veiled.[9]

Yet Middle Eastern travellers to Europe were equally fascinated by European women and just as ready to use them as a 'metaphor for delineating self and "Other"'.[10] Reversing the Orientalist dynamic, Mohamad Tavakoli-Targhi emphasizes the role played by the Occidentalist gaze and rejects Leila Ahmed's depiction of the passive absorption and reproduction of European prejudices. On the contrary, attributing the emerging gender discourse to an entirely indigenous ideological and cultural dynamic, he details Iranian constructions of an imagined European woman, either an unveiled and educated model for Iranian women, or a corrupt menace to Islam and Iranian society, and the centrality of these constructs to a range of Iranian political discourses.[11]

Introduction: coercion or empowerment? 7

Furthermore, as Marianne Kamp as argued, the analysis of gender modernism as exclusively a defensive response to European colonialism obscures the conflicts being played out within each Muslim society.[12] A Eurocentric view, privileging Western Europe, France and Britain in particular, as the true source of modernism around the world, underestimates the power of an emerging discourse of reform indigenous to the Muslim world.[13] The unprecedented rapidity of technological change in the late nineteenth–early twentieth century opened up enormous opportunities for communications and the exchange of ideas within the Muslim world, as much as or more than between the Muslim world and the West. The construction of railways, an explosion in the print media and large migrations encouraged the formation of what Khalid Adeeb has called a cosmopolitan community of the world's Muslims and contributed to the emergence of a pan-Islamic gender discourse.[14] In fact, in terms of their general outlook, their proposals for ameliorating the lot of women, and specifically their attitudes to veiling, reformers in the Muslim world were primarily influenced by each other rather than by the unmediated example of Europe. Travel was certainly of central importance to the ideological evolution of many leading reformers, but it was primarily travel between the great urban centres of the Muslim world. Travel within the Muslim world was infinitely greater than with Europe, available to much wider layers of society, and the example of change within Muslim societies far more powerful than the observation of alien customs in societies foreign in every sense and sometimes hostile. Many of the new generation of modernists found their outlooks transformed by movement between cities within the Muslim world.[15] In addition to human movement, the establishment of print media increased dramatically in these decades and led to the dizzying circulation of books, pamphlets and newspapers while Muslim communities such as the Tatars of the Russian empire, whose adoption of modernism had occurred at an early stage, constituted conduits for the transmission of such ideas across the Muslim world. Tatar reformers influenced other Muslim communities within the Russian empire, in the Caucasus and Central Asia, and beyond, in the Ottoman empire. Ottoman and Caucasian developments affected Iran, which in turn transmitted new ideas to Afghanistan. Arab reformers in Cairo and Muslims in the Balkans looked to Istanbul for inspiration. Across the Arab, Ottoman and Iranian worlds, across the Caucasus and Central Asia, and among the Muslim communities of the Balkans, reformers, operating within a newly integrated transnational Muslim intellectual environment, identified the same problem of 'backwardness' resulting from the same general and specific causes, and proposed the same remedies.

It was, however, not only those advocating change and critiquing the veil who drew sustenance from opinion across the Muslim world. As the reform agenda acquired a transnational character, so too did the opposition. Just as reformists might be encouraged by what they saw in Istanbul and Cairo, including changes in veiling practices, so might those of a more conservative cast of mind be horrified by the same phenomena.[16] Across the Muslim world a counter-discourse emerged, denouncing gender modernism, and the opposition to veiling in particular, as an effort to copy or mimic the West. It was argued that the modernists' treacherous embrace of European motifs hostile to Islam was a threat to the entire social order, endangering the moral purity of women and raising the spectre of chaos, of society being riven by *fitna* or turmoil.

By the early twentieth century a modernist gender discourse had taken shape and had immediately evoked a counter-discourse. The two sides often raised similar concerns and sometimes used similar methods of argument, although reaching diametrically opposed conclusions. Appeals to Islamic legitimacy, for example, were invoked by both those in favour of veiling and those opposed, both sides swapping verses from the Quran. On the one hand, it was asserted that the *Shari'a* required women to veil. Islamic modernists, on the other hand, most notably the famous Egyptian Muhammad Abduh, refuted the view that Islamic legal texts demanded any particular form of face-veil. Some went even further, concluding that, in fact, veiling was actually an un-Islamic practice, and should be discarded in favour of a more authentic piety cleansed of non-Islamic accretions. The argument went beyond religious prescription. Both sides also expressed concern about the moral health of society. Conservatives believed that not only religion but social custom and family honour demanded veiling, which protected women from moral corruption. Their opponents retorted that veiling in reality encouraged and facilitated such corruption, either because women remained ignorant and unschooled in true morality, or because, more crudely, the anonymity of the veil facilitated illicit contact between men and women.[17]

The struggle over the meaning of veiling took place between those in favour and those against, but also within the modernist camp, which was far from monolithic.[18] Different elements of the modernist programme were adopted in different places at different speeds and in different combinations. The need to educate women, for example, was much more readily accepted than the need to end veiling, and veiling was not always seen as an impediment to education. Kathryn Libal shows in Chapter 1 how, as modernism evolved, it increasingly attempted to freeze the debate in revolutionary and absolute terms through binary constructions: 'traditional' or 'backward' versus 'modern'; 'reformist' versus 'conservative'; 'old' versus 'new'.[19] Yet, in reality, in each concrete Muslim society opinion changed among different social groups at different rates, prioritized different concerns and was more variegated than a simple division into stark opposites would indicate.

Islamic modernism, which argued that veiling was not mandated by religion, was a powerful trend and might be found across the Muslim world. In the late nineteenth century, however, a clear-cut fracture appeared in the pan-Islamic reformist discourse regarding the veil. Iranian, Turkish and Balkan nationalist ideologues began to allocate opposition to the veil a role in the construction of new and specifically national, as opposed to religious, identities. These thinkers began to lay increasing emphasis on the differences between themselves and the larger Arab and Muslim worlds, and on the uniqueness and even superiority of their national cultures, sometimes expressed in racial terms. For the Iranians Mirza Fath Ali Akhundzadeh and especially Mirza Aqa Khan Kirmani, for example, the Arab invasions and the imposition of Islam on the Iranians had been a disaster, and veiling was a sign of the backwardness of a social order resulting from the submission of the Iranians to Arab and Muslim hegemony.[20] Ziya Gökalp, the preeminent ideologue of Turkism, also argued that Turkish culture needed to be protected from the deleterious impact of Islam and of Arab and Persian cultural practices and advocated returning to the pre-Islamic past to build a future in harmony with an authentic national identity. According to Gökalp, women were the equals of men in pre-Islamic Turkish societies and did not veil.[21] In the Balkans, where Muslims were often minorities and the developing nationalisms were formulated in direct opposition to Muslim Ottoman rule, the identification of the veil, and also other items of women's 'Eastern' clothing such as the baggy trousers known as *shalvari*, as foreign was even stronger. The 'foreign' clothing of both women and men was centrally located in the new Balkan nationalist discourse, visible markers of a legacy of alien, Ottoman, rule, this discourse being shared by secular Balkan reformers, Muslims as well as Christian.

Such ideas naturally began to produce some degree of divergence in the debates over veiling as they unfolded in the Arab, and in the Turco-Persian, worlds. In Arabic-language discussions, veiling, however heavily criticized as backward, was rarely deemed to be a cultural import, imposed on Arab society by an alien conqueror. In Turkey, Iran and the Balkans, on the contrary, notions of the veil as alien and foreign entered into mainstream thinking. It may perhaps be these differing configurations of veiling within nationalist discourses which explain why it was only in the Turco-Persian environment, not the Arab Middle East, that opposition to veiling became a state policy. No Arab country, even in the heyday of secular nationalism, officially attempted to change sartorial practices in any systematic way, yet such efforts may be found throughout the Turco-Persian world, including Central Asia, the Caucasus and the Balkans. It may be noted, in parentheses, that these arguments were ahistorical ideological constructs, veiling probably being common to elite women in all ancient Middle Eastern and Mediterranean societies. Arguments contrary to these nationalist constructs, based perhaps more securely on available historical evidence, might just as easily have been made, whereby veiling was, for example, a Persian or Byzantine imposition on Arab societies, and integral to pre-Islamic Iranian culture.

Although Islamic modernist arguments were important in developing an anti-veiling discourse, the Turco-Persian nationalist construction of the veil as alien carried within it the seeds of hostility to religion. In Iran, in particular, opposition to veiling began to be associated with religious scepticism, heresy and unbelief, sometimes taking on an aspect not just of secularism but of anti-clericalism. Unveiling became associated with the Babi heresy, the theatrical unveiling in 1848 of the Babi woman leader, Qurrat al-Ayn, having entered popular mythology, while the shocking caricatures of mullahs abusing veiled women in the radical journal *Mulla Nasr-al-Din* would have been unthinkable in an Arabic-language publication.[22] The conscious use of the veiling issue to attack Islam and clerics naturally took the issue into new political territory. Elsewhere, too, although perhaps less violently, unveiling possessed similar unwelcome connotations of unbelief. In Cairo, Christian women had pioneered unveiling, while Tatar women immigrants to Central Asia, who acted as conduits of modern ideas and practices of all sorts and had largely abandoned veiling by the late nineteenth century, were generally regarded as existing at the 'outer limits of Muslimness'.[23]

At first, the debates over veiling were an exclusively male concern, women the objects of both discourse and counter-discourse. Gradually, however, the voices of women began to make themselves heard. In the major cities of the Muslim world, women began to make themselves both visible and audible, contributing to newspapers and even founding newspapers and magazines of their own. Indeed, the two decades between 1890 and 1910 saw a flourishing of intellectual, literary and educational activity among elite women, nowhere more than in newly constitutionalist Istanbul and Tehran. Although most women advocated the reforms which had become traditional to modernism, there was no absolute unanimity among women on the veil. Some women remained vehemently opposed to unveiling, while others, perhaps sometimes motivated by a tactical prudence, declared they considered veiling no impediment to learning.[24] Some considered the issue of veiling a distraction from the real tasks such as education and family law reform, others pointed out that veiling avoided an otherwise total confinement to the home. Nonetheless, the unprecedented audibility of women's voices transformed women from merely objects of modernist reform agendas into active participants, and announced the arrival of the wearing or discarding of the veil as an issue of female agency.

In Muslim societies of the late nineteenth century, forms of *hijab*, or modest dress, certainly varied, from country to country, class to class and context to context. The modernist preoccupation centred, however, on the form of dress worn by urban women with some social status, almost invariably consisting of voluminous body and head coverings, and some form of face-veil. The Egyptian Qasim Amin's critique, for example, was focused very much on the face-veil. What mattered to modernism was not variation in style and significance, nor what was culturally specific, nor its anthropological significance.[25] It was rather the perceived function of veiling, of the role played by the veil in the perpetuation of segregation, seclusion and all their attendant evils, which was crucial. Veiling was defined as operating as an extension of female seclusion, veiled women simply taking their seclusion with them, symbolically and actually, wherever they went. In this respect, in terms of its allotted place within the modernist critique, full veiling was remarkably similar across the Muslim world.[26] In Iran, it was the body-enveloping *chador* and the *picheh*, a face-veil of black horsehair mesh worn under the *chador* and tied over the head with a ribbon, or *niqab/ruband*, a face-veil of rectangular white cloth with a latticework panel at one end covering the eyes. In the Ottoman Empire, including the Balkans, it was a cloak, either the *çarşaf* or the *fereçe*, *şalvar* trousers and the *peçe*, or face-veil; in Egypt, a cloak, with a *burqu'* or face-veil and a *habara* or shawl or wrap worn over the head; in central Asia, the *paranji* and *chachvon*, a combination head-and-body-covering robe with horsehair face-veil.[27] Such garments were collectively and indiscriminately the target of modernist attacks, although little interest was shown at this stage in what might replace them.

Yet women's clothing was not in fact the timeless enveloping covering of the modernist imagination but was already changing rapidly. Just as the late nineteenth/early twentieth centuries were decades of rapid and profound ideological, cultural and political change, so too did they witness actual changes in female dress, including the manner of veiling. European tastes were of course much in vogue among elites around the globe in the nineteenth century. An inclination for everyday life *alafranga* had spread like wildfire among the upper classes of the Middle East and beyond, encompassing not only public activities such as entertainments but also changing mundane domestic habits, the import of European furniture, for example, altering intimate personal behaviour such as table manners.[28] Dress was an area profoundly affected by such preferences. In the century's final decades, women of the Ottoman elite, especially in Istanbul, increasingly imported elements of European fashion into their own styles of clothing.[29] With this example, these fashions spread throughout the empire. Particularly striking was the adoption by upper-class women in Istanbul of a form of nominal face-veil consisting of a white chiffon yashmak, which covered only the lower face and through which the woman's features were clearly visible.[30] Within a few years this fashion was to be seen in other major urban centres, notably Cairo.[31] Most significantly, these changes were adopted independently of any male prompting, but were largely or perhaps entirely the result of innovative behaviour by women themselves.

Change operated, however, in both directions. In the same decades some women experienced an intensification of veiling practices. This might be produced by a range of different factors. It was sometimes a result of a new or renewed salience of Islam. In Ottoman cities, for example, in tandem with the transparent yashmak, a heavier and thicker form of veiling also appeared among some women as a feature of the newly politicized Islamic agenda of the Hamidian regime. Heavier veiling practices have also been associated with an increasing European colonial presence. Douglas Northrop has pointed out that the heavy covering of *paranji* and *chachvon* in Turkestani cities spread with the arrival of growing numbers of Russians after the conquest of Central Asia.[32] According to his account, the *paranji* and *chachvon*, which were later designated as definitive signifiers of Uzbek identity, were in fact then new,

12 *Stephanie Cronin*

having replaced a much lighter and less restrictive form of covering, the *mursak*, from the 1870s.[33] In the colonial context, the adoption by Turkestani women of fuller forms of veiling appeared to serve as a mechanism of cultural and psychological defence against Russian hegemony. Yet, even here, purely indigenous considerations remained important. Khalid Adeeb, for example, sees the spread of fuller forms of veiling in late-nineteenth-century Central Asia rather as symptoms of what might be called 'embourgeoisement'. A growing prosperity in the cities led to a general increase in seclusion and polygyny; the ability of a man to take more than one wife and to keep his female relatives secluded and economically inactive becoming a sign of wealth and status, a form of 'conspicuous consumption'.[34]

Although acting on their own initiative, women who introduced changes based on European fashions into their own dress were following the example of men, whose clothing and appearance had already undergone much more significant alteration. Again, change was most visible among, and perhaps largely confined to, the elites. In contrast to the innovations introduced by women into their dress, however, which were largely driven by women's own desire to follow European fashion, the Europeanization of male clothing in the nineteenth century had begun as a state-sponsored or state-led initiative, a mechanism of social engineering.[35] In the 1820s Sultan Mahmud 11 had launched a clothing revolution, epitomized by the introduction of the fez, headgear having special religious, cultural and social significance.[36] In Iran, the far-weaker Qajar state had no such tradition of legislating on the appearance of its subjects. Nonetheless in 1873, following earlier unsuccessful attempts in the 1830s and '40s, the frock coat and fez were made required dress for officials.[37] Even the Afghan amirs promoted European military uniforms and European dress at court. These governmental efforts were, of course, moving with the grain of broader change. In addition to policy and legislation, the example of sultan and shah and a deepening desire not only to be, but to be recognized as, modern, meant that, by the end of the nineteenth century, the frock coat and fez was almost universal dress among the official classes, Muslim and non-Muslim.

These changes to male attire provoked bitter controversies.[38] By the early twentieth century, the arguments over veiling were still largely theoretical and, in any case, men were far more visible, their status and consequently their choices about appearance of greater social significance. The struggle over meaning which swirled around male appearance was at least as intense as that which was later to engulf the veil. A levelling device as well as a disciplinary tool, the fez was resisted fiercely by those who felt their identity and economic position threatened, but was, on the other hand, as a homogenizing non-religious symbol, particularly eagerly embraced by the non-Muslims of the empire, including Christian elites across the Balkans.[39] For precisely this reason, the clerical classes in Iran staunchly rejected all such dress innovations, and were vocal in their criticisms of those who accepted them. As well as a general dislike of Europeanized dress, attacked as mimicking the infidel, clerics condemned specific elements of the new fashions. The trimming or shaving of beards was particularly condemned, men's beards, like women's veils, possessing complex meanings, signifiying status, gender identity and religious observance. During the nineteenth century the ulama produced a huge body of literature declaring that shaving was strictly forbidden, yet, by the 1920s, the advance of modernism meant that the controversy over the beard had subsided and the frock coat was being replaced by the suit and tie.[40] Modernism's sartorial triumph was not yet complete, however, and the European hat was everywhere avoided.[41] Nonetheless, the eager male embrace of European fashion, at least from the neck down, served to emphasize more than ever before the apparently widening gulf separating the modern man from the still veiled and therefore backward woman.

During the nineteenth century, a different kind of official attention was paid to women's dress, efforts to control women's appearance focusing on preventing, not encouraging, change.[42] The same authorities which encouraged and sometimes demanded the Europeanization and therefore modernization of men's dress were still dominated by an entirely unmodernized view of gender. In stark contrast to the much contested and sometimes harshly imposed male clothing policies, nowhere did the imperial regimes of the pre-First World War decades even propose reforms to women's dress. Even upon taking power, avowedly modernist regimes, such as that of the Committee of Union and Progress in the Ottoman Empire from 1908, were far from implementing, or even discussing, such steps.

The First World War and the collapse of the Ottoman and Russian empires transformed the political circumstances of vast numbers of the world's Muslims. In Turkey and Iran, dynamic nationalist elites led by Mustafa Kemal and Reza Shah, respectively, seized power, while the young King Amanullah placed Afghanistan on the same path. In the Caucasus and Central Asia, the new Soviet state gradually established its hegemony and in the Balkans, independent nationalist regimes consolidated themselves and sought a recognized place within the post-war European order. In each of these environments, modernism found itself suddenly and dramatically empowered, with an unprecedented opportunity to implement its broad agenda, including its prescriptions for women. The anti-veiling rhetoric of the past decades was now to be transformed into state policy.

But, for these new regimes, women's veiling was not the first priority. On the contrary, it was male dress which first attracted the attention of the authorities, where the most drastic reforms were implemented and where resistance was fiercest. In the 1920s Turkey and Iran legislated, and Afghan and Balkan nationalists strongly encouraged, further changes to men's dress within the context of a broader cultural transformation. These changes were still, as in the nineteenth century, aimed at homogenization, but their objective had now also expanded to reinforce bigger projects of nationalism, modernization and secularization through the creation of citizens marked by modernity and unmarked by symbols of ethnic or religious difference. The

14   *Stephanie Cronin*

male clothing reforms of the 1920s were not primarily concerned with gender, their adoption necessitating no wider transformation in male-female public interaction, as unveiling was to do. They did, however, possess a gender dimension. Nationalists everywhere remained wedded to the view that changes to women's lives could best be advanced by mobilizing the patriarchal structures of society. Women would unveil when encouraged or permitted to do so by their fathers and husbands. It was therefore necessary as a first step to effect a transformation in men's consciousness, and this process could be facilitated and hastened by changing men's outward appearance, ridding society of visible symbols of the backward past.[43]

Only in the USSR was there no attempt to transform male appearance and therefore consciousness as a prerequisite to tackling the veil. This was the first of several key differences between the Soviet approach and that of the nationalist regimes. Although Soviet officials occasionally resorted to using male domestic power to encourage unveiling, they understood the 1927 *hujum* (attack), of which the unveiling campaign was a major symbol, as an all-out battle against patriarchy. Furthermore, unlike Kemalist Turkey or Pahlavi Iran, the new Soviet authorities had no interest in the imitation of the European bourgeoisie. Their conceptualization of modernity was not hostile to national or ethnic cultural difference and they found nothing threatening or subversive in local 'folk' costume as they strove to create the new Soviet man and woman. On the contrary, they rather promoted it, even if only implicitly, as a signifier of authentic popular culture and in the course of a nationalities policy which actually involved the creation of nation-states across Central Asia and the Caucasus.

The Turkish republic was the first of the new states to embark on a project of 'sartorial social engineering'.[44] As an integral part of the drive to make Turkey resemble his vision of a secular and modern country, and as a sign of a rupture with the Ottoman past, Mustafa Kemal was determined to make the appearance of Turkish men conform to what he described as 'civilized' standards. Peaked caps were introduced into military uniforms, and in November 1925 the National Assembly passed the Hat Law banning the fez. In a striking example of the ability of simple clothing to carry varied and even contradictory meanings, the fez was turned by the republican authorities into the opposite of what it had been for the Ottomans. It was now redefined as 'an emblem of ignorance, negligence, fanaticism and hatred of progress and civilization', and the European hat, the headgear used by the 'civilized world' was made compulsory for men.[45] The Hat Law was part of a comprehensive and radical programme of political, social and cultural reforms aimed at eliminating the social and political presence of Islam, including the abolition of the sultanate and caliphate and the secularization of education and law, and this was clearly recognized by religious personnel and by the population in general. The Hat Law was popularly perceived, quite accurately, as an attack on religion, hats with brims being believed to be an infidel garment preventing the worshipper's forehead from touching the ground during prayer. It provoked

Introduction: coercion or empowerment? 15

widespread opposition which was dealt with by the draconian Independence Tribunals, established to deal with the recent Kurdish and religious uprising, and a number of men, including low-ranking clerics, were executed.

In 1927 Reza Shah embarked on a similar programme. In Iran, like Turkey, the peaked cap had already been introduced into the army and had also been adopted by some fashionable young men in Tehran.[46] In 1927 the Iranian cabinet decided to make the Pahlavi peaked cap, and not, in contrast to Turkey, the European hat, the official headgear for Iranian men. In 1928 the Majlis legislated to make the short coat and Pahlavi cap compulsory, with a few limited exceptions, with failure to comply punishable by fines and imprisonment. As in the Turkish case, in Iran too the clothing reforms took place in the context of a much wider programme of reform, including the secularization of the judicial and legal systems, conscription, economic *étatisme* and tribal settlement. As in Turkey, the Iranian Uniform Dress Law was, except among the small Westernized elite, very unpopular, especially among the ulama, for whom it was tainted with heresy. As in Turkey, its implementation produced serious opposition, including massive urban demonstrations led by low-ranking mullas which were suppressed with great harshness, and a swathe of tribal uprisings.[47] In 1935 the next episode of the hat story in Iran was written in blood. The government's attempt to replace the now outmoded Pahlavi cap with the 'international' or European hat, combined with other subaltern grievances, high taxation, poverty and low wages, and with rumours of unveiling, to produce an uprising in Mashhad which was only suppressed after several days by a veritable massacre by the army, sacrilegiously carried out within the precincts of the shrine of the Eighth Imam.[48]

Even in Afghanistan, where the state and the tradition of reform was far flimsier than in either Turkey or Iran, King Amanullah too appreciated the cultural power of clothing. Here, too, the earliest and most serious efforts at reform were in the area of male dress, not women's veiling. The late nineteenth/early twentieth century had seen the frock coat make some inroads at the Afghan court, usually coupled with an astrakhan hat. As Tom Wide describes in Chapter 6, in the 1920s Amanullah tentatively introduced some unenforceable policies which he hoped would spread the wearing of Western attire among men, beginning with the official and notable classes and moving on to the wider male population of Kabul.[49] These actions certainly contributed to Amanullah's burgeoning unpopularity outside the tiny modernist elite and aggravated the tribal crisis which was soon to overwhelm his regime. Tellingly, his opponents made the cancellation of the clothing reforms one of their first priorities.[50]

In the Balkans, male dress was also a target of nationalists and modernizers and became so at an earlier period than female dress. As in the Turkish republic, the fez was transformed into its opposite by modern nationalism.[51] As Mary Neuburger has described, in Bulgaria the fez, worn by Christian notables as well as Bulgarian Muslims (Pomaks) and Turkish-speaking Bulgarians, came to represent collaboration with the Ottoman state. Not only modernity but Bulgarian nationalism too demanded that it be abandoned in favour of either the hat or the peasant sheepskin *kalpak*. The first half of the twentieth century saw a long struggle to eliminate the fez and turban from Pomak and Turkish-speaking minorities. This struggle was enthusiastically embraced by Kemalists among the Turkish-speaking minority and Bulgarian nationalists among the Pomaks. A series of fragile interwar Bulgarian governments, lacking the stability of Kemalist Turkey, Pahlavi Iran and the Soviet Union, did little in legislative terms. When the Communist Party took power after the Second World War, it renewed the campaign against both the fez and the veil, but the change of hats for men was a clear priority and considered an essential prerequisite for unveiling.[52] Although the male clothing reforms were met by considerable resistance, this was of a 'weapons of the weak' character, which was inevitable given the minority and somewhat besieged status of the Muslim communities.

Only in the Balkans were the forms of dress typically worn by Muslim men, especially the fez, constructed as alien, relics of foreign rule, with their removal allowing the reappearance of the true European beneath. In Turkey, for example, the fez was defined as a symbol of the despised Ottoman past, but the rupture represented by the hat was with backwardness, not foreign rule, the hat itself a symbol of modernity. The designation of women's veiling as alien, as well as backward, was much more common, not only in the Balkans, but also in Turkey and Iran, where nationalist ideologues invented a pre-Islamic past where women's status was higher and they accordingly went unveiled. Only in the Soviet Union did the anti-veiling campaign make no use of motifs stressing the nationalist character of unveiling. Although the Soviet authorities were at ease with culturally specific national costume, their *hujum* was part of a wider drive against 'bourgeois' nationalism and the social groups that supported it. In the Caucasus and Central Asia, the project of imparting a nationalist dimension to the veil was adopted by those in favour, not those against.

The male dress reforms have usually been seen purely as initiatives of the newly established regimes, announced suddenly, divorced from their historical context and implemented in an authoritarian, top-down manner. In fact, as the above narrative shows, local elites had already eagerly adopted modern fashions. Their sartorial preferences framed by a discourse articulated by a modern intelligentsia, these elites ardently pressed the new nationalist regimes to oblige the rest of society to follow suit. By the early twentieth century, the spread of European-style clothing among the official and notable classes, symptomatic of a wider social and cultural modernism, had led to the appearance of an ever more visible gulf between elite and subaltern, town and country, educated and uneducated, religious and secular, with society increasingly losing sight of any shared cultural universe. The nationalist regimes saw their task as one of restoring a sense of social and national harmony through the forced imposition on the entire society of a modernism hitherto the preserve of the elites.

Introduction: coercion or empowerment? 17

Unveiling possessed a similar pre-history and occupied a similar position in the post-First World War agenda of both nationalist state and elite. Although the actual discarding of the veil had hardly occurred by the 1920s, ever lighter veils were being pioneered by upper-class women, and the intelligentsia was pressing support for unveiling on the new regimes. Unveiling was also essential to homogenize society and to complete male modernism. The image of the European suit- and hat-wearing man clashed more and more jarringly with that of his veiled wife.

Although male dress reforms had taken first priority, from the very beginning of their arrival in control of the state, modernists had begun to plan for changes to veiling practices. The issue remained controversial but the modernist voice was now infinitely more audible and authoritative as a result of its possession of the state. The counter-discourse and the social groups who articulated it, especially the clergy, were correspondingly disempowered and were increasingly cast, in this new official narrative, as historically redundant. Nonetheless, much greater caution was exercised everywhere in relation to unveiling than had been the case with male dress and hats.

In the first half of the 1920s, the new states refrained from active encouragement of unveiling but allowed the anti-veiling discourse to grow louder and to penetrate society more deeply. The importance of education and legal emancipation were still stressed but veiling was increasingly problematized. In addition to the damage it caused society through the constraints it placed on female education and employment, veiling was criticized ever more strongly on physical grounds. Modern medicine was mobilized to condemn veiling as directly injurious to health, causing vitamin D deficiency and tuberculosis, and indirectly, as an impediment to female participation in sports and gymnastics, an important innovation in the new schools.[53]

In Iran, Turkey and the Balkans, veiling was also more systematically problematized on moral grounds. In a striking illustration of the capacity of the veil, like the fez, to carry different, indeed contradictory, meanings, the modernist answer to the traditionalist assertion that unveiling would lead to corruption was to formulate the concept of the metaphorical 'veil of chastity'. Great emphasis was placed on the moral superiority of the unveiled woman who defended her own chastity through an internalized morality instilled through education.[54] In Iran, the sexually explicit poetry of Iraj Mirza contrasted the unchaste and sexually available veiled woman with the truly virtuous, enlightened and unveiled woman, while, as Nathalie Clayer discusses in Chapter 8, the Albanian intellectual, Mehdi Frasheri, argued that it was fanatical and reactionary Sunni Islam which imposed veiling on women, the locally influential Bektashi Sufism only requiring women to wear the 'veil of honour'.[55]

By the 1920s, veiling and seclusion were routinely being allocated another, highly significant, sexually corrupting role in the modernist discourse, allegedly contributing to newly problematized customs of male homoerotic relations. According to this novel, binary, view of healthy sexual mores, men were

18   *Stephanie Cronin*

driven into 'backward' homosexual emotional and physical attachments by the sequestration of women. Unveiling women and desegregating society would produce not only an educated wife and mother but an exclusively heterosexual man, able together to constitute partners in a companiate marriage, the building block of a modern society.[56]

In the infant Soviet Union, although a medicalized anti-veiling discourse was prominent, the redefinition of unveiling as a demonstration of a superior morality was completely absent. Indeed, for many of the Russian women activists who staffed the *Zhenotdel* (the Communist Party's women's department), the goal was not just the emancipation of the Soviet woman, but her complete liberation from the confines of a bourgeois morality, whether religiously underpinned or not. The leaders of the *Zhenotdel*, Alexandra Kollontai and Inessa Armand, were particularly associated with such views. This stance, and the rejection of such a redefinition of the unveiled woman as adhering more rigidly than her veiled sister to patriarchal moral codes, produced a greater ideological schism. It left Soviet women more ideologically exposed than unveiling women elsewhere and may have contributed to the uniquely violent backlash which greeted the *hujum*.

Under the umbrella of a sympathetic official discourse, women themselves began to intervene more energetically in the debate over veiling and to take practical steps on their own initiative. Lighter forms of veiling became more common as women continued the practical experiments in changing their attire of the kind which had begun the previous century.[57] Many more women simply quietly modified their veil into something entirely nominal. The face-veil became less common, and robes such as *chador* or *çarşaf* were worn more loosely over Western clothes. At the same time, dramatic episodes of public unveiling announced the new dress conventions to wider national and international audiences. Such theatrical performances of unveiling by elite women, largely protected from the consequences of public or family hostility, were epitomized by the action of the famous Egyptian feminist Huda Sha'rawi, who dramatically removed her veil when stepping down from a train in Cairo on her return from a women's meeting in Rome. The large crowd of women who had gone to meet her broke into applause and some imitated her, removing their veils.[58] Perhaps the most famous example of the performance of unveiling was by Queen Soraya of Afghanistan whose choice of apparel, including uncovered hair and décolletage, while accompanying King Amanullah on a tour of Europe and the Middle East in 1928, encouraged and scandalized in equal measures. The role of travel, or even only movement, in stimulating these episodes is clear and illustrates the depth of the changes wrought by the previous decades. Unlike the nineteenth century, the key experience was no longer travel within the Muslim world, but travel to Europe. It was, furthermore, no longer only men who could travel, but women, and even occasionally women independently of men, signifying the dramatic arrival of a degree of autonomy, at least for a minority. This ability to move between environments made available to women a strategy of flexibly

Introduction: coercion or empowerment? 19

adapting dress, this strategy easing the transition from fully veiled to fully unveiled. Uzbek women might veil in Tashkent and unveil in Moscow; Tehrani schoolgirls might veil in the street and unveil in school.

Women's contribution to the changing veiling praxis was important in another way. The early twentieth century had seen a new audibility of women's voices and the beginnings of a women's press and women's organizations.[59] In the 1920s, this new activism, notably in Iran and Turkey, continued to develop, charitable, educational and even political organizations mushroomed, transnational networks were established and the women's press contributed to the elaborations of new discourses and provided space for women themselves to discuss their own concerns about the shape and momentum of change. After 1928, for example, the Iranian women's journal, *Alam-i Nisvan*, became an advocate of unveiling, the debates reaching fever pitch by the early 1930s.[60] This activism was key to the reforming regimes, providing a bedrock of ideological and political support.[61] Its fate, however, was to be bleak. With the modernizing state intent on its own hegemony, the independent women's associations and publications of the 1920s succumbed to ever tighter state control, and ultimately to suppression during the later 1930s.

Gradually, country by country, the changes in veiling habits initiated and carried out by women themselves began to acquire more definite state backing. At the same time as the new states tolerated and encouraged ideological attacks on veiling, so they gradually began to offer protection to women who acted to lighten or discard their veils. In Iran, for example, the police were warned to cease their habit of detaining supposedly improperly dressed women and, in a dramatic episode in 1928, Reza Shah energetically defended his female relatives when they were criticized for visiting a shrine wearing only light *chadors*.[62]

Eventually this state support and protection for women who unveiled was transformed into an actual state-led campaign against veiling. The timing and context of such campaigns is highly significant as they were often synchronized with, and embedded within, much wider reform drives. Turkey had seen early examples of official initiatives in support of unveiling, although these remained only local and sporadic, taking place as a consequence of enthusiasm for the Hat Law of 1925 and its accompanying discussions of civilized and modern dress.[63] The next, much more significant stage took place from late 1934 when the Turkish state stepped up its campaign for change in women's dress directly after women's acquisition of the right to vote, when abandonment of the veil was presented as a necessary prerequisite to women's full exercise of their political rights. In Iran, unveiling also appears to have been mooted as an official policy immediately following the male dress reforms and in the throes of the legislative radicalism of 1927–29. But the discouraging example of the overthrow of King Amanullah in Afghanistan and the serious discontent inside Iran resulting from the imposition of a range of new and often very unpopular political, economic and cultural policies

20 *Stephanie Cronin*

apparently postponed the move. It then had to wait until 1936, 18 months after Reza Shah's visit to Turkey, his interest perhaps revived by the Kemalist example in full swing by 1935. Once more immediately following a male dress reform, the introduction of the 'European' hat to replace the Pahlavi cap, Reza Shah threw the resources of the state behind an unveiling campaign.[64] In Albania the Ministerial Council issued a perhaps rather ineffective ban on *peçe* and *fereçe* in 1929, following the introduction of the civil code the previous year and the political change from republic to monarchy. But it was in 1937, in the midst of a major reform drive, that parliament passed the 'law on the ban of face covering' which forbade women to cover their faces, totally or partially.[65]

Although the literature often contains claims to the contrary, recent research shows clearly that neither Turkey, Afghanistan, the Soviet Union nor even Iran ever passed legislation banning veiling. This historical reality contrasts strongly with conventional impressions. In Afghanistan, for example, despite Queen Soraya's acquisition of the status of an icon of modernity, and despite too the almost universal belief that one of the most important factors in Amanullah's overthrow was his advocacy of unveiling, in fact Afghanistan saw no legal change or official action. As Tom Wide shows in Chapter 6, Amanullah issued no decree, other than a rather obscure and completely unenforceable announcement that the *burqa'* be replaced by a light veil, and coat and hat.[66] Neither Iran nor Turkey had hesitated to use legislation as an instrument of general social engineering. Both had passed laws on male clothing as well as to advance a range of other cultural changes. But in Turkey, although local bodies such as municipal councils issued sporadic bans of the *peçe* and *çarşaf*, the government itself refrained from passing any anti-veiling laws. In Iran, as Rostam-Kolayi and Matin-asgari make clear, the Majlis passed no legislation nor is there any archival trace of a royal decree.[67] Even the Soviet Union resisted pleas from women activists that they needed the protection offered by legislation.[68] These regimes, avoiding the direct confrontation implied by legislation, relied rather on administrative measures combined with intensive propaganda campaigns.

Public opinion was carefully prepared. In her discussion of Turkey, Kathryn Libal describes the ways in which the Kemalist authorities used journals, newspapers, publications of People's Houses and photographs to encourage acceptance of the unveiled modern Turkish woman.[69] In Iran, too, the *kashf-i hijab*, as the unveiling campaign was known, was located firmly within a wider regime initiative of 'the Women's Awakening', and was preceded and accompanied by a press mobilization instigated and controlled by the government. As Camron Amin has shown, immediately before the launch of the *kashf-i hijab*, the regime ensured that the newspaper *Ettela'at*, Iran's main daily, was filled with images of unveiled Iranian women, the press hitherto having confined itself to showing only foreign women in its illustrations. The beginning of the campaign in early January 1936 saw the pages of *Ettela'at* full of coverage of unveiling ceremonies and editorials, articles and letters to the editor discussing 'the Women's Awakening'.[70]

Introduction: coercion or empowerment? 21

The press in both countries was also used to provide reassurance in the face of the profound anxieties aroused by the removal of face-veil and robe and to offer practical advice on how to cope with the far-reaching change in manners and behaviour necessitated by changing veiling practices. As Afsanah Najmabadi has explained, the abandonment of the physical veil entailed a complete re-ordering of gender relations in the public sphere.[71] This required not only that women, but that men too, introduce profound alterations to their everyday lives. Both women and men were required to familiarize themselves with an entirely new code of social intercourse, and publications offering advice on etiquette appeared to advise them.[72] Unveiling women also had to learn new ways of presenting themselves in terms of their physical appearance, and the women's press in particular devoted much space to discussions about fashion, clothing and the aesthetics of the body.[73] With unveiling, appearance, specifically conventions of beauty, became of infinitely greater importance to a woman's life-chances than hitherto.[74]

Unveiling propaganda took other forms. The launch of a campaign was often announced by a theatrical performance of unveiling. Huda Shar'awi's discarding of the veil at Cairo railway station, described above, was such a performance but was an individual independent initiative. Now the reforming state took over the tactic and paid great attention to choreographing in detail dramatic episodes of rejection. In Iran, for example, the *kashf-i hijab* was initiated by the appearance of Reza Shah and his wife and daughters, all without face-veil or *chador* and wearing hats, at a public occasion, a graduation ceremony at a teachers' training college in Tehran, in early January 1936.[75] This was the signal for unveiling ceremonies and celebrations to take place all over the country. In postwar Yugoslavia, following the passage of an anti-veiling resolution at the second congress of the Antifascist Women's Front of Bosnia-Herzegovina, a delegate made a demonstration of removing her veil to the applause of the other delegates, and at her urging other Muslim women followed suit.[76] But it was in the Soviet Union, most experienced and accomplished in the practice of mass mobilization through modern propaganda techniques, where the staging of unveiling was most elaborate. In the Soviet Union, furthermore, such theatre was not built around elite women, but was performed by ordinary and poor women mobilized by the *Zhenotdel*. Marianne Kamp has described one early episode when a delegation of Turkestani women to a Comintern meeting in Moscow in 1921 collectively unveiled to applause and tears of joy.[77] With the launch of the *hujum* in 1927, elaborate stagings of unveiling took place in Central Asia itself. Kamp narrates one such episode, replete with revolutionary symbolism, recalled by a female participant. The woman, then a teenager, gathered with other Komsomol members and together they marched, wearing *paranjis* and singing revolutionary songs, to the old city of Tashkent. The woman made a speech and thereupon she and her comrades removed their *paranjis* and threw them onto a bonfire.[78] The event took place on the occasion of International Women's Day, March 8 1927. Such public bonfires of *paranji* and *chachvon* came to typify the declaration of the *hujum* in each local area.

22 *Stephanie Cronin*

Governments had other methods of advancing the unveiling campaigns, part encouragement, part coercion. The modernist discourse had defined veiling as a symptom of a wider problem of female seclusion. It was, therefore, not sufficient to unveil. The attendant evils of segregation and seclusion has also to be targeted and vanquished. Accordingly the unveiling campaigns were everywhere accompanied by orchestrated efforts to organize mixed social gatherings of unimpeachable respectability. In Iran and Turkey, officials and army officers were invited and indeed obliged to attend mixed social functions with their unveiled wives at the risk of losing their positions.[79] In Central Asia, Communist Party members and Soviet officials were subject to similar pressures. These were certainly occasions which both men and women found difficult to navigate and often painful, but they did result, quite quickly, in a profound shift in attitude.

In Iran and Turkey, government efforts to encourage unveiling were aimed squarely at the new military and bureaucratic elites who were to provide exemplary leadership to the rest of society.[80] In these circles there was broad support for the modernist agenda of the regime, and changes in dress codes for men, and even to some extent for women, had already been accepted and even advocated. However Iran took a further step, mobilizing not only these, its natural, constituencies but also, crucially and perhaps surprisingly, the clerical classes. The press reported, for example, clerics and their unveiled wives attending unveiling ceremonies in Kirmanshah and Qazvin.[81] As Afshin Matin-asgari and Jasamin Rostami-Kolayi point out in Chapter 4, although members of the Iranian ulama were vocal in their defence of veiling in the debates of the earlier period, by the 1930s no senior cleric spoke out against the campaign.[82] The use of a docile ulama to provide legitimacy for unveiling was made possible by the fact that the clergy was, by the 1930s in both Turkey and Iran, firmly under state control, their leaderships successfully coopted. In the Balkans too, approval extracted from religious figures was an important strategy, clerics issuing pronouncements that revealing the face was not *haram*. In interwar Albania, the state's supervision and control over the activities of the ulama, who were, in any case, largely in the Islamic modernist camp, went so far as to produce the claim that the anti-veiling policy had actually been first suggested by the leadership of the Muslim community itself.[83] In Iran, Turkey and the Balkans, Islamic modernist arguments remained important to the construction of legitimacy for the unveiling campaigns. These were deployed alongside the apparently contradictory arguments appealing to notions of pre-Islamic national and cultural authenticity. Although, in ideological terms, the Islamic modernist and the secular nationalist discourses appeared to be dichotomous, politically they were both useful and were often used in tandem, amidst a general indifference to any theoretical contradiction.

Iran and Turkey were careful to present unveiling within a context of national and religious tradition. Here we find another stark contrast with the Soviet case, as described by Kamp. In Soviet Central Asia and the Caucasus,

Introduction: coercion or empowerment? 23

unveiling was presented in precisely opposite terms, as a revolutionary rejection of tradition. The absence from Soviet propaganda in the 1920s of the 'veil of honour' argument has been noted above. Although in Central Asia, some clergy and even some Communist Party activists were ready to express Islamic modernist arguments inherited from the *Jadidi* reformers, with the advent of the *hujum* the leadership actively rejected such arguments, insisting on locating unveiling within the context of a mortal struggle against Islam and clerical influence. Unveiling was a stage in the creation of the new Soviet woman. Attempts by clerics to offer support to unveiling were deemed subversive, insidious and more dangerous than outright opposition.[84] Thus, in contrast to Iran, Turkey and the Balkans, women in Soviet Central Asia and the Caucasus unveiled without the protection of a sympathetic modernist ulama, their action contextualized within an overt, class-based, anti-religious and anti-clerical struggle.

Only the Balkans saw legislation in favour of unveiling. Elsewhere governments concentrated on creating bureaucratic frameworks to shape and advance the campaigns and keep them within some sort of legal parameters. Both the Pahlavi and Kemalist regimes were, as is emphasized in the chapters by Matin-asgari and Rostam-Kolayi (Chapter 4), and Adak (Chapter 2), aware of the risk of provoking a backlash, and the educative element of their strategy was generally much stronger than it is usually assumed to have been. The scholarly literature and narratives drawn from memoirs and oral history have stressed the arbitrary, oppressive and sometimes violent character of state action, especially in Iran and Soviet Central Asia. The Iranian case, for example, certainly provides many examples of physical force being used by police.[85] Yet, as the new research below demonstrates, both Iranian and Turkish governments disliked such actions, and in fact emphasized the need for caution and restraint.[86] Contrary to the dominant conventional impression, the Turkish, Iranian and especially the Soviet regimes all supposed that the coercive power of the state, and specifically its legal mechanisms, would be exercised not against women but primarily against male opposition and in defence of women. Such an effort to extend legal protection to unveiling women reached its most extreme extent in Soviet Central Asia. As Kamp describes, here unveiling women faced extraordinary levels of violence from men. In the late 1920s, although there was no law forcing women to unveil, a number of laws were passed against male enforcement of certain traditional Uzbek gender customs, defined as 'crimes of everyday life'. It became illegal, for example, to coerce a women into wearing the *paranji* or remaining secluded.[87] As the violent reaction against the *hujum* gathered pace, attacks on women who unveiled were redefined as counter-revolutionary acts, carrying a capital sentence.[88]

The debates over veiling, which were now several decades old, had been complex, passionate and bitter. They consisted largely, however, of attacks on, and defences of, face-veil and robes. Surprisingly little attention was paid to the question of what forms of clothing and appearance might replace them.

24   *Stephanie Cronin*

Modernism did not problematize the new. It was as if it were only necessary to remove the old, and the new would then emerge like a butterfly from a chrysalis. In fact, it quickly became apparent everywhere that the abandonment, willingly or not, of face-veil and robe immediately gave rise to a host of unforeseen problems. In Turkey, the regime ideal, modelled on the Western European woman, was ardently advocated through various propaganda mechanisms. In practice, however, a great latitude was allowed to women in their choice of replacement dress.[89] Although it preferred hats and even bare heads, Kemalism was quite ready to tolerate headscarves and even subversive devices such as permanently unfurled umbrellas. The Soviet authorities were completely indifferent as long as the *paranji* and *chachvon* were abandoned. Indeed, throughout the USSR the headscarf had become a symbol of proletarian and peasant class identity. The confusion seems to have been greatest in Iran. Only here does there seem to have been a somewhat sporadic objection even to the headscarf and, perhaps given the prominence of the royal women as role models, a stronger determination to oblige the acceptance of 'civilized' European clothes and hats.[90]

Policy on women's dress was less positively prescriptive than had been the case with the male dress reforms. Nonetheless, the general tenor of public discussion on female appearance indicated a marked preference for a model drawn from Europe. Although female beauty, of a conventional stylized kind, had always been important and expressed especially in poetry, the conformity of the individual woman to this ideal was not a subject for discussion outside the immediate family. Now the veiling controversies gave rise to a new public preoccupation with female appearance. The press was filled with advice on beauty, fashion and hygiene, entirely new industries grew up to cater to the needs of the unveiled woman and, as Libal points out in Chapter 1, even beauty contests were introduced to accustom public opinion to the acceptability of openly regarding and commenting upon a woman's physical appearance.[91] The adoption of such new fashions, made necessary by unveiling, was an expensive project, and everywhere complaints could be heard from poorer women of the burden of this embryonic consumerism. The new habits were criticized on other grounds. The encouragement offered to women to become consumers of fashion, make-up, and related services, and to devote more attention to their personal tastes and preferences than previously, aroused new anxieties, or perhaps rather allowed older anxieties to reappear in a new guise. There seem to have been perennial concerns focused on women as possible conduits for a corrupting luxury and waste. These now emerged increasingly strongly into public discourse. As Afsaneh Najmabadi points out, in Iran in particular, the new consumerism, heralded by the unveiling policy, gradually produced a radical critique of modernism focused on women, who were denounced as the 'painted dolls' of the monarchy, the very essence of Westoxication.[92]

Everywhere, in Iran, Turkey, the Soviet Union and the Balkans, the new states took over a discourse which had gestated in civil society and themselves assumed responsibility and leadership in defining, shaping and enforcing unveiling policies. It has been argued that, in so doing, these regimes both disempowered women and turned unveiling into a target of a deeper opposition. Kamp, for example, suggests in Chapter 7 that it was the Communist Party's appropriation of unveiling which multiplied the meanings of the policy and accordingly, the acts of violence against it.[93] In the case of Iran too, it has been argued that the unveiling campaign contributed materially to the regime's wider unpopularity, and perhaps tarnished the image of the Pahlavi dynasty itself.[94] Yet much of the assessment of the unveiling campaigns has been undertaken in contexts where the regimes themselves have been discredited or even overthrown. Contemporary memories of the 1930s in post-Soviet Central Asia or post-Pahlavi Iran have inevitably been shaped by the powerful new discourses generated by the replacement regimes. One incontrovertible fact remains: in Iran, Turkey and the Balkans, opposition to unveiling *at the time* was muted, and far less than opposition to the male clothing reforms. Only in the Soviet Union did opposition result in violence, and there, as Kamp points out, such violence was directed at women themselves, not at the authorities responsible for the policy.

Camron Amin perhaps hints at the reasons for the stress laid in later accounts on the trauma caused by the unveiling campaign in Iran by pointing to the psychological effects, not on women, but on men. It was, after all, mainly men who recorded their impressions of unveiling and through male eyes that unveiling has been understood. Pointing to the sense of powerlessness induced in men by the new state's appropriation of control of female behaviour, hitherto the prerogative of male relatives, family and community, Amin describes the 'depths of male resentment' towards Reza Shah, a resentment which spread to encompass the entire regime and which left a deep mark on the collective memory, a memory nearly always articulated by men rather than by the unveiling women themselves.[95]

The appropriation by the state of the unveiling praxis raises especially acutely the question of women's agency. Certainly the reforming states were able to count on the support of numbers of women activists, particularly those who had already become involved in intellectual and educational activities and who shared a broad modernist outlook. Indeed, some women, as Shireen Mahdavi has argued in relation to Iran, welcomed the support of an authoritarian state as essential to overcome still powerful reactionary forces.[96] The Kemalist state made deliberate efforts to mobilize women as leadership for its campaigns; in Iran a new elite organization, the *kanun-i banuvan* (Ladies Society), was formed to promote the Women's Awakening in general and unveiling in particular; in the Soviet Union, leadership and organization of the *hujum* was provided by the women of the *Zhenotdel*. Indeed, sometimes radical women tried to push the state farther than it was prepared to go. In 1927 women activists wrote to the Soviet government asking for a decree calling for unveiling but were refused, the government insisting that unveiling should be voluntary.[97]

26 *Stephanie Cronin*

Yet, and this is the dimension that has usually been highlighted in the literature, women also resisted the unveiling campaigns. The negative impact on women of the authoritarianism of unveiling has been documented, particularly in the case of Iran, with even writers sympathetic to the broader project of female emancipation critical of the methods used by the Pahlavi regime. Yet recent research in this volume and elsewhere introduces a more nuanced view. Rostam-Kolayi and Matin-asgari conclude that, although forcible measures and even violence were used in Iran, 'their frequency and extent remains unclear' and they were opposed by the authorities directing the campaign.[98] In the case of Turkey, Sevgi Adak has argued that the very silence from the authorities about the type of clothing to replace veil and robe created a space within which women might negotiate and adapt the new sartorial requirements, making the change more complex and less radical. Between 'the poles of compliance and of resistance' women creatively devised a range of strategies for coping with the conflicting demands of state and society.[99] Perhaps Kamp's discussion of the Soviet Union most eloquently problematizes the question of women's agency.[100] She points out that, in such an era of authoritarian change, women often either remained veiled as a result of family pressure, or unveiled as a result of similar but opposite pressure from family, Party, and state, possibly in combination. These were not years, across the world, when the autonomous individual was easily able to stand against authority, from whatever source that authority emanated.

What, then, may be concluded about the similarities and differences between the various anti-veiling campaigns discussed in this collection? First, as Rostam-Kolayi and Matin-asgari point out, these narratives of unveiling appear to show that Kemalist Turkey and Pahlavi Iran were much closer in their discourse and their policy than has previously been thought.[101] They in turn deeply influenced Persian-speaking Afghan reformers and Muslim modernists in the Balkans. Soviet experience, however, diverges in significant ways.[102] The Soviet Union was the first state to launch a concerted anti-veiling drive, its *hujum* of 1927 coming earlier than either Turkish or Iranian campaigns. Mention has been made above of Kamp's calculation of the extraordinary level of violence directed by men towards women during the *hujum*, violence which is notably absent from the other case studies. She estimates that around 2,000 women were murdered in Uzbekistan in the years between 1927 and 1929.[103] In the Iranian case, by contrast, where the unpopularity of the measure has received almost all the scholarly interest, not a single case of serious violence has yet come to light. The unique context and radicalism of the objectives of the *hujum* may provide the beginning of an explanation. In Iran and Turkey, the policies of the interwar period flowed organically from an earlier and ever-deepening constitutionalism, nationalism and modernism. Both Mustafa Kemal and Reza Shah drew on ideological tropes drawn from these traditions and utilized elites which had been shaped by them. The reforms of the interwar period in general, and unveiling in particular, were advocated and supported by elites old and new, and occasionally the state even had to exert brakes on the zeal of reformers, women as well as men. In Central Asia before 1917, *Jadidism* had been a much weaker and more conservative phenomenon and, unlike Iran and the Ottoman Empire, had generated little in terms of women's activism. After 1917 the Communist Party, therefore, had only a very flimsy tradition on which to draw. In the 1920s, in both Iran and Turkey, an anti-veiling discourse was allowed to mature, and was even officially encouraged, and a transformation was effected in the way the state responded to women; rather than it harassing women deemed improperly dressed, as in the past, women were now offered protection when lightening their coverings. In Central Asia, Kamp points out, the Communist Party had done little to prepare public opinion for unveiling, nor had there been any critique of male dress to prepare the ground. Particularly important is the fact that Kemalist Turkey and Pahlavi Iran mobilized not only secular nationalism and the new bureaucratic and military elites in support of unveiling, but Iran in particular, perhaps surprisingly, was not afraid to invoke Islamic modernism and the active support of members of the ulama. Secular reformers reinforced the moral dimension to the campaign with the 'veil of chastity' rhetoric. In the Soviet Union, on the contrary, the *hujum* in general and unveiling in particular were an important part of the struggle against religion and against 'reactionary' elites of all kinds, including clerical, as part of the ongoing class war and revolutionary transformation. Unveiling was part of a wider and deeper attack on the old way of life, a step on the path to the creation of an entirely new Soviet woman, complementing the new Soviet man, and the *Zhenotdel* had no use for modernist mullas, deemed a fifth column, or the veil of chastity. Furthermore, not only did the authorities overtly reject the cooperation of elements compromised by class or politics, but the *Zhenotdel* based itself on the very poorest women, even those outcast from local society, thus making itself an even easier target for local doubters and resisters.

In the Balkans, anti-veiling campaigns suffered from something of a time-lag. An anti-fez and anti-veiling discourse was fully formulated during the interwar decades, building on older nationalist tropes. But the governments of those years, wracked by domestic political turmoil and regional chaos, lacked the stability which enabled regimes such as those in Turkey, Iran and Central Asia to embark on projects of social engineering. Such projects had to wait for the establishment of stronger post-war Communist regimes buoyed up by Soviet support. Although these regimes were based on local Communist parties, their clothing reform campaigns appear to have been hybrids, bearing similarities, both in terms of ideology and methods of enforcement, as much to the interwar nationalist drives as to the Soviet *hujum*. As well as the differing political context, a further specific feature of the Balkan campaigns was the position of Muslims as marginalized minorities within those societies. Only in Albania were Muslims a small majority and here the first legal prohibition on the face-veil was passed in 1937. In Yugoslavia the campaign began after the end of the Second World War, the prestige and legitimacy

28   Stephanie Cronin

of the new authorities high as a result of the victory over fascism. In Bulgaria, the new post-war Communist government at first soft-pedalled on the issue of women's dress, but an unveiling campaign began in earnest within the context of the 'Cultural Revolution' and 'Great Leap Forward' of the late 1950s.[104] Mary Neuburger describes in Chapter 9 the Bulgarian praxis, but unfortunately we have no studies of the discourse and policies of other post-war Balkan communist states, nor, incidentally, do we know anything about the attitude of the Chinese Communist Party to veiling among Muslim Chinese.

The narratives of unveiling in Turkey and Iran offer new ways of understanding not only the gender discourse of modernism in the Middle East but also the more general character of reforming regimes. Kemalism, for instance, appears, as Metinsoy points out, more flexible and even responsive to pressure from below than previously assumed, and Pahlavi Iran more connected to its own constitutionalist history and less dependent on the arbitrary will of the shah. The narratives of the *hujum* in Soviet Central Asia and the Caucasus also provide an opportunity to discuss the nature of Soviet rule in the non-Russian territories. For Douglas Northrop, the resistance to unveiling in Central Asia symbolized a wider resistance to Russian colonialism, and this explains the high level of violence against women.[105] Kamp, however, has disputed this, pointing out that the violence was against women and not directed at male Communist Party or State officials, and that the straightforward attribution of resistance to colonialism underestimates the importance of the profound and multifaceted conflicts taking place within Central Asian and Caucasian societies themselves.[106] It was patriarchy which was being defended by opponents of unveiling, not Uzbek identity. Adrienne Edgar, in a detailed comparative survey, has argued that Soviet gender policies in the 1920s resembled those of the independent state-builders in Iran and Turkey, but the response to them was closer to that of the colonized countries of the Middle East and North Africa.[107]

The debates over the character of the impact of the Soviet-organized *hujum* on its Muslim periphery takes us back to the controversies over the role of veiling in the nationalist and anti-colonial battles of the Middle East and North Africa. Northrop's analysis of Uzbekistan clearly echoes a view of the veil as a symbol of cultural authenticity and resistance to European hegemony, most famously articulated by Franz Fanon during the Algerian war of independence against French colonial rule. It appears easy, at least at first sight, to attribute an attachment to veiling to the trauma of the colonial presence. Yet this analysis is too simplistic. Unveiling proceeded gradually but relentlessly in Egypt during the period of British rule. By the 1960s almost complete among the urban elites and middle class, it was only to re-emerge with the rise of Islamic politics and the explosion in urbanization after 1967. In Nasserist Egypt, adherence to nationalist politics required no revalorization of the veil. On the contrary, although Nasser and the Free Officers originated from outside the old elite, still an attachment to modernism's gender discourse

Introduction: coercion or empowerment? 29

prevailed. Similarly, in Iraq under the British mandate, neither pan-Arab nor Iraqi nationalism was tempted to revive veiling. Among the Palestinians in the same period, veiling disappeared among the only social sector ever to have adopted it, the urban bourgeoisie. Certainly, in the course of the national struggle, Palestinian women's dress was imbued with a new symbolic significance, but here it was the 'national' embroidered dress which was mobilized to represent the collective identity. Down to the 1980s, despite the psychological as well as political impact of ethnic cleansing and the occupation of historic Palestine, and despite the intense mobilization of subaltern classes, peasants, refugees and migrant workers, veiling continued to diminish. In formally independent countries like Iran, which were, nonetheless, engaged in a bitter struggle with the old British imperial enemy, the issue of veiling also remained unproblematized in the 1940s and '50s, absent from the highwater mark of Iranian nationalism, Musaddiq's nationalization of the Anglo-Iranian Oil Company in 1951–53.

On the other hand, veiling certainly became symbolically important in Algerian decolonization. Rather than simply a function of the metropole–periphery conflict in general, the Algerian case may perhaps be explained by the specificity of French colonial rule and the mass, subaltern character of the independence struggle, quite unlike the peaceful transition to rule by local elites which took place elsewhere in North Africa. The deliberate Gallicization pursued by the French in Algeria, often focused on women as the vessels of a stubborn indigeneity, was quite different to the type of imperial control exercised by Britain in the countries mentioned above, with British control, in contrast to French, often reinforcing traditional culture as well as relying on traditional elites.[108]

The relationship between veiling and the search for cultural authenticity must therefore be problematized by reference to class and to historical period. We have seen above the attachment to and even adoption of veiling as a sign of embourgeoisement. Yet, in the 1920s and 1930s, notwithstanding veiling's value as a signifier of class identity and aspiration, and although the anti-veiling campaigns encountered opposition, the power of secularism and modernity on the European model throughout the region was irresistibly hegemonic and appeared to achieve an irreversible victory. Yet this victory was not in fact irreversible. Rather than in the struggle between metropole and colony, veiling appears to have been of greatest significance in the local struggles between secularism and Islam. It was not in the context of decolonization, but rather with the rise of political Islam from the 1970s that a generalized revalorization of the veil took place.

This revalorization took place everywhere, both in countries which had experienced official anti-veiling campaigns, such as Turkey, and where nationalist movements had left veiling largely unproblematized, such as Egypt. Perhaps the most dramatic example of such a revalorization took place in Iran. After several decades during which all forms of veiling had been largely replaced by European fashion in urban Iran, in the pre-revolutionary years a

30   Stephanie Cronin

modern form of *hijab* and the *chador* reappeared as a sign of opposition to the Pahlavi monarchy. Iranian Islamist currents of the 1970s, including and perhaps especially the Islamic Marxists of the *Mujahidin-i Khalq*, contextualized the veil as a weapon in the wider resistance to Westoxication and imperialism, yet in fact its primary relevance lay within Iran, in the struggle for dominance between secular and Islamic forces. This became sharply apparent immediately after the revolution, with massive demonstrations first against, and then in favour of, compulsory *hijab* in March 1979 becoming a flashpoint in the emerging post-revolutionary struggle for power.

Across the Muslim world, from the 1970s, veiling of various types, including the face-veil, reappeared in social milieux where it had disappeared and where it had never existed. But to what extent was this reaffirmation of veiling a resurrection of an older discourse or a completely new phenomenon? Certainly, in the case of Iran, the revolutionary re-appropriation of the *chador* implied precisely the opposite of its earlier meaning, signifying a very public activism rather than seclusion, and there was no revival of interest in the face-veil. Here too, as elsewhere, the decision to revert to *hijab* was, initially, the decision of women activists themselves although their autonomy was soon rejected in short order by the consolidating Islamic republic. By the twenty-first century, the voices of women themselves, including those who veil, had become ever more assertive and their agency more articulated. However, a fracture had developed in the discourse on the veil, between those women and men in countries where there was either a degree of freedom of choice or an official bias in favour of unveiling, for example, France or Turkey, and those in countries where veiling was obligatory and a denial of autonomy, such as Iran. The struggle over the definition of the meaning of veiling continues.

Much of the current pro-veiling discourse has been elaborated in environments where women who wished to veil, and the men who supported them, saw themselves as a minority discriminated against by the dominant cultural and legal systems. This was the case among immigrant communities in Europe, as well as among Islamist activists in Muslim-majority countries possessing secular governments, such as Turkey, Syria, Tunisia and Uzbekistan. Accordingly, pro-veiling opinion has mobilized arguments emphasizing the right of individual women to make their own active choice, their decision indicative of, variously, political allegiance, piety, education, modernity and upward social mobility.[109] Even in these communities, however, where modernity and agency have been emphasized, the logic of veiling has tended to bring in its train preferences for gender segregation. Of course, not all the pro-veiling discourse has been modernist. Perhaps the most obvious inheritors of the Uzbek opposition to the *hujum* are the Afghan mujahidin of the 1980s–'90s and their successors, the Taliban, who used veiling as one mechanism among others for the symbolic and actual reimposition of patriarchal and tribal gender codes within a domestic power struggle.

Can the discourse of the veil be better understood by wider comparisons? For the modernists of the late nineteenth–early twentieth century, veiling and seclusion strongly resembled other gender practices elsewhere in the world also identified as traditional, backward and an impediment to national progress. Chinese foot binding is a case in point. The resemblance in functional terms between nineteenth century foot binding and veiling is remarkable.[110] Both served to hide women from European view, thus heightening their eroticism and the 'otherness' of their society. Both controlled sexual access to females and ensured female chastity and fidelity. Both were important markers of status and sometimes ethnicity, were legitimized by reference to tradition and custom, were necessary to a good marriage and family honour, and were policed primarily by women themselves. Both were diffused downwards, from elite to middle classes and then to those merely aspiring to gentility, and both became more exaggerated over time.[111] Both were also initially opposed by a combination of indigenous Enlightenment modernists and European observers. Indeed, in the 1920s, the Soviet authorities explicitly linked these practices. Northrop describes how the Commission for the Improvement of Women's Labour and Daily Life (KUTB) studied the possibility of banning the veil in Central Asia and Transcaucasia, of forbidding foot binding among Chinese families in Siberia and of outlawing other harmful customs that were oppressive to women.[112] Yet foot binding disappeared quickly and completely and the Chinese Communist Party has shown no inclination to allow it to undergo any mutation into a vehicle for nostalgia or resistance. This contrasts with another practice, initially rejected but subsequently reinvented, that of female circumcision in Africa. Like foot binding and veiling, this too was a mechanism of controlling female sexuality and justified by reference to custom, and also first condemned by a combination of Europeans, especially missionaries, and African modernists. Unlike foot binding, but rather like veiling, female circumcision has experienced a revival and modernization and has been allocated a place in an emerging discourse of anti-colonialism and indigeneity, actually being newly introduced in parts of Africa as an 'imagined return to African traditions'.[113]

Attempts to assess the significance, let alone the 'success' or 'failure' of the unveiling campaigns raise fundamental questions about the nature of historical knowledge. There is often, for example, an unacknowledged proclivity to assume that history moves in one direction only. Yet, in this case, any judgement about the impact of unveiling made in the 1960s or '70s would have reached profoundly different conclusions to one made in the 2000s. The assessments of the long-term impact of the anti-veiling campaigns depend, to an alarming extent, on the political conjuncture from which they are viewed. But what of their impact *at the time*? The male dress reforms of the 1920s and '30s were more comprehensive, were imposed by law and provoked widespread resistance. Yet they have been relegated to a marginal curiosity in much of the literature. It is rather the unveiling policies, which provoked almost no major upheavals, which have attracted lasting attention and been most problematized. Have they achieved this significance only through the prism of the recent and current revalorization of veiling?

32   Stephanie Cronin

Changes in male dress were, in the long run, much less ambiguous in their results. With the rise of Islamic movements in Iran and Turkey, for instance, which saw the re-invention of veiling, there was no question of any reversion to earlier forms of male headgear, nor were beards more than a marginal issue. Despite the initial defence of the fez in the 1920s, it disappeared more or less completely, its disappearance was final and there has been no attempt to revive it. Only in Afghanistan under the Taliban did beards or their absence take on a dangerous political significance, shaving or even trimming the beard being perceived as indicative of political disloyalty and religious apostasy. Modern Islamic movements in general imbue male appearance with little or no emotional force. Women, it seems, must still bear alone the weight of 'representation'.

Notes

1 The National Assembly legislated against face-covering in July 2010, the Senate following suit in September. The ban came into force in April 2011.
2 The controversy in Turkey has been extensively covered in the press and the scholarly literature, the Tunisian case less so. For Turkey, see, for example, Nilüfer Göle, *The Forbidden Modern: Civilization and Veiling (Michigan, 1997); Emilie A. Olson, 'Muslim Identity and Secularism in Contemporary Turkey: "The Headscarf Dispute"'*, Anthropological Quarterly, *vol. 58, no. 4, October 1985. For Tunisia, see http://magharebia.com/en_GB/articles/awi/features/2006/10/27/feature-01; http://nawaat.org/portail/2006/11/23/the-war-over-the-veil-in-tunisia.*
3 For a recent discussion, see Leila Ahmed, *A Quiet Revolution: The Veil's Resurgence, from the Middle East to America* (New Haven, CT, 2011).
4 Several years ago Adrienne Edgar called for the elaboration of precisely such a comparative analytical perspective on gender policies in the interwar decades. See Adrienne Edgar, 'Bolshevism, Patriarchy, and the Nation: The Soviet "Emancipation" of Muslim Women in Pan-Islamic Perspective', *Slavic Review*, vol. 65, no. 2, Summer, 2006, pp. 252–72.
5 See the photograph of the woman selling oranges in Jaffa in the late nineteenth century, 'Marchant d'Orange á Jaffa', on the Library of Congress website, www.loc.gov/pictures.
6 See, for example, Reina Lewis, *Rethinking Orientalism: Women, Travel, and the Ottoman Harem* (London, 2004).
7 Leila Ahmed, *Women and Gender in Islam* (New Haven, CT, 1992).
8 Ahmed, *Women and Gender*, op. cit., p. 163
9 Ahmed, *Women and Gender*, op. cit., p. 165.
10 Mohamad Tavakoli-Targhi, 'Women of the West Imagined: The *Farangi* Other and the Emergence of the Woman Question in Iran', in Valentine M. Moghadam (ed.), *Identity Politics and Women: Cultural Reassertions and Feminisms in International Perspective* (Boulder, CO and Oxford, 1993), p. 98.
11 Tavakoli-Targhi, 'Women of the West Imagined', op. cit.
12 Marianne Kamp, *The New Woman in Uzbekistan: Islam, Modernity and Unveiling under Communism* (Seattle, WA, 2006); and Kamp (Chapter 7), this volume.
13 For a discussion of the general phenomenon of Eurocentrism in history, see J. M. Blaut, *The Colonizer's Model of the World: Geographical Diffusionism and Eurocentric History* (New York, 1993).

Introduction: coercion or empowerment? 33

14 Adeeb Khalid, *The Politics of Muslim Cultural Reform: Jadidism in Central Asia* (Berkeley, CA and Los Angeles, CA, 1998). See also Edgar, 'Bolshevism, Patriarchy, and the Nation,' op. cit.

15 For instance, the young Mahmud Behbudi, a member of the old cultural elite of Turkestan who was to become the founder of Central Asian *Jadidism*, found his outlook transformed by a journey on the Transcaspian railway from Samarquand via Transcaucasia, Cairo and Mecca. For Behbudi, see Khalid, *The Politics of Muslim Cultural Reform*, op. cit., p. 80.

16 Afsaneh Najmabadi, *Women with Mustaches and Men without Beards: Gender and Sexual Anxieties of Iranian Modernity* (Berkeley, CA, 2005), pp. 134.

17 Khalid, *The Politics of Muslim Cultural Reform*, op. cit., p. 228.

18 Najmabadi, *Women with Mustaches*, op. cit., pp. 137.

19 See Libal (Chapter 1), this volume.

20 Najmabadi, *Women with Mustaches*, op. cit., p. 134. Indeed, by the 1920s unveiling and the adoption of European dress could be presented not as a rupture with the past but, on the contrary, as a return to Iran's true Aryan identity. Houchang E. Chehabi, 'Staging the Emperor's New Clothes: Dress Codes and Nation-Building under Reza Shah', *Iranian Studies*, vol. 26, no 3/4, Summer–Autumn 1993, p. 223. For a recent critique of Aryanism in Iran, see Reza Zia-Ebrahimi, 'Self-Orientalization and Dislocation: The Uses and Abuses of the "Aryan" Discourse in Iran', *Iranian Studies*, vol. 44, no. 4, (June 2011).

21 Göle, *The Forbidden Modern*, op. cit., p. 45.

22 Najmabadi, *Women with Mustaches*, op. cit., pp. 134. For reproductions of some of these illustrations, see *Molla Nasreddin: The Magazine that Would've, Could've, Should've*, Slavs and Tartars (eds.) (Zürich, 2011).

23 Khalid, *The Politics of Muslim Cultural Reform*, op. cit., p. 227.

24 Najmabadi, *Women with Mustaches*, op. cit., p. 137; Beth Baron, 'Unveiling in Early Twentieth Century Egypt: Practical and Symbolic Considerations', *Middle Eastern Studies*, vol. 25, no. 3, (July, 1989), p. 372.

25 For a discussion of veiling stressing the actually almost infinite variety of styles and their sociological meaning, see Nancy Lindisfarne-Tapper and Bruce Ingham (eds.), *Languages of Dress in the Middle East* (Richmond, VA, 1997); Fadwa El Guindi, *Veil: Modesty, Privacy and Resistance* (Oxford and New York, 1999).

26 The Anahita Gallery has a large collection of photographs of veiled women from the Middle East and Central Asia, www.anahitagallery.com.

27 Jasamin Rostam-Kolayi, 'Expanding Agendas for the "New" Iranian Woman: Family Law, Work and Unveiling', in Stephanie Cronin (ed.), *The Making of Modern Iran: State and Society under Riza Shah, 1921–41* (London and New York, 2003); Baron, 'Unveiling in Early Twentieth Century Egypt', op. cit., p. 370. Not all women in Central Asia wore the face-veil. For a discussion of the significance of the Soviet anti-veiling campaign among the un-face-veiled but yashmak-wearing women of Turkmenistan, see Adrienne Lynn Edgar, *Tribal Nation: The Making of Soviet Turkmenistan* (Princeton, NJ, 2004).

28 H. E. Chehabi, 'The Westernization of Iranian Culinary Culture', *Iranian Studies*, vol. 36, no. 1, March 2003.

29 Baron, 'Unveiling in Early Twentieth Century Egypt', op. cit., p. 373. See also Nancy Micklewright, 'Women's Dress in 19th Century Istanbul: Mirror of a Changing Society', PhD thesis (University of Pennsylvania, 1986).

30 For examples of this style, see Figure 6.

31 Baron, 'Unveiling in Early Twentieth Century Egypt', op. cit., p. 375.

32 For an illustration of *paranji* and *chachvon*, see Figure 1.

33 Douglas Northrop, *Veiled Empire: Gender and Power in Stalinist Central Asia* (Ithaca, NY, 2004,) p. 44. For a photograph showing the progressively heavier forms of veiling being adopted, see p. 45.

34 *Stephanie Cronin*

34 Khalid, *The Politics of Muslim Cultural Reform*, op. cit., p. 223.
35 A similar connection between state- and nation-building and clothing regulation may be observed around the world, including in Europe. See Donald Quataert, 'Clothing Laws, State and Society in the Ottoman Empire, 1720–1829', *International Journal of Middle East Studies*, vol. 29, no. 3, August 1997, p. 405. Peter the Great's beard tax and the banning of the 'feudal' pigtail by the new Chinese republic after the overthrow of the Manchus are apposite examples.
36 Quataert, 'Clothing Laws, State and Society', op. cit., p. 405.
37 Patricia L. Baker (1997), 'Politics of Dress: The Dress Reform Laws of 1920–30s Iran', in Lindisfarne-Tapper and Ingham (eds.), *Languages of Dress*, op. cit., p. 179.
38 See Najmabadi, *Women with Mustaches*, op. cit., p.144.
39 Quataert, 'Clothing Laws, State and Society', op. cit., p. 414.
40 Najmabadi, *Women with Mustaches*, op. cit., pp. 142–43.
41 Chehabi, 'Staging the Emperor's New Clothes', op. cit., p. 210.
42 Madeline C. Zilfi, *Women and Slavery in the Late Ottoman Empire* (Cambridge, 2010).
43 Mary Neuburger has documented this thinking particularly clearly in the case of the Bulgarian Communist Party. See Mary Neuburger, *The Orient Within: Muslim Minorities and the Negotiation of Nationhood in Modern Bulgaria* (New York, 2004), p. 101, and Chapter 9, this volume.
44 Chehabi, 'Staging the Emperor's New Clothes', op. cit., p. 222.
45 Mustafa Kemal's speech of 15–20 October 1927, John Norton (1997), 'Faith and Fashion in Turkey', in Lindisfarne-Tapper and Bruce Ingham (eds.), *Languages of Dress*, op. cit., pp. 149–77, pp. 161–62.
46 Stephanie Cronin, *The Army and the Creation of the Pahlavi State in Iran, 1910–1926* (London and New York, 1997), p. 208.
47 Stephanie Cronin, *Soldiers, Shahs and Subalterns in Iran: Opposition, Protest and Revolt, 1921–1941* (Basingstoke, 2010), pp. 180–200.
48 Cronin, *Soldiers, Shahs and Subalterns*, op. cit., pp. 32–34.
49 See Thomas B. Wide (Chapter 6), this volume.
50 Wide (Chapter 6), this volume.
51 See Neuburger, *The Orient Within*, op. cit.
52 Neuburger, *The Orient Within*, op. cit., p. 103.
53 See Janet Afary, *Sexual Politics in Modern Iran* (Cambridge, 2009), pp. 142–73; Camron Michael Amin, *The Making of the Modern Iranian Woman: Gender, State Policy, and Popular Culture* (Florida, 2002), pp. 80–113. For an illustration of the new athleticism, see Figure 12.
54 Amin, *The Making of the Modern Iranian Woman*, op. cit., pp. 92.
55 Iraj Mirza quoted by Afsaneh Najmabadi, 'Veiled Discourse-Unveiled Bodies', *Feminist Studies*, vol. 19, no. 3, (Autumn, 1993), pp. 510–11. Nathalie Clayer (Chapter 8), this volume.
56 Afary, *Sexual Politics in Modern Iran*, op. cit., pp. 111–41; Najmabadi, *Women with Mustaches*, op. cit., pp. 146–50.
57 See Figures 7 and 8.
58 Margot Badran *Feminists, Islam and Nation: Gender and the Making of Modern Egypt* (Princeton, NJ, 1995), pp. 92–93.
59 Ellen L. Fleischman, 'The Other "Awakening": The Emergence of Women's Movements in the Modern Middle East, 1900–1940', in Margaret L. Meriwether and Judith E. Tucker (eds.), *A Social History of Women and Gender in the Modern Middle East* (Boulder, CO, 1999).
60 Rostam-Kolayi, 'Expanding Agendas for the "New" Iranian Woman', op. cit., p. 168.

Introduction: coercion or empowerment? 35

61 Charlotte Weber, 'Between Nationalism and Feminism: The Eastern Women's Congresses of 1930 and 1932', *Journal of Middle East Women's Studies*, vol. 4, no. 1, (Winter 2008).
62 Rostam-Kolayi, 'Expanding Agendas for the "New" Iranian Woman', op. cit., p. 170; Chehabi, 'Staging the Emperor's New Clothes', op. cit., p. 213.
63 Sevgi Adak (Chapter 2), this volume.
64 Amin, *The Making of the Modern Iranian Woman*, op. cit., pp. 94–95.
65 Clayer (Chapter 8), this volume.
66 Wide, (Chapter 6), this volume.
67 Jasamin Rostam-Kolayi and Afshin Matin-asgari (Chapter 4), this volume.
68 Northrop, *Veiled Empire*, op. cit., p. 299.
69 See Libal (Chapter 1), this volume.
70 Amin, *The Making of the Modern Iranian Woman*, op. cit., p. 96.
71 Najmabadi, *Women with Mustaches*, op. cit., pp. 152–55.
72 Najmabadi, *Women with Mustaches*, op. cit., p. 153.
73 Afary, *Sexual Politics in Modern Iran*, op. cit., pp. 157.
74 Afary, *Sexual Politics in Modern Iran*, op. cit., pp. 157.
75 Amin, *The Making of the Modern Iranian Woman*, op. cit., p. 94.
76 Robert J. Donia, *Sarajevo – A Biography* (London, 2006), p. 218–20.
77 Kamp, *The New Woman in Uzbekistan*, op. cit., pp. 141–42.
78 Kamp, *The New Woman in Uzbekistan*, op. cit., p. 158.
79 See Figure 11.
80 For a vivid description of the efficacy of obliging members of the elite to conform to the new policy, see Sattareh Farman Farmaian and Dona Munker, *Daughter of Persia: A Woman's Journey from Her Father's Harem through the Islamic Revolution* (London, 1992), pp. 95–96.
81 Amin, *The Making of the Modern Iranian Woman*, op. cit., p. 97.
82 See Rostam-Kolayi and Matin-asgari (Chapter 4), this volume.
83 Clayer (Chapter 8) this volume.
84 Kamp, *The New Woman in Uzbekistan*, op. cit., p. 182.
85 See Mansoureh Ettehadieh, 'The Origins and Development of the Women's Movement in Iran, 1906–41', in Lois Beck and Guity Nashat (eds.), *Women in Iran from 1800 to the Islamic Republic* (Urbana, IL and Chicago, IL, 2004), p. 99.
86 See Rostam-Kolayi and Matin-asgari (Chapter 4), this volume.
87 Kamp, *The New Woman in Uzbekistan*, op. cit., p. 244.
88 Kamp, *The New Woman in Uzbekistan*, op. cit., p. 257.
89 See Adak, (Chapter 2, this volume) and Libal (Chapter 1, this volume).
90 Chehabi, 'Staging the Emperor's New Clothes', op. cit., p. 226.
91 See Firoozeh Kashani-Sabet (Chapter 5), this volume and Libal (Chapter 1), this volume. See also A. Holly Shissler, 'Beauty is Nothing to be Ashamed of: Beauty Contests as Tools of Women's Liberation in Early Republican Turkey', *Comparative Studies of South Asia, Africa and the Middle East*, vol. 24, no. 1, 2004, pp. 109–26.
92 Najmabadi, *Women with Mustaches*, op. cit., p. 154.
93 Kamp (Chapter 7), this volume.
94 H. E. Chehabi, 'The Banning of the Veil and its Consequences', in Cronin (ed.), *The Making of Modern Iran* (London, 2003), p. 204.
95 Amin, *The Making of the Modern Iranian Woman*, op. cit., p. 111. The immense increase in state power resulting from the male clothing reforms was already apparent. In Iran, for example, state exemption boards were established, in effect to grant 'turban licences'. For the boards, see Bianca Devos, *Kleidungspolitik in Iran: Die Durchsetzung der Kleidungsvorschriften für Männer unter Riżā Šāh* (Würzburg, 2006).

36 *Stephanie Cronin*

96 Shireen Mahdavi (2003), 'Reza Shah Pahlavi and Women: A Re-evaluation', in Cronin (ed.), *The Making of Modern Iran*, op. cit. Indeed, so enthusiastic were some elite women about the prospects for emancipation under Reza Shah that they took the opportunity of his coronation in 1926 to go onto the streets unveiled, an initiative for which they were promptly arrested. *Persidskaya Zhenschina i Rezhim Reza Shakha Pekhlevi*, April 2, 1928, Archiv Rossiiskij Gosudarstvennyj Arkhiv Sotsial'no-politicheskoj Istorii (RGASPI) Fond 495, Op 90, Delo 174. I am grateful to Lana Ravandi-Fadai for this reference.
97 Kamp, *The New Woman in Uzbekistan*, op. cit., pp. 157–58.
98 Rostam-Kolayi and Matin-asgari (Chapter 4), this volume.
99 Sevgi Adak, 'Women in the Post-Ottoman Public Sphere: Anti-Veiling Campaigns and the Gendered Reshaping of Urban Space in Early RepublicanTurkey' in Nazan Maksudyan (ed.), *Women and the City, Women in the City: A Gendered Perspective to Ottoman Urban History* (Berghahn Books, forthcoming September 2014).
100 Kamp, *The New Woman in Uzbekistan*, op. cit., pp. 157–58; and Chapter 7, this volume.
101 Rostam-Kolayi and Matin-asgari (Chapter 4), this volume.
102 See Edgar, 'Bolshevism, Patriarchy, and the Nation,' op. cit. For a wider comparative discussion of interwar modernity, see Stephen Kotkin, 'Modern Times: The Soviet Union and the Interwar Conjuncture', *Kritika: Explorations in Russian and Eurasian History*, vol. 2, no. 1, (Winter 2001).
103 Kamp (Chapter 7), this volume.
104 Neuburger, *The Orient Within*, op. cit.
105 Northrop, *Veiled Empire*, op. cit.
106 Kamp, *The New Woman in Uzbekistan*, op. cit.
107 Edgar, 'Bolshevism, Patriarchy, and the Nation,' op. cit.
108 Edgar, 'Bolshevism, Patriarchy, and the Nation', op. cit.; Elizabeth Thompson, *Colonial Citizens: Republican Rights, Paternal Privilege, and Gender in French Syria and Lebanon* (New York, 2000).
109 Göle, *The Forbidden Modern*, op. cit., pp. 4–5; Ahmed, *A Quiet Revolution*, op. cit.
110 The link between veiling and foot binding has been explored by Farzaneh Milani, 'Hijab va Kashf-i Chini', *Iran Nameh*, vol. 2, 1990. See also Northrop, *Veiled Empire*, op. cit., p. 38.
111 Gerry Mackie, 'Ending Footbinding and Infibulation: A Convention Account', *American Sociological Review*, vol. 61, no. 6, (December, 1996), pp. 999–1017.
112 Northrop, *Veiled Empire*, op. cit., p. 298.
113 Mackie, 'Ending Footbinding', op. cit., p. 1015.

Part I
Turkey

1 From face veil to cloche hat

The backward Ottoman versus new Turkish woman in urban public discourse

Kathryn Libal

> It is rumoured that a general order to unveil may be passed but whether this be true or not, the famous injunction of Kamal Ataturk to the women of Turkey uttered in the early days of the Republic has already been widely followed. "Show your faces to the world, and look the world in the face." The essential fact about the veil in Turkey to-day is not that some women still retain the veil but that wearing it has become entirely a matter of personal choice and hence it has lost its traditional significance.[1]

Although Ruth Woodsmall, a social worker who spent more than a decade in Istanbul working for the Young Women's Christian Association, exaggerated the extent to which women's dress in public had become a matter of individual choice, her assessment that the veil had lost some of its "traditional significance" for many women by the mid-1930s was fair. Her quote of President Mustafa Kemal Atatürk, who was overwhelmingly regarded as the champion of women's rights in the early republic, underscored the idea that women's participation in the new republic was critical—the labors of women, as citizen subjects, both within the household and public sphere were vital to assuring the young country's progress.

Turkey's republican regime of the 1920s–1930s is renowned for its modernizing and secularizing reforms, many of which targeted women as objects of social transformation.[2] State-sponsored efforts to accord women new rights in the public sphere, sometimes labeled as state feminism,[3] included efforts to encourage women to give up traditional forms of dress and head and body coverings.[4] Yet the state did not criminalize veiling at the national level or launch a high-profile campaign to force rapidly a shift to a particular mode of dress among all women in the young country.[5] Instead, officials at the national level promoted a change to Western-style dress, especially among the growing middle class and urban elite, through education, popular media, and consumerism. Regulations were instituted in the workplace, and pressure to conform for public figures was intense.[6] Yet in the 1930s a diversity of head and body coverings persisted, even among republican elites. Clothing practices in public ranged from being bare-headed to wearing tightly bound

40   *Kathryn Libal*

fashionable scarf wraps covering much of the hair. Amongst the middle class and elites in urban areas in particular, the *manto*, or long coat, supplanted the *çarşaf*, or more traditional outerwear.

Although officials did regulate and even criminalize some specific women's covering practices at a local level in the 1930s, as Murat Metinsoy and Sevgi Adak address in their chapters (Chapter 3 and Chapter 2, respectively) for this volume, in this chapter I examine pervasive and less overtly coercive techniques. Blurring the lines of what may be cast as an "official anti-veiling" campaign, I focus on promoting public support among the emerging middle class and elites through early republican public culture. I outline the construction of two dominant opposing figures—the backward Ottoman vs. modern Turkish woman—as they were deployed in popular culture, professional journals, publications of the "people's houses," and in photographs. Drawing upon domestic and international discourses on Turkish women's emancipation, I highlight some of the widespread cultural assumptions about women's position prior to the founding of the republic and an emerging imaginary of the "modern Turkish woman" that undergirded the "woman question" (*kadın meselesi*) and feminism in the 1930s. Some of the highest stakes within this debate concerned reformist condemnation of middle-class or elite women who did not conform to expectations of the figure of the Turkish woman. Even among educated elites debating modernizing reforms, significant contention existed about the meanings of so-called traditional covering practices and Western women's attire.[7] In sum, the question of how middle- and upper-class women dressed in this era operated as "shorthand" for contention over women's roles within all realms of life, both public and private—their access to education, political participation, rights within the workplace, and roles within the household as wives and mothers. And for some activists of the era, campaigning to change how women dressed diverted from more pressing questions of poverty and hardships that working class and rural women faced, including recognition within their communities and society as citizens with legitimate claims on the state for support.

The symbolic work of "modernizing" women's dress in the early republic

By the time the Turkish republic was founded in 1923, women in urban locales had already shifted dress practices considerably from what had been "traditional" conservative urban women's dress in the eighteenth and nineteenth centuries. The *peçe* and *çarşaf* appear most often in discussions of "backward" dress among urban and town women. As Hale Yılmaz notes in her work on efforts to regulate women's dress at local levels in the 1930s, the *çarşaf* referred to a woman's clothing worn outdoors, "consisting of a top piece covering the head and the upper part of the body, and a skirt covering the body from the waist to the feet."[8] The *peçe*, or face cover, could be worn with the *çarşaf*. During the 1930s these articles of clothing are often referred to together, though they were two separate pieces of clothing and not necessarily worn at the same time.

Eradicating the *peçe* and *çarşaf*—visible signs of "women's liberation"— was symbolically critical to state authorities and social reformers as an measure of modernity and progress. Officials were deeply invested in portraying Turkey as a modern society and securing its legitimacy as a nation-state within the West. As Çınar notes, since the nineteenth-century clothing served as a means of conveying national belonging; as early Turkish republican leaders sought to build a new state and craft a citizenry loyal to that state, clothing and dress practices became one social field through which to establish a sense of nationhood. Revolution (*inkılap*) entailed creating "a sharp break from the Ottoman past, an inscription of a historical rupture, an insistence on disjunctive change, on a revolutionary diversion from Ottoman ways."[9] The "national self could be constituted as new and modern" against the image of the traditional, the backward, and the degenerate Ottoman past.

Ruth Woodsmall noted in her widely published travelogue that a vanguard of civil servants and wives of officials were having an effect even in more remote towns and "typical cities of the Interior," where social change was still slow with regard to dress, marriage practices, gender relations, and expectations regarding education for girls. She notes based on observations while traveling throughout the country in the early to mid-1930s:

> In the towns off the railway line, perhaps a large majority and in a railway centre probably half of the women are still veiled. In all of these places there is, of course, the advanced minority, the so-called 'foreign groups' of unveiled teachers, wives of officials and business men from Istanbul, who lead quite a separate social life. The prevailing atmosphere is conservative but the presence of this 'foreign' group undoubtedly has its effect; for each year the number of veils in the Interior decreases.[10]

Women's attire in public was a touchstone of Turkish modernity in the early republic—and, like men's attire, sartorial practices were a matter of public policy and political campaigning.[11] Yet state officials were aware of the dangers of bald enforcement of regulations and standards for women's dress, wary of being accused of employing "terroristic methods" of reform,[12] even while seeking to promote a public image of Turkish transformation, development, and progress both domestically and internationally. Shortly after the Turkish republic was founded, Halide Edip Adıvar, prominent writer and activist who gained renown during the Turkish War of Independence (Greco–Turkish War), became a strong critic of Atatürk's one-party regime and heavy-handed reforms. Although she ostensibly deplored dictatorial and "terroristic methods" to impel social change, Halide Edip mused about whether or not such change could have happened otherwise. She asserted that "On the whole, within the last twenty years women in Turkey as elsewhere have profited by changes more than men," citing the replacement of Sharia

42   *Kathryn Libal*

law with a civil code and women's greater access to education and work in professions. But, Adıvar derided efforts to enforce the "Hat Law" passed in 1925:

> In a week it made the Turks don European hats (the only part of the city dwellers' outfit which had not been westernized) and made them look like westerners, although the manner in which it was accomplished was utterly un-western. The westernization of Turks is not and should not be a quest of mere external imitation and gesture. It is a much deeper and more significant process. To tell the Turk to don a certain headdress and 'get civilized' or be hanged or imprisoned, is absurd, to say the least.[13]

Reformist zeal to convey an image of modernization at work through changing men or women's outerwear is clearly reflected in nationalist publications of the 1930s. The image of the "new Turkish woman" freed from the *kafes*,[14] *peçe, and çarşaf* was unabashedly grounded in a nationalist effort to establish the legitimacy of Atatürk's and the Republic People's Party's authority. The regime waged a "campaign of propaganda" on two fronts— domestically to hasten Westernization of dress, and internationally to counter Orientalist discourses on the backwardness or weakness of the Turks and secure inclusion within the club of "civilized" nation-states.

Turkish nation-state making was a defensive measure in a global era of heightened militarism and nationalism. The intensity of Turkey's efforts rapidly to "modernize" derived from its history of near-colonialism and defeats in successive wars in the late nineteenth and early twentieth centuries. Atatürk and his allies within the Republican People's Party suppressed internal social and political dissent, arguing that they sought to promote national unity so that Turkey's foreign "enemies" would not be emboldened to invade again.[15] Leaders regarded nation-building efforts predicated on a program for rapid "modernization" and economic and population growth as a means to secure national boundaries. Establishing universal mass education, promoting literacy among adults, modernizing factory work and agricultural practices, minimizing the public role of religion in daily life, and fostering women's participation in public life all marked progress and signified the legitimacy of the new state. Republican reformers zealously instituted numerous measures, institutions, and practices that would effect a transformation in the way people lived their daily lives and considered themselves to be connected (in urban centers in particular). In "solidifying" the notion of nation-state, national elites also sought to create a new sense of citizenship, subjectivity, Turkishness. The process in the 1920s and 1930s was an incomplete realization of modernity, yet remarkable in its movement and achievements.[16]

Scholarship on gender in the early republic has flourished in response to Deniz Kandiyoti's call in the late 1990s to "gender the modern."[17] This chapter represents an effort to attend more carefully to elite constructions of debates over women's dress and their role in public life in the early republic. The "women's question," of which debates over dress were a part, was initiated during the late Ottoman Empire, appearing in the press, literature, and associational life, and in politics. These debates carried over into the "new republic," where social reformers (including professional elites, writers and journalists, as well as politicians, civil servants, and educators) juxtaposed ideals of the "modern republic" with a vilified Ottoman era through the figures of the "backward Ottoman woman" and the "new Turkish woman." While locally instituted policies to regulate the *çarşaf* and *peçe* were enacted at the local and provincial level (with varied impacts and effects) in the 1930s,[18] national-level officials were reluctant to ban women's traditional head coverings or other forms of dress associated with Islam or "backwardness."[19] Rather than legislating against "veiling" through campaigns to force women to conform to Western, secular norms for women, reformers at the national level pressed for change through education and example. As the Minister of Interior, Şükrü Kaya expressed in a circular to governors and inspectors general in 1934:

> At a time when our women are in fact following the requirements of our revolution, one should be wary of carrying this matter [of unveiling] to excesses that might cause unwanted reactions. We should get them to accept the requirements of the revolution not through police force but by way of well-managed inculcation. Therefore, it would be appropriate to be content with propaganda in the *peçe* and *çarşaf* matter as well.[20]

Central to such "inculcation" was education—both formal schooling and popular education—as well as promoting the image of the "new Turkish woman" through an expanding popular media, including newspapers, serial publications and magazines, and radio broadcasts, and through film.[21]

Discourses on Ottoman pasts and Turkish futures

> In the houses in which we were born, in the schools in which we studied, in the thoughts, feelings, and customs by which we were raised, in our clothing, our common understandings, and the way that we carry ourselves, from top to bottom everything has changed. Neither a man nor a generation can emotionally absorb such widespread chaos that has taken place in the past eight to ten years, no matter how much he has every intention of doing so. The wound of being Oriental has encrusted us. There yet exists a scab on our skin. With a vigorous brush of this scab, it can again be infected. We are half humans. Our correct ideas are still fighting against our wrong feelings. We still have a considerable number of brave revolutionaries who won't let their wives emerge from the *kafes*. The *sarık*[22] that we cast off winds itself around our feet and trips us.[23]

In 1929 Falih Rıfkı (Atay), a well-known nationalist writer and editor of the Republican People's Party newspaper, *Ulus*, highlighted the dangers of "being

44 Kathryn Libal

of the past" or "being Oriental" in Turkey's child welfare annual. The author depicted an elder generation that refused efforts to embrace "modern" Turkish values as a threat to nationhood. Being associated with "Orientalness" referenced both a state of being and time: "being other," "being backward," "being degenerate," "aged," "outdated," and "reactionary," to name a few characterizations.[24] Atay indicted the "considerable number of brave revolutionaries" who refused to be seen in public with their wives, signalling resistance among male leaders to embrace reformers' expectations that male political leaders be accompanied by their wives at public events.

Atay's stance on women's seclusion among the elite was not new. A decade earlier, prominent sociologist, Ziya Gökalp ardently pressed for the end of seclusion and veiling practices during the Young Turk era, just prior to the founding of the republic. According to Ahmed Emin (Yalman), Gökalp authored a pamphlet against veiling that was "at that time too radical to be given general publicity in the press."[25] Circulated privately, Gökalp's views would become much more commonly expressed in public a short decade later:

> The forms of social life have nothing to do with religion, whose field is the world to come, and those problems which as yet reason cannot solve. A social usage such as veiling is easily traceable to certain instincts, and to primitive social origins. Its perpetuation in the present century is the greatest possible insult to our women. It is based on the supposition that they are fundamentally immoral, and must constantly be kept by physical barriers from taking wrong steps. An ethical system which is based on external guardianship, and not on confidence in one's character and self-respect is not worthy of the Turkish nation. The discarding of veils can have no immoral consequences, and will be, on the contrary, the starting point of a higher ethical development."[26]

Gökalp challenged women's subordination in his famous treatise, *Principles of Turkism*, as well.[27] The sociologist rooted women's subordinate status not to religious grounds, but rather in "primitive origins." He does not address veiling explicitly in this longer text, but underscores the necessity of women's full engagement in the workplace, politics, and all facets of public life. Gökalp's concern with promoting "higher ethical development" by removing physical barriers such as the *peçe* or seclusion practices reflect a modernist faith in the individual's capacity to act within family, community, or social world. Though, ostensibly, campaigns to afford women access to schooling, work outside the home, and to participate in leisure activities in public must be as much directed towards men as women.

Gökalp is renowned for efforts to locate the impetus for social change in (mythic) understandings of a social past that predated the influence of late Ottoman Islamic norms. Columnists for the popular and influential magazine, *Yedigün*, also endeavoured to chart a reference point for Turkish modernization projects that did not merely attempt to mimic the West. According to

Nereid, editors for the magazine often referred to pre-Abdülhamid practices as a source of women's liberation and gender equality.[28] She cites one op-ed published by Mahmut Yesari in 1934 as an example:

> In some districts in Turkey women are still veiled. But this must come to an end: why are women still dressed that way, eleven years after the revolution? Even in the Ottoman days, before Sultan Abdülhamid II, women would show more of their face than they do today. But Abdülhamid imposed his zeal on the whole population and made them cover up. If women were caught with uncovered hair, their hair would be cut off. But now we have a republic! Women should not stay in the shadow, or be veiled. Turkishness is a sun that penetrates even the darkest shadow![29]

Rooting women's covering practices in "primitive social origins," as Gökalp does, or in the "zeal" of Sultan Abdülhamid II, as Yesari does nearly two decades later, illustrates attempts to explain women's status and gender relations at the pivot of new nationhood. Yet, by the 1930s balder juxtapositions of "old" and "new" abounded in a variety of print media, in political speeches, and in radio broadcasts. Below I illustrate just a few of these instances as they related to women's dress, arguing that the construct of "old" and "new" did serve a powerful ideological goal to create distance between reformers and those from the immediate Ottoman past who may challenge the new elite's goals for modernization and social change.

Juxtaposing "old" and "new" in the 1930s

Emerging scholarship on efforts to enforce dress codes for women in the early republic is an important corrective to the often cited claim that Atatürk's regime only outlawed the fez and turban, both articles of male headgear. Alongside such research, it is important to examine other ways in which promoting so-called Western women's dress was accomplished and to what effect. As Yılmaz notes, for some officials "inculcation" (*telkin*) was preferred, as was the case for the Minister of the Interior, Şükrü Kaya (cited above).

The weekly, *Yedigün* (Seven Days), published a column highlighting the distance travelled between "old" and "new" in honour of Turkey's tenth anniversary.[30] Contrasting the ruins of a destroyed Ottoman state with the achievements of the Republic, the column notes considerable strides in education, the economy, and formation of modern legal institutions. In terms of "yesterday," the column notes that the people "floated in ignorance and neglect." "Women were a (form of) property ... and even our clothes were absurd." By contrast, today's Turkey is a place where

> all our needs are met by the country. Schools have been created to teach even the retired to read. The Republic gave Turkish women their rights

46 *Kathryn Libal*

and created the civil code and genuine courts. The Revolution even took up [the ways in which] dress differentiated us from the civilized realms.

A black and white illustration by Münif Fehim accompanying the narrative underscored visually the gulf between the Ottoman past and Turkish present. On the left of the page Fehim depicted Ottoman citizens walking toward the reader, led by the Sultan, followed by men wearing the fez or turban and women in headscarves, *peçe*, and *çarşaf*. On the right of the page, Atatürk, dressed in tuxedo and top hat, led urban women and men dressed in Western attire. Men sported the latest Western hats; male workers donned caps with brims, and youth wore the hats of boy scouts. Women were adorned in stylish cloche hats or were bare-headed.

A poster produced by Turkish Village Publications in the 1930s illustrated visually arenas of transformation from "old" (Ottoman) to "new" (republican).[31] Highlighting reforms in law, marriage, measurement (weights, measures, and time), agricultural production, educational styles, science and medicine, the military, and dress, the poster portrayed the break between the Ottoman past and the republican present as a radical one. In the panel titled "Turkish Civil Code," a drawing of "yesterday's" wedding couple was contrasted with that of "today's." On the left, the creator Mustafa Koç depicted a husband wearing a fez with his first wife and toward the foreground in headscarf and diaphanous veil was his second wife. Neither woman smiled. On the right, Koç drew the same man and one of the women. Dressed in tuxedo and white wedding dress, the couple smiled at the viewer. In another panel titled "Dress Reform," a polygamous couple with young child wear traditional headgear, contrasted with the man–wife–male-child unit of "today" where the nuclear family is clad in Western attire and has no head covering.

Akbaba, a weekly satirical magazine, ran numerous cartoons throughout the 1930s lampooning changing dress practices and the perceived gulf between "old" and "new." In one cartoon by Ramiz, the top panel depicted an elderly couple dressed in "traditional" clothing staring at a young couple in Western dress.[32] Dated "Carnival in 1915," the older couple ridicules the young couple in Western dress, saying, "Look at those clowns!" In the lower panel identified as "Carnival in 1935," the young couple (apparently a bit more aged) has reversed the formula, ridiculing the elder couple for their outlandish attire.

The magazine also satirized the divide between classes, often depicting "the poor" of Istanbul's streets struggling amidst the nouveau riche who seemed more concerned with consuming the latest fashions than thinking about the lives and well-being of the working class and poor within the city. A cover for *Akbaba* in 1936 depicted two women walking near a mosque where a beggar had his hand out for alms.[33] The women, wearing skirts below the knees, short sleeves, white gloves, and fashionably angled hats, strode by. The beggar said, "My arms and legs don't work, I cannot see and cannot hear" and one of the women replied, "Here, take this address. (And to her friend said) An

The backward Ottoman versus new Turkish woman   47

ideal husband for your daughter." Juxtaposing the mosque with women striding through Istanbul's streets, and a confident (and dismissive) interaction with a male beggar of lower class drew *Akbaba*'s readers' attention to the contradictions being lived out on a daily basis within Istanbul. Changes both in wealth, class structure, and gender relations and norms, as well as relations with religious institutions such as the mosque, were matters for commentary and debate.

The device of deploying binary constructions to depict Turkey's national struggle—of "old" and "new," "decrepit" and "vital," "backward" and "progressive," pervades not only the Turkish press in the era. The changing role of Turkish women and their "condition" was a matter of considerable interest within the US and European press in the 1920s and 1930s as well. Women leaving behind the *kafes* and *peçe* was a dominant referent in Western journalistic accounts of Turkish nation-building. Turkey's 10-year anniversary in 1933 was commemorated publicly as a marker of triumphant progress and the achievement of rapid modernizing gains. This discourse on monumental strides and the transformation of "the old" Ottoman Empire to "new" nation-state was highlighted in the Turkish and Western press.

Accounts in US and British papers in many ways mirrored the republican regime's narrative of women's liberation, reinforcing the image of Atatürk as "benevolent dictator." A *New York Times* article contrasted the revolutionary transformation with images of a mosque-filled Istanbul skyline and a wide street of the Ankara capital lined with modern buildings, street lights, and sidewalks.[34] The article title and byline, "Kemal's New Turkey Is Ten Years Old: While Bringing Vast Changes to His People, the Dictator Has Raised the Republic's Standing in World Affairs," heralded Turkey's growing stature as a nation-state. The text narrated a description of the new regime's reforms, highlighting changes in men's head coverings and women's dress as "remarkable":

> Once they [women] wore black dresses, were heavily veiled, lived in harems, took no care of their figures and never even thought of working. Today they vie with one another in being chic and smartly dressed and thousands of them have clerical and other jobs. They appear to be emancipated in the fullest sense of the word.

The theme of women's emancipation is addressed in many of the *New York Times* articles throughout the 1930s, usually depicting a radical break from past practices. The idea of women confined to harems and veils is often invoked as a backdrop to new achievements and frontiers attained by Turkish women. In an article titled "Turkish Women Still Striding Onward," Charles Pound asserts that a fundamental change had occurred in Turkey, best depicted in women's Westernizing attire and upper-class women's increasing participation in public life.[35] Pound pointed to a growing republican theme of the necessity of women's work for the good of the nation, pointing to the new commemorative statue of Turkish womanhood displayed in Ankara in 1933

48   *Kathryn Libal*

as symbol of Turkish womanly strength that could not be limited to harems and veils. In place of the *çarşaf* and *peçe*, the sculptor chose the "kerchief, pantaloons and turned-up slippers which were originally worn by all Turkish women but have survived in modern times only among the peasants of the fields." Pound emphasized, "It is a statue of a Turkish woman without the veil and the flowing charshaf that have been worn in the towns for the last two or three centuries." He noted, as well, that

> there are conservatives to whom it is still a sin to expose the face and hair to the gaze of strangers; in fact, the covering of the hair is still a wide-spread custom. No upper-class Turkish woman of good position would appear at an embassy function in Pera without a small colored kerchief, frequently of black embroidered gold, just large enough to cover the hair. The same custom persists among large numbers of middle-class women and girls who still wear neat black kerchiefs exposing no more than a stray curl in front of the ear. But the use of the hat is spreading and, where colored hats are worn, the last memory of the shrouding black of the past seems to have vanished.[36]

Journalists profiled women who were "the first" to take part in an activity, such as in the photo of Mouamer Hanoum (*hanım*) who was the first woman to earn a chauffer's license. Shown in the driver's seat of a Chevrolet, the caption underscored her "liberation" from Ottoman pasts: "In a Taxi Instead of the Harem."[37] Another photo in the *New York Times* depicted a small group of women standing at attention during national anniversary cere-monies.[38] The women were participating ostensibly in what the *New York Times* called compulsory military training. Sporting rifles over their right shoulders, the young women were bare-headed and clad in black dresses fall-ing below the knee. They completed their uniform with thick stockings, Wes-tern shoes, and a white scarf tied over the shoulders in the style of youth scouts. The photo conveyed the impression that Turkish women were ready to be "equal" even in the most dangerous realm of public service. In actuality, however, women were not recruited into military service during the 1930s. The experience of Sabiha Gökçen, Atatürk's adopted daughter, who trained as an airplane pilot, was an exception to this. And, though she participated in some of the first aerial military operations within Turkey when Turkish forces suppressed Kurds who were rebelling in Dersim, she was denied the right to join the military and take a commission. According to Gökçen's memoirs, Chief of the General Staff Mustafa Fevzi Çakmak refused her petition to allow women into the military.[39]

Following the decision of the Grand National Assembly to allow women to serve in parliament, Turkey gained considerable acclaim in the international press and from women's organizations world-wide. *The Times* (of London) noted that the move was important because of the "influence" that women were likely to have in shaping social change: "No more than 12 years ago most Turkish women lived behind latticed windows, and ventured abroad only when heavily veiled; their sole ambition was to please their lords and masters. To-day they enjoy equal civic rights with men."[40]

New republic women in popular culture and public discourse

The early republican regime relied upon discursive constructions of Ottoman backwardness to legitimate the new national leadership and construct a new Turkish citizen subject. As Çınar eloquently states, "the veil was projected as a mark of the oppressive Ottoman-Islamic rule that had subjected the nation, represented by the female body, to backwardness, barbarism, and uncivilized, degrading conditions."[41] For Çınar the "unveiling of the female body came to be the ultimate sign of the emancipation of women and the liberation of the nation."[42] Yet, as scholars have pointed out, this symbolic "revealing" of the face and body operated within constraints recognized and accepted by authorities prompting dress reform. Though bathing at the beach, participating in sport, or attending school was encouraged through popular press and educational materials, images of women with some form of head covering (whether "Western" or as a form of modified "turban") were also commonplace in the same media and educational outlets.

The co-occurrence of "old" and "new" in women's dress in the early republic underscored how fraught the process of government-sponsored change was in that era—regardless of whether or not compliance was mandated through legislation or promoted through the "softer" kinds of pressure that came with regulation and exhortation. The President himself exemplified in his own family life the kinds of transitions being made—through example Atatürk called on his closest allies to embody the new norms not only in public pronouncements but also in their own family practices.

Atatürk and the new Turkish woman

> In some places I have seen women who put a piece of cloth or a towel or something like it over their faces … when a man passes by. What is the meaning and sense of this behavior? Gentlemen, can the mothers and daughters of a civilized nation adopt this strange manner, this barbarous posture? It is an object of ridicule. It must be remedied at once.[43]

Images of Atatürk and other state officials relating to "the people" throughout their travels and campaigning became infused in the political and social imaginary of Turkish citizens. Press coverage of Atatürk's adopted daughters, Sabiha Gokçen, Ayşe Afet İnan, and Ülkü, formed part of the mythic narrative of Atatürk's regard for women and girls. The blending of paternalism and nationalism, symbolized in his surname, which meant "Father of the Turks," further added to the myth of the benevolent dictator who seemingly single-handedly emancipated women.

50   *Kathryn Libal*

Atatürk is renowned for his admonitions to men, particularly within parliament and the Republican People's Party, to encourage women and girls in their households to wear Western-style clothing in public. Woodsmall cites in her widely read account of travels in Turkey in the 1920s and 1930s that Atatürk encouraged Turkish women to "Show your faces to the world, and look the world in the face."[44] In 1924, shortly after the founding of the republic, photos of Atatürk in official public functions with his wife, Latife Hanım, underscore that traditional coverings could still officially be worn.[45] Latife Hanım was also depicted in fully Western dress at the same time period.[46] Images of girls and women who played a central role in Atatürk's life in the 1930s, however, reflect a major shift to and valorization of Western women's dress.

Photos of official functions show diverse head-covering practices, such as in a photo depicting a reception committee for Atatürk at Çolak İbrahim Bey's factory in Seferhisar (Izmir Province) in 1926.[47] The older women wore a fashionable scarf tied closely to the head and younger women at the forefront of the picture wore (school) uniforms and hats. Two young women with bow ties and bobs had no head coverings whatsoever. The long coat (*manto*) and soft scarf tied as a turban over the hair prevails as a style in a number of photos of women meeting Atatürk in the late 1920s. In Izmit representatives of the local women's association greeted the President with handshakes, adorned in manto and scarf.[48] Photos of a 1929 reception committee at Pendik train station show a half-dozen women wearing the cloche hat and no scarves.[49] Women lining streets to see Atatürk in Arifiye (Sakariya Province), however, reveal the mixture of older practices (*peçe/çarşaf*) and newer dress norms of western Turkey.[50]

The symbolic work of portraying the "new Turkish woman" extended into many realms, including the vital leadership role of middle-class and elite women in associational life, new roles as parliamentarians and municipal-level political figures, in advertising for consumer goods linked to the household, in public commemoration including notably Youth and Sport Day on May 19, and through beauty pageants and photo contests that underscored a form of Turkish feminine beauty to be remarked upon, noticed, and even valorized. I highlight a number of examples of this symbolic effort to inculcate through example below.

Becoming "Miss World": Keriman Halis (Ece) as Turkey's model woman

Beauty contests (and contests in general) gained in popularity in urban areas and many towns in Turkey throughout the 1930s. In 1929 initial contests were sponsored to identify Turkish beauties (as adults) as well as beautiful and robust children (in celebration of the first children's day).[51] Beauty contests were new arenas for displaying Turkish femininity—and again were intended to have effects at both the domestic and international levels. Local contests to identify women conforming to the republican model helped to translate—or "inculcate" in the words of Interior Minister Şükrü Kaya—acceptance of the new ideal. Among young women with access to such imagery, it helped foster desire to conform as a matter of national pride and consumption.

Shissler provides a nuanced analysis of the ideological work of the first beauty pageants.[52] She argues that such contests opened new spaces for women to participate in public life and thus radically "shifted the parameters of where women could go and what they could do." At the same time, Shissler notes that beauty contests represented a "redefinition of the concept of respectability or honor, *namus*, and an expansion for women of the limits of the social contract."[53] This redefinition process was uneven, however, as evidence of verbal attacks and slights against women who participated in the contests shows. For example, Keriman Halis's selection as Miss World in Belgium in 1931 stirred reaction within Turkey—some newspapers reported that Miss Halis's family wanted to marry her off right away to secure her respectability now that the whole world "knew her." Keriman and her family strongly denied that she expressed regret over being exposed to everyone's gaze and sought retractions from the newspapers in question.[54] In an article in *The Times* (of London), the correspondent asserts that Keriman Halis' selection as "Miss Universe" in 1932 is emblematic of Turkish women's rapid move "towards complete emancipation."[55] According to the reporter she received a warm reception upon her return to Turkey, and her

> triumph was regarded rather as a symbol of the new freedom which Turkish women have won, and a proof to the world that Turkey has finally shaken off the shackles which kept her so long from taking her place among civilized nations.

The Times reinforced the dominant idea circulating throughout the 1930s that women's progress was due to Atatürk's aim to emancipate women through state decree. The internationally recognized beauty queen was quoted as saying to Atatürk, "My success is the result of the ideas inspired by you in the women of the country." For the correspondent the event marked "a swift change from the Age of the Veil!"

Securing a national image of modernity and civility: the 1935 Istanbul Women's Congress

The dominant narrative of Turkish women's emancipation as tied to unveiling and emerging from the *kafes* into public life can be seen in publications, reports, and press releases of the International Alliance of Women for Suffrage and Equal Citizenship (IAW). The IAW leadership had initially refused an invitation by representatives of the Turkish Women's Union (*Türk Kadın Birliği*) to host its 1935 World Congress in Istanbul.[56] In the lead up to the 12th Congress of the International Alliance of Women for Suffrage and Equal Citizenship held in Istanbul on April 18–25, 1935, the IAW leadership lauded

52 *Kathryn Libal*

Turkish women for the strides made and commended Atatürk and the government for affording women the right to vote and serve in national and local office, and expanding opportunities for women in education and the workforce.[57] Holding the IAW Congress in the Yıldız Kiosk on the grounds of former Ottoman sultans signalled globally Turkish women's liberation: "No more striking example could be given of the transformation of the position of the Oriental woman, from age-old bondage to their present freedom."[58] The Turkish government issued a series of commemorative stamps in honour of the 1935 Congress—including one stamp of Mustafa Kemal Atatürk in the series because of his role in advancing women's suffrage in Turkey. The IAW heartily endorsed the series, commending Atatürk for promoting women's suffrage world-wide.

In April 1935, during the Istanbul Congress, the journalist and writer, Suad Derviş, ran a series of articles in *Cumhuriyet* (The Republic) foregrounding the views of Congress delegates from a variety of countries. Derviş was most interested in assessing IAW delegates' views on women's role within the military and how the IAW actually worked to promote world peace. She also asked delegates their views on the criminalization of abortion and how the state should respond to public health risks associated with prostitution. She did not take up the issue of women's dress directly, but consistently asked IAW delegates from abroad their opinion of Turkish women's status and legal rights. Delegates expressed how impressed they were with the progress of Turkish womanhood. In one example, Katherine Bompas, British delegate and General Secretary of the IAW replied,

> As you know for us Westerners (*garbliler*), Istanbul is the 'dream of 1001 nights.' But I came here not to see the reality of beautiful Istanbul. I wanted to see the free and happy Turkish womanhood saved from the yoke of slavery by Atatürk. The rights you have been given and your freedom offers the world's women a lot of courage and helps them to have courage in their own struggle."[59]

Throughout the week of the IAW meetings in Istanbul, the Istanbul and Ankara press reiterated this theme, quoting both international and Turkish delegates on the importance of Turkey's strides to accord women political rights.

Numerous photos published alongside reports of the Congress showed Turkish delegates in fashionable Western attire, wearing dark colored cloche hats and donning dresses that fell just above the ankle. Turkish delegates in *peçe* or *çarşaf* were not shown in the press, though a much fuller examination of photographic archives of the event would be necessary to determine whether or not Turkish members of the audience were admitted in more traditional attire. And, when US delegates returned to the United States to report on the 1935 Istanbul Congress, they emphasized the rapid progress that Turkish women had experienced, particularly in dress and political rights.

Delegate Josephine Schain conveyed in a radio address from July 1935 that the changes she had seen in Ankara since her travels there in the 1920s to the mid-1930s were "almost impossible to believe." She notes, albeit in an exaggerated way, that social change in Turkey and the entire region is dramatically exemplified in the status of women: "It illustrates the depths to which the new movement has gone. On this trip I saw only two veiled women in my travels throughout the whole of Turkey. (By the way, this includes not only my wanderings around Istanbul and my trip to Angora [Ankara] but also a trip through some Turkish villages near Brusa [Bursa])."[60]

New sensibilities for dress and domesticity in magazines and advertising

Yedigün, a popular weekly, portrayed Turkish women in clothing and hairstyles indistinguishable from other European counterparts, though for commemorations or holidays the serial also depicted women in "local costumes" idealizing peasant dress from particular regions. The cover of a 1935 issue celebrating 23 Nisan (April), or National Sovereignty and Children's Holiday, portrayed a young blond mother, with bobbed short hair, holding a chubby, naked toddler who has curly blond locks.[61] The mother figure, idealized in popular culture and political discourse during the 1930s as protector and nurturer of Turkey's future, was shown outdoors wearing a short-sleeved dress.

Weeklies such as *Yedigün* and the large newspapers such as *Cumhuriyet*, *Ulus*, and *Tan* ran advertisements for Western consumer products depicting women as symbols of "modern" domesticity and sociability. A Frigidaire ad in *Yedigün* featured the same woman and child from the 23 Nisan cover; in this ad they were dressed for outdoor recreation.[62] The mother sported a summer hat, bare arms, and wide-legged pants. Such clothing was still "unconventional" by contemporary standards, only worn by a small elite in private settings, but the growing number of images such as these in newspapers and advertising conveyed a notion of the cultural acceptability of such practices. Nereid assesses *Yedigün*'s impact in the 1930s, asserting that the magazine, which had the largest readership of any magazine in the era, "provided a large public state for women, literally unveiling them," and later notes that the magazine provided numerous instances where young women were "given a narrative voice asserting women-centered interests and points of view."[63] Nereid claims, however, that *Yedigün*, unlike other publications, allows a space for continuity between Ottoman pasts and the modern present and in a sense "domesticates" the modern in its pages.

> The fact that the public image of women as educated professionals was always combined with the reassurance that they were not neglecting their family responsibilities did not consign women to the domestic sphere, but was rather a necessary part of the domestication of modernity, in 1930s Turkey as well as in the rest of the West.[64]

54 *Kathryn Libal*

Conclusion

Metinsoy and Adak's analyses of anti-veiling campaigns at municipal and local levels illustrate that, though a national ban on particular forms of veiling never occurred in the early Turkish republic, a variety of local anti-veiling campaigns were waged locally from the mid-1920s through 1930s. Adak argues that varied bans on *peçe* and *çarşaf* signaled efforts by local elites to have a measure of control over the process of modernization. Moreover, these local campaigns offered opportunities for women to participate in Kemalist modernization as full citizens, as shapers of the women's liberation. As Metinsoy notes, however, local communities were also sites of coercion and were often environments in which women resisted casting off the *peçe* and *çarşaf* due to social pressure, rumour, and public humiliation for those who took up wearing modern hats and overcoats in public. Both these accounts illustrate the dynamic interplay between the central state, local elites, and Turkish society, and the high stakes of contestation, control, and social change revealed in efforts to transform norms for women's dress in public.

I have outlined some of the arenas in which reformist elites shaped socially acceptable standards of women's dress in the early Turkish republic, examining especially efforts to foreground images of the "modern Turkish woman" as iconic of the new nation's progress. Through technologies of print media that were increasingly accessible to urban publics, visual representations of women dressed in Western-style clothing and without the headscarf conveyed a message of social transformation and modernity achieved in the new republic. Images of Turkey's first beauty queens, newly elected women parliamentarians, female doctors, teachers, and mothers conveyed a notion of the modern Turkish woman as a central subject in the new nation-state. As importantly, the continued portrayal of women dressed in *peçe* and *çarşaf* as particularly backward operated to shape public awareness of the desirability of forgoing such practices and taking up the modern *manto* (coat) and hat. The clothing practices of working-class, poor, and rural women were also subjects of commentary in public media, signaling backwardness yet to be reformed through education. But reformers were as troubled by perceived laggards among the urban middle classes, exemplified by the frustrations expressed by Falih Rıfkı Atay over failures of even the most respected "revolutionaries" to permit their wives to be seen in public. Thus, throughout the 1930s, women's attire was a pronounced political and social question.

While Turkish women's appearance was one of the dominant symbols of Turkish modernity,[65] both within the country and in international discourse regarding Turkey in the 1930s, women's dress was only one dimension of the "woman question" debated within the early republic. As importantly, public discourse centred on the role of women as mothers and wives in the domestic realm and as potential defenders of the nation should a regional or world war break out again. And, for leftist social reformers, such as Suad Derviş and Sabiha Zekeriya Sertel, focusing on dress was a distraction. Far more

The backward Ottoman versus new Turkish woman 55

important were efforts to build support for women's rights within the work-place and family, especially for women who were raising families with no husband or family member able to provide for their economic needs. Similarly, effectively tackling public health issues, such as the spread of communicable diseases like tuberculosis and cholera, would do far more to help women from the working classes than concern over their attire.

Yet, as I have argued elsewhere, constructing an image that the state and its allied reformers were engaged in projects of social transformation performed a kind of ideological work that yielded reputational benefits and reinforced the legitimacy of the state.[66] The image of Turkey as a progressive state which had accomplished much in the 10–15 years after its founding was in large part effected by depictions of Turkish women "modernizing" their attire, becoming educated, and entering the paid workforce in much larger numbers. The fact that Orientalism operated in the construction of a radically "modern" and "new" Turkey cannot be ignored, of course, for this helped to inform the very policies, laws, and regulations that were created in the name of "revolution," and debates about their justness or efficacy that were published in Turkey's press in the 1930s.

Notes

1 Ruth Frances Woodsmall, *Moslem Women Enter a New World* (New York: Round Table Press, Inc., 1936), 57–58.
2 Yeşim Arat, "The Project of Modernity and Women in Turkey," in *Rethinking Modernity and National Identity in Turkey*, eds. Sibel Bozdoğan and Reşat Kasba (Seattle, WA: University of Washington Press, 1997), 95–112; Deniz Kandiyoti, "Gendering the Modern: On Missing Dimensions in the Study of Turkish Modernity," in *Rethinking Modernity and National Identity in Turkey*, eds. Sibel Bozdoğan and Reşat Kasba (Seattle, WA: University of Washington Press, 1997), 113–32.
3 Şirin Tekeli, *Kadınlar ve Toplumsal Hayat* (Istanbul: Birikim, 1982); Nilüfer Göle, *The Forbidden Modern: Civilization and Veiling* (Ann Arbor: University of Michigan Press, 1997).
4 See Kemal Yakut, "Tek Parti Döneminde Peçe ve Çarşaf," *Tarih ve Toplum*, 231 (Nisan 2002), 23–32; Hakkı Uyar, "Çarşaf, Peçe, ve Kafes Üzerine Bazı Notlar," *Toplumsal Tarih*, 6/33 (Eylül 1996), 6–11.
5 Metinsoy and Adak (Chapters 3 and 2, respectively, this volume) both develop insights into local and provincial efforts by governmental authorities to wage anti-veiling campaigns that included fines and criminalization. See also Yakut, "Tek Parti Döneminde Peçe ve Çarşaf," op. cit., pp. 27–31. The Republican People's Party debated whether or not to legislate acceptable parameters of women's dress at a national level episodically in the mid-1930s, but ultimately did not pass such legislation, Yakut, "Tek Parti Döneminde Peçe ve Çarşaf," op. cit., p. 28.
6 According to Yakut, the Ministry of Education provided the first platform for such regulations, issuing a dress code forbidding female teachers from covering their faces with veils during class, Yakut, "Tek Parti Döneminde Peçe ve Çarşaf," op. cit., p. 26.
7 I do not fully develop here reflections on strong reactions to practices of seclusion and covering in Turkey's southeast provinces. See Hale Yılmaz, *Reform, Social*

56 Kathryn Libal

Change, and State-Society Encounters in Early Republican Turkey (unpublished dissertation, University of Utah, 2006) for insights from some archival sources on zealous Turkish civil servants seeking to criminalize Kurdish women's dress. See also Lilo Linke's observations on the relatively widespread practices of women's continued preference for *peçe* and *çarşaf* in her tours of towns in Turkey's Black Sea region, the southeast, and central Anatolia in the mid-1930s. Lilo Linke, *Allah Dethroned: A Journey Through Modern Turkey* (New York: Alfred Knopf, 1937).

8 Yılmaz, *Reform, Social Change, and State-Society Encounters*, op. cit., p. 59, fn.6. Yılmaz's work also shows that traditional village attire for men and women depicting affiliation with a particular locale, such as *zeybek* clothing in Aydın, was subject to a ban. Yılmaz argues, however, that these bans had little effect, as can be seen from the repeated efforts to create ordinances that were then in turn ignored, ibid, pp. 58–59.

9 Alev Çınar, *Modernity, Islam, and Secularism in Turkey* (Minneapolis: University of Minnesota Press, 2006), 62.

10 Woodsmall, *Moslem Women Enter a New World*, op. cit., p. 57.

11 Göle, *Forbidden Modern*, op. cit.

12 Halide Edip Adıvar, *Turkey Faces West* (New York: Arno Press, 1973, reprint edition), 223–29.

13 Ibid, p. 224.

14 Literally, *kafes* is often translated as "cage," but in this instance it better refers to the wooden lattices over windows of an Ottoman-style house or, figuratively, to seclusion within the home.

15 Halide Edip Adıvar's memoir, *Turkey Faces West*, op. cit., narrates her perspective on the repression of political contention and efforts to promote a vital democracy. See also Sabiha Zekeriya Sertel's memoirs pertaining to the same period in which she interprets severe political repression from a socialist standpoint, Sabiha Zekeriya Sertel, *Roman Gibi* (Istanbul: Belge Yayınları, 1987 [1969]). For an excellent secondary analysis that outlines the significance of Kurdish resistance to Turkish homogenizing policies, see Mete Tunçay, *T.C.'nde Tek Parti Yönteminin Kurulması (1923–1931)*. 3d ed. (Istanbul: Cem Yayınevi, 1992).

16 While nation-state making was translated to Turkish citizenry as a unique process in which their "true" cultural heritage would be valorized and preserved, the entire modernization project shared much with other nationalisms and nation-state-making efforts. Turkey's proximity to Europe and the historical roots of nationalism and Westernization in the nineteenth century shaped the republic's orientation for reforms in a westerly direction. Nergis Canefe reminds us that the roots of Turkish nationalism were inspired in large part by movements in the Balkans during the nineteenth and early twentieth century. These regionally related nationalisms in turn drew upon political programs, philosophies, social sciences, and socio-cultural trends in France, Germany, Italy, United Kingdom, United States, and at times the Soviet Union in particular. See Nergis Canefe, *Sovereign Utopias: Civilisational Boundaries of Greek and Turkish Nationhood (1821–1923)* (unpublished PhD dissertation, York University, North York, Ontario, 1998).

17 Kandiyoti, "Gendering the Modern," op. cit.; Kathryn Libal, "Specifying Turkish Modernity: Gender, Family, and Nation-state Making in the Early Turkish Republic," in G. Brockett (Ed.), *Towards a Social History of Modern Turkey: Essays in Theory and Practice* (Istanbul: Libra Kitap, 2011), 81–96.

18 At local and provincial levels some authorities did criminalize women's head coverings, with varied effects. See the work of Metinsoy and Adak (Chapters 3 and 2, respectively, this volume) and Yılmaz, *Reform, Social Change*, op. cit., for

The backward Ottoman versus new Turkish woman   57

insights into local campaigns to change women's covering practices and resistance to these campaigns.

19 Yılmaz, *Reform, Social Change*, op. cit., traces the politics of central government authorities in Ankara trying to moderate provincial and local level efforts to enforce bans of the *çarşaf* and *peçe*. She argues that in the mid-1930s the Republican People's Party officials and the Ministry of Interior opposed outright bans and harsh enforcement measures given fears of backlash from "the people." See especially Chapters 1 and 2.

20 As cited in Yılmaz, *Reform, Social Change*, op. cit., pp. 60–61. Translation is also that of Yılmaz.

21 At this stage I have not incorporated analysis of films available for popular consumption in urban locales.

22 A *sarık* was a fez with a turban wrapped around it.

23 Falih Rıfkı (Atay), "Bizim Çocuğumuz" (Our Children), *Cocuk Haftası* 1 (1929), 30.

24 Reformist elites often used terms such as "Orientalism" or "Easternism" in public discourse and, in distancing themselves from "the Orient," struggled to demarcate spheres of reform, influence, and create new parameters of socio-political activity. Reformers often valorized the initiatives, policies, and practices of Europe and the United States of America, though reworking such practices to mark a specifically Turkish modernity. See also Göle, *The Forbidden Modern*, op. cit., and Irvin C. Schick, *The Erotic Margin: Sexuality and Spatiality in Alterist Discourse* (New York: Verso Press, 1999).

25 Ahmed Emin (Yalman), *Turkey in the World War* (New Haven, CT: Yale University Press, 1930).

26 As quoted in Ahmed Emin (Yalman), op. cit, pp. 234–35.

27 Ziya Gökalp, *Principles of Turkism*, trans. Robert Devereux (Leiden, ND: E.J. Brill, 1968).

28 Camilla Trud Nereid, "Domesticating Modernity: The Turkish Magazine Yedigün, 1933–39," *Journal of Contemporary History*, 47/3 (2012), 483–504.

29 As translated by and quoted in Nereid, "Domesticating Modernity," op. cit., p. 502.

30 "Dün Bugün," *Yedigün*, 2/33 (Birinciteşrin 1933), 3.

31 As depicted in the front matter to Touraj Atabaki (Ed.), *The State and the Subaltern: Modernization, Society, and the State in Turkey and Iran* (New York: I.B. Tauris, 2007).

32 Ramiz. Untitled cartoon. *Akbaba*, 13/63 (14 Mart 1935), 13.

33 *Akbaba*, 14/140 (12 Eylül 1936).

34 J. Walter Collins, "Kemal's New Turkey Is Ten Years Old: While Bringing Vast Changes to His People, the Dictator Has Raised the Republic's Standing in World Affairs," *New York Times*, October 29, 1933, SM7.

35 Charles Pound, "Turkish Women Still Striding Onward," *New York Times*, April 16, 1933, SM8.

36 Ibid.

37 *New York Times*, July 27, 1930.

38 *New York Times*, November 12, 1937, 18.

39 As cited in Şule Toktaş, "Nationalism, Modernization, and the Military in Turkey: Women Officers in the Turkish Armed Forces," *Quaderni di Oriente Moderno*, 28/84 (2004), 254.

40 "Women Deputies in Turkey: The New Assembly," *The Times of London*, February 12, 1935.

41 Çınar, *Modernity, Islam, and Secularism*, op. cit., p. 63.

42 Ibid.

43 As quoted in Çınar, *Modernity, Islam and Secularism*, op. cit., p. 62.

44 Woodsmall, *Moslem Women*, op. cit., p. 58.

45 S. Eriş Ülger, *Mustafa Kemal Atatürk I* (Ankara: Verlag Anadolu, 1994), 67.

58 Kathryn Libal

46 Ibid, p. 68.
47 Ibid, p. 71.
48 Ibid, p. 98.
49 Ibid, p. 119.
50 Ibid, p. 100.
51 On contests to demonstrate health and beauty in children see, Kathryn Libal, "Realizing Modernity through the Robust Turkish Child, 1923–38," in Daniel Thomas Cook (Ed.), *Symbolic Childhood* (New York: Peter Lang, 2002), 109–30.
52 A. Holly Shissler, "Beauty Is Nothing to Be Ashamed Of: Beauty Contests as Tools of Women's Liberation in Early Republican Turkey," *Comparative Studies of South Asia, Africa, and the Middle East*, 24, 1 (2004), 109–26.
53 Ibid, p. 107.
54 Ibid, pp. 114–15.
55 *The Times*, November 12, 1932, 11.
56 Seniha Rauf and Lâmia Tevfik attended a conference sponsored by IAW in Marseilles in 1933. While there they conveyed the Turkish Women's Union's (and Turkish government's) invitation to hold the 1935 Congress in Istanbul. Margery Corbett Ashby reportedly expressed interest in the offer, but asserted no decision could be made without having first determined dates for the meeting. "Türk Kadınlar Birliği Üyelerinden Seniha Rauf ve Lâmia Tevfik'in, Marsilya'da Toplanan Kadın Kongresi'ne Ait Raporları" (Reports of the Turkish Women's Union Representatives Seniha Rauf and Lâmia Tevik to the Women's Congress Held in Marseilles). May 5, 1933. Başbakanlık Cumhuriyet Arşivi 30.10.229.541.11.
57 Kathryn Libal, "Staging Turkish Women's Emancipation: Istanbul, 1935," *Journal for Middle East Women's Studies*, 4/1 (2008), 31–52.
58 "For Immediate Release." Press Department—International Alliance of Women for Suffrage and Equal Citizenship. IAW Papers, Box 1, Folder 7, Sophia Smith Collection, Smith College, Northampton, MA.
59 Suad Derviş, "Dünya Feministlerle Görüşmeler: 'Biz Türk Kadınlarına Cidden Gıpta Ediyoruz,'" *Cumhuriyet*, April 10, 1935, 5.
60 Josephine Schain. Script of a Radio Broadcast (July 3, 1935). Josephine Schain Papers, Box 5, Folder 6, Sophia Smith Collection, Smith College, Northampton, MA.
61 *Yedigün*, 5, 118 (24 Nisan 1935).
62 *Yedigün*, 5, 118 (12 Haziran 1935), 28.
63 Nereid, "Domesticating Modernity," op. cit., p. 495.
64 Nereid, "Domesticating Modernity," op. cit., p. 496.
65 See Göle, *The Forbidden Modern*, op. cit., and Yılmaz, *Reform, Social Change, and State-Society*, op. cit.
66 Libal, "Staging Turkish Women's Emancipation," op. cit.

2 Anti-veiling campaigns and local elites in Turkey of the 1930s

A view from the periphery

Sevgi Adak

Women's un/veiling has been an issue of controversy in Turkey since the late Ottoman Empire. However, beginning in the second half of the 1920s and especially with the advent of organized anti-veiling campaigns in the mid-1930s, it became a battleground on which various actors came to debate the issues of religion, secularism, modernization and women's role in society under the new republican regime. As such, it can be argued that the anti-veiling campaigns of the formative years of the republic have constituted the historical context within which the meanings of veiling and unveiling have been contested in Turkey until today. Yet, despite their significance, we know strikingly little about the details of the anti-veiling campaigns. The discourse of the secular Kemalist elite in Ankara on creating a new and modern (therefore unveiled) Turkish woman has received more attention than the specific content, implementation and consequences of these campaigns.[1]

In Turkey, in contrast to what is usually thought, anti-veiling campaigns only aimed at the removal of the *peçe* (face veil), the *çarşaf* (a full-body cloak)[2] and, in some places, local equivalents of the *çarşaf*, and thus did not openly target all forms of veiling. In other words, although the Kemalist imagination of the modern Turkish woman entailed total unveiling as an ideal, anti-veiling campaigns did not openly try to eliminate the various headscarves that women used to cover their hair, for example. The use of the *peçe* and the *çarşaf* was never outlawed, and the campaigns against these forms of veiling were organized at the local level, mainly by the efforts of the local elite and by the indirect involvement of the central authority. The Republican People's Party (RPP) administration in Ankara and the Ministry of Interior tried to coordinate the campaigns by mobilizing the provincial administrators. Hence, anti-veiling campaigns were country-wide phenomena in the second half of the 1930s. However, the lack of a well-formulated central policy and a systematic reform agenda resulted in a rather loose process of change, whose main dynamics were rooted in the provinces. As local initiatives, the anti-veiling campaigns in early republican Turkey thus varied in different cities, leaving a space for negotiation of the regime ideals at the local level as well as for the involvement of various local actors in the shaping of the campaigns.

60   Sevgi Adak

The first examples of anti-veiling campaigns in Turkey were organized during the second half of the 1920s. A decision made by the members of the Trabzon Turkish Hearth (*Türk Ocağı*) in October 1925 that women members should remove their *peçe*s and *çarşaf*s and men should wear a hat is the earliest example we know.[3] The city council of Eskişehir prohibited the use of the *peçe* and the *peştamal*[4] in 1926; the provincial councils (*Vilayet Genel Meclisi*) of Trabzon, Muğla and Rize issued bans on the use of the *peçe*; and in Aydın, in 1927, the provincial council prohibited the use of the *peçe*, the *çarşaf* and the *peştamal*.[5] These early examples seem to be uncoordinated, local initiatives, which had been motivated by the Hat Law of 1925 and the uncompromising manner in which it was put into practice by the Kemalist regime. Although it only concerned men's headgear, the Hat Law triggered a public debate on civilized dress and the importance of modernizing the outlook of the Turkish nation, stigmatizing certain clothes as uncivilized and backward. Attempts to modernize women's dress by the local elite of some provinces had emerged as part of this general momentum.[6] However, these early initiatives remained limited, and the main wave of anti-veiling campaigns began in the 1930s in a much more comprehensive manner both in terms of content and the scope and the intensity of the propaganda regarding it. The fact that similar bans were issued in the 1930s by the city councils of the same cities that had initiated a campaign in the 1920s can be seen as an indication of the limited and weak impact of the earlier attempts.

This paper aims at providing a general overview of the main wave of anti-veiling campaigns in the 1930s under the Kemalist regime based on extensive research in local newspapers, complemented by Turkish state and police archives and British consular reports. I will try to explore the Kemalist ideals on women's dress by concentrating on the reflections of these ideals at the local level as put into practice during the anti-veiling campaigns, and the relations between the local and national dimensions of these campaigns. I will particularly concentrate on the role of the local elite, namely the initiators of the campaigns in the provinces. In doing this, the focus will be on the periphery, on places other than Ankara and Istanbul, where state control was more difficult to exercise and less consistent. Rather than providing a complete story of an anti-veiling campaign in a particular city or discussing the wave of anti-veiling campaigns throughout the country in a comprehensive manner, the paper will try to illustrate the local dynamics and agents that shaped the process, based on the examples of various cities. The argument of the paper is that, despite the involvement of the central authority and the degree of coordination that the RPP and the Ministry of Interior aimed to achieve, the formulation and implementation of anti-veiling campaigns in Turkey were shaped by discussions, negotiations and concessions at the local level. This allowed a range of possibilities for manipulating or compromising the new dress codes, leaving a space for the influence of various local actors, men and women alike.

Anti-veiling campaigns in the 1930s

Placed in a larger context, anti-veiling campaigns can be seen as part of the Kemalist cultural modernization project. From the beginning of the 1930s onwards, the Turkish state extended its control over society and increased its interventions in the cultural and social life of its citizens in an unprecedented manner. Cultural reforms were put into practice in many areas, from music to language, which aimed at a more determined break with the Ottoman past, and with all habits and norms coded as traditional, uncivilized, false or backward.[7] In other words, the anti-veiling campaigns of the 1930s should be seen and analysed as an aspect of the Kemalist regime's consolidation as an authoritarian single-party regime.

In terms of the historical debates on women's rights and social role in Turkey, they can be seen as a chapter in women's emancipation as it was envisioned, propagated and put into practice by the Kemalist leadership.[8] The abolition of gender segregation and women's participation in public life as modern citizens of the nation came to be seen as essential elements of modernization, continuously emphasized and promoted in public discourse, especially in the press. For many Kemalist men and women, traditional women's clothing seemed unfitting to the new picture of Turkish women. Removal of the *peçe* and the *çarşaf*, stigmatized as backward and uncivilized attire alien to Turkish national culture, came to be perceived as an indispensable part of women's civilized status and, therefore, a *sine qua non* for the image of the new republic as a modern and civilized (read Western) regime.

Particularly significant in terms of the timing of the anti-veiling campaigns was women's acquisition of their political rights in December 1934. Women's right to elect and to be elected was seen as the final and most important step in the new regime's effort to modernize women and to improve their status in society. Many interpretations of this development, both at the national and local level, emphasized its (supposed/expected) effect of relegating Turkish women's backward image as 'hiders behind the *peçe* and the *çarşaf*' to the pages of history.[9] An article published in a Trabzon newspaper shows how this link was reinforced at the local level: 'The news agency notes the removal of the *peçe* and the *çarşaf* in Muğla. Does the women's right to elect and to be elected to the parliament ... not mean the abolition of the *peçe* and the *çarşaf* anyway?'[10] Likewise, in his report on the yearly performance of the local party administration of Antalya, which was read at the local party congress, the head of the Antalya party branch pointed to the particular significance of the upcoming national elections because of women's participation and their liberation from centuries-old segregation symbolized by the *peçe* and the *çarşaf*:

> The Turkish revolution had found the Turkish woman behind the *kafes*[11] [lattice] at home, in the *peçe* and the *çarşaf* in the street and in a servile situation in the family. But now, the Turkish woman is among us, equipped with rights that her sisters lack in the most civilized countries.[12]

62 *Sevgi Adak*

It seems that there was a widespread assumption on the part of the Kemalist elite, both at the centre and in the periphery, that women's acquisition of political rights meant their increasing participation in public life and, therefore, modernization of their dress. Women's participation in the public sphere wearing *peçes* and *çarşafs* was a contradiction; having gained all their rights, modern Turkish women had to be modern in dress as well. It should also be mentioned that the existence of a significant number of women who had already removed their *peçe* and *çarşaf* was also important for legitimizing the new forms of clothing as the modern and national norm, and for consolidating them as symbols of these norms.[13]

The strategy that the Kemalist elite used in dealing with the issue of veiling has been generally analysed in the literature as a moderate one compared to some of its contemporaries, such as early Pahlavi Iran.[14] As a close look at the anti-veiling campaigns in the Turkey of the mid-1930s reflects, the Kemalist regime saw the issue as something that should be handled at the local level, through public propaganda, guidance and mobilization of women, and mainly with the initiatives of the local elite. In other words, the lack of a law, a decree or a central party decision did not mean that there was no state intervention. Nevertheless, it can be argued that it provided a relatively wider space for discussion, opposition, negotiation and, therefore, local variation. The fact that the anti-veiling campaigns in Turkey openly targeted only the *peçe* and the *çarşaf* and thus allowed a certain range of possibilities to maintain traditional dress norms was also a factor significantly contributing to the end result of the campaigns as a complex and relatively less radical transformation.[15] Thus, despite obvious attempts on the part of the central authority to coordinate and intervene in local efforts, local communities could influence the process.

In the 1930s, the earliest attempt to remove the *peçe* and the *çarşaf* that I could trace is the banning of the *çarşaf* in Safranbolu, then a district of the province of Zonguldak, in August 1933.[16] Similar decisions were taken in many cities throughout the country from 1934 onwards, accelerating in 1935.[17] As far as can be followed from the local newspapers and archival documents, a large number of anti-veiling campaigns resulted in the declaration of outright bans. Although some of them were issued by the provincial councils led by governors, most of the bans were achieved through city councils, as part of the legal capacity of municipalities. With the Municipal Law issued in 1930 and following legal regulations concerning the provisions about municipal penalties and the use of municipal police, municipalities were legally and politically equipped with the capacity to modernize social life in their localities.[18] It seems that this idea of positioning municipalities as initiators of civilized urban life overlapped in the case of anti-veiling campaigns with the perspective of Ankara of leaving the issue of unveiling mainly to the local administrators.

The content of the bans and the actors involved varied in different cities. Some cities only banned the *çarşaf*; others, both the *peçe* and the *çarşaf*; while in yet others, the ban also included the *peştamal* or other local varieties of veil. In Antalya and Erzincan, for example, the ban also included the *kafes*, in addition to the *peçe* and the *çarşaf*. The campaigns that included the removal of the *kafes* indicate that the eradication of gender segregation and the elimination of all barriers to women's visibility were among the significant motivations behind the anti-veiling campaigns. In Rize, the city council even asked women to remove their umbrellas, which they were using to hide themselves.[19] In most of the decisions declared, women were given a certain period to adapt to the new norms and advised to replace their *çarşaf* with an overcoat.[20]

The process leading to a decision to ban the *peçe* and the *çarşaf* most often began as an initiative of a group of local elites in a certain local institution, supported by a propaganda campaign in the local newspapers and, in most cases, eventually followed with an outright ban. In Bursa, for example, where the ban on the *çarşaf* came in in 1935, some women had tried to initiate a campaign to remove it as early as October 1933 by their own efforts.[21] Particularly People's Houses and their members played a significant role in the organization of the campaigns.[22] In Aydın, the People's House members began discussing the removal of the *peştamal* veil in early 1934, while the actual ban came a year later.[23] In the case of Diyarbakır, for which we lack information as to whether an outright ban on the *peçe* or the *çarşaf* was issued or not, the anti-veiling campaign began by the efforts of the members of the People's House, who were all men, as understood from the news. They organized a meeting where they decided to be the first to remove their family members' *peçe* and *çarşaf* so as to be the vanguards of the struggle.[24] Similarly, in Çankırı, the anti-veiling campaign was first initiated at a meeting of the members of the People's House, followed by a more organized meeting, including delegates from all institutions and party members, where they decided to abolish the *peçe* and the *çarşaf* in order to open the way for the women of the city to follow Atatürk's path.[25] In some cities, propaganda in the press was considered enough to initiate a change in women's dress. The lack of any decision in Istanbul, for instance, became an issue in some newspapers. Rumours emerged that the *peçe* and the *çarşaf* would also be banned in Istanbul, like in many Anatolian cities, but the governor of the city declared that there was no need for any decision or ban for the enlightened and progressive people of Istanbul and that they expected women of this advanced city to remove their *peçe* and *çarşaf* by themselves.[26]

Ankara on the anti-veiling campaigns

To an ordinary citizen in the mid-1930s, following the newspapers of the time, anti-veiling campaigns would seem to be entirely local initiatives. They would look like they stemmed from the vanguard role of provincial administrators as well as from the mobilization of local people to celebrate women's newly gained political rights, their increasing social status and the modernization of the country in general. There was no indication of the direct involvement of

64 *Sevgi Adak*

the government, or any trace of a central action by the party administration in Ankara. However, Ankara was in fact involved in the process, yet quite cautiously and ambivalently, sometimes even inconsistently, only to intervene more actively on certain occasions, especially when some local administrators acted over-zealously or indifferently, as well as in case of opposition and resistance in certain cities.

The first document indicating the Kemalist regime's involvement is a directive sent from the Minister of Interior to all governors and inspectors general in December 1934, right after the decision on women's acquisition of their political rights. Mentioning some measures that were already put into practice by some provincial administrators to fight against the *peçe* and the *çarşaf* in some cities, and the intention of some others to take stronger actions, such as preventing women wearing the *peçe* and the *çarşaf* from entering public places by using the municipal police force, the directive of the minister was inviting the local elite to be more responsible and moderate in dealing with this issue. Writing on the modernization of women in general, the minister indicated that the governors had to focus on propaganda activities only and stay away from taking extreme measures related to the reform efforts:

> At a time when our women are in fact abiding by the requirements of our revolution, it is necessary to avoid carrying this issue too far by taking some measures that might cause undesirable reactions. The requirements of the revolution should not be enforced by municipal police force, but they should be got accepted through well-administered inculcation. Therefore, it would be suitable to be content with propaganda in the *peçe* and *çarşaf* issue as well.[27]

The circular of the minister is crucial in clarifying the initial position of the regime on the question of unveiling, one favouring a moderate and gradual transformation, with the aim of avoiding 'undesirable reactions' on this sensitive issue. On the one hand, it can be read as an invitation for the local administrators to promote propaganda for unveiling, and thus clearly indicates the involvement, or at least the encouragement of the centre regarding the anti-veiling campaigns. On the other hand, this correspondence also demonstrates that some anti-veiling campaigns did begin as local initiatives, as it mentions some measures already taken by some administrators. It also indicates the will of the centre to limit the tendency of some local administrators to be more radical in interpreting and putting regime ideals into practice, and points to the ambiguity and potential disagreements regarding how to struggle against the *peçe* and the *çarşaf*.

These disagreements became visible at the 4th Congress of the RPP, in May 1935. The idea of issuing a law banning the *peçe* and the *çarşaf* country-wide was suggested to the congress by the delegates of Muğla and Sivas, triggering a debate on the proper form of action.[28] The commission that prepared a report on the appropriateness of the request took a negative position, maintaining that these veils had been gradually removed without any measures being taken and they had survived only because of women's respect for their fathers and husbands. Having discussed the suggestion of the commission to leave this issue to the work of the party branches and local institutions, the congress rejected the idea of resorting to general legislation, despite the urging of a few opposing delegates who argued that it was not the *çarşaf* but rather the *peçe* that must be eliminated by adding an article to the Police Law.[29] One of these delegates, Hakkı Tarık Us, referred to the decisions already made and implemented in some cities as indicators of a general need and desire existing in the country to eliminate this form of dress, asserting that these local efforts must be supported with a revolutionary (not evolutionary) attitude on the part of the party. At the general meeting, it was argued that such a move would be unnecessary, since the number of women wearing the *peçe* and the *çarşaf* was low in the cities, and in villages, where the majority of the population lived, women were not segregated and their faces were uncovered. The Minister of Interior, Şükrü Kaya, claimed that this was a minor problem that should be left to the decision of women and that if such a law were needed, the leader of the revolution would have issued it already, referring to the unwillingness of Mustafa Kemal to intervene on this issue.[30] Nevertheless, Kaya suggested that the struggle against the *peçe* and the *çarşaf* should be led by the local administrations, local party cadres and People's Houses and that they should enlighten people on this issue.

In fact, two months later, on 22 July 1935, the minister sent a circular to all governors and inspectors general underlining, very explicitly, the will of the Kemalist revolution to remove the *peçe* and the *çarşaf* and to provide Turkish women with a civilized social status. He indicated, however, that in Kemalist social policy, this reform was left to the civilized taste of women and men, and, thanks to this taste, in the ten years since the establishment of the republic, an impressive transformation had been achieved. He also mentioned the contribution of the work of the municipal and provincial councils in achieving this transformation. Trusting in the revolutionary and modernist character of the Turkish nation, he underlined the approach of the government as being content with propaganda, but nevertheless suggested that a few encouraging steps could complement this reform and could result in the total removal of the *peçe* and the *çarşaf*, which could still be seen here and there: 'Our state officials must take the lead in this. If everyone influences his family members and his immediate circle, this issue will then be solved naturally.'[31] He urged the police to be alert to those who were wearing the *peçe* and the *çarşaf*, but only if this caused a security concern, i.e., that they were trying to hide their identity.[32] He also mentioned that, on occasions related to issues of security, the police should be watchful in big cities and should make sure that women wearing the *peçe* avoid public places such as trams, coffee houses and music halls.[33] On 9 September, 1935, the general secretary of the RPP sent a circular to local party administrators asking them to help the governors on this matter and inform the party centre about the situation.[34]

66 *Sevgi Adak*

These circulars certainly opened the way for the acceleration of the anti-veiling campaigns. As is understood from the replies of some of the local party branches to the letter of the general secretary of the party, the influence of the debate at the party congress in May had already been felt at the local level through the participating delegates. In Sinop, for example, the party decided to ban the *çarşaf* after having listened to the impressions of their delegates about the party congress.[35] However, it should be emphasized that these circulars were sent to the local authorities *after* the *peçe* and the *çarşaf* had already been prohibited in some cities and, in some others, *after* an anti-veiling campaign (although without an outright ban yet) had already been initiated. Even the first circular of the interior minister in December 1934, which was less imperious compared to the ones sent after the party congress, came after the initiation of campaigns in a number of cities. In other words, the local initiative had been playing a significant role right from the very beginning, and the involvement of the party centre and the government accelerated gradually and, as will be discussed below, never reached a level that completely determined the process at the local level. Left vague and sometimes even incoherent in terms of the policy guidance of the regime, the anti-veiling campaigns were shaped by the local circumstances, particularly by the role of local elites.

Anti-veiling campaigns and the role of local elites

What is clear from the overall picture regarding the anti-veiling campaigns in Turkey is that the role and attitude of local elite were critical in fashioning the practice of the campaigns. Apart from most of the state officials and members of both the state and party administration, a cluster of local elites was formed by local notables and the prominent members of the People's Houses, sport clubs, professional organizations, associations and the leading contributors to the local newspapers. Some of these people were appointed officials; but there were a considerable number of people in every city who were locals and were part of this local elite cluster. Simply put, they were the people who formed the educated and/or high-status groups at the local level, characterized and represented as the 'enlightened' segments of the population, but they were far from being homogeneous politically, and the shape that regime ideals would take in practice at the local level was as much a product of the conflicts and negotiations within these local elites as they were of the central policies.

The regime expected local elites to lead the way in social and cultural modernization, and many of their members also envisioned themselves in this role. Therefore, for some members of the local elites at least, men and women alike, there was no need for a directive to come from the centre for every attempt made in the modernization process.[36] Women in particular were in a critical position as agents of change. Local women's associations and women members of People's Houses and some other institutions were actively involved in the anti-veiling campaigns.[37] Many of these women were state officials themselves, or members of local elite families. They supported unveiling by organizing gatherings, giving speeches and encouraging and helping ordinary women to adopt new clothes.[38] Thus, as a result of these efforts, many women did remove their *peçe* and *çarşaf*, sometimes even at the expense of facing verbal and physical harassment.[39]

The most apparent initiative of the local elites was the leading role they had in propaganda efforts, especially by using the local newspapers. Given the difficulties the regime was facing to penetrate society fully through established institutions such as the party branches because of limited state capacity, the local newspapers had gained an important function in 'convincing and leading' the masses on the necessity to reform and 'civilize' women's dress.[40] They were the platform on which local elites tried to initiate and promote the anti-veiling campaigns at the local level. As seen above in the circulars sent from Ankara, the propaganda efforts of local elites were in line with the suggestions of the regime; they were advised to do so. But some local newspapers began to publish articles written by local authors about the need for the removal of the *peçe* and the *çarşaf* earlier. Women were also writing in the local newspapers to promote unveiling, directly addressing the women of the city. One crucial character of this propaganda was that, although their pro-regime stance was obvious, there was nevertheless an effort to represent the desire for such a reform as a genuinely local one, voiced by the elites of the cities themselves. In other words, most of the local authors and journalists were representing the removal of the *peçe* and the *çarşaf* as a natural end result of the modernization of Turkish society and themselves as the natural agents of this modernization. Formulated as 'we the new Turkish youth', 'the enlightened people of the city', 'the women of our city' or sometimes simply 'the people' (of Trabzon, of Konya, etc.), this self-representation of the local elite had the aim of portraying the initiative as something expected from the historical position of their city as the 'vanguard' city and something their city had to do to be worthy of the revolution or not to fall behind the other cities in this struggle. This idea of being the vanguard city was an argument frequently used by local elites in mobilizing the public in various cities.[41]

There were cases where the initiative did in fact originate locally, especially concerning the right way to organize and implement an anti-veiling campaign. One example of such an initiative can be followed in a letter of the acting governor of Antalya to the Minister of the Interior towards the end of 1934, where he was curious about the opinion of the government and the party on the proper way of struggling against the *peçe* and the *çarşaf*. Conveying his opinion that the Kemalist revolution attained yet another major achievement by granting women the political rights that they lack in the most civilized nations, he suggested that it would be inappropriate for Turkish women to welcome this achievement by wearing the *peçe* and the *çarşaf*.[42] Convinced that these veils were showing Turkish women to foreigners in a primitive condition, he asked whether the government had made a decision or was planning to make a decision on the issue, and requested the permission of

68 *Sevgi Adak*

the ministry to use the municipal police to prevent women wearing the *peçe* and the *çarşaf* from entering public places. This was *before* the circular of the minister urging the governors not to use the police force and to use propaganda and inculcation only. The letter of the acting governor of Antalya was in fact one of the reasons for the minister's circular. On the same day that he issued a circular to all governors and inspectors general on the issue, the minister also replied to the letter of the governor of Antalya separately:

> It is not appropriate to prevent women wearing the *peçe* and the *çarşaf* from entering any place, from walking here and there. One should attain this goal only through well-administered inculcation. Therefore, it is also necessary to be content with propaganda in this matter.[43]

Showing the determined will of a local administrator to initiate a forceful campaign, the letter of the acting governor of Antalya also points to the tendency of some of the local actors to solve the issue by taking stronger measures. Despite the warnings of the minister, this tendency continued to guide the actions of some local administrators. This was partly because the circular sent from the Ministry of the Interior was clear about the regime's position regarding the use of the *peçe* and the *çarşaf*, but unclear about how to fight them apart from propaganda and state officials' vanguard role. Once these efforts did not work or were found ineffective or insufficient, some local administrators saw themselves in a position to devise a stronger framework of action and could easily go beyond propaganda activities. The governor of Ordu, for example, informed the Ministry of Interior on 5 March 1937 that he banned the *peçe*, the *çarşaf* and the *peştamal* in Ordu as of 23 April 1937, since decisions and measures taken by some institutions in the province had proved ineffective over the years. He also noted that those who did not abide by the decision would be fined, based on the Law on the Provincial Administration, and they would not be allowed to enter public offices and courts.[44] The minister, in response, reminded the governor of the earlier circulars and warned him that he had no right to enforce a punishment based on the mentioned law. Since there was no law including a ban on the *peçe* and the *çarşaf*, explicitly or implicitly, and since, under a republican administration, every decision and circular should be based on law and all state offices and courts should process the appeals of the citizens regardless of their clothing, the minister urged the governor not to practise any punishment and not to limit women's access to public offices. The minister had a margin for the right to remove women's *peçe* in state offices where there was a need to identify them, but rejected the measure of ignoring women's appeals on the basis of their use of the *çarşaf* or the *peştamal*. He advised the governor to find other measures suitable to local circumstances, without hinting at what these measures might be.[45]

In fact, even after the circular of the minister and contrary to his order, some local authorities did use the municipal police to implement the decision

Anti-veiling campaigns in Turkey of the 1930s 69

to impose a ban on the *peçe* and the *çarşaf*. In a few instances, such as in Denizli and Bursa, women who continued to wear the *peçe* and the *çarşaf* had to pay fines for not obeying the municipal regulations.[46] In some of the notices published in local newspapers concerning the bans, women were warned of the possibility of municipal police intervention in cases of non-compliance.[47] In Bergama, a district of the province of Izmir, the city council announced that not only women who did not comply with the decision, but also shopkeepers who employed women wearing the *peçe* and the *çarşaf*, and persons who harassed women wearing 'national' attire, would be fined.[48] In some cities, decisions of the city councils to ban the *peçe* and the *çarşaf* were put into practice by charging the police to patrol in the main streets, checking women's compliance.

There were some among the local elites who tried to complain to the authorities in Ankara about the way the anti-veiling campaign was implemented in their cities. Having received a letter complaining that in Tosya, a district of the province of Kastamonu, the gendarmerie forcefully removed some women's *peçe* and *çarşaf* in the streets after the decision of the district municipal council on 17 July 1935, and stating that, because of this, people of the district were offended, the Ministry of Interior asked the governor of Kastamonu to report on the issue.[49] The governor of Kastamonu replied by assuring the minister that the decision of the municipality had been made with the help of state officials and enlightened people of the town and that no action by the municipal police was needed. According to the governor, only some prostitutes who continued to wear the *peçe* and the *çarşaf* were called to the police station and warned; no honourable woman was forced by the gendarmerie.[50]

Such cases imply that Ankara was indeed aware of these actions of the local authorities, tried to limit them, but could not get them under full control. This may hint at the limited capacity of the regime to coordinate the campaigns. It may also hint at the fact that, particularly in cases like the anti-veiling campaigns of the 1930s, where policy guidelines from the centre were loose and ambiguous, disagreements both among the elite in Ankara as well as between Ankara and the provinces tended to come to the surface and thus created an ambiguous situation in terms of how to turn a reform ideal into reality.[51] What seems clear is that the lack of definite guidelines from the central authority on how to remove the *peçe* and the *çarşaf* significantly increased the space of action for the local elite. They were in a position to decide the mechanisms through which people would be mobilized, the methods through which they would be 'convinced' or the social occasions where new forms of dress and gender relations would be promoted. For example, the mobilization to fight against the *peçe* and the *çarşaf* in Antalya had in fact been accelerated before the letter of the governor of the city to the interior ministry and predominantly by the involvement of the local party and People's House elite. The party branch had organized a tea party on September 13, 1934, specifically to 'encourage women to engage in social activities'.[52] At the

70 *Sevgi Adak*

tea party, the head of the party branch, Şerafettin Bey, gave a speech that explained the duties of the 'enlightened' women of Antalya, one of which was to eliminate the '*peçe* and *çarşaf* mentality' symbolizing 'backward womanhood' and to encourage and spread civilized clothing.[53] This first initiative was followed by a meeting at the Antalya People's House.[54] Three days later, the formation of a committee to fight the *peçe* and the *çarşaf* by the women members of the Antalya People's House themselves was announced in an Izmir newspaper, with the comment that this fight was seen as necessary since women had to work hand in hand with men for the good of the nation.[55] In Siirt, after the decision of state officials to remove the *peçe*, women who removed their *peçe* were invited, along with their husbands, to a special movie screening organized by the People's House. The way found in Çankırı to create a mixed-gender environment where women could participate without the *peçe* and the *çarşaf* was to organize a New Year's celebration at the People's House, to which members of the House would all come with their wives and daughters who had removed their *peçe* and *çarşaf*.[56]

Local elites also played a leading role in organizing efforts to help women to adapt to the new dress codes. In some cities, local institutions and associations, such as the local branches of the Red Crescent, provided poor families with overcoats, since new clothing was more expensive than the *çarşaf* or the *peştamal*, and this was one important factor contributing to women's inability to adapt.[57] In Trabzon, a special committee was formed with the collaboration of the People's House, the municipality, the Red Crescent, the RPP and the Chamber of Commerce for the same purpose.[58] In Antalya, a similar committee was established under the authority of the provincial council to help those women in need.[59] The committee helped women convert their *çarşaf* into an overcoat and, if this was not possible because of the fabric of the *çarşaf*, to obtain a new one. The head of the committee was the wife of the governor of the city and she led the efforts every day at the party office, where the committee worked. The committee also tried to collect money from charitable donors to help poor women and to support the sewing expenses. In Akşehir, a district of the province of Konya, the tailors were assiduously sewing overcoats while the party inspector visited the city at the peak of the mobilization for the removal of the *peçe* and the *çarşaf*.[60]

In the relatively wide space of action that they enjoyed on the issue of anti-veiling campaigns, some local elites tended to follow a more gradual strategy, while trying to convince the centre that they had taken all the necessary measures to promote unveiling. The governor of Çorum, for example, first tried to mobilize the minor officials who were locals of the province and gave them a certain period of preparation to adopt the new dress codes.[61] At the end of this period, on 15 September 1935, he organized a meeting at the People's House to which all minor officials were invited with their family members, who had now replaced their *çarşaf* with an overcoat. In the meantime, having carefully observed the reception of this mobilization by the general public, he then invited the leading members of the local party branch and the municipality to a joint meeting, where they had decided to ban the *çarşaf* by 29 October 1935, Republic Day. Writing to the Minister of Interior on 22 November 1935, the governor reported that the ban was mainly successful in application through 'official intervention and action'. However, due to the heavily conservative character of the people of Çorum, it was still possible to encounter women wearing the *çarşaf*, mostly women from poor neighbourhoods or older women, and hence one should only expect a gradual transformation in Çorum on the issue of unveiling. Likewise, the governor of Kırklareli also informed the Minister of Interior that all officials and their families had removed their *peçe* and *çarşaf* in the centre of the province, while only some of the women in the district capitals and villages had began wearing overcoats because of poverty. Therefore, he added, this job would be tackled slowly.

One common tendency of the local elites was to represent the anti-veiling campaign in their city as successful and as an effort that found acceptance especially from the women of the city. This image was reinforced by the local newspapers as well. 'The women happily welcomed the decision of the city council' was a very common expression attached to the news reports about the bans on the *peçe* and the *çarşaf*. On 1 July 1934, a local newspaper, *Yeni Mersin*, reported the beginning of the *çarşaf* ban in Mersin, informing the readers how easily and happily the new ban had been accepted by the people of the city.[62] Since the *peçe* ban had begun 20 days earlier than the *çarşaf* ban, the newspaper emphasized that not even a single woman had faced investigation because of non-compliance, and almost half of the women had already removed their *çarşaf* right after the decision of the council, without waiting for the ban to be applied. Claiming that the decision to ban the *peçe* and *çarşaf* had originated from public demand in the city, whose most significant sign was women's willingness to remove these veils, the newspaper announced 1 July as the 'day of liberty for the women of Mersin'. Next day, only one day after the *çarşaf* ban came into effect, *Yeni Mersin* was announcing the total disappearance of the *çarşaf* in Mersin.[63]

Likewise, on 2 May 1935, the local newspaper *Antalya* informed its readers that the campaign against the *peçe* and the *çarşaf* in the city of Antalya was continuing with great success, and that women's willingness to abide by the decision to remove these veils, despite the financial difficulties, deserved to be appreciated.[64] The report of the party inspector Adnan Menderes on Antalya at the end of 1935 in fact confirmed these accounts given by the newspaper. He indicated in his report that the *peçe* and the *çarşaf* had been removed in the city quite easily, without any reaction or gossip, and that this could be interpreted as a lack of opposition to the revolution.[65] One of the few women members of parliament and a deputy of Antalya, Türkân Baştuğ, also reported on 27 November 1935 that the issue of veiling, 'which divides the life into two spheres', had been settled, especially in the city centre in Antalya, as well as in some district capitals. She had seen no veiled women in the city centre, and women were living a normal life together with men in the public sphere.[66]

72 Sevgi Adak

Such reports by the party inspectors and deputies indicate the state of the anti-veiling campaigns and the attitudes of local elites; thus, the regime had certain means to monitor what was going on at the local level. However, the inspectors were not specifically asked to report on the issue. In other words, we do not see information on the anti-veiling campaigns in all reports. Rather, the governors reported to the Minister of Interior after receiving his circular on 22 June 1935, and many of them reported a very positive picture, without mentioning the measures they had taken in detail.[67] As mentioned above, it was the general secretary of the RPP who had asked its local branches to report on the situation themselves, and the local party administrators rarely mentioned any obstacle, problem or hesitation regarding the process.[68] On 5 November 1935 the head of the party branch in Maraş informed the general secretary that, together with the governor of the city, he had explained the necessity of reforming women's clothing to the members of the city council and they all happily accepted and signed the decision banning the *peçe* and the *çarşaf*, and, as had been done everywhere in the country, these veils would be removed in Maraş by 1 January.[69] Writing on 10 January about the result of the ban, he reported that it had been applied successfully and not even a single woman went onto the streets or into the markets of Maraş wearing the *peçe* and the *çarşaf* anymore, and that the *çarşaf* had been replaced by the overcoat.[70]

However, in Maraş, the effect of the anti-veiling campaign was in fact very limited. In 1936, the party inspector reported that even the leading families of the city seemed to be unwilling to abide by the decision to ban the *peçe* and the *çarşaf*, linking this attitude to the same attitude that they had developed a decade ago against the hat reform:

> No reactionary tendency or counter-revolutionary activity is detected. There are people who are cursing their fellow townsmen for blackening the name of their hometown since they were formerly condemned for their opposition to the hat; but there are also people who think that those who were condemned were ignorant and naïve, and that that movement [against the hat] was overplayed. What is certain is that the people are extremely religious (*koyu bir tassup içinde*) and even the wealthy of today acquired their wealth by appearing religious (*mutassıp görünmekle*). As it was the rich, even the members of the administrative board of the party, who were the last people to wear the hat back then, today, they are still the same rich families who do not remove the *peçe* and the *çarşaf* because of the same concern [for appearing religious].[71]

According to another report written in 1940, in Maraş, apart from two or three local families, women from families that were supposed to be liberal and young-minded were wearing long overcoats to the heels and carrying umbrellas to hide themselves, day and night. There were even women coming from upper-class families who were not going out, or visiting the hamam or

Anti-veiling campaigns in Turkey of the 1930s 73

their neighbours at night only, regardless of how enlightened these families were.[72] In 1943, the report of the party inspector mentioned the negative image of the only woman member of the local party administration, Nuriye Bülbül, in the eyes of the religious residents of the city, since she was the first woman to remove the *çarşaf* in Maraş and thus played an important role in the anti-veiling campaign.[73]

Some local elites were deliberately opposed to the anti-veiling campaigns or unwilling to participate actively, and thus there was a struggle within the local elite in some cities on the proper way to approach the issue. One main conflict that arose in a number of city councils was over issuing an outright ban, since some members openly resisted this idea.[74] In Alanya, for example, a district of the province of Antalya, there had been a debate among the members of the municipal council on whether the municipality should issue a decision on the removal of the *peçe* and the *çarşaf.* As the party inspector reports, some members of the council rejected the idea by arguing that the municipality should not intervene in this issue and that they had no right to interfere with the feelings of the people.[75] As a result, the decision of the municipal council of Alanya only mentioned that 'the municipality would encourage the removal of the *peçe* and the *çarşaf*', a decision the inspector characterized as vague and meaningless.[76] A member of the council, Kâmil Kemal, who was also a member of the party administration in Alanya, opposed this decision of the council and attached an annotation. The district governor of Alanya had also intervened in the situation to revise the decision. Although we lack information concerning the result of this attempt, it seems that pro-regime members of the city councils had played an active role in trying to achieve a strong decision on the issue in council meetings, and in cases where they were ineffective or there was a reluctance to issue a decision, governors or local party administrators were involved in convincing the council members accordingly. In the same report, the party inspector mentioned a similar example in the Hadim district of the province of Konya, where the local party president had complained about the difficulties he faced in trying to get a decision on the removal of the *peçe* and the *çarşaf* because of the opposition coming from the fanatically minded (*softa kafalı*) members of the local party administration, who were seemingly supportive of the decision but would most probably be unwilling to encourage the people accordingly and to promote regime ideals. Similarly, in Mersin, some people opposed the idea of banning the *peçe* and the *çarşaf* by arguing that it would be very difficult to apply such a ban and that this issue should be handled by an evolutionary approach.[77]

In cases of opposition, the attitude of the central elite in Ankara changed considerably, favouring direct involvement, mainly through pressuring the governors, or by having the inspectors general intervene in the situation. Any attempts at questioning, complaining or negative propaganda regarding the anti-veiling campaigns were associated with a potentially more general ideological opposition to the regime, and were thus approached with great

74   *Sevgi Adak*

suspicion. Having learned that a certain Ahmet had circulated a rumour that a policeman and two gendarmes had been killed because they tried to remove women's *çarşaf* in the middle of the street in the city centre of the province of Konya and in one of its villages, the Minister of Interior asked the governor of Konya to investigate Ahmet's ethnic origin and whether he had any connections from outside, and to send Ahmet's picture and fingerprint.[78] Similarly, when a certain *peştamal* weaver in Aydın, Dokumacı Ahmet Şevki, sent a telegram directly to the President Mustafa Kemal Atatürk complaining about the use of force by the gendarmes in the application of the ban on the *peçe*, the *çarşaf* and the *peştamal* in Aydın, the Ministry of Interior asked the governor of Aydın to report, very urgently, who this person was. The governor replied, claiming that no such incident had happened, the veils were removed in Aydın very easily and uneventfully, and the telegram of Ahmet Şevki was a result of his fear of losing his job as a *peştamal* weaver. The Minister then warned the governor that there might be a possibility that Ahmet Şevki had reactionary aims, and thus it should be investigated whether he was a member of any religious order (*tarikat*).[79]

The case of Trabzon is perhaps one of the best examples illustrating the tensions between local actors and the ways in which the anti-veiling campaigns were shaped at the local level through their struggles and negotiations, and how Ankara intervened if the result of the tensions risked a backlash. In Trabzon, the anti-veiling campaign first began with propaganda efforts in the local newspapers from October 1934 onwards, followed by a petition of the members of the youth and sports clubs, led by the Trabzon Home for Adolescents (*Erginler Yurdu*), to the city council requesting a ban on the use of the *peçe* and the *çarşaf* in February 1935.[80] Some members of the city council had opposed the idea by arguing that such a ban would be disgraceful for the city.[81] The opposition in the council continued for a year and they were able to postpone the talks in the council meetings several times in order to prevent a decision.[82] The sport clubs had to give the same petition to the provincial council due to the reluctance of the city council and its tendency to postpone the process.[83] Meanwhile, in his reply to the circular sent by the secretary general of the party in October 1935, the head of the local party branch did not mention the council's opposition and indicated that the *peçe* had disappeared in Trabzon and that to remove the *çarşaf*, of which only a few examples remained, he would consult the governor and they would together take the necessary measures.[84] In fact, the situation was quite different; the *peçe* had not disappeared and the *çarşaf* was still an issue. During this year, Trabzon newspapers published several articles, commentaries and news reports trying to mobilize the people of the city, especially the women, to support the anti-veiling campaign, to remove the *peçe* and the *çarşaf*, and to pressure the council to obtain a decision.

In the end, with the pressure coming from the local party administration and the governor, the city council banned the *peçe* and the *çarşaf* on 4 February 1936 with a majority decision, declaring 4 May as the enforcement

Anti-veiling campaigns in Turkey of the 1930s 75

date.[85] However, the tension in Trabzon probably had its reflection in Ankara since the recently appointed inspector general of the region, Tahsin Uzer, took a firm position in controlling the situation and making sure that the aims of the anti-veiling campaign were achieved. As the British Pro-Consul in Trabzon informed the British Embassy in Ankara in March 1936, Tahsin Uzer's main aim since his arrival in the city had been to develop a modern social life in Trabzon, and especially to increase women's participation in the social activities organized and encouraged by the inspector general, and hence to fight against women's seclusion. The inspector criticized the failure of the Trabzon municipality to initiate a ban on the wearing of the *peçe* and the *çarşaf*, regretting that the ban had been delayed until 4 May. Inspector General Uzer also added that if he had been in Trabzon at the time he would not have allowed the delay. The Pro-Consul noted the plan of the inspector general to arrange an evening party to which would be invited only those renowned for their religious fanaticism and their wives.[86] It seems, however, that the attitude of the inspector general increased the tension rather than alleviating it. A few weeks later, the British Pro-Consul reported to the embassy in Ankara that the reaction against the anti-veiling campaign had accelerated in the city and he was informed that the mayor of Trabzon was receiving anonymous letters threatening him with murder. The wife of the mayor was attacked and other instances of violence also occurred because of the way the anti-veiling campaign was put into practice:

> On the 13th of April the wife of the President of the Municipality was assaulted and injured in the street by a man who tore her dress and underclothes, calling them immoral. The police are now searching for the culprit who, if found, will, it is stated, be punished in an exemplary manner. It is reported that at Palatane [today's Akçaabat, a district of the province of Trabzon S.A.] a man killed a gendarme who according to the regulations obtaining there had forcibly removed his wife's veil. I understand that great animosity prevails locally against the municipality as a result of the decision regarding women's dress, and especially against the Third Inspector General and his staff who, owing to the conduct of most of them, are considered unfitted to the task of civilising the region, being commonly referred as 'a band of debauchees'. I am informed that the recent visit of the Fleet to Trebizond and its surroundings was made with the object of cooling the reactionary feelings of the local population and of reminding them that force was behind the authorities.[87]

The case of Trabzon shows that 'undesirable reactions' were not avoided as was advised by Ankara. The possibility of such tensions might have concerned many local elites so that, even though a decision was made to remove the *peçe* and the *çarşaf* in some cities, its implementation was carried out rather reluctantly. Reporting from the Kadınhan district of the province of Konya in the fall of 1935, the party inspector indicated that no action had yet

76 *Sevgi Adak*

been taken on the issue of *peçe* and *çarşaf* despite the existence of a decision to abolish them.[88] There were also cases where the local elite avoided issuing an outright ban by claiming it unnecessary for their city. In Akseki, a district of the province of Antalya, no measure was taken on the issue of *peçe* and *çarşaf* because the guidance that would be given in houses and neighbourhoods was considered sufficient given that the level of awareness concerning this issue among the people of Akseki was in fact high.[89]

This argument that the people of the city were in fact 'conscious' regarding revolutionary ideals and the necessities of modern life had been used by many local elites. Reporting to an Izmir newspaper, one of the columnists of a Konya newspaper, *Babalık*, was arguing that three-fourths of the women of Konya were in civilized clothes and the rest of them were using a white veil called *şelme*, which they wove themselves, and this was the reason why Konya had not been vocal about the campaigns against the *peçe* and *çarşaf*.[90] Concerned that this could be interpreted as resistance or a sign of backwardness, the author was trying to convince the readers that there was only a small number of women in Konya who were wearing the *peçe* and the *çarşaf* and the use of *şelme* was only due to poverty. The women of Konya had proven their social maturity; they were conscious enough so that there was no reason to worry about their will to progress further.[91] Part of the reason behind these efforts was related to the aim of representing the image of the city as already modern and civilized, as mentioned above. However, the intention of such propaganda was also to remind women of their responsibility in making this image a reality by becoming the agents of social change in their society.

Concluding remarks

In his article dated 23 December 1934, a local columnist in one of the Trabzon newspapers, Cevdet Alap, addressed the local authorities. After mentioning a circular of the governor of Trabzon to all state officials advising them not to process the petitions of women wearing the *peçe* and the *çarşaf*, Alap requested that this decision be turned into a general ban including all public places:

> This ban can gradually be expanded to the following: A woman cannot sit in the park wearing the *peçe* and the *çarşaf*, cannot enter Güzelhisar Park, cannot come to the movie theatre, and finally, cannot wander in the market or bazaar. If we do not issue such a ban today, the revolution, the regime will, perhaps not today or next year, but soon. The regime, the revolution, which has given women the right to elect and to be elected, will totally eliminate the *peçe* and the *çarşaf*, which are now a sign of being uncivilized, through a law like the one on the dress of the priests and hodjas.[92]

This call of a local voice for the realization of regime ideals through a local initiative, without waiting for an order or a central regulation, is an example

Anti-veiling campaigns in Turkey of the 1930s   77

of how the anti-veiling campaigns in Turkey were shaped by local agents as much as they were shaped by the will and involvement of the central authority.

As I have tried to show in this paper, this was a complicated process, fashioned by the interplay between ordinary people, local elites and the regime. Attempts by the central authority to encourage, monitor and intervene in the making of the anti-veiling campaigns, albeit critical, did not determine the form they took in practice. In the absence of a common blueprint, local elites were in a critical position to shape the campaigns, which opened a space for negotiation, compromise and, thus, variation. As a result, the case of the anti-veiling campaigns can be considered as illustrative of the complexities of the process of modernization in Turkey, which can only be partially understood by looking at the discourse and policies of the Kemalist regime as seen from Ankara. It shows the necessity of looking at the local level, at what the state actually could do in practice and to the occasions where different agents encountered, interacted and transformed the project of modernity.[93]

As such a process, the anti-veiling campaigns in Turkey in the 1930s took different forms in different cities and varied significantly in terms of effectiveness. However, it should also be emphasized that they affected many women. They caused a decrease in the use of the *peçe* and the *çarşaf*, at least for a certain period of time after the initiation of the campaigns, and contributed to their replacement with overcoats and various types of headscarf.[94] Therefore, they created a considerable change in women's clothing throughout the country. This change was not determined by the policies of the regime, or by the efforts of the male actors in the provinces only. Women's responses were critical at all levels. In particular, those women who supported and were involved in the campaigns acquired the opportunity to reinforce their place as equal citizens in the society. The deliberate decision of the Kemalist elite in Ankara to avoid radical measures in dealing with women's clothing can also be understood within this framework. They had trusted, especially at the local level, in the support and agency of women in promoting the ideal of 'modern Turkish woman'.

Notes

1 There are articles focusing on the anti-veiling campaigns organized in some cities. See Mesut Çapa, 'Giyim Kuşamda Medeni Kıyafetlerin Benimsenmesi ve Trabzon Örneği', *Toplumsal Tarih* 30, June 1996, p. 22–28; Hakkı Uyar, 'Çarşaf, Peçe ve Kafes Üzerine Bazı Notlar', *Toplumsal Tarih* 33, September 1996. See also Kemal Yakut, 'Tek Parti Döneminde Peçe ve Çarşaf', *Tarih ve Toplum* 220, April 2002, p. 23–32. Yılmaz has an important chapter on the regulation of women's clothes in the early republic based on archival documents as well as oral historical sources. See Hale Yılmaz, 'Reform, Social Change and State-Society Encounters in Early Republican Turkey', unpublished PhD dissertation, The University of Utah, 2006. For an early work discussing the changes in women's clothing from the Ottoman Empire to the republic, see Muhaddere Taşçıoğlu, *Türk Osmanlı Cemiyetinde Kadının Soyal Durumu ve Kadın Kıyafetleri*, Ankara: Kadının Sosyal Hayatını Tetkik Kurumu, 1958. See also Cihan Aktaş, *Tanzimat'tan 12 Mart'a*

78 Sevgi Adak

Kılık-Kıyafet ve İktidar, Istanbul: Kapı, 2006; Bernard Caporal, *Kemalizmde ve Kemalizm Sonrasında Türk Kadını (1919–1970)*, Ankara: Türkiye İş Bankası Kültür Yayınları, 1982; John Norton, 'Faith and Fashion in Turkey', in Nancy Lindisfarne-Tapper and Bruce Ingham (eds.), *Languages of Dress in the Middle East*, London: Curzon Press, 1997, p. 149–77.

2 The Turkish *çarşaf* is similar to the Iranian *chador*, but it is either gathered at the waist or in two pieces, consisting of a long skirt and a cloak covering also the head. It is usually black, but it can also be in other colours.

3 Mustafa Reşit Tarakçıoğlu, *Trabzon'un Yakın Tarihi* [1986], reprinted in Hikmet Öksüz and Veysel Usta (ed.), *Mustafa Reşit Tarakçıoğlu, Hayatı, Hatıratı ve Trabzon'un Yakın Tarihi*, Trabzon: Serander, 2008. It seems that this was a genuinely local initiative and an example of how the local elite were seeing themselves as the vanguards of the modernization project. The Turkish Hearth was an association founded in 1912 to promote Turkish nationalism. For more, see Füsun Üstel, *İmparatorluktan Ulus-Devlete Türk Milliyetçiliği: Türk Ocakları (1912–1931)*, Istanbul: İletişim, 1997.

4 *Peştamal* is a local fabric cover that has been used especially by rural women. Its colour and pattern are different in different regions.

5 See Çapa, 1996, op. cit; Yakut, 2002, op. cit.; Caporal, 1982, op. cit.; From RPP Muğla Administration to RPP Secretariat General, The Turkish Republic Prime Ministry Republican Archives (hereafter PMRA) 490.01/17.88.1, 15 October 1935; from the Governor of Aydın to Prime Minister İsmet Paşa, PMRA 030.10/ 53.346.6, 3 February 1927. Yakut mentions that similar anti-veiling campaigns were organized in Bursa and Ordu in the 1920s, but he does not provide any details about the time and content of these campaigns. See Yakut, 2002, op. cit.

6 The statement of the mayor of Eskişehir was in fact referring to this link. See Çaha, 1996, op. cit. Aktaş also points to the relationship between the Hat Law and the regime's message on veiling. See Aktaş, 2006, op. cit., p. 185.

7 As part of this wave of reforms in the 1930s, a law in 1934, known as the Dress Law (*Kisve Kanunu*), prohibited the clergy from wearing their religious dress outside service. The law applied to the people of all religions, including Jewish and Christian clergy. Thus anti-veiling campaigns were not the only attempts at the regulation of clothing in the 1930s.

8 For more on the Kemalist perspective on women's emancipation, see Deniz Kandiyoti, 'Emancipated but Unliberated? Reflections on the Turkish Case', *Feminist Studies* 13: 2, Summer 1987, p. 317–39 and Yeşim Arat, 'The Project of Modernity and Women in Turkey', in Sibel Bozdoğan and Reşat Kasaba (eds.), *Rethinking Modernity and National Identity in Turkey*, Seattle: University of Washington Press, 1997, p. 95–112.

9 Mustafa Kemal himself also hinted at a connection between women's political rights and the removal of the *peçe* and the *çarşaf*. See 'C.H.F. Grup Kararları', *Yeni Asır*, 6 December 1934. See also 'Atatürk Ulusal Savaşında Kadından Saylav Yapacağını Söylemişti', *Yeni Asır*, 16 December 1934. In fact, Mustafa Kemal never directly addressed the issue of unveiling or referred to the necessity of anti-veiling campaigns, but it was obvious in a number of his speeches that, for him, general habits of dress widespread among women in Turkey in the early years of the republic did not have a national and civilized character. As seen in his speeches, his main concern was with women's segregation and exclusion from the public sphere, and his direct criticisms targeted covering of the face, thus, the use of the *peçe*. Interestingly, he also criticized women who tried to imitate European women and carried the change in their style to extremes, and urged Turkish women to maintain their modesty. For his speeches, see *Atatürk'ün Söylev ve Demeçleri*, Ankara: Atatürk Araştırma Merkezi Yayınları, 1989.

10 Cevat Alap, 'Ayinesi iştir kişinin Lafa bakılmaz', *İkbal*, 13 December 1934.

Anti-veiling campaigns in Turkey of the 1930s 79

11 *Kafes* is a lattice or a window grill, used to enclose windows for privacy.
12 Report of the administrative board presented at the RPP 1934 Congress of the Province of Antalya, PMRA 490.1/618.28.1, 11 December 1934. The provincial chairman of the party also indicated that during 1934 the efforts of the party administration in Antalya to increase the number of party members in the city were particularly focused on gaining women as members.
13 In fact, the change in women's dress had already begun in the late Ottoman period and continued gradually in the republican era. The debate on the *peçe* and the *çarşaf* had also started in the late nineteenth century, especially with the increasing influence of the West and the rise of the Ottoman women's movement. For the change in women's attire from the Ottoman Empire to the republic, see Aktaş, 2006, op. cit.; Melek Sevüktekin Apak, Filiz Onat Gündüz and Fatma Öztürk Eray, *Osmanlı Dönemi Kadın Giyimleri*, Istanbul: İş Bankası Yayınları, 1997; Nora Şeni, 'Fashion and Women's Clothing in the Satirical Press of Istanbul at the End of the 19th Century', in Şirin Tekeli (ed.), *Women in Modern Turkish Society*, London: Zed Books, 1995, p. 25–45.
14 For example, see John Norton, op. cit., p. 149–77.
15 The cases of Iran and especially Uzbekistan, for example, can be considered as more radical attempts to change women's clothing. See the chapters in this volume. For the Iranian case, see also Patricia L. Baker, 'Politics of Dress: The Dress Reform Laws of 1920–30s Iran', in Nancy Lindisfarne-Tapper and Bruce Ingham (eds.), *Languages of Dress in the Middle East*, London: Curzon Press, 1997, p. 178–92; Jasamin Rotsam-Kolayi, 'Expanding Agendas for the 'New' Iranian Woman: Family Law, Work, and Unveiling', Shireen Mahdavi, 'Reza Shah Pahlavi and Women: A Re-evaluation' and H. E. Chehabi, 'The Banning of the Veil and Its Consequences', all in Stephanie Cronin (ed.), *The Making of Modern Iran: State and Society under Riza Shah, 1921–1941*, London: Routledge, 2003. On the Uzbek case, see Marianne Kamp, *The New Woman in Uzbekistan: Islam, Modernity and Unveiling under Communism*, Seattle: University of Washington Press, 2006.
16 'Safranboluda çarşaf menedildi', *Cumhuriyet*, 21 August 1933.
17 The list of the cities where there was an outright ban include: Giresun (April 1934), Mersin (July 1934), Kayseri (November 1934), Bolu (December 1934), Muğla (December? 1934), Antalya (February 1935), Bursa (February? 1935), Adana (February? 1935), Erzincan (February 1935), Rize (February 1935), Artvin (March 1935), Nevşehir (May? 1935), Aydın (August 1935), Kastamonu (August, 1935), Konya (August 1935), Afyon (August 1935), Sivas (August 1935), Isparta (August 1935), Yozgat (September 1935), Denizli (September 1935), Elâziz (September 1935), Sinop (September 1935), Uşak (October 1935), Bitlis (October 1935), Siirt (October 1935), Maraş (November 1935), Gümüşhane (November 1935), and Trabzon (February 1936). The list is based on the time that the decisions were taken and declared, rather than the time that the ban became effective, except for Mersin and Yozgat. Caporal gives different dates for some cities. See Caporal, 1982, op. cit., p. 649. A Trabzon newspaper indicates a ban in Muğla on 13 December 1934, but the exact date of the decision is unclear. However, the ban was effective as of 1 June 1935. See RPP Muğla Administration to RPP Secretariat General, PMRA 490.01/17.88.1, 15 October 1935. In Bursa, on 1 February, the first decision of the city council was to prohibit tailors from sewing the *çarşaf*. In the next meeting of the city council on 10 February 1935, the *kafes* was banned. I could not identify the date of the decision in Bursa that banned the use of the *peçe* and the *çarşaf*, but some news reports later that year indicate that there was such a ban. See 'Çarşaflar kalkıyor ... ', *Hakkın Sesi*, 10 October 1935.

80   *Sevgi Adak*

18 İlhan Tekeli, *Cumhuriyetin Belediyecilik Öyküsü (1923–1990)*, Istanbul: Tarih Vakfı Yurt Yayınları, 2009, p. 50–116. The number of decisions taken by city councils can be interpreted as Ankara's tacit consent for dealing with the unveiling issue through municipalities and within the legal framework of the Municipal Law.

19 See 'Rizede Peçeler ve Çarşaflar Kalkıyor', *Yeni Asır*, 1 March 1935.

20 This period was different in every city, but the general tendency was to grant a shorter time for the removal of the *peçe*, and a longer one for the *çarşaf*. This was probably because the *peçe* was considered easier to remove, since women did not need to replace it with other clothing, unlike the *çarşaf*. It is also related to the fact that uncovering women's faces was considered as a more urgent task.

21 'Bursada artık çarşaf giymeyecekler', *Cumhuriyet*, 29 October 1933.

22 Founded in 1932, People's Houses was perhaps the most important cultural institution of the Kemalist regime aiming at educating and mobilizing people in line with its ideals and policies. For a recent study on People's Houses and their role in the domestication of Kemalist reforms at the local level, see Alexandros Lamprou, 'Between Central State and Local Society. The People's Houses Institution and the Domestication of Reform in Turkey (1932–51)', unpublished PhD dissertation, Leiden University, 2009.

23 'Aydında peştemalı kaldırmağa çalışıyorlar', *Cumhuriyet*, 14 April 1934.

24 'Diyarbekir kadınları da çarşafı atıyorlar', *Cumhuriyet*, 29 December 1934.

25 'Çankırıda çarşaf kalkıyor', Cumhuriyet, 31 December 1934; 'Çankırı'da Peçe Çarşafların Atılması Kararlaştırıldı', *Yeni Asır*, 1 January 1935.

26 'İstanbulda da çarşaf çıkarılacak', *Cumhuriyet*, 4 September 1935; 'İstanbul münevver kadınları bu garip örtüyü kendiliğinden atacakdır', *Halk*, 16 September 1935. A news report published in an Izmir newspaper did indicate the total removal of the *kafes* in Istanbul, though. No ban or decision by the municipality was mentioned. See 'Kafesler Kaldırılıyor ... ', *Anadolu*, 21 September 1934. Rumours in fact played an important role in the anti-veiling campaigns, especially in mobilizing opposition. However, they also sometimes helped in increasing compliance with the bans. In the 1920s, for example, some women removed their *peçe* and *çarşaf* because of a rumour that Atatürk had ordered their removal. See Aktaş, 2006, op. cit., p. 210–11.

27 From the Minister of Interior to all provinces and general inspectorships, Turkish National Police Archives (hereafter TNPA) 13216–17/1, 17 December 1934.

28 For the discussion on the *peçe* and the *çarşaf* issue at the congress, see *C.H.P. Dördüncü Büyük Kurultayı Görüşmeleri Tutulgası, 9–16 Mayıs 1935*, Ankara: Ulus Basımevi, 1935.

29 It is interesting to note that even those delegates who were in favour of a general ban made a distinction between the *çarşaf* and the *peçe*, considering the latter completely unacceptable while the former more tolerable. See ibid.

30 Kaya also mentioned that such a law would put the party in a difficult situation, again referring to the intention of the regime to avoid reactions.

31 From the Minister of Interior to general inspectorships and provinces, TNPA 13216–7/1, 22 July 1935.

32 Especially the attempts at theft by people who were using the *çarşaf* as a way to hide themselves were the major concern, and these attempts were also used in the propaganda against the *peçe* and the *çarşaf*. For news on such attempts based on municipal police reports, see for example 'Bir Çarşaflı Kadının Hırsızlığı', *Antalya*, 10 January 1935; 'Çarşaflı Hırsız Tutuldu', *Babalık*, 6 March 1935; 'Mersin'i Soymak İstediler', *Yeni Mersin*, 2 July 1934.

33 In the directive, the Minister of Interior particularly mentions the need for the removal of the *peçe*, especially in marketplaces by referring to the example of Istanbul. He suggests that if women continue to wear the *peçe* after they are given

Anti-veiling campaigns in Turkey of the 1930s 81

a notice to remove it, then they can be banned from selling their goods in the market.

34 See the letter from the RPP Yozgat Administration to the RPP Secretariat General, PMRA 490.01/17.88.1, 13 November 1935.

35 From the RPP Sinop Administration to the RPP Secretariat General, PMRA 490.01/17.88.1, 30 September 1935.

36 For expressions of such ideas in local newspapers in the 1920s, see Çapa, 1996, op. cit. Similar views were voiced during the anti-veiling campaigns of the 1930s in the local newspapers.

37 Some of the campaigns were in fact initiated by women. In Bursa, for example, removal of the *kafes* from windows was suggested to the city council by the deputy mayor, Zehra Hanım. See 'Belediye Meclisinde', *Hakkın Sesi*, 3 February 1935. In Antalya, the anti-veiling campaign began with the formation of a women's committee composed of the women members of the People's House. See 'Antalyada Çarşaf ve Peçelerle Mücadele Başladı', *Yeni Asır*, 23 December 1934.

38 For some examples of women's efforts, see 'Diyarbekir kadınlar derneği ... ', *İkbal* 27 January 1935; Hayriye Ural, 'Çarşafları Atalım', *Halk*, 30 Mart 1936.

39 There is evidence that such events happened in a few places. Some municipalities had taken measures to prevent them. See Yakut, 2002, op. cit.; Yılmaz, 2006, op. cit. It should be noted that women tried to handle this change in various ways, and many of them also resisted unveiling. The most common way of resisting unveiling was disobedience and trying to avoid the authorities, but women also tried to domesticate new clothes by adapting them to local circumstances and by adopting long overcoats, various kinds of headscarves and turbans to replace the *çarşaf*. Poverty, social pressures in and outside the family and the patriarchal social structure also played a significant role in women's responses to unveiling. For more on resistance to anti-veiling campaigns, see Murat Metinsoy's contribution (Chapter 3) in this volume, entitled 'Everyday resistance to unveiling and flexible secularism in early republican Turkey.'

40 The local party branches were also using local newspapers to inform people about the party programme and ideals. For the efforts of the Antalya party branch to use the local newspaper, *Antalya*, for propaganda activities, see the 1935 Report of Adnan Menderes, deputy of Aydın, PMRA 490.1/618.27.1, 2 December 1935.

41 In this sense, apart from the struggle within local elites to be the leading agents of change, one can point to competition among the cities to be the vanguards regarding the anti-veiling campaigns. For examples of this kind of propaganda, see 'Trabzon kadınları ve çarşaf', *İkbal*, 29 October 1934; 'Halkevinde dün akşamki toplantı', *Antalya*, 20 December 1934; 'Eni konu konuşmalar', *Halk*, 11 April 1935. Likewise, introduction of a campaign in a certain province soon came to affect the districts of that province, creating a snowball effect and an atmosphere of competition. The way in which campaigns were reported in provincial newspapers shows how this comparison created pressure on district administrations to follow the province in banning the *peçe* and the *çarşaf*. *Yeni Mersin*, a newspaper of the province of Mersin, for example, was reporting the inability of the district of Tarsus to launch a successful campaign against the *peçe* and the *çarşaf* during the year 1933, celebrated the renewal of the efforts to issue a municipal ban in 1934, following the decision in Mersin, and published commentaries inviting the members of the Tarsus municipal council to support the ban. See 'Çarşaflar Tarsustada kalkıyor', *Yeni Mersin*, 16 September 1934; 'Tarsus Belediye M. toplantısı', *Yeni Mersin*, 4 February 1935. See also Rıza Atila, 'Yeni Çağın Artığı', *Yeni Mersin*, 4 February 1935.

42 From the Acting Governor of Antalya to the Ministry of Interior, TNPA 13216–7/1, 17 November 1934. It is also interesting to note that the main concern of the

82   *Sevgi Adak*

governor about the issue of veiling was the kind of image that it represented in the eyes of foreigners. This was in fact a very widespread concern in public discussions throughout the anti-veiling campaigns. It is also crucial that the governor was characterizing the struggle against the *peçe* and the *çarşaf* as a struggle of many years, which refers to a degree of continuation between the earlier examples of the anti-veiling campaigns in the 1920s and the later ones in the mid-1930s.

43 From the Minister of Interior to the Province of Antalya, TNPA 13216–17/1, 17 December 1934.

44 Copy of the letter of the Governor of Ordu to the Ministry of Interior, TNPA 13216–7/1, 5 March 1937.

45 Copy of the letter of the Minister of Interior to the Province of Ordu, TNPA 13216–17/1, 14 May 1937.

46 Hakkı Uyar, 'Tek Parti Döneminde Denizli'de Siyasal Hayat', in Ayfer Özçelik *et al.* (eds.), *Uluslararası Denizli ve Çevresi Tarih ve Kültür Sempozyumu: Bildiriler I-II*, Denizli: Pamukkale Üniversitesi, 2006. Uyar does not give any information about precisely how many women were fined in Denizli. A news report in a Bursa newspaper mentions that more than 100 women were fined in a few months by the city council. See 'Çarşaflar Kalkıyor', *Hakkın Sesi*, 10 October 1935.

47 See 'Çarşafların yasağı hakkında Belediye Riyasetinden', *Halk*, 30 April 1936.

48 'Bergama'da Çarşaf, Peçe ve Kıvraklar Kaldırılıyor', *Anadolu*, 6 December 1934.

49 From the Ministry of Interior to the Province of Kastamonu, TNPA 13216–7/1, 14 September 1935. For a similar complaint about the use of force in Aydın, see a copy of the telegram from Dokumacı Ahmet Şevki to Atatürk, TNPA 13216–17/1, 16 August 1935. For another complaint from Ödemiş, a district of the province of Izmir, reporting the mistreatment of those women who continued to wear the *çarşaf* by the gendarmerie in 1937, see Yılmaz, 2006, op. cit., p. 78.

50 From the Governor of Kastamonu to the Ministry of Interior, TNPA 13216–7/1, 17 October 1935.

51 Because of this ambiguity, some local administrators were at pains in trying to promote unveiling while balancing the concerns mentioned by Ankara and the demands stemming from the local environment. The governor of Sinop, for example, asked for the guidance of the Minister of Interior since some members of the local party branch and the municipal council of Sinop were pressuring for a council decision to ban the *çarşaf*, while the governor was concerned that this would be against the circular of the Ministry of Interior. From the Governor of Sinop to the Ministry of Interior, TNPA 13216–17/1, 4 March 1935. The city council of Sinop banned the *çarşaf* in September 1935.

52 'Bu akşamki çay', *Antalya*, 13 September 1934.

53 'Fırkamızın çay gecesi', *Antalya*, 20 September 1934.

54 'Halkevinde dün akşamki toplantı', *Antalya*, 20 December 1934.

55 See 'Antalyada Çarşaf ve Peçelerle Mücadele Başladı', *Yeni Asır*, 23 December 1934; 'Antalyada kafesler ve çarşaflar yasak edildi', *Yeni Asır*, 14 February 1935. The city council of Antalya banned the *peçe*, the *çarşaf* and the *kafes* on 12 February, 1935. See 'Kent Kurultayının Bir Kararı', *Antalya*, 16 February 1935. For a similar committee formed by the women of Muğla, see 'Muğla Kadınları Çarşafları Kaldırıyor', *Halk*, 31 December 1934.

56 'Çankırıda Peçe Çarşafların Atılması Kararlaştırıldı', *Yeni Asır*, 1 January 1935.

57 See 'Kızılay fakirlere 50 manto dağıttı', *Halk*, 30 April 1936; 'Kızılay bugün 150 manto daha dağıtıyor', *Halk*, 4 May 1936; 'Kızılay mantoları dağıttı', *Halk*, 11 May 1936. See also PMRA 490.01/17.88.1.

58 See 'Halkevi çok fakir ailelere Manto yaptıracak', *Halk*, 27 February 1936. See also 'C.H. Partisi 100 Manto dağıtacak', *Halk*, 11 May 1936.

59 'Kentimizde kadın kılığı işi bütün hızıyla yürüyor', *Antalya*, 2 May 1935.

Anti-veiling campaigns in Turkey of the 1930s   83

60 See 1935 Report of Adnan Menderes, deputy of Aydın, PMRA 490.1/618.27.1, 2 December 1935.
61 From the Governor of Çorum to the Ministry of Interior, TNPA 13216–7/1, 20 August 1935. Minor officials who were locals of the cities in which they were living and working were particularly under pressure from the provincial administrators. They were the first people who were expected to support the anti-veiling campaigns. For the pressure that was put by the governors on those minor officials whose family members were wearing the *peçe* and the *çarşaf*, see also the letter from the Governor of Maraş to the Ministry of Interior, TNPA 13216–17/1, 13 August 1935.
62 'Kadın Umacı Değildir', *Yeni Mersin*, 1 July 1934.
63 'Çarşaflı kadına rastlanmıyor', *Yeni Mersin*, 2 July 1934.
64 'Kentimizde kadın kılığı işi bütün hızıyla yürüyor', *Antalya*, 2 May 1935.
65 1935 Report of Adnan Menderes, deputy of Aydın, PMRA 490.1/618.27.1, 2 December 1935. For example, in Korkuteli and Serik districts of the province of Antalya, where the inspector saw no trace of fanaticism or reaction to the revolution, the issue of the *peçe* and the *çarşaf* was easily settled. He characterized these districts as village-like, small and newly established, and without any tradition of religious reactionaries because of the lack of a *medrese* tradition and the influence of religious hodjas. It seems that, in his judgment, these were crucial factors in determining whether the *peçe* and the *çarşaf* could easily be removed in a certain city.
66 Report of Türkân Baştuğ, deputy of Antalya, PMRA 490.1/618.28.1, 27 November 1935.
67 For examples of letters from the governors that reported total acceptance of the new dress codes in their provinces, see TNPA 13216–7/1.
68 One common complaint that was mentioned in the reports of the local elites was the reaction of the weavers of the *çarşaf* or the *peştamal* that they would lose their job if the decisions to ban these clothes were applied. See correspondence from RPP Maraş Administration to RPP Secretariat General, PMRA 490.01/17.88.1, 24 January 1936.
69 See PMRA 490.01/17.88.1. The city council of Maraş also banned the use of some of the local men's clothes.
70 From RPP Maraş Administration to RPP Secretariat General, PMRA 490.01/17.88.1, 10 January 1936. For the report of the Governor of Maraş to the Minister of Interior along the same lines, see TNPA 13216–7/1. The governor was also reporting that the implementation of the ban was very successful and the transformation was very smooth.
71 1936 Report of Şevket Ödül, deputy of Kırklareli, PMRA 490.01/686.328.1, 2 November 1936.
72 Copy of the Report of Mitat Aydın, deputy of Trabzon, PMRA 490.01/612.125.2, 12 June 1940. It seems that the *çarşaf* was in fact replaced by the overcoat in Maraş, but the length of the overcoat was a concern.
73 Copy of the Report of Mitat Aydın, deputy of Trabzon, PMRA 490.01/273.1091.2, 7 May 1943.
74 In two cases, the local elite also debated whether the city councils had indeed the right to take a decision to ban the *peçe* and the *çarşaf*. The city council of Bergama settled on forming a committee to investigate the municipal law. Having come to the conclusion that the municipalities had the legal capacity to issue such bans, the city council of Bergama banned the *peçe* and the *çarşaf* eventually. A similar debate arose in the Ereğli district of the province of Konya. See 'Bergama'da Çarşaf, Peçe ve Kıvraklar Kaldırılıyor', *Anadolu*, 6 December 1934.
75 1935 Report of Adnan Menderes, deputy of Aydın, PMRA 490.1/618.27.1, 2 December 1935.

84 *Sevgi Adak*

76 Because of this reluctance of the city council (in addition to other factors), the inspector reported that there were regressive-minded (*geri kafalı*) people in Alanya, and that the mayor was particularly so with his old and agha mentality (*eski ve ağa kafalı*). See Ibid.
77 'Mersin'in başardığı iki mühim iş', *Yeni Mersin*, 18 July 1934.
78 From the Ministry of Interior to the Governor of Konya, TNPA 13216–17/1, 14 October 1935.
79 From the Minister of Interior to the Governor of Aydın, TNPA 13216–7/1, 7 September 1935. Dokumacı Ahmet Şevki had also sent a telegram to President Atatürk a year before, complaining about the efforts of the municipality to remove the *peştamal*, and in fact received a reply to his telegram. His insistence on directly complaining to the President had probably made the Ministry of Interior uncomfortable. The governor of Aydın replied that he could find no relationship between any religious order and Ahmet and that he was a person of no significance; he was only encouraged by the reply he had received from Atatürk. See the letter of the Governor of Aydın to the Ministry of Interior, TNPA 13216–17/1, 1 October 1935. We have no information about the content of Atatürk's reply to the telegram of Dokumacı Ahmet Şevki.
80 'Kadın Peçe Çarşaflarının kaldırılması hakkında erginler yurdu belediye meclisine muracaat ediyor', *Halk*, 11 February 1935.
81 'Trabzon Gençliği', *İkbal*, 13 February 1935.
82 'Peçe ve çarşaf meselesinin konuşulması Nisan toplantısına kaldı', *Halk*, 18 February 1935; 'Belediye Meclisi Dağıldı', *Halk*, 16 May 1935; 'Belediye Meclisi', *Halk*, 23 September 1935.
83 'Çarşaf ve Peçeler', *Halk*, 18 April 1935.
84 From the head of the RPP Trabzon Administration to the RPP Secretariat General, PMRA 490.01/17.88.1, 4 October 1935.
85 It is crucial to note that the decision was not unanimous; some members still opposed the decision. For the news indicating the pressure of the local party administration on the city council in Trabzon see 'Halkevinde Peçe ve Çarşaf mes'elesi görüşüldü', *Halk*, 26 March 1936. For the case of Trabzon, see also Çapa, 1996; Uyar, 1996.
86 Memorandum from the British Pro-Consul in Trabzon to British Embassy in Ankara, British Foreign Office (hereafter FO) 371/20087, 28 March 1936.
87 British consul in Trabzon to British Embassy in Ankara, FO371/20087, 16 April 1936.
88 See 1935 Report of Adnan Menderes, deputy of Aydın, PMRA 490.1/618.27.1, 2 December 1935.
89 'Akseki Mektubu', *Antalya*, 15 August 1935.
90 See A. Evren, 'Konya Kadınlığı Uyanıktır', *Yeni Asır*, 19 December 1934. See also 'Peçe ve Çarşaf', *Babalık*, 20 December 1934.
91 However, it seems that such arguments and propaganda proved ineffective since the city council of Konya had to ban the *peçe*, the *çarşaf* and the *şelme* in August 1935, probably following the acceleration of the campaigns after the party congress and the circular of the party secretary. See 'Peçe, Çarşaf, Şelme Yasak', *Babalık*, 7 August 1935.
92 Cevat Alap, 'Çarşaf, Peçe Artık Yok Olmalıdır', *İkbal*, 23 December 1934.
93 For more on the significance of studying such occasions to understand social change, see Joel Migdal, 'Finding the Meeting Ground of Fact and Fiction: Some Reflections on Turkish Modernization', in Sibel Bozdoğan and Reşat Kasaba (eds.), *Rethinking Modernity and National Identity in Turkey*, Seattle: Washington University Press, 1997, p. 252–60. For a recent study that draws on a similar perspective and focuses on the gap between what the state planned to achieve and what it actually could achieve in the Kurdish provinces, see Senem Aydın,

'Everyday Forms of State Power and the Kurds in the Early Turkish Republic', *International Journal of Middle East Studies* 43:1, February 2011, pp. 75–93.

94 For various examples of women's adaptation to new clothing and to new forms of covering their hair, see Oya Baydar and Feride Çiçekoğlu (eds.), *Cumhuriyet'in Aile Albümleri*, Istanbul: Tarih Vakfı Yurt Yayınları, 1998.

3 Everyday resistance to unveiling and flexible secularism in early republican Turkey

Murat Metinsoy

The secularizing reforms of the early Turkish republic during the interwar period were one of the most comprehensive modernization attempts in world history. Historical studies are largely united in their appraisal of these reforms. They examine the reforms in respect of elite motives, state policies and a few widely known mass protests and political dissenters. As the climax of the Turkish modernization project, the secularizing reforms conventionally have been evaluated as a strict, repressive, uncontested and uncompromising intervention of the Kemalist single-party state into society, along the same lines as the coercive policies of Reza Shah in Iran.

Both nationalist-secularist and critical accounts have shared this view, underestimating the people's complex interaction with the reforms in daily life. The nationalist-secularist accounts have eulogized these reforms as a progressive step and merciless struggle against religiosity and backwardness,[1] whereas critical approaches have emphasized their repressive, exclusionary and authoritarian aspects.[2] Particularly Islamist accounts criticized these reforms as a blind imitation of Western culture and symptomatic of the alienation of the Kemalist elite from the Muslim-Turkish population.[3] Recent studies have put forward the idea that the Kemalist elite pursued an assertive and strict kind of secularism like that of the French secularism of the Third Republic, in contrast to the passive and moderate secularism of the Anglo-Saxon countries. Furthermore, these accounts regarded the Kemalist secular reforms as the main reason for the rise of political Islam which showed a legitimate reaction to the strict secular policies.[4]

This is mainly due to the dominant state-and-elite-centred historiography and culturalism that dominate the history writing on early republican Turkey. Another reason for such an approach is the fact that the sources are richer and more easily accessible for the analysis of state policies, political thought and openly organized actions. Therefore, most scholarly studies focus on high politics, elite discourse and legal and organizational developments and events. The 'revolution from above' paradigm captures the studies on early republican Turkey. Emphasizing the state's use of propaganda and coercion, scholars generally argue that the people were either brainwashed into conformity or intimidated opponents of the regime. Society is reduced to an

Everyday resistance to unveiling in Turkey   87

inert object shaped by the active intervention of the strong and transformative state. These studies barely notice the difference between the state image, which was represented in conventional sources as a strong and uncompromising polity, and the state reality, that is, the everyday performance of state actors and its daily interaction with its citizens.[5] Due to the preoccupation with formal-legal politics, political thought and organized movements and protest, historical accounts overemphasize a few open rebellions, and the thoughts and activities of intellectual and religious dissenters, with good or bad connotations.[6] The people are thus written out of the history of the early Turkish republic.

These ideologically conflicting but theoretically parallel accounts fail to notice ordinary people's everyday forms of resistance and selective-adaptation to the secular reforms, which ushered in a covert negotiation between the state and society. Furthermore, both nationalist-secularist and critical accounts barely touch on the social, economic, psychological and gender underpinnings and dynamics that evoked public resentment of the reforms. The culturalist perspective deeply ingrained in the literature reduces the people's critical response to the reforms to the conflict between tradition and modernity. Whereas the modernization-development narratives label the discontent with the secular regime as religious backlash (*irtica*); the critical, especially Islamist, accounts explain the discontent with secularism with reference to the state's assault on people's religious integrity.

Finally, most of these studies, drawing parallels between the secularism of the early Turkish republic and the secularizing policies pursued by Reza Shah and King Amanullah, classify the Turkish single-party polity on the same continuum as these regimes. Despite the similarities in their interventionist and state-led secularizing attempts, putting these regimes in same pot blurs the nuanced but crucial differences between them, particularly in respect of anti-veiling policies. Therefore, these approaches give little attention to the distinctive hallmarks of the Turkish secularization experience.

This paper brings into question these widely accepted views regarding Kemalist secularism through the 'history from below' of the people's experience with anti-veiling policies during early republican Turkey. Turkish historiography hardly examines the Kemalist anti-veiling policies of the interwar period in detail.[7] In many studies, the anti-veiling policies are evaluated within the conventional frameworks mentioned above. The literature on the subject centres on state intervention, elite motives, legal regulations and narratives of the 'liberation' or 'repression' of Muslim-Turkish women.[8] This paper suggests three changes in emphasis which bring out aspects that have so far received less attention. These are, first, ordinary people's negative perceptions, everyday resistance and selective-adaptation mechanisms in localities that contested and negated the reforms in practice; second, contrary to a culturalist perspective, the socioeconomic, gender and psychological underpinnings of social discontent with secular reforms; and third, the influence and role of social control by neighbours and local men, which, I argue,

88 *Murat Metinsoy*

outweighed the state's influence. Finally, the paper briefly evaluates how the government dealt in a flexible manner with the social response to the anti-veiling campaigns and compares it with the unveiling policies of Reza Shah and King Amanullah.

Unveiling Muslim-Turkish women

After a successful military campaign for independence and the establishment of a republican regime in 1923 led by Mustafa Kemal (hereafter Atatürk), the Turkish modernizing elite sought to transform Muslim-Turkish society into a modern, secular and Western nation under an authoritarian single-party regime dominated by the Republican People's Party (RPP) during the inter-war period. Many of the reforms undertaken by the new republican regime were in fact the culmination of modernization efforts over a long time span from the Tanzimat era to the First World War.[9] However, the Turkish single-party era was by all means an extraordinary period marked by modernizing reforms. One of the most spectacular modernization attempts was the cloth-ing reforms, which culminated in the unveiling campaigns starting with female civil servants in 1925.[10] Henceforth, the government began to encou-rage the unveiling of Turkish women and promoted a Western image of women in a gradual manner. The anti-veiling policies gained new momentum especially after the RPP consolidated its power in the mid-1930s. In 1934, the central government stimulated the provincial governments to launch official anti-veiling campaigns. The local governments began to conduct special ceremonies during which several educated and elite women publicly took off their veils and subse-quently these unveiled women were celebrated by the local authorities so as to encourage other veiled women to discard theirs.[11] However, the central gov-ernment never attempted to make a juridical legislation banning the veil or to use physical force against women veiled, as Reza Shah attempted.

The people gave various responses to these anti-veiling campaigns, ranging from vigorous support to active resistance, and sometimes took heterogeneous positions by leaving old types of veils and adopting new forms of covering head and face or by combining the new and old styles. Some educated and middle-class women, representing a minority of Turkish women, welcomed the clothing reforms, readily or half-heartedly. The newspapers and some conventional official documents, exaggerating this picture, declared how Turkish women had bravely discarded their veils, and thereby emancipated themselves *en masse*. The critical accounts, especially those by Islamists, emphasized the coercive action against those women who were attached to their religious feelings and veils at heart, pointing out some police cases in which veiled women had quailed before the state repression.

However, contrary to the conventional accounts which depicted women as 'supporters' or 'victims' of this 'libertarian' or 'oppressive' campaign, ordin-ary Turkish women's experience of the unveiling reform, especially in the Anatolian provinces, was far more complex than these oversimplifications of

Everyday resistance to unveiling in Turkey 89

the republican or anti-republican accounts. The majority of men and women resorted to several negotiation and contestation strategies in the face of the unveiling campaigns in a wide spectrum ranging from selective-adaptation and passive resistance to active confrontation. A considerable number of women withdrew from public life in order to protest against the anti-veiling policies and to make no concession of their clothing habits. Many, paying no mind to the unveiling campaign, continued to wear their usual veils, even in public places. Some women openly entered into confrontations with interfering police and gendarme officers, and insisted on veiling in spite of warnings and fines. Those women who were determined to cover their heads and bodies did not hesitate to resort to the law courts to seek their rights when they met with harsh and unfair treatment by the police. Another strategy to circumvent both the official fines and local social sanctions was to create new forms of veiling through an eclectic combination of the new and usual clothing styles.

This was not due to the people's ignorance or strength of their religious bonds, but was a result of multiple overlapping socioeconomic, gender and psychological determinants. Women's clothes and head coverings remained largely under the influence of the local social norms, customs and social relations rather than the republican government's principles and rules. More precisely, the influence of the social milieu, in other words, local men, cultural bonds, and social control, for example being afraid of condemnation and exclusion by neighbours and relatives, outweighed the rules, measures and principles of the government. Clerics especially, who lost their status and income due to the republican reforms, vented their anger on the anti-veiling policies and the official image of Turkish women promoted by the state through criticizing unveiled women. Ordinary men, who were worried about maintaining their authority over their women, played a crucial role in resistance to the dress reform by encouraging or even forcing women to continue wearing the veil. Furthermore, by disturbing the modern-looking and uncovered women verbally and physically, men, particularly poor and marginalized men, obstructed the unveiling efforts of local governments. Some poor men wreaked their anger stemming from poverty and economic inequality on modern-looking women who were seen as symbols and representatives of the new social and political order. In addition, the anti-veiling campaigns outraged the makers and traders of veils and traditional clothes due to the possible loss of a huge market. Furthermore, the new image of women constituted a financial burden for many low-income families and women because the new fashionable clothing was expensive, whereas the usual clothing and especially the charshaf[12] was both easily made and cheaper. The charshaf functioned to hide the poor clothes of women as well. Finally, it was quite stressful and uncomfortable to walk in the street for a woman without a veil. Unveiling was a source of anxiety for both many ordinary women and their men.

Many women thus were exposed to the double-sided pressure of the local milieu and men on the one hand, and the security forces on the other. In the face of these multilayered pressures, however, they developed cunning coping

90   *Murat Metinsoy*

strategies in several ways. For example, some of them left their old-style veils in order to avoid a possible fine or bad treatment by police officers, but covered their heads and bodies with different types of clothes and headscarves in order to prevent any criticism from their neighbours, especially the rough menfolk. Even educated and middle-class women needed to use headscarves tied under their chins. Consequently, ordinary women's customary ways of dressing persisted almost everywhere, except for a limited change in a few big city centres, where a transformation in the clothing habits of middle-class women had already been underway before the republican regime.

Tenacity of the veil

Numerous native or foreign eyewitness accounts during the late 1920s and 1930s point out the tenacity of the Turkish women's usual ways of dressing. According to these remarks, the great majority of women in Anatolia continued to wear the traditional 'old-fashioned' clothes. In other words, what was called 'old-fashioned clothing' in the elite discourse and press was still popular and fashionable among ordinary women. Joseph Grew, the first US ambassador to Turkey, for example, wrote in his memoirs of his impressions of how far the reforms had affected the women in the early 1930s as follows:

> It is obvious that there is no change in importance of religion in women's lives … . Almost all the women living in Turkey, except for women in bigger cities, are veiled or covering their heads with headscarves. While men are passing by women, they hide their face with clothes and turn their back to these men.[13]

Harold Armstrong, another foreign observer, who travelled throughout Anatolia in the late 1920s, described similar scenes. In his visit to Anatolian towns, almost all of the women he saw were in the traditional clothing. He wrote,

> The townswomen were shapeless masses of black clothes with their black charshaf cloaks drawn over their heads and shoulders down to their wrists, and thick veils: peasant women in baggy striped bloomers, blouses and brocaded coats, and a white towel drawn across their faces, leaving one eye only exposed.[14]

Armstrong found the situation similar in Kayseri, an important province of central Anatolia. 'In Kayseri', he wrote, 'women were not unveiled. I never saw a Turkess unveiled.' He continued to tell of his observations about the women in Kayseri as follows:

> They wore thick, black veils drawn down, and shapeless dresses, consisting of cloaks to the wrists and skirts to the heels, and made of white and blue print with a heavy blue edge, which was characteristic of Kayseri.[15]

Everyday resistance to unveiling in Turkey 91

The province where he saw women unveiled for the first time was Ankara. 'I saw for the first time in the street', he wrote, 'the emancipated Turkish women. Perhaps fifty percent of the women I passed were uncovered and dressed as Europeans.'[16] However, according to him, İstanbul had changed little. In the great part of İstanbul, women continued to cover their faces with veils especially when a man looked at them or talked to them.[17] One day when he visited his old friends in Yeniköy, a veiled woman opened the door shyly.[18]

Another foreign journalist, Lilo Linke, toured Turkey in 1935 and collected her observations in a book, titled *Allah Dethroned*. In spite of the title of her book, her account purports to say that the old lifestyles, forms, and practices had been dethroned in the legal and political realms, but not yet in the everyday life of the countryside, especially in women's lives. Linke tells of her first impression of women in İstanbul by writing about the Turkish women she had seen in a government office in April 1935.

> Most women, more strongly tied to tradition, were wrapped from head to foot in their black cotton charshafs which some of them had even half drawn across their faces.[19]

Beginning her travel with a voyage in the Black Sea from İstanbul to Samsun, she shared a cabin with two wealthy Turkish women who wore black silk charshafs.[20] When she travelled to Sivas, she saw that 'most women were veiled by a straight piece of black cloth tied round their heads underneath their charshafs.' In the provincial government office (*valilik*), she came across 'the women in their cotton charshafs checked in red and white'.[21]

One of the important centres in Anatolia that she visited was Mersin. Here she visited a textile factory in the Tarsus district. Although Tarsus was a developing region comparatively, in which some women began to work in the textile factory, almost all of the women were veiled with cotton charshafs:

> In spite of the blazing heat the women on the platform were all closely wrapped in large checked cotton charshafs which they held across their faces so that only one eye could peep out. Apparently, Tarsus had not made its 'big jump forward' yet.[22]

In Alanya, another southern region, the situation was similar. As Arif Balkan, a contemporary entrepreneur wrote in his memoirs, women did not take off their black charshafs even in the sweltering days of summer in Alanya in the 1930s. They also strolled through the streets with their black umbrellas. Some who dared to uncover their faces used these black umbrellas in order hide their faces and heads.[23] In her memoirs, Pakize Türkoğlu, who spent her childhood in Alanya in those years, confirms Balkan's observation. She also briefly addresses the widespread use of umbrellas by women to cover their faces and head.[24] Another contemporary, the wife of a staff officer who had

92 Murat Metinsoy

been appointed from İstanbul to Elazığ in the mid-1930s, tells how all the women continued to wear black charshafs in the city centre.[25] According to a monographic study on Safranbolu conducted by a folklorist of the time, Enver Beşe, even in this town near the capital city, as elsewhere in Anatolia, the young girls were expected to don black charshaf as soon as they turned 11.[26]

The reports of the local governments and the police departments about the implementation of the clothing reforms in Anatolian towns indicate that women's clothing in public and private places had not changed in the direction prescribed by the government. In a report dated 1930, for example, the Gaziantep governor admitted that the great deal of effort made to modernize women's clothing and to struggle against the charshaf had fallen short of the targets. Even after the ban on veils by the city council of Adana in 1934, the police reports indicate that many women covered themselves with charshafs and headscarves or used black umbrellas to hide themselves in the main streets. It was reported from Sinop in 1935 that the women in the province had not abandoned their traditional clothes. Even those unveiled women who had come to vote in the previous elections in their modern clothes continued to wear their charshafs in daily life.[27] A general situation report penned by the Ordu governor in 1935 stated that the struggle against the veil and charshaf had proved unsuccessful. Despite all the efforts of the local government, 80 percent of women continued to cover their head and body in one way or other. The number of unveiled women was quite small.[28] Towards the end of the decade, in 1939, it was reported that women in Tokat continued to wear charshafs and other kinds of veils. In the same year, the Urfa governor also reported that the number of women who wore charshaf and scarves was considerably high. It is possible to give further examples.[29]

Newspapers of the time also reported in a complaining manner the tenacity of customary women's clothing in the Anatolian provinces. For example, in January 1934, a newspaper reported that women in Kütahya could not go out of their houses without their veils and charshafs.[30] Similarly, it was reported in April 1934 that the number of women with veil and charshaf was quite high in Aydın.[31] According to a newspaper report dated 23 June 1934, the women in Amasya had not given up wearing the veil and charshaf.[32] One year later, another newspaper wrote that many women in a western coastal town like Ayvalık kept to wear the veil and charshaf.[33]

Social dynamics of resistance to unveiling: the role of Anatolian men, and opposition to the secular regime

Who resisted the unveiling? What were the underlying reasons for their resistance? In what ways did they contest the unveiling campaigns? The most important actor in this resistance was not women, but men. As mentioned above, the first response against the anti-veiling campaigns came from the ordinary male population of Anatolia. Together with a great body of religious

Everyday resistance to unveiling in Turkey 93

men like *imam*s (Muslim priests), *hoca*s (Muslim religious instructors), *müez-zins* (those who recite the call to prayer and say prayers) and *şeyh*s (Islamic scholars and sect leaders), the male population by and large opposed the anti-veiling efforts of the government. In particular the clerics and average men who were alienated by the new order championed the passive resistance to unveiling and other reforms regarding gender relations. The unveiling policy annoyed especially the clerics. For them, the veil symbolized the chastity, piety and sexual identity of Muslim women. Using religious discourse and these usual meanings attributed to veiling, those clergymen who hated the new regime delivered anti-unveiling sermons in their mosques. They often criticized unveiled women, their lifestyle and the end of gender segregation.

As a matter of fact, as Leslie Peirce has shown in the Ottoman context, the clerics' and other religious men's objection to women's equal status or rights under cover of religious terminology was to some extent a tactic aimed at preserving their own authority. 'The debate over women', Peirce writes, 'was thus not always about women; rather, they were often a metaphor for order'.[34] Therefore, under cover of the 'morally degenerative effects' and 'irreligiousness' of the new appearance of women, in fact, the clerics targeted the secular regime and its new rulers who had disempowered them.

From the initial phases of the republican reforms, critical sermons were delivered in mosques. One of them was given in the Trabzon Central Mosque by its *vaiz* (preacher), Hacı Hafız İsmail Hakkı Efendi, during the Friday prayer in February 1928. Referring to a verse of the Koran, he declared that Islam required men to control their wives by beating them and keeping them away from modern civilization.[35] Likewise, the *vaiz* of the Yozgat Central Mosque, Ethem Hoca, expressed his animosity toward the republican reforms, particularly the unveiling of women. He insulted 'bareheaded women' and accused all modern-looking women of being prostitutes. He also alleged that all women would become prostitutes at that rate.[36]

Comparing the republican regime with the rule of Reza Shah in Iran, an *imam* in İstanbul had accused both of them of being infidels. In both countries, he said, the men shaved their moustaches like women, women uncovered their heads like infidels, and the political leaders put on their heads something like chamber pots instead of the sacred Islamic turban.[37] Another *imam* in Mersin talked against the new image of Muslim women as well as the hat reform in his sermons.[38] In Beyşehir, a preacher named Abdülkadir Hoca in the mosque located in the city centre often sounded off against the reforms in his sermons. In 1933, Abdülkadir Hoca had damned the ballrooms in the People's Houses and modern hotels, where women and men came together to have fun or dance. He said, 'those people who dance are pimps in this world and devils in the afterworld'.[39] These seditious sermons delivered in the mosques continued in the following years. In 1938, the Ministry of Internal Affairs received numerous intelligence reports and denunciation letters about anti-regime sermons, especially during the month of Ramadan, when men flooded the mosques.

94 Murat Metinsoy

Men's worries about their authority over women and competition from female labour

Ordinary men were not passive consumers of the ideological bombardment of the clerics. Nor were they fanatical opponents of any novelty. They had their own subjective reasons. Above all, the republican reforms like the Civil Code forbidding polygamy and equating women with men before the law, the entrance of some women into public and working life without any official restriction, the compulsory education of school-age girls, the legal abolition of sexual segregation in public life and the promotion of modern-looking women by the state, along with other secular practices, frightened the vast majority of Anatolian men. Therefore, they were first to react to the unveiling campaigns. As a contemporary female observer stated, 'there were many men who objected to seeing their wives or their daughters appearing in public without the traditional clothes'.[40]

For many ordinary men, these developments posed the potential risk of reducing their authority and challenging the existing hierarchy within the family. Therefore, they did not take kindly to the Kemalist discourse behind the reforms, i.e., the 'equality of men and women'. A contemporary observer remembers how a man who visited his home criticized the reforms as follows:

> The distaff side [eksik etek] cannot be considered equal to men. If there are no men to control their families, the dependent women will go astray. What the hell is that equality?[41]

Some men thought that the republican reforms concerning women made Turkish men henpecked.[42] They disliked and frequently criticized harshly the reforms modernizing women's appearance but, in fact, they implicitly opposed the probable liberalization of strict patriarchal gender relations through the new clothing codes.

Another likely reason behind men's opposition to unveiling was the possible adverse economic effects of the liberation of women for men. It is not surprising to see that working and unemployed men perceived the easier entrance of women into public and working life as further competition for employment. Undoubtedly, the female workforce was an indispensible component of the growing capitalist industrial development under the republican regime. Many sectors such as textiles, cotton, food processing and tobacco needed a female workforce for several reasons. Perhaps the most important economic rationale for the employment of female workers was that they could be paid less. Since they were mostly not the heads of their families, they could be more content with lower wages. Besides, they were more obedient than male workers. Especially, given the drastic decrease in the male population due to the First World War and the National Struggle, which had resulted in a huge labour deficit during the interwar period, one of the prerequisites of the developing Turkish capitalism led by state enterprises was to free women from

Everyday resistance to unveiling in Turkey 95

the bonds of traditional gender relations which debarred them from joining the labour market.[43]

According to official statistics, the number of women workers slightly increased during the 1930s. In view of the shortcomings of the state administration in collecting demographic and sociological facts and figures throughout the country, the official statistics should be taken with reserve. However, it is reasonable to think that the number of working women increased to some extent, particularly in government offices, because the modernizing ideology of the government allowed a relatively limited number of educated women to work in state offices more easily than in the past. Furthermore, the decrease in the male population due to the successive wars one decade earlier and the economic crisis of the 1930s had also pushed some women to work for their very survival.[44]

Therefore, those men who saw the female workforce as a threat to their jobs grumbled about the idea of women's free entrance into work life. According to a newspaper article titled 'Male Workers Complain about Women', men, particularly unemployed men in Bursa, complained of female workers because their employment had resulted in a decrease in average wages. The male workers blamed above all the textile factories that mostly preferred to employ female workers because they were paid less than their male counterparts on average. One unemployed man criticized the employment of female workers by saying,

> We [men] are obliged to pay the Road Tax, but they [women] are employed in factories. If women replace us in factories, how will we pay the taxes?[45]

What is more, women workers were susceptible to sexual harassment and rape by their employers and foremen. Sexual harassment aggrieved not only the female workers, but also their families. For instance, in a tobacco factory directed by the state monopoly, the workers complained of frequent sexual harassment by the foremen and factory directors.[46] Again, a 1933 report about working life in the industrial enterprises of İzmir drew attention to the widespread sexual abuse of female and child workers. According to the report, most of the women and even children in the factories of İzmir could not help but became prostitutes and morally depraved.[47] Undoubtedly, this situation was not peculiar to İzmir factories, but widespread in other industrialized regions as a universal fact of industrial capitalism exploiting not only the labour of women and children, but also their sexuality.[48] For that reason, many women did not welcome the modernization of their own appearance and the legal removal of the sexual segregation system. Even in the capital city, the people did not take kindly to women who were working outside their homes.[49] Likewise, although the Kayseri textile factory, one of the largest public enterprises of the time, needed a female workforce, most of the women and particularly their male relatives disliked the idea of women working side

96　*Murat Metinsoy*

by side with men and, therefore, the factory had to employ children about 12 years old.[50]

Veil traders: fear of the possible loss of a huge market

The small manufacturers and merchants of veils and other traditional women's clothes also seem to have been terrified of the state policies that sought to transform the appearance of Turkish women. They generally perceived the anti-veiling campaigns as detrimental to their business. Many of them were aware that, if their female consumers did not need their products in the near future, they would most likely die out or have to adapt their business to the new fashions. This last option would be costly and not so easy for these small-scale and low-income craftsmen. For that reason, they raised their complaints and criticisms about state intervention in women's clothing.

A textile manufacturer named Ahmet Şevki from Aydın was one of these opponents of the official image of women and unveiling. According to the information about him collected by the police, his only source of income was producing and selling charshafs and headscarves. His main interest was thus to ensure his income by the continuation of this old fashion. Upon the start of the anti-veil campaigns, he sent long petitions complaining of these campaigns to Atatürk and to the RPP government. Addressing the individual rights of citizens rhetorically, he wrote, 'The law of individual freedom has been trampled on.'[51]

In a similar vein, the RPP organization in Maraş reported in 1936 that the handloom weavers, tailors and sellers who for a long time had produced and marketed the black cotton fabrics and traditional women's clothes opposed the elimination of the veil. They requested the government to lift the veil ban imposed by the city council; otherwise, they would lose their jobs.[52]

Women's reasons for resistance: social and economic costs of unveiling

Women were not passive bystanders in this process. They had their own subjective reasons for their resistance to the anti-veiling efforts of the local governments. One of the important sources of discontent with the city councils' ban on the veil and charshaf that led many women to resist unveiling was the fact that poor families were not able to afford the new fashion outfits. Therefore, the majority of destitute and low-income women saw unveiling as an additional and unnecessary cost for their family budgets. Some of them wrote to newspapers. The following letter sent from Çorum complained about the financial burden of unveiling for families living at subsistence level:

> The veil has been banned. That is okay. However, women in villages and towns so far have met their need for clothing by buying a few meters of cheap native fabric and sewing charshafs easily. Is it easy to afford an overcoat?[53]

Everyday resistance to unveiling in Turkey   97

A group of women from the Milas district of İzmir also wrote to a newspaper and complained that the city council's ban on the charshaf had made things extremely difficult for them because they were not able to afford overcoats.[54] It is most probable that the financial cost of unveiling distressed low-income men. They also expressed their complaints about the matter by writing to newspapers. For example, in a newspaper report titled 'Overcoat or Bread?', it was stated that a group of men in the Akseki district of Antalya had written a letter and said, 'We are poor people, who lived on bread. In spite of this, the authorities here have ordered us to buy new outfits for our wives.'[55]

Furthermore, veiling was an egalitarian practice in some respects. The black charshaf especially was a relatively egalitarian garment because of its uniformity except for the differences of fabric quality, and sometimes colour. Its modest and uniform appearance was very functional for low-income women, enabling them to conceal their old and dirty clothes under their charshafs when they were in public. That is, the black charshaf made all women who wore it, whether poor or wealthy, beautiful or ugly, equal in the street.[56] This also must have played a role in women's strong attachment to such clothes.

The role of local community control over women

Perhaps one of the most important factors that discouraged women from discarding their veils and accepting the new clothes was local social control or community pressure.[57] The local beliefs about veiling as a symbol and requirement of piety and chastity, and negative perceptions and word of mouth about unveiled women, and the close monitoring by neighbours and especially men in the streets outweighed the state's control and the RPP's principles. Not only men, but also women played an important role in this regard. As a study on Pakistani women points out, 'women were susceptible to other women's evaluations regarding their responsibilities … . Women carried patriarchal tenets and gender expectation into ritual environment. Mutual sur-veillance – subtle or projected – kept each other within the proper boundaries.'[58]

In contrast to the official image of Turkish woman, in many Anatolian towns, the seclusion of women and sexual segregation continued in open or covert forms. Any woman who broke these rules most likely faced fiercest public criticism or sometimes verbal and physical attack. Especially in the poor quarters of even big cities and in the countryside, both men and women fixed their eyes on uncovered and modern-looking women in the streets. The monitoring by the neighbours and especially astonished gazing by the men in streets, shopping districts and markets kept many women from adopting the clothes officially promoted.

The Anatolian people, particularly men and old women, frowned on unveiled women. According to İbrahim Yasa's observations in a village named Hasanoğlan in Ankara during the late 1930s and early 1940s, an old woman he interviewed had expressed her dislike of bareheaded girls and

98 *Murat Metinsoy*

women. According to her, God would punish in the afterlife those women who uncovered their heads and legs.

> In the good old days, ... they had never used to walk in the street bareheaded; they used to make preparation for the afterlife. There are no such things nowadays. They are walking in the street bareheaded ... . They [demons of hell] will burn you in hell.[59]

As Pakize Türkoğlu writes in her memoirs, when she wanted to enrol in a school during her childhood in the early 1930s, her relatives and neighbours told her, 'What the hell do girls have to do with school? Female students do not cover their head there; if you go to school, you will burn in hell tomorrow.'[60] Mediha Esenel, who conducted several village surveys in central and western Anatolia in the early 1940s, wrote that Turkish peasants, even in relatively developed regions of the country, continued to believe that angels did not visit those homes in which the women were not covered. She also personally witnessed a peasant woman being beaten by her husband because she had forgotten to cover her head even at home.[61]

The main reason triggering such behaviour toward women was a common popular understanding of the ideal woman, which was at odds with the Kemalist perception of the ideal woman. The customary perception of women still maintained its influence among ordinary people despite the government's efforts to reverse it. For example, according to the majority of ordinary people, the new image of the Turkish woman promoted by the government was so nasty that they looked like prostitutes and whores. In an official notice sent to the Ministry of Internal Affairs, the General Directorate of Security (*Emniyet Umum Müdürlüğü*, that is, the Turkish Police Department) reported that among the people were heard plenty of inflammatory conversations and subversive statements, like 'A woman should wear her black cloak and her soles should be cracked. Nowadays they have made women look like whores.'[62]

Similarly, Adnan Binyazar wrote in his memoir that his low-income master running a diner in the Kasımpaşa district of Istanbul in those years also criticized unveiled women and their men for being 'whores' and 'cuckolds', respectively.[63] According to police documents, 'certain reactionary men spread reactionary ideas about women during the official campaigns for unveiling in Eskişehir'. Accusing the anti-veiling campaigns of going against moral values and traditions, they aimed to discourage women from being unveiled. Interestingly, some of them were the administrators of the local party branches. In Eskişehir, for instance, the party directors in some districts refused to make a move against the veiling.[64] Likewise, as Adnan Menderes, a party inspector of Konya and Antalya provinces, reported, some party administrators and members in Konya also were unwilling to carry out an unveiling campaign.[65] Menderes also criticized the party administrators in the Alanya, Serik and Korkuteli towns of Antalya for avoiding an official unveiling campaign because of either their narrow mindedness or fear of public criticism. Menderes wrote that many

Everyday resistance to unveiling in Turkey 99

party members, disapproving the anti-veiling policies, had said, 'We have no right to hurt people's feelings.'[66]

Revolutionary communist party members also occassionally tried to benefit from this religious-based negative popular perception of the unveiling reform to mobilize the masses against the government. Despite their sympathy with the secular reforms, members of the Communist Party of Turkey (*Türkiye Komünist Partisi*), the major underground opposition movement in these years, generally did not hold with the republican elite's admiration of Western culture, rituals and bourgeois lifestyle. They saw these as cultural imitations of the West that were not beneficial to the poor. In 1929, during the communist trials held in İzmir, for example, a group of communist artisans and workers were arrested for writing on a placard 'Hapless and Poor Brothers Who Have Been Deceived and Poisoned Everyday by the People's Party's Opium!' (*Halk Fırkasının Her Gün Yeni Bir Ayfonla Uyutulan ve Zehirlenen Yoksul ve Bedbaht Kardeşler!*). Addressing the religious feelings of the people, this placard criticized the clothing reforms, and modern-looking women and men, and their leisure activities like dancing and sports as well as the other secular reforms. The placard, claiming that young virgin women were forced into prostitution in this new era, called for a popular struggle against the government.[67]

In parallel to such perceptions of women, the segregation of the sexes continued in open or covert forms throughout Anatolia, except in the big centres. This shows the tenacity of society's view of women. For example, in the Gebze district of Kocaeli, the shops frequented by women were still separate by 1934. It was reported that it was impossible for a woman to walk in the street alone.[68] Similarly, it was reported that, in the district of Balıkesir, women were not allowed to go shopping in the bazaar. Even those women who passed by the main street were criticized by the public.[69] As stated above, society in central Anatolia generally took a dim view of women working outside their homes.[70] In the eastern regions, seclusion of women was more intense. There women were not permitted even to go shopping in the town centres. In many families, the male children and especially adult male members of families could not sit and chat with women in the same rooms. Men and women were supposed to stay in different rooms and welcome their guests in the special rooms assigned to them.[71]

As noted by a contemporary eyewitness, the sexual segregation (*haremlik selamlık*) continued in Gaziantep as an important rule of domestic life. The *selamlık* part of the home, where the men talked, smoked and discussed social, political and economic matters, was the basic socialization space of influential and middle-class men in the province.[72] Again, as reported from Giresun, a province in the Black Sea Region, the sexual segregation in public life and homes was still a principle in a great part of the province by December 1936.[73]

In most of the Anatolian villages and towns, wedding feasts, too, were held in different places for women and men.[74] In public places such as cinemas, men and women had to attend at different hours or on different days. As reported from Manisa in 1931, women had not discarded their veils and charshafs, and the men and women were unable to go to the cinema together. A special day was assigned for women only at the cinemas.[75] Similarly, although local governments had abolished the separation of the sexes in public transportation, women and men preferred to travel in different parts of the public vehicles. For instance, a national newspaper reported in 1936 that there was still a kind of *haremlik selamlık* on the tramways of İstanbul. The women got into the tramways from the front door, whereas the men from the back door.[76]

Based on police intelligence, the governor of Çankırı addressed the question of the adverse impact of the negative popular perception of bareheaded women on the performance of unveiling campaigns in small districts. According to the report, the monitoring each other and the communal pressure in towns were so strong that the efforts of the governorship to eliminate the veil encountered the moral constraints imposed by local social milieux on women. Therefore, except for women belonging to a few cultured families of state officials, most of the women in Çankırı did not dress according to the regulations prescribed by the city council. 'The main reason for this', the governor wrote, 'is that the local people live in fear of each other, rigid customs and religious fanaticism.'[77]

The governor was not wrong to a certain extent. After the ban on veil and charshaf, owing to the fear of a possible prosecution or fine by the security forces, the areas of activity for veiled women decreased to some extent. However, in a similar vein, the physical and social mobilization of unveiled and modern-dressed women also was limited. These women were exposed to social sanctions in the forms of gossip, criticism, exclusion, and verbal and physical assaults by neighbours and men. Therefore, both veiled and unveiled women felt the need to withdraw from public places. Police reports dated 1935 noted that women in the Tosya district of Kastamonu could not go out of their homes just after the commencement of anti-veiling campaigns. Many women in villages also hesitated to go to the town market.[78] It was reported that women in the counties of Aydın still could not walk in the streets easily even three years after the beginning of the campaigns.[79]

For women who were not ready or not willing to go outside their homes unveiled, idea of going out in public without a garment that covers the head and face constituted a distressing emotional problem rather than a religious question. Many unveiled women felt shame when they appeared in public places. Walking in streets or shopping in markets and bazaars were sources of anxiety for newly unveiled women. The eyes of all the men were on these women. Hence, these women were generally confused over what to do, how to walk and where to go in the streets. Dropping their eyes, perspiring suddenly and blushing, they had great difficulty in finding their way when walking in the street. When shopkeepers and artisans in the shopping district gawped at them, some of these bareheaded women stumbled due to their increasing anxiety.[80]

Intimidating into veiling: verbal and physical attacks on unveiled women

Unveiled and modern-looking women frequently encountered harassment and verbal attack by men in the streets. Some of those men who disturbed and molested them were only vagabonds; however, some men deliberately treated bareheaded women discourteously owing to their resentment of unveiling as an extension of secularism, the government and well-to-do people, mostly equated by the vast majority. In that sense, disturbing a modern-looking woman was a popular expression of hostility toward the secular reforms and socio-political order as well as the new look of women. Furthermore, it was a way to intimidate women into veiling and remaining at home.

Some poor people exploited and marginalized by the republican regime targeted fashionably dressed and especially elite women who were seen as symbols and representatives of the government. Given the symbolic forms of popular protest and resistance as addressed by Robert Darnton in *The Great Cat Massacre*,[81] the modern-looking women were the Kemalist elite's symbols on which the dissenters vented their anger. There were several cases of verbal and physical assaults on unveiled women in the streets. In his memoirs, Kılıç Ali noted that this trend appeared especially right after the clothing reforms, in this way:

> When we came to Adana, we heard that there appeared a mob called *kül-hanbeyler*, wearing jodhpurs and breeches, in those days. Therefore, the virtuous women of Adana could not go out of their homes because of these people's extreme wickedness ... . Neither the gendarmes nor the police were able to cope with them. Despite all the measures taken by the governor and the police department, they were not able to prevent such events.[82]

Anatolian towns were full of such men. In one example, a rough man troubled bareheaded female teachers in Sivas. According to a telegram sent by three female teachers from Sivas to the government authorities, a person named Nergiszade Boyacı Ahmed, threatening the female teachers and other unveiled women, was trying to intimidate them into to taking off their hats and wearing the charshaf as before.[83] Likewise, it was reported from Afyon in November 1935 that, with the appearance of bareheaded women in public places right after the unveiling campaign, some men began to harass them by shouting at them 'What wonderful "domestic goods" we have!' (*Ne eyi yerli mallarımız varmış!*). According to the authorities, such rude behaviour kept the women of the province from discarding their veils.[84]

Another widespread slander against a woman in modern dress was to call her 'infidel' (*gavur*) when she was walking in the street.[85] In addition, some men harassed and verbally attacked unveiled women and even men wearing modern hats by calling them 'tango' in the streets. In the eyes of the people, tango was an immoral dance performed together by women and men who were dressed 'indecently' during the balls and receptions of the Kemalist elite

102 *Murat Metinsoy*

or of the non-Muslim minorities. Therefore, non-elite people at times called modern-dressed people 'tango' by shouting at them from behind, 'look at you, tango!'.[86]

It was not rare that verbal attacks turned into physical ones. In Zile, for example, a group of men who frequently criticized a female teacher for her acceptance of modern clothes ultimately raped her.[87] Similarly, in İzmir, a rude person verbally and physically attacked a married woman who had recently taken off the veil, when she was walking in the main street.[88]

The memoirs of Adnan Binyazar are a good example of how poor, marginalized and desperate young men vented their anger on modern-looking women. Binyazar, a poor boy who had migrated from Diyarbakır to İstanbul in those years, worked in several jobs under heavy and exploitative conditions. He vented his resentment of wealthy people on elite-looking women and fancy and pampered girls by troubling them in several ways. Once, he threw a rotten tomato at a woman mincing along in a smart dress in a shopping district of İstanbul.[89]

These incidents must have been so widespread that the government, aware of the adverse impact on the anti-veiling campaigns of such behaviour towards bareheaded women, decided to take stringent measures. The Ministry of Justice issued a circular in September 1929 ordering the local judicial authorities to launch legal action immediately against those rude persons who attempted to molest or accost women.[90] In the following years, numerous men who verbally attacked women in the streets were sentenced to imprisonment or a heavy fine.[91]

Rumours about unveiled women

One important form of popular challenge to the state's intervention in women's clothes was popular culture, particularly rumour.[92] Compounded by the popular dislike of the anti-veiling campaigns, rumours as informal media served to express and to disseminate competing and negative views about the secular reforms, to be more specific, anti-veiling policies, thereby creating a counter public opinion. Furthermore, rumours stimulated resistance to or discouraged support for the regime. Numerous rumours predicted a forthcoming retreat to the previous regime, and thereby to the older forms of dress, and disseminated unfounded stories such as the murder of police and gendarme officers who had offended veiled women, casting doubt on the future of the regime and its reforms, and thus encouraging women's insistence on maintaining the veil. Again, as will be stated below, rumours that frightened people by claiming that 'the state would export Muslim women to foreign countries' and 'the state would import bells and Christian crosses', also shook the people's, particularly women's, trust in the government's intentions behind the anti-veiling policies.

Right after the introduction of local anti-veiling campaigns in 1925 and 1926, the rumour mill began to work by circulating various baseless stories

Everyday resistance to unveiling in Turkey   103

about the regime's ill-intentioned plans for women. In October 1925 and March 1926, just after the clothing reform, a rumour spread on the grapevine throughout central Anatolian towns and villages according to which the government would soon collect all young virgin girls and virtuous widows and export them to foreign countries. Informed about the rumour, the local authorities had to warn the government about this phenomenon and its catastrophic results. In some villages, this rumour caused social disorder by leading ill-intended adult peasant men to rape virgin females as young as 10 years of age.[93]

Women also both produced and disseminated rumours at gatherings of close friends. Some women in Mersin, for example, expressed their objection to the dress reforms via a rumour of the ghost of a dead person who had been resurrected from his grave due to the 'bareheaded' and 'whorish-looking' women. This rumour reached the Mersin police in April 1928. According to police reports, the wives of some working-class men such as porters and tinsmiths had been saying that some people had heard a dead body sitting and wailing in his grave. Upon this, according to the rumour, a doctor and a public prosecutor had also visited the grave and heard what this ghost had said. The ghost had said, 'I am a living ghost and I am burning in fire, because neither mothers nor fathers take care of their children; women in the streets are nude, and getting their hair cut, and wearing overcoats.' At the end of the investigations, the police prosecuted four women, Ayşe, who was the wife of the porter Mustafa; Katibe, who was the wife of the tinsmith Bilâl; and two other women named Semra and Fatma. They were accused of spreading this rumour in the region. Undoubtedly, this rumour was a manifestation of the discontent of ordinary people in Mersin with unveiling and the new secular lifestyle. It was also a form of resistance discouraging unveiled women by making them feel guilty and full of remorse.[94]

In another case, according to a police report from Konya in 1935, local people were arguing that 'policemen and gendarmes had been killed by the people because they had attempted to remove women's veils'. According to the report, such an incident had never happened in the province. The people who had deliberately disseminated this groundless rumour had been brought before the court.[95] Probably this rumour had also been manufactured by dissenters in order to encourage women and men to disregard the anti-veiling campaign or to discourage the government agents who were supposed to take part in struggle against the veil.

Some rumours expressed negative opinions, frightening women into keeping away from public life, and thereby from unveiling. For example, in Gaziantep, a rumour began to circulate among the people upon the start of the anti-veiling campaign. This rumour had it that the police officers had begun to tear off charshafs and scarves whenever they saw them. Upon hearing this rumour, women stopped going outside their homes.[96] Another rumour that circulated in Hınıs in 1939 was more fear-provoking. This rumour alleged that the government was preparing Turkish girls to put them

104 *Murat Metinsoy*

into the service of Russian men as wives. People were saying, 'A few years later, all Muslim girls would be sent to Russia.'[97]

Especially after the death of Atatürk, according to the police records, various rumours claiming that radical policy changes were forthcoming in the near future circulated everywhere. At a home reception of women in Eskişehir on 28 November 1938, for example, the guests talked about what would happen after Atatürk's death, saying, 'Atatürk is dead. Henceforth the western hat will be discarded. We will easily wear our charshafs. The old clothes will be reinstituted and the dervish lodges will be reopened.'[98]

The İstanbul police department also reported similar rumours heard in schools, mosques and coffeehouses. Some of them were like these: 'Girls will not be allowed to go to high school'; 'Those girls who graduated from university will not be allowed to work'; 'İsmet İnönü will not force women to wear a hat, but will reaccept the veil'; and 'Working women will be fired and men will be hired instead of them.'[99] Likewise, in İzmir, it was rumoured that the government would dismiss all the female employees in state offices and state establishments. In Edirne, many people were talking about the probable removal of the city council's ban on the black charshaf.[100] The National Security Service (*Milli Emniyet Hizmeti*) also notified the government that for 15 days all people and students in Adana had been saying, 'The government will shut down the girls' high schools' and 'Women officials will be fired.'[101] The police departments and the security officials of the intelligence agency in Ankara, Bolu, Çoruh, Elazığ, Erzurum, Giresun, Isparta, İstanbul, Kırklareli, Konya, Malatya, Maraş, Mardin, Mersin, Muğla, Ordu, Seyhan, Van and Yozgat reported similar rumours in November 1938.[102]

Everyday resistance: open disobedience, petitioning, and threatening letters

Concordantly, many women who were torn between communal pressure for veiling and the official anti-veiling drive strived to get rid of this dilemma by resisting mostly the latter. Despite the intimidation measures of the police such as levying fines, giving warnings or taking women to police stations in a limited number of cases, the state authorities did not insist on such measures in the face of women's massive insistence on keeping their usual way of dressing. From the beginning, the vast majority of women firmly refused to yield to the local governments' ban on veils and resisted the officious security officers who attempted to take off their veils forcibly. In the Tirebolu district of Giresun, for example, the municipality decided to eliminate the veil on 7 October 1926, but obtained no result in the face of women's resistance. The women in the province continued to cover their heads and faces.[103] In Trabzon, the city council banned the veil in December 1926, but the majority of women disregarded the ban, wearing their usual clothes and head coverings. Although the police prosecuted a few veil wearers for intimidating other women with head coverings, most stood up to these measures. Even those

Everyday resistance to unveiling in Turkey 105

women who were taken or invited to the police station continued to wear their veils. Some withdrew from public life to avoid any official sanction or confrontation with the security forces.[104]

One of these determined women was Sakine Arat. In spite of several warnings and fines by the police, she did not give up wearing her charshaf. When the police attempted to rip up her charshaf, she openly raised her voice against the police officers, saying, 'Even if you tear off my charshaf ten times, I will not give up veiling. This is my tradition.' In the end, the police stopped warning her.[105]

The resistance to the anti-veiling campaigns also took the form of writing complaints or threatening letters to the central government authorities. Many letters were sent to the RPP headquarters. Those women who were offended or fined by the police sought their rights by writing to the central government. Some women knew that their clothes were not against the law, because the Grand National Assembly of Turkey (*Türkiye Büyük Millet Meclisi*) had never passed a law banning the veil. Therefore, they did not hesitate to resort to the central government to complain against officious police officers and to demand corrective action against bad or unjust treatment by the security forces. One such case involved two sisters in Sivas, named Azime and Mehri, who were fined for disobedience to the city council's ban on the veil. Upon their entering the government office with their black charshafs, police officers had declared their garments illegal and imposed a fine of five piasters on each of them. However, writing to the government, they refuted the police officers' arguments and claimed that their clothes were not contrary to the law.[106]

Some people directly criticized the anti-veiling campaigns by writing to the central or local government authorities. For example, the government received from Ordu province a huge number of letters of complaint against the anti-veiling campaign. Police sources reported that the local population had greeted the anti-veiling campaign organized by the provincial administration with general aversion.[107] Among the documents in the police archive are also warning letters sent by prominent and influential figures in the provinces. These people, who had kept their fingers on the pulse of public opinion in their regions, openly warned the politicians not to force veiled women to change their clothes. One of these letters, sent to the Minister of Internal Affairs, was penned by a prominent farmer of Ödemiş named Çiftçi İsmail Efe. He had stated that, because of a night watchman's physical intervention in not only women's charshafs, but also the headscarves and overcoats, furious conflicts had erupted between the security forces and women or their husbands every day.[108]

An incident that occurred in the Nazilli district of Denizli indicates that the misery and grievances of women – and of their husbands – had reached an unbearable level and shows how they resisted the anti-veiling policies of the district governor. The firmness of the district governor in striving against the women's cloaks and charshafs spurred a group of women to write an

106 *Murat Metinsoy*

anonymous complaint letter and to leave it at the door of the district governor's house. One of these women, named Pakize, suspected of writing the letter, was prosecuted by the court. The letter was as follows:

> Mister District Governor, the Kind and Truthful,
>
> For the sake of God and the Prophet, for the sake of your youth and your children, all of the women in the district have lost their sense of shame and bashfulness. The men also are out of patience with this situation. Please save the women from the hands of cruel persons tearing off their clothes. You would receive our and all the women's blessings. We wish to have our own longstanding customs. We are poor, and cannot dress in the way you want. We do not have suitable outfits to wear outside the home.[109]

Likewise there was widespread discontent stemming from the tough measures taken against the veil in Gaziantep. A significant number of people who were displeased with the anti-veiling campaigns of the city council petitioned the local authorities. In their anonymous letters, they warned the local administrators, in a threatening manner, to give up the struggle over women's clothing. In the face of these threat letters, the Gaziantep governorship was to put off the campaigns in June 1936 and let the women have their way.[110]

Selective adaptation and eclectic clothing styles: combining traditional with modern

Another strategy to deal with the anti-veiling campaigns was to find a middle course between the official rules and the accustomed clothing styles. As mentioned above, the double-sided pressure from the police and gendarmes on the one hand, and neighbours and men on the other hand, generally distressed the women psychologically. The security forces viewed women from the standpoint of the government directives and warned them to change their traditional clothes or sometimes fined them, whereas neighbours and especially men observed the local customs, traditions and basic expectations from women such as decency (*edeplilik*) and chasteness (*iffetlilik*), symbolized primarily by veiling. In this tight situation, many women pursued other methods to escape from both the police pressure and neighbours' criticisms: they wore stylistically eclectic clothes, reaching a compromise between the religious-traditional-social prerequisites and necessities, and the official rules and principles. Indeed, many women managed to solve the problem by wearing large-sized overcoats covering the neck to the ankles and the shoulders to the wrists and headscarves covering the head and neck completely. Some only covered their hair by using a headscarf tied under chin. These were new combinations that were, as compared to black charshaf with face veil, more suitable to both the decisions of local governments and their customary way of life.[111]

For those women who were not content with the overcoat and headscarf, another alternative way to hide the head and face was to use an umbrella. As noted above, many women who discarded the veil or who adopted the overcoat and headscarf resorted to umbrellas in order to further conceal their faces. Its use was quite practical and functional to hide the face, hair and sometimes the whole upper part of the body. For instance, according to a newspaper report titled 'You Cannot See Any Woman without Umbrellas in Alâiye', almost all of those women who went unveiled in the district had begun to use black umbrellas to hide their faces and heads, even at night.[112] In another case, upon the commencement of the official anti-veiling campaign in Gaziantep, women who still wanted to cover their hair and faces substituted large umbrellas for their charshafs.[113]

The memoirs of Nahid Sırrı Örik, a Kemalist bureaucrat who toured many Anatolian towns in the late 1930s, also indicate how Anatolian women circumvented the anti-veiling policies through partly incorporating these policies into their usual clothing system. His first impressions in Kayseri were of the absence of women in public places. Many women had withdrawn from public life. After quite a while of waiting in the city centre, he saw a small number of women wearing black overcoats and black gloves. Some women also had black umbrellas with which they managed to hide their faces completely. He wrote that he could not see the face of even one of these women.[114]

Another contemporary observer, Necla Pekolcay, a young woman of the period from a middle-class family in İstanbul, witnessed how her mother began to wear an overcoat with a scarf to cover her head and another scarf to hide her neck.[115] That is, although the form of headscarf currently preferred most by Islamist and traditional Turkish women, called the *sıkmabaş* or *türban*, emerged somewhat later in a different historical and sociological context, its prototypes appeared in the earlier period as an eclectic/adaptive form of veiling, but not as a symbol of a religious-political movement in the sense used by today's Islamist women.

As a final example, in Ordu, upon the local government's anti-veiling measures in 1934, many women gave up their black charshafs but invented interesting forms of veiling methods. They wrapped around their waist a large towel (*peştemal*), and covered their heads and shoulders with another large towel. It was reported that many women replaced the black charshaf with these towels, which spread throughout the Black Sea region.[116]

The flexible response of the government

From the beginning of the anti-veiling policies, neither the central government nor the local governments resorted to the systematic use of physical force, except in a limited number of cases, these mostly stemming from the officiousness and ignorance of rude police and gendarme officers. The single-party government was aware of the possible dangers of forcible intervention into gender relations, especially into women's private lives. In 1934, after the

108 Murat Metinsoy

political consolidation of the single-party regime, the government encouraged local party administrations and municipalities to take locally suitable measures to promote the elimination of the veil. On the other hand, the central government did not pass a law forbidding the veil; nor did the local governments strictly forbid it. Although the city councils in many provinces banned the veil, they never strictly observed the implementation of this ban. When zealous and revolutionary governors asked permission from the Ministry of Internal Affairs to resort to the security forces against those women who were defying local veil bans, the Ministry decidedly refused their demand and warned them to avoid such outrageous measures. The Antalya governor was, for example, one of those radical provincial bureaucrats who were eager to exercise physical force against veiled women as a last resort. Due to women's widespread indifference to the local veil ban, he sent a telegram to the Ministry of Internal Affairs in November 1934. In his telegram, after complaining that some women did not obey the veil ban, the governor argued that it was impossible to wipe out the veil through enlightening propaganda in a gradual manner. He asked the Ministry for the authorization to employ police force against those women who challenged the veil ban.[117] However, the Ministry firmly ordered the governor not to use police force and advised him to persuade such veiled women and their husband though propaganda and education.[118] On 14 December 1934, the Ministry of Internal Affairs sent a circular to all provincial governors, ordering them to keep away from forcible measures against veiled women.[119]

In view of widespread discontent, ordinary women's unwillingness to change their clothes, and insistence on veiling or several eclectic veiling forms combining the new and old, the government had to soften the measures further toward the end of the decade. On 14 November 1938, the Minister of Internal Affairs, Şükrü Kaya, issued a circular to all the local governors, according to which security officers and other state servants should by no means force or even warn women and girls to take off the headgear that they had been using since old times. Kaya recommended the provincial governorships and party organizations to take social measures appropriate to local social conditions so that such clothing habits would fade away in a gradual manner.[120]

One year after this circular from Kaya, the new Minister of Internal Affairs, Refik Saydam, also issued another similar circular and ordered that all local governors, party administrators and security forces be much more calm and tolerant in the face of resistance and disobedience to clothing laws:

> In these days in which we are seeking to prosecute reactionaries, I kindly request that neither the police organization nor the other state institutions resort to physical force against or put pressure on women – even verbally – to take off their veils. Do not depreciate our struggle against the veil and black charshaf.[121]

Everyday resistance to unveiling in Turkey 109

Concluding remarks

This article contemplates the veiling issue in interwar Turkey by drawing on new sources and by focusing on the everyday realities of the Turkish unveiling experience, particularly in the provinces. It shifts the focus from Islamic or secularist discourse and laws, or the experiences of a few dissidents, which have obscured the analysis of crucial determinants of both veiling and anti-veiling practices, to a more complex matrix of socioeconomic, psychological, sexual and gender determinants.[122] Thus, it unveils the everyday forms of people's negative perception of and response to the anti-veiling campaigns and the various reasons and dynamics other than religiosity behind the people's approach to local governments' attempts. It also points out that women's veiling practices and Turkish secularism's handling of veiling were shaped by the mutual interplay and compromises between the state and society, but not by the state's top-down decrees and forcible measures.

My first conclusion is, in this sense, that the resistance to secular reforms was not limited to a few well-known subversive activities by the regime's opponents or some open uprisings, which were eliminated by the state. Ordinary men and women contested the anti-veiling policies and the Kemalist image of modern women in everyday life in more covert, subtle and anonymous ways. Women occasionally openly resisted the local governments' directives ordering them to discard their veils. Moreover, in order to avoid police pressure, fines, or local communal pressure, an overwhelming majority of women creatively adopted new and eclectic styles of veiling. In addition, the pressure of the local society on women to cover their heads outweighed the influence of official anti-veiling campaigns.

Accordingly, the second point this article makes is that modernization did not overcome provincial society's local cultures and lifestyles. People under the influence of local social and cultural norms generally insisted on their usual ways of living. Consequently, women's usual clothing codes persisted throughout Turkey, except in the big city centres. Yet, modernity and local cultures were not always necessarily exclusive to each other. Most women eclectically combined veiling with the modern clothing codes promoted by the state. That is, Turkish women managed to incorporate veiling in more acceptable forms in an eclectic manner by creatively finding a compromise between their traditional clothing styles and the officially promoted ones.

Third, women's insistence on wearing the veil and public dislike of the official image of modern women stemmed from more complex variables rather than simply religious conservatism. In this regard, this article argues that both men's and women's identities and agency were shaped not only by religiosity, but also by sexuality, class position, economic status, local social relations, culture and psychology.[123] In other words, multiple complex dynamics underpinned and set the stage for the people's negative or hesitant response to the anti-veiling policies.

110　*Murat Metinsoy*

Fourth, a closer look at the anti-veiling campaigns shows that the everyday practices of republican secularism were not determined by top-down decrees, rigid principles and coercive measures. The everyday discontent, resistance and selective-adaptation, not challenging the political order directly, but alarming the government, compelled the Turkish reformers to seek compromise by leaving the approval of the reforms to time, unless people challenged the political order and reforms directly and in an organized manner. The government was aware of its fragile hegemony, and this self-awareness compelled it to take a more flexible and tolerant attitude towards the individuals who insisted on their old lifestyles and practices.[124] Well aware of the people's great sensitivity to gender relations and women's clothing as an extension of gender relations, the Turkish government avoided any strict and direct intervention in women's way of dressing during the interwar era. Atatürk personally admitted the hazardous effects of radical state interference with gender relations and accordingly with women's clothing.[125] This flexible and moderate authoritarianism of the republican regime distinguished it from the extremely interventionist and repressive contemporary regime in Iran, which encountered serious challenges and legitimacy crises.[126] The republican regime's approach to the issue, as Kandiyoti also argues, was pedagogic and indirect, compared to Reza Shah's drastic ban on veiling in 1936.[127] The Iranian authorities did not permit even the wearing of a headscarf.[128] The Turkish government, however, gave passive consent to such alternative formulations created by people and even the black charshaf in many cases, unless they directly undermined the political order. In this regard, these findings open to question the conventional approaches which have described Turkish secularism as assertive and uncompromising.

Acknowledgment

I would like to thank Ferdan Ergut and Elif Mahir Metinsoy for their invaluable comments, and TÜBİTAK for financial support to this research.

Notes

1　See Bernard Lewis, *The Emergence of Modern Turkey* (London; New York: Oxford University Press, 1961); Niyazi Berkes, *The Development of Secularism in Turkey* (Montreal: McGill University Press, 1964); Niyazi Berkes, *Batıcılık, Ulusçuluk ve Toplumsal Devrimler* (İstanbul: Cumhuriyet Kitap, 1997); Stanford Shaw and Ezel Kural Shaw, *History of the Ottoman Empire and Modern Turkey* (Cambridge: Cambridge University Press, 1977); Tarık Zafer Tunaya, *Türkiye'nin Siyasi Hayatında Batılılaşma Hareketleri*, Vols 1 and 2 (İstanbul: Cumhuriyet, 1999); Tarık Zafer Tunaya, *Devrim Hareketleri İçinde Atatürk ve Atatürkçülük* (İstanbul: Baha Matbaası, 1964). In addition, see Çetin Özek, *100 Soruda Türkiye'de Gerici Akımlar* (İstanbul: Gerçek Yayınevi, 1968). Although Binnaz Toprak, political scientist and currently the deputy of the Republican People's Party in the Turkish parliament, criticizes political Islam and the rise of the veil, she reproduces implicitly political Islam's approach to the secularism of early republican Turkey by calling it 'militant secularism', which is radical and

Everyday resistance to unveiling in Turkey 111

unbending. See Binnaz Toprak, 'Women and Fundamentalism: The case of Turkey', in *Identity Politics and Women: Cultural Reassertions and Feminisms in International Perspective*, ed. Valentine M. Moghadam (Boulder, CO: Westview Press, 1993), pp. 298–99.

2 For instance, according to Mete Tunçay, Mustafa Kemal's main motivation for the abolition of the Caliphate was to reinforce his own personal authority. See Mete Tunçay, *Türkiye Cumhuriyeti'nde Tek Parti Yönetiminin Kurulması* (İstanbul: Tarih Vakfı Yurt Yayınları, 2005), pp. 72–73. See also Erik Jan Zürcher, *Turkey: A Modern History* (London; New York: I. B. Tauris, 2004), p. 167, 179. Ayşe Kadıoğlu, *Cumhuriyet İdaresi, Demokrasi Muhakemesi* (İstanbul: Metis Yayınları, 1999); Levent Köker, *Modernleşme, Kemalizm ve Demokrasi* (İstanbul: İletişim Yayınları, 1990).

3 For Islamist accounts of early republican secularism, see Necip Fazıl Kısakürek, *Son Devrin Din Mazlumları* (İstanbul: BD Yayınları, 1974); Sadık Albayrak, *İrtica'ın Tarihçesi*, Vol. 4, *Devrimler ve Gerici Tepkiler* (İstanbul: Araştırma Yayınları, 1990); Sadık Albayrak, *İrtica'ın Tarihçesi*, Vol. 5, *Tek Parti Dönemi ve Batıcılık* (İstanbul: Araştırma Yayınları, 1990); *Sadık Albayrak, Türkiye'de Din Kavgası* (İstanbul: Sebil Matbaacılık, 1975); Şükrü Karatepe, *Tek Parti Dönemi* (İstanbul: İz Yayıncılık, 1997); Abdurrahman Dilipak, *Bir Başka Açıdan Kemalizm* (İstanbul: Beyan Yayınları, 1988); Yavuz Bahadıroğlu, *Osmanlı Demokrasisinden Türkiye Cumhuriyetine* (İstanbul: Nesil Yayınları, 2008); Hasan Hüseyin Ceylan, *Cumhuriyet Dönemi Din-Devlet İlişkileri I* (İstanbul: Risale Yayınları, 1991). For a classical Marxian account criticizing the secularizing reforms for alienation and blindfold imitation of the West, see İdris Küçükömer, *Düzenin Yabancılaşması: Batılaşma* (İstanbul: Ant Yayınları, 1969).

4 Since the Turkish political elite and especially Mustafa Kemal Atatürk intellectually were inspired by the French secularism of the Third Republic, this inspiration has been taken for granted in evaluation of Turkish secularism as Jacobin secularism. The everyday interactions between the state and society, and everyday practices of secular reforms have not been examined in depth. For instance, in his recent book, Ahmet Kuru labels the republican Turkey's secularism as assertive, rigid and exclusionary, inspired from France. See Ahmet Kuru, *Secularism and State Policies toward Religion: The United States, France, and Turkey* (New York: Cambridge University Press, 2009). Both Ahmet Yaşar Ocak and Nilüfer Göle argue that the emergence of Islam in the post-1980s was a challenge to the strict and authoritarian Kemalist secularism. They also see the early republican secularism as inflexible and uncompromising. See Ahmet Yaşar Ocak, *Türkler, Türkiye ve İslam* (İstanbul: İletişim Yayınları, 1999), pp. 111–14; Nilüfer Göle 'The Civilizational, Spatial, and Sexual Powers of the Secular', in *Varieties of Secularism in a Secular Age*, ed. Michael Warner, Jonathan Van Antwerpen and Craig Calhoun (Cambridge: Harvard University Press, 2010), p. 255. In contrast to these ahistorical and essentialist arguments, which blame Kemalist secularism and unveiling policies for the rise of political Islam in Turkey, I think that the origins and dynamics of the current veiling issue as a symbol of political Islam are far more complex. For a more nuanced analysis of the socio-economic, political and international context of the Islamist policies regarding women and the veil in Islamic countries, see Deniz Kandiyoti, 'Women, Islam, and State', in *Political Islam: Essays from Middle East Report*, ed. Joel Beinin and Joe Stork (New York: I. B. Tauris, 1997).

5 For the most prominent examples of the strong-state theory, see Şerif Mardin, *Türkiye'de Toplum ve Siyaset, Makaleler 1* (İstanbul: İletişim Yayınları, 2002); Metin Heper, *The State Tradition in Turkey*, (Walkington: The Eothen Press, 1985); Ahmet İnsel, *Düzen ve Kalkınma Kıskacında Türkiye* (İstanbul: Ayrıntı Yayınları, 1996).

112 *Murat Metinsoy*

6 See Gavin. D. Brockett, 'Revisiting the Turkish Revolution, 1923–38, Secular Reform and Religious "Reaction"', *History Compass* 4 (2006), pp. 1060–72. Umut Azak, 'A Reaction to Authoritarian Modernization in Turkey: The Menemen Incident and the Creation and Contestation of a Myth, 1930–31', in *The State and the Subaltern: Modernization, Society and the State in Turkey and Iran*, ed. Touraj Atabaki (New York: I.B. Tauris, 2007); Mahmut Gologlu, *Devrimler ve Tepkileri (1924–1930)* (Ankara: Gologlu Yayınları, 1972); Çetin Özek, *Türkiye'de Gerici Akımlar* (İstanbul: Gerçek, 1968); Hülya Küçük, 'Sufi Reactions against the Reforms after Turkey's National Struggle: How a Nightingale Turned into a Crow', in *The State and The Subaltern: Modernization, Society and the State in Turkey and Iran*, ed. Touraj Atabaki, op. cit., pp. 123–42; Binnaz Toprak, 'Dinci Sağ', in *Geçiş Sürecinde Türkiye*, ed. Irvin Cemil Schick and Ertuğrul Ahmet Tonak (İstanbul: Belge Yayınları, 1998), pp.246–47.

7 A limited number of studies specifically focused on the veil issue of the interwar period. They describe particularly legal aspects of the unveiling campaigns, debate among elites and intellectuals, and motivations behind the unveiling politics; see for example, Kemal Yakut, 'Tek Parti Döneminde Peçe ve Çarşaf', *Tarih ve Toplum* 220 (April 2002), pp. 23–32; Hakkı Uyar, 'Çarşaf, Peçe ve Kafes Üzerine Bazı Notlar', *Toplumsal Tarih* 33 (Sept. 1996), pp. 6–11.

8 For the 'liberation' account, see the above-mentioned studies of Niyazi Berkes, Bernard Lewis and Tarık Zafer Tunaya and many other modernist narratives mentioned above. As an example of the 'repression' account, see Elisabeth Özdalga, *The Veiling Issue: Official Secularism and Popular Islam in Turkey* (Richmond: Curzon Press, 1998); Murat Aksoy, *Başörtüsü-Türban: Batılılaşma-Modernleşme, Laiklik ve Örtünme* (İstanbul: Kitabevi Yayınları, 2005); Nilüfer Göle, *The Forbidden Modern: Civilization and Veiling* (Ann Arbor: University of Michigan Press, 1996); and see also the other Islamist and critical accounts mentioned above.

9 See İlber Ortaylı, *İmparatorluğun En Uzun Yüzyılı* (İstanbul: İletişim Yayınları, 2003).

10 The main motives of the republican elite for the clothing reforms are beyond the scope of this paper. For a recent discussion about the subject, see Murat Metinsoy, "Everyday Resistance and Selective Adaptation to The Hat Reform in Early Republican Turkey", *International Journal of Turcologia* 8–16 (Autumn 2013), pp. 7–48.

11 For the role of local families and women in the anti-veiling campaigns, see the article of Sevgi Adak in this volume.

12 In Anatolia, the charshaf was the most common form of veil, resembling the Iranian chador. Though varying from place to place in length, style, colour and fabric, it generally covered the body from head to foot, knees or waist. It sometimes covered the face or was combined with another veil covering the face of the wearer. The veiling practices in the form of wearing a long, black chador with a niqap covering the face had begun to lose their popularity in some provinces of the Ottoman Empire during its last decades. Yet, albeit in varying styles, the veiling in the form of charshaf, sometimes combined with niqaps concealing the faces and even eyes, continued throughout Anatolia. See İkbal Elif Mahir-Metinsoy, *Mütakere Dönemi İstanbul'unda Moda ve Kadın, 1918–1923* (İstanbul; Libra Yayınevi, 2014). And see İ. Elif Mahir-Metinsoy, *Poor Ottoman Turkish Women During World War I: Women's Experiences and Politics in Everyday Life, 1914–1923* (PhD Dissertation, Université de Strasbourg and Boğaziçi University, 2012).

13 Joseph C. Grew, *Atatürk ve Yeni Türkiye (1927–1932)* (İstanbul: Gündoğan Yayınları, 2002), p. 159.

Everyday resistance to unveiling in Turkey   113

14 Harold Armstrong, *Turkey and Syria Reborn: A Record of Two Years of Travel* (London: J. Lane, 1930), p. 121.
15 Ibid., p. 176.
16 Ibid., p. 200.
17 Ibid., p. 221.
18 Ibid., p. 223.
19 Lilo Linke, *Allah Dethroned* (London: Constable & Co. Ltd., 1937), p. 5.
20 Ibid., p. 8.
21 Ibid., p. 18.
22 Ibid., p. 267.
23 Arif Balkan, *Cumhuriyet Türkiye'sinin İnşası: Anılar* (İstanbul: Papirüs Yayınları, 1996), p. 53. Umbrellas were used by women who dared to wear the new fashioned charshafs not hiding the face in the late Ottoman period. For more information about women's fashion during the late Ottoman period, see İkbal Elif Mahir-Metinsoy, 'Fashion and Women in the İstanbul of the Armistice Period, 1918–23 (MA thesis, Boğaziçi University, İstanbul, 2005), p. 4.
24 Pakize Türkoğlu, *Kızlar da Yanmaz: Genç Cumhuriyet'te Köy Çocuğu Olmak* (İstanbul: İş Bankası Kültür Yayınları, 2011), p. 480.
25 Oryal Gökdemir, *Annemin Anlattıkları* (İstanbul: Arkın Kitabevi, 1998), p. 108.
26 M. Enver Beşe, 'Safranbolu'da Bir Köylünün Hayatı', *Halk Bilgisi Haberleri*, No. 91 (May, 1939), p. 104.
27 For these reports and correspondence between the Ministry of Internal Affairs, the provincial governors and the General Directorate of Security (Turkish Police Department), see the Archive of the General Directorate of Security (Emniyet Genel Müdürlüğü Arşivi [EGMA]) [13216–17] and EGMA [13211–16].
28 For the General Situation Report on Ordu Province, see Başbakanlık Cumhuriyet Arşivi-Muamelat Genel Müdürlüğü Katalogu (Prime Ministry Republican Archive-Catalogue of General Directorate of Transactions [BCA-MGM]) [30.10/65.433.5.] (1935).
29 See EGMA [13216–17] (7 November 1939) and EGMA [13211–16] (18 March 1939).
30 'Kütahya Hanımları', *Köroğlu* (27 January 1934).
31 'Peçeli, Peştemallı Kadınlar', *Köroğlu* (25 April 1934).
32 'Çarşaf-Peçe!' *Köroğlu* (23 June 1934).
33 'Çarşaf, Peçe ve Yabancı Dil', *Son Posta* (21 April 1935).
34 Leslie P. Peirce, *The Imperial Harem: Women and Sovereignty in the Ottoman Empire* (New York: Oxford University Press, 1993), pp. 267–72.
35 Minister of Internal Affairs, Şükrü Kaya, BCA-MGM [30.10/102.668.9] (28 February 1928).
36 Minister of Internal Affairs, Şükrü Kaya, BCA-MGM [30.10/102.668.8] (25 February 1929).
37 'Bir Ahûnd Tutuldu', *Son Posta* (23 May 1935).
38 'Vay Yobaz!' *Köroğlu* (8 January 1936).
39 Prime Ministry Republican Archive-Catalogue of Republican People's Party [BCA-CHP] [490.01/677.288.1] (19 April 1933).
40 Selma Ekrem, *Turkey, Old and New* (New York: C. Scribner's Sons, 1947), p. 81.
41 Mitat Enç, *Selamlık Sohbetleri* (İstanbul: Ötüken Neşriyat, 2007), p. 204.
42 İbrahim Yasa, *Hasanoğlan Köyü'nün İçtimaî-İktisadî Yapısı* (Ankara: Doğuş Ltd. O. Matbaası for Türkiye ve Orta Doğu Amme İdaresi Enstitüsü, 1955), p. 165.
43 For the enormous losses in the Ottoman-Turkish male population during the First World War and the National Struggle, see İkbal Elif Mahir-Metinsoy, 'Poor Ottoman Turkish Women during World War I: Women's Experiences and Politics in Everyday Life, 1914–23 (PhD dissertation, Université de Strasbourg and Boğaziçi University, 2012), pp. 103–11. For the shortage of labour in industry

114   Murat Metinsoy

during the interwar period, see Ahmet Makal, 'Türkiye'nin Sanayileşme Sürecinde İşgücü ve Sosyal Politika', *Toplum ve Bilim* 92, (Spring 2002).

44 Hikmet Kıvılcımlı, *Türkiye İşçi Sınıfının Sosyal Varlığı* (İstanbul: Sosyal İnsan Yayınları, 2008) p. 57; Erdal Yavuz, 'Sanayideki İşgücünün Durumu, 1923–40'. *Osmanlı'dan Cumhuriyet Türkiye'sine İşçiler, 1839–1950*, ed. Donald Quataert and Erik Jan Zürcher, trans. Cahide Ekiz (İstanbul: İletişim Yayınları, 1998), p. 190.

45 'Erkek İşçiler Kadınlardan Şikayetçi', *Köroğlu* (23 October 1935).

46 *Orak Çekiç*, No.11 (1 October 1936), quoted in Mustafa Özçelik, *1930–1950 Arasında Tütüncülerin Tarihi* (İstanbul: TÜSTAV Yayınları, 2003), pp. 101–02.

47 İzmir'in Esnaf ve İşçi Teşkilatında Bir Buçuk Senelik Mesâi ve Tetkikatıma Ait Umumi Rapor' (General Report on My One-and-a-Half Year Investigations about the Organizations of Workers and Artisans in İzmir) BCA-CHP [490.1/1446.26.1] (17 June 1933).

48 For brief information about the sexual abuse of female and children workers by their employers in early industrial society, see Karl Marx, *Kapital*, Vol. 1 (Ankara: Sol Yayınları, 2000), pp. 378–88.

49 Levent Cantek, 'Kabadayıların ve Futbolun Mahallesi: Hacettepe', *Sanki Viran Ankara*, ed. Funda Şenol Cantek (İstanbul: İletişim Yayınları, 2006), p. 187.

50 Linke, *Allah Dethroned*, op. cit., p. 312.

51 Ahmet Şevki wrote: 'Hürriyet-i Şahsiye Kanunu ayaklar altına alınmaktadır'. EGMA [13216–17] (22 August 1935).

52 President of the RPP Provicial Administration Board. BCA-CHP [490.1/17.88.1] (14 January 1936).

53 'Çarşaf, Peçe', *Köroğlu* (9 January 1935).

54 'Çarşaf ve Peçe', *Köroğlu* (10 August 1935).

55 'Manto mu Ekmek mi?' *Köroğlu* (14 October 1935).

56 See Bernard Newman, *Turkish Crossroads* (London: Robert Hale Ltd, 1951), p. 88. Pakize Türkoğlu also writes in her memoirs that the two main functions of the headscarf for peasant women were to protect them from cold and to hide their dirty long hair. See Türkoğlu, *Kızlar da Yanmaz: Genç Cumhuriyet'te Köy Çocuğu Olmak*, op. cit., p. 173.

57 Şerif Mardin used this concept for the first time. By this concept, Mardin referred to indirect social control and pressure exerted by Muslim people over their neighbours to make them conform to their lifestyles and existing social, moral and religious norms. See Şerif Mardin, 'Religion and Secularism in Turkey', in *Atatürk: Founder of a Modern State*, ed. Ali Kazancıgil and Ergun Özbudun (London: C. Hurts, 1981), p. 214.

58 Mary Elaine Hegland, 'The Power Paradox in Muslim Women's Majales: North-West Pakistani Mourning Rituals as Sites of Contestation over Religious Politics, Ethnicity, and Gender' in *Gender, Politics and Islam*, ed. Therese Saliba, Carolyn Allen, Judith A. Howard (Chicago, IL: The University of Chicago Press, 2002), pp. 117–19.

59 Yasa, *Hasanoğlan Köyü'nün*, op. cit., p. 214.

60 Türkoğlu, *Kızlar da Yanmaz: Genç Cumhuriyet'te Köy Çocuğu Olmak*, op. cit., p. 5.

61 Mediha Esenel, *Geç Kalmış Kitap: 1940'lı Yıllarda Anadolu Köylerinde Araştırmalar ve Yaşadığım Çevreden İzlenimler* (İstanbul: Sistem Yayıncılık, 1999), p. 135.

62 From General Directorate of Security to the Ministry of Internal Affairs, EGMA [22552–33] (25 October 1937).

63 Adnan Binyazar, *Masalını Yitiren Dev* (İstanbul: Can Yayınları, 2003), pp. 124–28.

64 EGMA [13216–17] (7 February 1936).

Everyday resistance to unveiling in Turkey 115

65 Inspection Report by Adnan Menderes on Konya Province, BCA-CHP [490.1/ 677.289.1] (16 February 1936).
66 Ibid.
67 Kerim Sadi, *Türkiye'de Sosyalizmin Tarihine Katkı* (İstanbul: İletişim Yayınları, 1994), p. 790.
68 'Gebze Hanımları', *Köroğlu* (7 April 1934).
69 'Amma İş Ha!', *Köroğlu* (22 March 1933).
70 See Levent Cantek, 'Kabadayıların ve Futbolun Mahallesi: Hacettepe', op. cit., p. 187; Linke, *Allah Dethroned*, op. cit., p. 31.
71 Şehmus Diken, *İsyan Sürgünleri* (İstanbul: İletişim Yayınları, 2005), p. 88.
72 Enç, *Selamlık Sohbetleri*, op. cit., p. 16.
73 'Harem Selamlık Kalkmalıdır', *Yeşilgireson* (26 December 1936).
74 Reşat Nuri Güntekin, *Anadolu Notları* (İstanbul: İnkılâp Kitabevi, 1998), p. 104.
75 'Kadın Erkek Birlikte Sinemaya Gidemiyorlar', *Milliyet* (28 July 1931).
76 'Hala Harem-Selamlık Zihniyet Var!' *Son Posta* (3 January 1936).
77 From Çankırı Governor Hüsnü Uzgören to the Ministy of Internal Affairs, EGMA [13211–16] (18 March 1939).
78 Report of Police Chief Tahsin from Tosya, EGMA [13216–17] (1935).
79 EGMA [13216–17] (1937).
80 Enç, *Selamlık Sohbetleri*, op. cit., p. 200.
81 See Robert Darnton, *The Great Cat Massacre and Other Episodes in French Cultural History* (New York: Vintage Books, 1985). Darnton describes how the poor printing house apprentices in eighteenth-century Paris vented their wrath and anger in the face of harsh exploitation by their masters on the highly favoured cats of their masters. Darnton interprets these acts as symbolic forms of workers' protests.
82 Hulûsi Turgut (ed.), *Atatürk'ün Sırdaşı Kılıç Ali'nin Anıları* (İstanbul: İş Bankası Kültür Yayınları, 2005), p. 391.
83 BCA-MGM [30.10/104.679.4] (16 February 1926).
84 EGMA [13216–17] (13 November 1935). By the way, in parallel to the industrialization policies in the 1930s, the government encouraged the citizens to consume 'domestic goods'. For this purpose, the government launched a 'domestic good campaign' to promote the items made in Turkey. See *Cumhuriyet Ansiklopedisi, 1923–2000*, Vol. 1, *1923–1940* (İstanbul: Yapı Kredi Yayınları, 2005), p. 133, 238.
85 Barbro Karabuda, *Goodbye to the Fez: A Portrait of Modern Turkey*, trans. from Swedish by Maurice Michael (London: Denis Dobson Books, 1959), p. 74. Not only those women who were bareheaded or who wore fashionable female hats, but also men who wore homburg or derby hats were vulnerable to people's attacks in streets.
86 Sinan Korle, *Kızıltoprak Günlerim* (İstanbul: İletişim Yayınları, 1997), p. 42.
87 BCA-MGM [30.10/101.654.15] (16 November 1925).
88 EGMA [13216–17].
89 Adnan Binyazar, *Masalını Yitiren Dev*, op. cit., pp. 124–28.
90 'Kodese', *Köroğlu* (14 September 1929).
91 '1 Lafa 15 Gün', *Köroğlu* (31 October 1936).
92 Historians of popular culture have shown that people deployed rumour as a device to articulate their aspirations and to create public opinion. According to them, rumour shaped and vented the ordinary people's dissent when the space of open confrontation was not easily available. For the role of rumour as a politically communicative tool and informal media, see Robert Darnton, 'An Early Information Society: News and Media in Eighteenth-Century Paris', *American Historical Review*, 105–1 (Feb. 2000); Arlette Farge and Jacques Revel, *The Vanishing Children of Paris: Rumor and Politics before the French Revolution*

116   Murat Metinsoy

(Cambridge, MA: Harvard University Press, 1991); Arun Kumar, 'Beyond Muffled Murmurs of Dissent? Kisan Rumour in Colonial Bihar', *The Journal of Peasant Studies* 27–1 (Oct., 2000).
93 Prime Ministry Republican Archive – Catalogue of Presidency of Religious Affairs (Başbakanlık Cumhuriyet Arşivi-Diyanet İşleri Reisliği Katalogu [BCA DİR]) [51.V05/2.2.3] (11 March 1926); Prime Ministry Republican Archive – Catalogue of Cabinet Decisions (Başbakanlık Cumhuriyet Arşivi-Bakanlar Kurulu Katalogu [BCA BKK]) [30.18.1.1/16. 71.14] (23 October 1925).
94 BCA MGM [30.10/88.580.6] (2 May 1928).
95 EGMA [13216–17].
96 Enç, *Selamlık Sohbetleri*, op. cit., p. 199.
97 Ministry of Internal Affairs Archive (İçişleri Bakanlığı Arşivi [İBA]) [12213–69] (1939).
98 İBA [12212–14] (28 November 1938).
99 Ibid.
100 EGMA [12212–14] (23 January 1939); İBA [12212–14] (27 January 1939); İBA [12212–14] (16 February 1939).
101 İBA [12212–14] (27 January 1939).
102 İBA [12212–18] (22 November 1938); and İBA [12212–14].
103 *Yeşilgireson* (29 October 1926).
104 *Yeşilgireson* (6 January 1926).
105 Şehmus Diken, *İsyan Sürgünleri*, op. cit., p. 52.
106 EGMA [13216–4].
107 EGMA [13216–17].
108 EGMA [13216–17] (8 January 1938).
109 EGMA [13216–17] (1940).
110 From the Gaziantep Governorship to the Minister of Internal Affairs. EGMA [13216–17] (1 June 1936).
111 From the Deputy Governor of İstanbul, Sahip Örge, to the Ministry of Internal Affairs, EGMA [13211–16] (20 March 1939).
112 'Alâiye'de Şemsiyesiz Gezen Kadın Göremezsiniz', *Son Posta* (3 May 1932).
113 'Hala Eski Kafa!' *Köroğlu* (21 December 1935).
114 Nahid Sırrı Örik, *Anadolu'da: Yol Notları – Kayseri, Kırşehir, Kastamonu – Bir Edirne Seyahatnamesi* (İstanbul: Arma Yayınları, 2000), p. 92.
115 Necla Pekolcay, *Geçtim Dünya Üzerinden* (İstanbul: L&M Yayınları, 2005), p. 163.
116 *Ayın Tarihi*, June 1937, (Ankara: Basın Yayın Genel Müdürlüğü, 1937), quoted from Vâlâ Nurettin, *Haber* (1 May 1937).
117 From The Governor of Antalya to the Ministry of Internal Affairs, EGMA [13216–17-1] (17 November 1934).
118 From Minister of Internal Affairs to the Governor of Antalya, EGMA [13216–17-1] (17 November 1934).
119 Circular from Minister of Internal Affairs to all the Governors and Inspectors General EGMA [13216–17-1], (14 December 1934).
120 Circular Letter of the Minister of Internal Affairs, Şükrü Kaya, to the Provincial Governors, EGMA [13211–10] (14 November 1938).
121 Circular Letter of the Ministry of Internal Affairs to the Provincial Governors, EGMA [13216–17] (22 November 1939).
122 For criticisms of essentialism, lack of class perspectives and ahistorical approaches, see Nikki R. Keddie, 'Problems in the Study of Middle Eastern Women', *International Journal of Middle East Studies* 10 (1979), pp. 225–40.
123 For a volume consisting of several essays using such an approach, see Therese Saliba, Carolyn Allen, Judith A. Howard (eds), *Gender, Politics, and Islam* (Chicago, IL: The University of Chicago Press, 2002).

124 See Murat Metinsoy, 'Fragile Hegemony, Flexible Authoritarianism, and Governing from Below: Politicians' Reports in Early Republican Turkey', *International Journal of Middle East Studies* 43–4 (November 2011), pp. 699–719. On the other hand, Taha Parla and Andrew Davison criticize the Kemalists' flexible and moderate approach toward religion in private and individual realms. They argue that 'Kemalism made and continues to make official and established concessions to religion'. See Taha Parla and Andrew Davison, 'Secularism and Laicism in Turkey', in *Secularisms*, ed. Janet J. Jakobsen and Ann Pellegrini (Durham: Duke University Press, 2008), pp. 58–75.

125 Atatürk argued that the use of physical force against women to impose modern clothes on them might spur social reactions and endanger all of the reforms. In his words, 'The man's strong and tight concern for woman originates from completely unconscious and unreasonable feelings. The fact that near friends, brothers, and even father and sons became deadly enemies of each other because of a woman is a well-known daily incident all along. From this standpoint, it is not true and fruitful to use force even against a small number of them to transform their clothes'. See Hasan Rıza Soyak, *Atatürk'ten Hatıralar* (İstanbul: Yapı Kredi Yayınları, 2004), p. 270.

126 For a comparative analysis of the authoritarian modernization attempts in Iran and Turkey during the interwar period, see Touraj Atabaki and Erik Jan Zürcher (ed.), *Men of Order: Authoritarian Modernization under Atatürk and Reza Shah* (London: I. B. Tauris, 2004). The Iranian historians in this volume argue that the Iranian state implemented the secular reforms in a more repressive manner. Especially when Reza Shah visited Turkey in 1935, he was impressed by the Turkish modernization and sent orders to Tehran for stricter measures to impose the hat reform and ban on veiling. The Turkish government, however, deliberately avoided repressive intervention in women's clothes.
For Reza Shah's strict anti-veiling drive and tougher use of physical force against veiled women through security forces, see Ashraf Zahedi, 'Concealing and Revealing Female Hair: Veiling Dynamics in Contemporary Iran', in *The Veil: Women Writers on Its History, Lore, and Politics*, ed. Jennifer Heath (Berkeley and Los Angeles: University of California Press, 2008), pp. 254–55. See also H. E. Chehabi, 'Dress Codes for Men in Turkey and Iran', in *Men of Order: Authoritarian Modernization under Atatürk and Reza Shah*, ed. Touraj Atabaki and Erik Jan Zürcher, op. cit., pp. 221–23; H. E. Chehabi, 'The Banning of the Veil and Its Consequences', in *The Making of Modern Iran: State and Society under Shah, 1921–1941*, ed. Stephanie Cronin (New York and London: Routledge-Curzon, 2003); Homa Katouzian, 'State and Society under Reza Shah', in *Men of Order: Authoritarian Modernization under Atatürk and Reza Shah*, ed. Touraj Atabaki and Erik Jan Zürcher, op. cit, p. 34; Ruth Frances Woodsmall, *Women and the New East* (Washington, DC: The Middle East Institute, 1960), p. 49.

127 Deniz Kandiyoti, 'Women, Islam, and the State', op. cit., p. 187.

128 Zahedi, 2008, op. cit., pp. 255.

Part II
Iran and Afghanistan

4 Unveiling ambiguities: revisiting 1930s Iran's *kashf-i hijab* campaign

Jasamin Rostam-Kolayi and Afshin Matin-asgari

Iran's 1930s "unveiling campaign," *kashf-i hijab* in Persian, has been addressed in a number of books dealing with gender and women in Iranian history, most prominently by Janet Afary, Camron Amin, Firoozeh Kashani-Sabet, and Parvin Paidar.[1] Houchang Chehabi has also treated this subject in several articles on the Reza Shah-era national dress reforms.[2] However, an overview of the above scholarship reveals important conceptual ambiguities, as well as gaps in information. These can be grouped into four main areas, which the present chapter will identify and clarify in light of primary sources and narratives on unveiling recently published in Persian. First, the absence of comprehensive documented historical studies of variations in women's dress codes and styles in pre-modern Iran causes uncertainty in the meaning of "traditional" veiling, including the extent to which it may have been "Islamic." Given this problem, it becomes difficult to ascertain exactly what changes the 1930s "unveiling" brought about. Second, contrary to common assumptions, even in scholarly literature, Iran's *kashf-i hijab* was neither legislated nor "decreed" by Reza Shah. Below, we identify the legal and institutional frameworks and actors responsible for the project's conception and implementation. Third, we argue that *kashf-i hijab* was carefully conceived not to contradict the *shari'a* or be forced on women throughout the country. Forcible measures and even violence were occasionally used, but their frequency and extent remains unclear, while documentary evidence shows such actions were opposed by higher authorities in charge of the project's implementation. Fourth, archival evidence does not show *kashf-i hijab* being categorically and directly rejected, for example through *fatwas*, by Reza Shah-era high clerical authorities. Nor is there conclusive evidence to know how most women, the majority of whom lived in small towns and rural areas and therefore were not directly affected by *kashf-i hijab*, reacted to the project. All of the above leads to our study's seemingly ironic conclusion, i.e. that the core thrust of the 1930s "unveiling," essentially calling for women's faces to be uncovered and the discarding of the *chador*, was not only accepted as compatible with Islam in the post-Reza Shah era, but continued as "Islamic *hijab*" even under the Islamic Republic.

This chapter also argues for revisions to scholarly comparisons between Iran's *kashf-i hijab* and a similar contemporary campaign in the Turkish

122   Jasamin Rostam-Kolayi and Afshin Matin-asgari

Republic. While scholars consider Republican Turkey as an inspiration and model for Reza Shah's modernizing reforms, it is often assumed that Iranian and Turkish unveiling campaigns differed significantly in both intent and implementation. For example, Chehabi notes that the Kemalist Turkish government prohibited the wearing of the veil for teachers and government employees and merely discouraged it for other women, whereas the Pahlavi state under Reza Shah banned it outright and forcibly for all Iranian women. He writes, "[T]here was never any forced unveiling in Turkey. Ataturk discouraged veiling ... [and] physical force was not used on Turkish women." The Iranian case, which "used physical force," therefore appears more radical, far-reaching, and oppressive than the Turkish one.[3] However, our revisiting the Iranian case, in light of recent scholarship on Turkish unveiling such as the chapters included in this volume,[4] suggests that unveiling campaigns in Iran and Turkey, both in terms of intent and implementation, had more in common than previously appreciated.

Diverse meanings and practices of *hijab* in pre-1930s Iran

A fundamental problem of the vastly proliferating English-language literature on *hijab* is that the term's complex and multi-layered meaning is lost when it is rendered simply as "veil/veiling." In Iran, as well as other Muslim countries, *hijab* refers not only to comportments in women's dress, but also to codes of behavior and physical barriers or "separations" between genders in public space.[5] This problem is compounded by the fact that even when used only for women's dress codes, *hijab* historically has taken a variety of meanings, both religious and secular, referring to a wide range of different and at times contradictory practices.

In the Iranian case, scholarly discussions of pre-1930s veiling range from brief explanations to comprehensive descriptions. For example, Kashani-Sabet explains traditional veiling by citing Western travel writers observing that women in public covered their faces and bodies with a "cloak, which descends from their head to their feet,"[6] referring to what is commonly known as the *chador*. Afary offers a detailed account of pre-1930s Iranian veiling practices, noting the urban–rural, tribal, ethnic, and social class differences of women's public dress. She notes, "tribal women went about their work unveiled, and poor rural women wore a modified form of the veil, [while] elite urban women strictly observed the practice." In addition to the fully encompassing *chador*, some urban Iranian women wore *rubandeh* (literally "face-cover"), which left most of the face, except the eyes, covered. Afary also discusses the regional and ethnic differences in veiling practices, for example among Gilani, Kurdish, Arab, Tehrani, and Kashani women, as well as variations of dress among different socio-economic classes. "Poor urban women ... often wore a loose veil (and sometimes no face veil)."[7] Thus, while some, mostly upper-class, urban women wore face-veils and/or donned the *chador*, most women, i.e. the urban poor and working class, as well as those in rural and tribal areas, were not "separated" from men in public and wore a variety of tight- and/or loose-fitting dress, often including headscarves that did not cover the face or strictly the hair.

Chehabi, too, details the various types of women's face, head, and body coverings, such as *picheh* and *chador*, before the 1930s. *Picheh*, for example, was a facial mask worn under or over the *chador*, "a loose, enveloping, sleeveless piece of cloth that covered the whole body."[8] Chehabi also suggests that *picheh* was gradually going out of fashion in Tehran and elsewhere in Iran even before state-mandated unveiling.[9] Thus, most "traditional" or premodern Iranian women, from lower and working classes and living in rural and tribal areas, were already "unveiled," that is if *hijab* is taken to mean women's social segregation and the covering of their head and face in public. This point was noted and cited approvingly by early Iranian advocates of "unveiling," as well as in 1930s official pronouncements, but is not sufficiently addressed in academic studies.

The ambiguity of *hijab*'s "traditional" meaning is compounded by the fact that, considered as a dress code, its religiously mandated (*shar'i*) definition differed from what local customs and social conventions (*urf*) prescribed. For example, while the majority of Iranian women, in rural and tribal areas, appear not to have observed strictly *shari'a* codes on *hijab*, the rural and urban women who did wear face-masks (*niqab* or *rubandeh*) practiced *hijab* more stringently than the *shari'a* mandated. The lack of clear distinction between customary (*urfi*) and religious (*shar'i*) practices of *hijab* was related to the fact that "Islamic *hijab*" was itself subject to various juridical interpretations.

The legal status of Iran's *kashf-i hijab*: Was it decreed or legislated?

Scholarly writings on Iran's 1930s "unveiling" reveal different, and at times contradictory, explanations of what exactly it entailed. Afary suggests it primarily involved urging women to wear "European suits and hats."[10] Without a clear description of "traditional" veiling, Paidar defines Reza Shah's compulsory dress policy as prohibiting women to appear publicly in "*chador* and scarf."[11] Kashani-Sabet equates the 1930s unveiling with the prohibition of *chador* and "headgear" and the push to wear European hats.[12]

Amin and Chehabi offer the most careful and detailed examination of the Iranian "unveiling" campaign under Reza Shah. According to Amin, Iran's early-twentieth-century discourse on "unveiling" focused on the removal of women's face coverings, as advocated by Egyptian reformer Qasim Amin in his 1899 *Liberation of Women*, rather than the discarding of the *chador* or all head coverings. However, the 1930s state-led unveiling campaign and its implementation focused on the removal of the *chador*, the face veil, and headscarf and the adoption of European-American dress and hats. In reference to the 1935 government directive on unveiling, Amin writes, "The memorandum conflated the Qasim Amin standard of unveiling (that is, the

124 *Jasamin Rostam-Kolayi and Afshin Matin-asgari*

removal of the face veil) with contemporary Euro-American standards of public dress, with the hair completely uncovered."[13]

Chehabi too equates the 1930s unveiling with the prohibition of *chador* and the headscarf, as well as encouraging Western-style dress for women. Reza Shah envisioned unveiling as a "complete westernization of dress" rather than the mere uncovering of a woman's face, which implied that women's hair would be uncovered as well.[14] Though some women, especially in the provinces, circumvented unveiling by "wearing long dresses and headscarves," local authorities were pressured to prevent such practices as tantamount to wearing the *chador*.[15] However, Chehabi and other sources are not clear as to what exactly "Western-style" dress for women implied and whether it was mandated or recommended. An abundance of photographic evidence of the period, for example those showing government employees ordered to appear with their "unveiled" wives, illustrates that officially sanctioned "unveiling" included the wearing of Western-style brimmed hats along with long coats and dresses.[16] Thus, scholarly consensus suggests that 1930s unveiling aimed at banning the *chador*, *picheh*, and headscarf, while mandating the adoption of Western-style dress. However, the scholarship remains vague on exactly how, and by whom, the 1930s unveiling campaign was conceived, as well as on how and in what language it was presented to the public and enforced on the ground.

A major point of confusion in scholarship is whether the 1930s unveiling campaign came about via legislation and/or a decree by Reza Shah. Kashani-Sabet, for example, writes that Iranian unveiling was nationally "legislated" and "decreed,"[17] while Paidar and Afary suggest it was only decreed by the shah.[18] In fact, while national dress codes for Iranian men were mandated through 1928 *Majles* legislation, modern dress codes for Iranian women came neither by national legislation nor via executive decrees, thus making Iran's unveiling campaign similar to that in Republican Turkey.[19] Chehabi and Amin note correctly that unveiling was not "enshrined in a law." According to Chehabi, this was because unveiling violated the tenets of Shi'i Islam, which Reza Shah had sworn to uphold when he took office.[20] In fact, however, Iran's 1930s *kashf-i hijab* was carefully conceived and presented as properly Islamic. Nonetheless, Chehabi rightly points out that, by this time, dress reform for both women and men was not legislated through the *Majles* but decreed by other state organs in an authoritarian fashion.[21] Furthermore, Iran's official "unveiling" campaign was launched in December 1935 when female teachers and students in girls' schools were mandated to "unveil" by the Ministry of Education.[22] Similarly, Amin locates the origin of state-mandated women's dress codes in "directives" issued by the Ministry of Education concerning the comportment of female government employees, such as public school teachers, and their students, later expanding it to require high- to mid-level civil and military officials to attend official gatherings and ceremonies with their wives "unveiled."[23]

Implicit, yet insufficiently noted, in the above accounts is the point that the 1935 directives did not mandate countrywide unveiling of Iranian women, since they were aimed only at a small minority of urban women who were

Revisiting 1930s Iran's kashf-i hijab *campaign* 125

either married to or themselves government employees. Moreover, scholarship seems to have missed the crucial point that government directives presented these new dress codes for women as fully compatible with Islamic and *shar'i* norms. In this respect, scholars appear influenced by official narratives under the Islamic Republic, which consider the 1930s unveiling a foreign-sponsored anti-Islamic conspiracy, forcibly imposed by Reza Shah on all Iranian women. Interestingly, the above narrative is undermined by a growing body of Pahlavi-era documents made available since the 1990s by research and archival institutions affiliated with the Iranian government. This contradiction is reflected in recently published source-based Persian-language studies of *kashf-i hijab*, which are more nuanced on its intellectual background, actual conception, and implementation, while still awkwardly toeing the official line. For example, studies by Mehdi Salah and Maryam Fathi frame the 1930s campaign in a larger Iranian project of modernization, noting that "unveiling" advocacy originated as a reformist project a generation before Reza Shah but was reformulated to be put into practice under the authoritarian conditions of the 1930s.[24] Salah also notes how modernist discourses critical of veiling had already converged on the removal of *chador* and *picheh*, which he agrees were dress styles not necessarily identical to Islamic notions of *hijab*.[25] Moreover, and similar to English-language scholarship, Salah and Fathi pay considerable attention to institution building and political developments preceding the 1935–36 launching of the "unveiling" campaign.

Background events, legislation and politics of *kashf-i hijab*

The events often listed as direct background to *kashf-i hijab* trace back to March 1928 (Noruz 1306), when, during a visit to Ma'sumeh Shrine in the city of Qom, the queen and a few women of the royal family were admonished by a cleric and told to leave because their face-veils were partially removed. The next day, Reza Shah went to Qom and personally punished the cleric and a few others.[26] Later in spring 1928, Reza Shah publicly received visiting Afghan King Amanollah Khan, ignoring clerical objections to the Afghan queen's "unveiled," i.e. without the chador, appearance. Amanollah Khan's overthrow the same year was seen as related to his modernizing reforms, including women's unveiling.[27] More important was the 1928 legislation mandating national dress codes for Iranian men, an event that was not only unpopular itself, but hinted at similar plans in store for Iranian women. At the same time, official conservatism with respect to women was reflected in the Marriage Law of 1931, which essentially codified *shari'a* family injunctions. The political elite's caution and hesitations regarding the "woman question" was apparent also during the Second Eastern Women's Congress officially hosted by Iran in 1932. The semi-official daily newspaper *Ettela'at* covered the congress and its goals with considerable distortion, falsely implying that Iran had accomplished everything the gathering stood for. Similar apprehensions are attributed to Reza Shah himself, who allegedly told his

126 *Jasamin Rostam-Kolayi and Afshin Matin-asgari*

advisors that even though unveiling might be necessary for "the progress of the country," he would divorce both of his two wives when the change actually came.[28]

Pahlavi-era narratives tend to cite Reza Shah's 1934 visit to Turkey as the turning point focusing his attention on "women's liberation."[29] While this visit was important in many ways, its impact on Iran's unveiling campaign must be understood in the context of legal and institution-building projects already underway, paving the ground for Iranian unveiling. In March 1934 (Esfand 1312), a few months prior to Reza Shah's departure for Turkey, the Ministry of Education announced the opening of 25 modern Teachers' Training Colleges for young men and women in Tehran, Tabriz, Isfahan, Mashhad, Shiraz, Urumieh, Kerman, and Ahvaz. Female students in these colleges were unveiled and encouraged to engage in physical activities and sports events in public. More importantly, in May 1935, the government established the Ladies' Center (*Kanun-i Banuvan*), "supported and supervised by the Ministry of Education" and with Princess Shams as its honorary head. A few years earlier, all private initiative on women's issues was banned, independent women's publications were closed, and a few vocal women activists were imprisoned. Now, the Ladies' Center was to be the sole official organization spearheading the government's version of "women's liberation." The main goals of the Ladies' Center included:

1 the intellectual and moral cultivation of women; and teaching them the scientific principles of home economics and child rearing, via lectures, publications and adult education;
2 promoting sports activities suitable to [women's] physical education according to health standards;
3 establishing charitable institutions for helping poor mothers and parentless children;
4 promoting simplicity in living [standards] and the use of national products.[30]

Studies published under the Islamic Republic, including those by Salah and Fathi, insist that the main goal of the Ladies' Center was *kashf-i hijab*, something that is also mentioned by some of the women who led the organization.[31] While this may have been the case, the organization's other goals were nevertheless real, thus framing *kashf-i hijab* within a broader authoritarian nationalist project of modernizing women's education, physical health, and moral cultivation.

Apart from the activities and goals of the Ladies' Center, English- and Persian-language narratives on *kashf-i hijab* converge on a 1935 event that immediately preceded, and hence is argued to have precipitated, its official launch. This was the 1935 violent repression in Mashhad of popular protests against the imposition of new dress codes for men. In June 1935, a Ministry of Interior directive mandated the wearing of European-style brimmed hats for all Iranian men. On July 4–6, scattered protests and strikes against this

Revisiting 1930s Iran's kashf-i hijab *campaign*   127

directive, which was rumored soon to be followed by women's unveiling, occurred in the Tehran bazaar, but were contained without much difficulty. Led by the politically complacent Ayatollah Abdolkarim Ha'eri Yazdi, Qom's clerical establishment remained quiet. However, a few days later, serious protests broke out at Gowharshad Mosque near the shrine of Imam Reza in Mashhad, which were violently crushed first by local security forces and then more forcefully by special military units from Tehran. Reported casualties vary from hundreds to several thousands, the higher figures coming from sources published under the Islamic Republic, which also interpret the Mashhad protests to have been primarily against unveiling. However, the dress code legally imposed preceding the July 1935 protests was the wearing of European-style hats by men, whereas the *kashf-i hijab* campaign remained to be inaugurated officially about six months later in January 1936. Nor does documentary evidence directly connect the Gowharshad protests to the push toward unveiling already underway in the Ladies' Center, girls' schools, and certain official events.[32]

Kashf-i hijab as defined by late 1935 ministerial directives

The first legal documents officially launching *kashf-i hijab* were two "confidential directives" (*motahhad al-mal mahramanih*) issued in mid December 1935, signed by Prime Minister and Minister of the Interior Mahmud Jam and by Minster of Education Ali-Asghar Hikmat. These documents stipulated important general definitions, guidelines, and rationale, laying the foundation for a series of further directives that were to follow. These two major directives, however, were preceded by a brief confidential Ministry of Interior directive (no. 1442) issued a few days earlier, on December 9, 1935, which stated:

> [To local] governments of Arak, Hamidan, Garrus, Malayir, Kirman-shah, Sanandaj and Golpaygan: The subject of *kashf-i hijab* must be encouraged by [local] governments and the police without forcing *kashf-i hijab* on anyone. Preachers or others who might oppose or talk against it must be immediately arrested and punished by the police. Act in a very prudent and dignified manner. Report the progress of this matter routinely via secret code.[33]

Despite its brevity, the above directive lists several key features of the *kashf-i hijab* project, including its flexibility, as well as the arguably intentional ambiguity of its objective and scope. First, as this document shows, the *kashf-i hijab* campaign originated and legally stayed within the parameters of a series of ministerial directives, primarily issued by the Ministry of Education. In other words, as argued earlier, it was neither legislated by the *Majlis* nor decreed by Reza Shah. Second, the project was a joint venture whereby the Ministry of Education set the general guidelines, whose implementation then became the responsibility of the Ministry of Interior, acting through

128 *Jasamin Rostam-Kolayi and Afshin Matin-asgari*

provincial governments and the police. The latter feature underscored the project's bureaucratic and forcible side, including punitive measures against its vocal opponents, who, as correctly anticipated by the above document, were mostly lower-ranking clerics ("preachers"). Third, according to this document, *kashf-i hijab* must be implemented in a "prudent and dignified manner," without being forced on anyone. Thus, despite punitive measures taken against its male opponents, and its forcible imposition on some women, unveiling was not to be implemented coercively or indiscriminately throughout the country. The arguably deliberate conceptual ambiguity of *kashf-i hijab* allowed for flexibility in its implementation and adaptability to various local conditions and contingencies.

Within days, the December 9 directive was followed by two longer confidential directives, the first issued by the Minister of Education (on December 16) and the second (on December 18) by the Minister of Interior who signed also as the Prime Minister. These are the most important documents on *kashf-i hijab*, whose closely overlapping content and language reveal how the project was originally conceived and presented for implementation at the highest governmental level. Signed by the Prime Minister, Directive No. 623 (December 18) was a long rejoinder to the two previous directives (December 9 and 16) of the Ministry of Education. Its preamble declared "reforming education and women's condition" among the government's top priorities. The country's "progress and civilization" was impeded as long as half of society was "covered up" (*mastur*) and barred from "science, education and social life." "Governors and administrators" were identified as primarily responsible for responding to the above challenges. The term *kashf-i hijab* appeared only once, at the end of the document. However, the directive did not explain the term's meaning beyond "the sacred goal" of educating women "to enter society," instead of being "ignorant *pardeh*-dwellers."[34] It went on to say:

> to achieve this goal, one must begin with the educational environment, meaning with female elementary school principals and their students, gradually reaching other classes. (To this effect, the Ministry of Education has given comprehensive orders to those locally in charge of education.) Elementary and other girls' schools must begin first, with government officials organizing gatherings of respectful cultivated families, where they can advance their objective in a dignified manner via morally beneficial conferences and discussions concerning chastity, hygiene, proper conduct and simplicity of dress ... . Specifically, officials must insist such actions are not mere imitation of foreigners, but necessary for the benefit of Iranian families and their country ... individuals and women of ill repute must be barred from these gatherings, and, to prevent damage to this sacred cause, prostitutes must strongly be prevented from *kashf-i hijab*.[35]

The above reference to "comprehensive orders to those locally in charge of education" apparently alluded to a more comprehensive confidential directive, issued two days earlier (December 16) by the Minister of Education. About three times longer and more detailed than the one signed by the Prime Minister, the December 16 directive had explained the objectives of *kashf-i hijab*, while also setting specific guidelines for its implementation. Moreover, it included an important physical description of what *kashf-i hijab*, as a dress code for women, meant. Addressed to those locally in charge of education across the country, the December 16 directive began with a preamble on the necessity of saving women from age-old "ignorance" and social indolence:

> similar to women in other civilized countries, [Iranian] women, who are the mothers of tomorrow's men, must enjoy the benefits of science, civilization and education, enabled to establish healthy useful families, educating brave patriotic children for the nation. To realize this noble objective, the Ministry of Education pursues a specific systematic program, a copy of which is confidentially sent to you below, so that educational endeavors within your purview follow the same program, without undue haste or sluggishness.[36]

The directive then explained the various points of its "program." The first concerned children, calling for public elementary schools across the country to be co-educational and taught by female teachers. The second focused on a dress code for female public school students, requiring that, "without exception, girls in elementary and secondary schools must wear uniforms, per instructions already given." No particular description of the "uniform" was provided, except that it had to be "clean and simple," not allowing apparent distinctions among rich and poor girls. "Whether at school, on the street or at home, they must appear in the same dress, chosen with utmost attention to chastity and good taste." It was obvious that schoolgirls' dress codes excluded the use of the *chador*, something that was mentioned implicitly: "They should know that women's moral virtue is their strongest cover/protection [*pardeh*]."[37]

The bulk of the December 16 directive consisted of its third point, centering on adult women (*khanomha*). Here, local Ministry of Education officials were to proceed in "two steps." First, they had to "educate this [particular] class of women" by organizing conferences in elementary and secondary schools, with "female teachers appearing in uniform" along with "other respectable ladies attending with their husbands," to hear lectures and presentations on "scientific, moral and social" topics. In addition to expert guest lecturers, these gatherings were to feature female high school students giving speeches and/ or reciting morally uplifting poetry. Such conferences were to teach both women and girls "socialization and dress etiquette, as is common among chaste and noble families in civilized countries." At this point, the directive explained how the newly mandated dress code was fully in accord with Iran's ancient history and Islamic character, and not an imitation of foreign norms:

In particular, you must try to impress upon them that women's dress in today's world is the same as what was customary in ancient Iran and up to the first two centuries of Islam. This is the same manner the sacred Islamic *shari'a* ordains for prayers and the *hajj*, i.e. the face and palms must remain uncovered and open. Today's revival of this beneficent old tradition is because of the innate natural and social utility of this style of dress, and not in imitation of other countries.[38]

Although these new dress codes applied only to female public school teachers and students, the directive indicated this was part of a broader national campaign to promote women's participation in society at large. To that end, the program's "second step" required local heads of police and civil government to participate in social gatherings bringing along their wives. Such family gatherings were meant to teach both men and women to interact in carefully controlled, "dignified" social settings. The directive concluded:

In carrying out this task, you must take utmost care to exclude certain unmarried, superficial young men, since these social gatherings are to be the foundation of high moral standards; otherwise, they will lead to evil consequences. This has been a summary of an extensive program, which, according to orders, is already underway in the capital and is to be implemented in the provinces, according to judgments of Ministry of Education officials, who are responsible for cultivating public morality.

Following his signature, the Minister of Education added in handwriting:

Respecting this important cause, it is specifically reiterated that you must remain within the bounds of prudence and dignity, avoiding all pretention, vulgarity, and brazenness.[39]

Numerous government documents show how the basic instructions outlined in the above two 1935 directives reached the lower echelons of the government bureaucracy across the country. For example, a December 30, 1935 confidential directive from the provincial government of Khorasan to the city government of Nishapur read:

Since, per the prime minister's orders, women's enthusiasm for modernity and cultivation, and their progress towards perfection, are to be vigorously encouraged, the following instructions are to be implemented with utmost care and attention. (Attached is a copy of the prime minister's order):

1 As in everywhere, begin by acting via education, in public schools and through the Girl Scouts and girls' physical education.
2 Acting through heads of government bureaus, encourage women's gatherings, not ostensibly for unveiling (*raf'-i hijab*), but in fact for that purpose.

Revisiting *1930s Iran's* kashf-i hijab *campaign*   131

3 Make local preachers and [religious] leaders explain the campaign's purpose to the public, proving it is not contrary to religion, and that the spirit of Islam is far from this [existing] kind of *hijab*.
4 Preachers or others opposing or speaking against *raf'-i hijab* are to be arrested and punished by the police.
5 Wives of high government officials must lead the implementation of this cause, advancing women's renewal in a reasonably appropriate manner by the simplicity of their own dress.
6 The above steps must be undertaken with utmost prudence and dignity, without forcing *kashf-i hijab* on anyone. Police and educational employees have received necessary and proper instruction from the Ministry of Education and the General Bureau of the Police. Regularly report on these undertakings' results and the advancement of this objective.[40]

Another directive, dated January 14, 1936 and signed by Minister of Finance Ali-Asghar Davar, stated explicitly that the wives of government employees in the provinces were required to attend public gatherings without the *chador*.

> Encourage the removal of *chador* by all means, especially concerning government employees ... . It is imperative that government employees attend [official] events with their wives not wearing the *chador*. Per this order, any employee of the Ministry of Finance responding to invitations without his wife, or with the wife in *chador*, must be immediately placed on leave, the matter to be taken up with the capital.[41]

The January 1936 official launch of *kashf-i hijab* and its implementation

The turning point invariably cited in narratives of Iran's *kashf-i hijab* is an event, dated January 7, 1936 (Day 17, 1314), during which Reza Shah publicly inaugurated the "unveiling" campaign. Emphasizing this event, Pahlavi-era narratives have obscured the complexity of the *kashf-i hijab* campaign, reducing it to a single symbolic act, credited entirely to Reza Shah. A paradigmatic example is *Mission for My Country*, where Mohammad-Reza Pahlavi, writes:

> My father initiated the unveiling of women (*raf'-i hijab*) ... . In 1935, veiling was banned to teachers and female students, while military officers were banned walking alongside women with hijab. Finally, on January 7, 1936, announcing *kashf-i hijab*, my father took the final step on this path, asking my mother and sisters to accompany him unveiled (*bidun-i hijab*) at an important official celebration.[42]

In the same book, Mohammad-Reza Shah defined *kashf-i hijab* as a ban on the *chador* and face veil, imposed forcibly by his father, but something he himself preferred to promote in "a democratic manner":

132 *Jasamin Rostam-Kolayi and Afshin Matin-asgari*

My father issued the order (*dastur*) for unveiling (*raf'-i hijab*). According to this order (*dastur*), women and girls were not allowed to wear *chador* or *niqab*, and women appearing with *ruband* and *chador* in public ... had their *chadors* removed forcibly (*jabran*). As long as my father ruled, this ban was observed all over the country ... . It would have been more reasonable to pursue reformist measures in a democratic manner ... . As soon as my father left the country, given the chaotic conditions of war, some women went back to their old ways, violating the rules of *kashf-i-hijab*. However, my government and I ignored such violations, preferring this issue to follow its natural course, without us resorting to force.[43]

Mohammad-Reza Shah's description of *kashf-i hijab* echoed official Pahlavi propaganda declaring January 7, 1936 as the day Reza Shah inaugurated *raf'-i hijab*, thereby "liberating" Iranian women. This event was indeed important politically in demonstrating the kind of women's public comportment, including dress, approved by Reza Shah. As we have seen, however, *kashf-i hijab* was a broader, multifaceted national project, initiated before and continuing after this event.

A few Reza Shah-era statesmen also have written about the 1934–36 unveiling campaign.[44] Arguably the most important testimony is by Ali-Asghar Hikmat who, as Minister of Education, was directly responsible for the campaign's conception and presentation to the public, as well as for supervising its initial implementation. Hikmat's account begins with a summer 1935 conversation when Reza Shah inquired about what the Ministry of Education had done regarding "uncovering women's faces" (*raf'i ru-pushidan-i zanan*). Promising quick results, Hikmat conceived and implemented a two-tiered plan. First, he gathered a group of "intellectual" women involved with the Ministry of Education to form The Ladies' Center. His second move came via a Ministry of Education program, which, acting through girls' school principals, would bring about female student participation in mixed-gender public events with "uncovered faces" (*ru-yi baz*).[45] Hikmat then related how, in early fall 1935, Reza Shah again asked him about the progress of "unveiling" (*raf'-i hijab*). At that point, he requested the shah become personally involved, setting an example:

We have acted, according to plan, and some progress has been made in preparing public opinion. Young girls now attend school with faces uncovered, but such projects by the Ministry of Education do not suffice where adult women are concerned. Here, decisive action is to be undertaken by the country's most excellent families. If His Imperial Majesty takes the initiative, everyone will follow.

Reza Shah responded: "Very well, since others don't act, I myself, though an old man, am prepared to step forward and become their example."[46] Hikmat then wrote an official letter inviting the shah, along with the queen and

Revisiting 1930s Iran's kashf-i hijab *campaign* 133

princesses, to attend that year's graduation ceremony at Tehran's Teachers' Training College. With female teachers and principals also in attendance, this would be announced "the Day of Women's Liberation."[47]

Hikmat thus claimed direct responsibility for planning the unveiling campaign, including its official inaugurating event featuring Reza Shah's public appearance with royal women unveiled. According to him, the first phase of his plan unfolded during 1935 as girls and young women participated in sports events and gave lectures at school gatherings and graduation ceremonies attended by government officials in Tehran and other cities. Reza Shah had planned the royal family's appearance at the graduation ceremonies of spring 1936. Hikmat reported, however, that on December 15, 1935, the shah ordered him to convene the ceremony sooner to show further decisiveness in confronting conservative religious forces in the wake of that summer's uprising in Mashhad.[48]

Preparations were made for this event to take place on January 7, 1936, when both male and female graduates of Tehran's Teachers' Training College were to receive their diplomas. Reza Shah presented diplomas and prizes first at a gathering of male graduates and then at a separate hall where female graduates and educational employees had gathered "unveiled" in dark-colored long dresses and hats, similar to the way in which the queen and the two princess were dressed. Hajar Tarbiyat, headmistress of the Women's Teachers' Training College, welcomed the monarch, who spoke briefly and in general terms about Iranian women's accomplishments and ability to enter society, without making references to *kashf-i hijab*, or even using the term. The "unveiled" appearance of his wife and daughters, however, showed his personal endorsement of the project.[49]

Hikmat's final recollections of January 7, 1936 record a lingering note of ambivalence on the shah's part about that day's significance. According to him, "a very pleased and jubilant" Reza Shah told a cabinet meeting that evening:

> Today the Iranian nation joined the rank of civilized countries. Europeans always criticized and scolded us because of women's hijab, their ignorance and illiteracy. Thank God, we overcame this defect too, rendering the country yet another service.

After listening to ministers expressing gratitude for his various accomplishments, the shah told them: "And yet, my greatest service to this country was instituting conscription."[50]

Finally, Hikmat's memoirs admitted to difficulties in the implementation of *kashf-i hijab*, including problems related to the use of coercion:

> Following orders by the Ministry of Interior, police and municipal officials in Tehran and government officials in other cities, bothered women, forcing them to unveil (*kashf-i hijab*), and even tearing their chadors and face-masks (*niqab*).[51]

134   *Jasamin Rostam-Kolayi and Afshin Matin-asgari*

Hikmat then recalled a meeting with the shah, soon after January 7, where he argued:

> These days the police and some civil authorities forcibly impose *kashf-i hijab* on the streets, causing women many difficulties. They bother respectable families and women who are unaware [of *kashf-i hijab*] in public, forcibly and violently removing *chadors*. Such behavior causes [negative] reactions. Thousand-year-old habits must be handled delicately, so that women can be educated gradually and willing to show their face and hands, as permitted by the *shari'a*, thus becoming naturally prepared for *kashf-i hijab*.[52]

Hikmat's memoirs did not address *kashf-i hijab*'s more long-term consequences, except for declaring it a resounding success.[53] While published government archives similarly reflect the occasional use of violence and coercion by local police, they also show, as does Hikmat's memoir, that higher government officials saw coercion as an impediment to *kashf-i hijab*. For example, a 1938 directive issued by the Minister of Interior to all provincial governors and city mayors hinted at major difficulties that the campaign faced two years into its implementation, repeating, as remedy, the official line on prudence, flexibility and non-coercion:

> Obviously, one must act with the best of intentions, propriety, and prudence. This means one cannot act the same way in Qom and Mashhad as in Rasht. However, reports indicate in certain locations, instead of being prudent, police action has been violent and impolitic, leading to complaints. Apparently, police agents have used extreme violence in removing women's headscarves *that do not cover the face to cause hijab* [emphasis added] but are worn to protect against winter cold or summer heat, as is common also in other countries. Such behavior is bound to cause problems and misunderstandings.[54]

Overall, published government documents show that, while coercion and violence against women occurred, they were discouraged officially. The official recommendation of flexibility, including the use of different approaches in dealing with particular regions and social groups, was related also to the fact that imposing a uniform dress code on Iran's entire female population would have been a practical impossibility.

Iran's *kashf-i hijab* in comparative perspective

Our closer investigation of Iran's *kashf-i-hijab* makes it appear differently in comparative perspective. First and foremost, we conclude that in three important respects, i.e. intellectual conception, legal-juridical articulation, and practical implementation, Iranian and Turkish unveiling campaigns are more similar than hitherto assumed by scholarship. First, in their intellectual

Revisiting 1930s Iran's kashf-i hijab *campaign* 135

conception, both Iranian and Turkish unveiling campaigns were carefully articulated not to violate the *shari'a*. In other words, neither campaign technically rejected Islamic *hijab* per se. While Iran's *kashf-i hijab* verged on a total ban of the *chador* and *picheh* (face-veil), the Kemalist case discouraged, without banning, the Turkish *pece*, equivalent to the Iranian *picheh*, and the Turkish *charshaf*, an overcoat-headscarf garment, similar to the Iranian *chador*.[55] As in the Iranian case, Turkish officials assumed that rural women, i.e. the majority of the population, did not cover their faces or wear the *charshaf*. Second, both Iranian and Turkish unveiling became legal not through national legislation or executive decrees, by Ataturk or Reza Shah, but via ministerial directives. Third, and again similar to Iran, the Kemalist regime began unveiling selectively, first at the level of female students, teachers, and the wives of government employees. Central authorities directing unveiling campaigns in Iran and Turkey understood the project's sensitivity, recommending to local administrators a gradualist and non-coercive approach in its implementation. The Turkish case, like the Iranian one, shows that ambiguous guidelines were provided by higher authorities to local officials, granting them considerable leeway in interpreting and enforcing the directives on unveiling.[56] Documents on Iranian *kashf-i hijab* appear to conform to what scholars of unveiling in Turkey have argued, i.e. that in practice dress reform was carried out differently throughout the country, depending on the orientation of the municipal government and realities on the ground.[57] Last but not least, the assumption that Reza Shah's unveiling campaign was more violent and far-reaching and Ataturk's less coercive and radical is not supported by available archival evidence for the Iranian case.

Related to the dearth of archival records of resistance to *kashf-i hijab* is the lack of documented opposition to the project by Iran's clerical establishment, specifically at its highest echelons. This issue is not addressed in English language studies, but admitted to in Salah's document-based study of *kashf-i hijab*. According to Salah, although prior to the 1930s several prominent clerics had intervened in debates on the veil, defending Islamic *hijab*, no major cleric issued a *fatwa* against the 1936–41 campaign.[58] He attributes this to the clerical establishment's fear of Reza Shah, who dealt with them with increasing harshness. This explanation, however, is unconvincing on two grounds. First, had the entire clerical establishment perceived the 1930s campaign as categorically anti-Islamic, it would have registered some serious opposition, at least in the form of mild complaints to Reza Shah or his officials. The complete absence, during the 1930s, of recorded clerical pronouncements against *kashf-i hijab* weakens the claim that the campaign was vehemently opposed by the clerical establishment. Second, post-1941 *fatwas* and declarations in relation to *hijab*, for example by Ayatollahs Hossayn Borujerdi and Mohammad-Taqi Khunsari, did not specifically reject 1930s laws and governmental decrees. The most specific of such documents is a 1941 letter from Ayatollah Kashani to the Ministry of Interior, in which he complained about the forcible removal of women's *chadors*.[59]

Conclusion: Reza Shah's legacy and the modernization of Islamic *hijab* (1930s–1970s)

In an important sense, Iran's 1930s *kashf-i hijab* was an enduring success, surviving the fall not only of Reza Shah but of the Pahlavi dynasty. In fact, what arguably was the core concern of 1930s *kashf-i hijab*, i.e. the uncovering of women's faces in public, has remained in effect to the present. This was accepted as Islamic by Reza Shah-era high clerics, as well as the next generation of Iran's modernizing clerics. The latter were best exemplified by the influential Ayatollah Mortiza Motahhari, whose clear endorsement of Islamic *hijab* allowing uncovered faces helped pave the way for the adoption of the same practice by the Islamic Republic of Iran. Motahhari's most direct, detailed, and specific work on this topic is *The Question of Hijab* (*Mas'alih-i hijab*), a book based on lectures he delivered to the Islamic Association of Physicians several years before the 1978–79 revolution.[60] Superficially engaged with contemporary debates on feminism and women's rights, Motahhari was apologetic regarding Iranian women's existing social status and participation in public life. On the other hand, he was quite thorough and in full command of his subject when discussing juridical (*fiqhi*) matters. Deploying a seemingly secular utilitarian argument, his narrative generally contended that uncontrolled mixing of genders leads to social corruption and women's sexual objectification and exploitation. Hence, Islam reasonably requires certain limitations on contact between genders in public, including a dress protocol for women.[61]

Motahhari's final pronouncement on Islamic *hijab*, however, was clear and well articulated. First, he noted the original meaning of *hijab* in Arabic as "curtain" (*pardih* in Persian), as well as "separation" and/or "covering." Therefore, *hijab* referred to dress only in its secondary meaning, for which Motahhari identified a clear technical definition in Islamic jurisprudence (*fiqh*).[62] According to him, there was indisputable *fiqhi* consensus, among both Sunnis and Shi'i jurists, that women's face and hands, i.e. the palm and fingers, need not be covered. Therefore, he argued, while traditional Iranian practices such as "face covering" (*ru-giriftan*) may be customary (*urfi*), they are not *fiqhi*. Motahhari's reasoning therefore was the same as Reza Shah-era directives on *kashf-i hijab*, drafted by individuals who were equally cognizant of what *fiqh* had pronounced on the subject.[63]

Thus, the ultimate irony of *kashf-i hijab* in twentieth-century Iran is its curious continuity to the present. In other words, the currently mandated *hijab* under the Islamic Republic of Iran bears more resemblance to Reza Shah-era dress codes than to pre-1930s "traditional" dress styles of Iranian women. Although the *chador*, the nemesis of the 1930s *kashf-i hijab*, continues to be worn by many Iranian women, it is in practice going out of style. Despite some early attempts, the *chador* did not become part of the mandatory dress code in the Islamic Republic, which officially adopted overcoats and various forms of "modern" head covering. Last but not least, the overlap

Revisiting 1930s Iran's kashf-i hijab *campaign* 137

in the appearances of 1930s-era forcibly unveiled Iranian women (uncovered faces, plus coats and hat) and women's current forced veiling (uncovered faces, coats and headscarf) demonstrates the similarity of Reza Shah's regime to the Islamic Republic in denying women the right to participate in social and political decision making, including in matters of dress, as free and equal citizens.

Notes

1 See Janet Afary, *Sexual Politics in Modern Iran* (Cambridge: Cambridge University Press, 2011); Camron Amin, *The Making of the Modern Iranian Woman* (Gainseville: University Press of Florida, 2002); Firoozeh Kashani-Sabet, *Conceiving Citizens* (New York: Oxford University Press, 2011); and Parvin Paidar, *Women and the Political Process in Twentieth-Century Iran* (Cambridge: Cambridge University Press, 1995).
2 Houchang Chehabi, "The Banning of the Veil and its Consequences," in *The Making of Modern Iran: State and Society under Riza Shah, 1921–1941*, ed. Stephanie Cronin (London: Routlege, 2003) and "Staging the Emperor's New Clothes: Dress Codes and Nation-Building under Reza Shah," *Iranian Studies*, vol. 26, nos. 3–4 (Summer/Fall 1993): 209–29.
3 Chehabi, "The Banning of the Veil," op. cit., p. 193.
4 See, for example, Sevgi Adak, "Anti-Veiling Campaigns and Local Elites in Turkey of the 1930s: A View from the Periphery" (Chapter 2, this volume) and Murat Metinsoy, "Everyday Resistance to Unveiling and Flexible Secularism in Early Republican Turkey" (Chapter 3, this volume).
5 Chehabi, for example, notes that *hijab* "refers not merely to the piece of clothing that protects women from the gaze of men, but also to the proper mode of interaction between the sexes." Chehabi, "The Banning of the Veil," op. cit., p. 193.
6 Edward Scott Waring, *A Tour to Sheeraz, by the Route of Kazroon and Feerozabad* (1807), p. 62, quoted by Kashani-Sabet, op. cit., p. 148.
7 Afary, op. cit., p. 44–45.
8 Chehabi, "The Banning of the Veil," op. cit., p. 194.
9 Chehabi, "The Banning of the Veil," op. cit., p. 196.
10 Afary, op. cit., p. 157.
11 Paidar, op. cit., p. 107.
12 Kashani-Sabet, op. cit., pp. 159–60, 162.
13 Amin, op. cit., p. 91.
14 Chehabi, "The Banning of the Veil," op. cit., p. 199.
15 Chehabi, "The Banning of the Veil," op. cit., p. 202.
16 See, for example, photographic images at the end of Mehdi Salah, *Kashf-i Hijab: Zamineha, Payamadha va Vakonesh* (Tehran: 2005).
17 Kashani-Sabet, op. cit., pp. 153, 156, 157, 161.
18 Paidar, op. cit., pp. 106, 107 and Afary, op. cit., p. 156.
19 See, for example, Chehabi, "Dress Codes for Men in Turkey and Iran," in *Men of Order: Authoritarian Modernization under Ataturk and Reza Shah*, eds. Touraj Atabaki and Erik J. Zürcher (London/New York: I.B. Tauris, 2004). On Turkish unveiling, see Adak (Chapter 2) in this volume.
20 Chehabi, "The Banning of the Veil," op. cit., p. 193.
21 Chehabi, "Staging the Emperor's New Clothes," op. cit., p. 215.
22 Chehabi, "Staging the Emperor's New Clothes," op. cit., p. 216.
23 Amin, op. cit., pp. 90, 99.

138 *Jasamin Rostam-Kolayi and Afshin Matin-asgari*

24 Salah, op. cit., p. 61. Maryam Fathi, *Kanun-i banuvan* (Tehran: 2002), pp. 113–20.

25 Salah begins with a discussion of the women's journal *Zaban-i Zanan* (Women's Word) and its editor and publisher Sediqeh Dowlatabadi as the first woman who discarded the *chador* in public. The women's journal *Alam-i Nesvan* (Women's World) called for Iranian women to follow the example of Turkey: "It is better that Iranian women, like those in Turkey, discard the shroud which is called *hijab* but is in fact an innovation in Islam." Salah, op. cit., pp. 27, 30, and 35.

26 Salah, op. cit., p. 130. Baqer Aqeli, *Ruzshomar-i tarikh-i Iran*, vol. 1 (Tehran: 1990), p. 155 and Fathi, op. cit., pp. 120–21.

27 Aqeli, op. cit., pp. 164–65 and Amin, op. cit., p. 82.

28 See Amin, op. cit., pp. 189–97. Reza Shah's personal aversion to unveiling was reported by Mehrangiz Dowlatshai, whose father was among the few close advisors recommending unveiling to Reza Shah. See Amin, op. cit., p. 83.

29 Issa Sadiq, *Yadigar-i omr*, vol. 2, (Tehran, 1345), pp. 301–5.

30 Fathi, op. cit., pp. 129–30.

31 Fathi, op. cit., p. 131–32 and Salah, p. 121.

32 Aqeli does not mention unveiling among the causes of the Gowharshad event, which he explains as a popular protest against the imposition of uniform dress and the "international hat." He reports the number of casualties at about 2,000. See Aqeli, op. cit., pp. 205–6. Chehabi narrates the Gowharshad event in a section titled "Veiling and the Pahlavi State," while Amin's account reflects the ambiguity of this event's relation to unveiling. See Chehabi, "The Banning of the Veil," op. cit., pp. 196–99 and Amin, op. cit., pp. 86–89. For a recent example of narratives connecting the Gowharshad protests to *kashf-i hijab*, see Hasan Shamsabadi, "Qiam-i Gowharshad" in *Faslnamih-i motali'at-i tarikhi* (Tehran), vol. 7, no. 29 (Summer 2010), pp. 115–41. This article estimates the event's casualties to have been hundreds, but less than 2,000. Like previous studies, however, the article cites no documentary evidence showing *kashf-i hijab* as a main issue during the Mashhad protests. In fact, it refers to an official government report saying the unrest began with protests against new men's dress laws. See Shamsabadi, op. cit., p.124, 128.

33 We will trace official documents as presented in a 1993 volume, most of which also appear in other collections. Iranian National Archives Organization, *Khoshunat va farhang: Asnad-i mahramanih-i kashf-i hijab* (Tehran: 1993), p. 1.

34 *Khoshunat*, p. 1.

35 *Khoshunat*, pp. 1–2.

36 *Khoshunat*, pp. 2–3.

37 *Khoshunat*, p. 3.

38 *Khoshonat*, pp. 3–4.

39 *Khoshonat*, p. 4.

40 *Khoshunat*, pp. 4–5.

41 *Khoshunat*, p. 8.

42 Mohammad-Reza Pahlavi, *Ma'muriyat baray-i vatanam* (*Mission for My Country*), quoted in Salah, op. cit., pp. 48–49.

43 Mohammad-Reza Pahlavi, *Ma'muriyat baray-i vatanam*, quoted in Center for Researching Historical Archives (Information Ministry of the Islamic Republic of Iran), National Archives, *Taghir-i lebas*, (Tehran: 2000), pp. 419–20.

44 See Isa Sadiq, *Yadigar-i 'omr*, vol. 2 (Tehran: 1965) and Ali-Asghar Hikmat, *Si khatirih az asr-i farkhondih-i Pahlavi* (Tehran: 1975). Hikmat claimed personal responsibility for the conception and legal presentation of the *kashf-i hijab* project. He wrote: "Since this author was personally involved in those events, being a witness and playing a part in that great reform, I feel obligated to summarize my extensive notes on the subject, thus presenting to history an overview of what was among that era's great accomplishments." Hikmat, *Si khatirih*, op. cit., p. 88.

Sadiq, who, at the time, was head of Tehran University and the Teachers' Training College, did not claim direct involvement in the unveiling campaign. According to him, beginning in the academic year 1935–36, the use of *chador* was banned to female students now required to wear uniforms. He also provided an eyewitness account of the January 7, 1935 event, noting how Reza Shah was accompanied by the queen and daughters Shams and Ashraf in "long black overcoats and black hats." See Sadiq, op. cit., pp. 306–10.

45 Hikmat, *Si khatirih*, op. cit., p. 89.
46 Hikmat, *Si khatirih*, op. cit., p. 91.
47 Hikmat, *Si khatirih*, op. cit., p. 92.
48 Hikmat, op. cit., pp. 92–93.
49 The event, including the shah's speech, was covered in the daily newspaper *Ettela'at* and *Ta'alim va Tarbiyat*, the official organ of the Ministry of Education. Hikmat, op. cit., pp. 92–97 and Sadiq, op. cit., pp. 310–14. The full text of Reza Shah's speech is in *Taghir-i lebas*, op. cit., pp. 132–35.
50 Hikmat, *Si khatirih*, op. cit., pp. 97–98.
51 Hikmat, *Si khatirih*, op. cit., pp. 98–99.
52 Hikmat, *Si khatirih*, op. cit., p. 100.
53 Hikmat, *Si khatirih*, op. cit., pp. 101–02.
54 *Khoshunat*, op. cit., pp. 26–27.
55 However, as Adak argues (Chapter 2, this volume), some Turkish provincial towns and cities did in fact call for a ban without central government approval.
56 See Adak (Chapter 2, this volume).
57 See Adak and Metinsoy (Chapters 2 and 3 in this volume).
58 Salah, op. cit., pp. 26–30.
59 Salah, op. cit., pp. 185–89 and 278–88.
60 See Morteza Motahhari, *Mas'alih-i hijab* (Tehran: n.d.), a widely influential book that had reached its forty-first printing in 1993, 15 years after Motahhari's death.
61 Motahhari, op. cit., pp. 51–65, 92–95.
62 Motahhari, op. cit., p. 78. Furthermore, he noted that the Qur'anic use of the term *hijab* occurs in verse 54 of the chapter "*Ahzab*," where it is not clearly defined, yet has a specific context and application referring to the prophet's wives, op. cit., pp. 80–81.
63 Motahhari, op. cit., pp. 184–86, 192.

Figure 1 Women of Kokand, Uzbekistan, wearing *paranji* and *chachvon*, early twentieth century
Source: (Mary Evans / John Massey Stewart Collection)

Figure 2 Man in traditional clothing accompanied by two women with their face veils drawn aside, Iran, late nineteenth / early twentieth century
Source: (Courtesy of the Institute for Iranian Contemporary Historical Studies)

Figure 3 Egyptian woman on a donkey
Source: (Fotografia Egiziana / Luigi De Michele, c. 1890, Anahita Gallery, Inc. Santa Fe, New Mexico, USA)

Figure 4 Two Egyptian women heavily veiled
Source: (Fotografia Egiziana / Luigi De Michele, c. 1890, Anahita Gallery, Inc. Santa Fe, New Mexico, USA)

Figure 5 Veiled African Muslim women, presumably ex-slaves, photographed in Constanta, Romania, c. 1910s / 1920s
Source: (Mary Evans / Grenville Collins Postcard Collection)

Figure 6 Turkish woman from Smyrna (Izmir), 1907, wearing the newly fashionable transparent white chiffon yashmak
Source: (Mary Evans / Grenville Collins Postcard Collection)

Figure 7 Three veiled Turkish women showing their ankles and with semi-transparent veils, early 1920s
Source: (Mary Evans / Grenville Collins Postcard Collection)

Figure 8 Schoolgirls wearing *chadors*, but without face-veils, over fashionable Western clothing
Source: (Maynard Owen Williams, National Geographic Creative, October, 1931)

Figure 9 Veiled Muslim women at Sarajevo market, Bosnia, 1930s
Source: (Mary Evans Picture Library)

Figure 10 Veiled Muslim women, Bulgaria, 1930s
Source: (Mary Evans Picture Library)

Figure 11 Some leading figures and army commanders with their wives in an official ceremony held in Iran on the anniversary of removal of veils
Source: (Courtesy of the Institute for Iranian Contemporary Historical Studies)

Figure 12 Women athletes parading, Turkey, 1936
Source: (Mary Evans / Grenville Collins Postcard Collection)

5 Dressing up (or down)

Veils, hats, and consumer fashions in interwar Iran

Firoozeh Kashani-Sabet

Iranians of the interwar era expressed some of their ambivalence about culture and politics through attire. The unveiling campaign of 1936 was perhaps the most controversial expression of this culture war. As new textile industries and institutes of fashion design opened up, Iranians had to confront the economic impact of these businesses on ordinary citizens. The unveiling campaign represented more than just a break with religion. It created new career opportunities and commercial possibilities for Iranian women and men in an increasingly global and interconnected market.

The literature on veiling has understandably centered on the religious framework in Iran and reflects the tug of war between secularism and religion. This essay, while acknowledging the salience of Islamic dress, and its rejection, as a statement of Iran's uneasy transition to a more secular society during the interwar era, also considers the new economic processes that seemingly facilitated the modern Iranian fashions of this period. As consumers, women and men showed an eagerness to experiment with new modes of dress and appearance, and these choices guided the growth of fashion industries during the interwar years.

Fashion became a revealing political statement because of its public visibility and because the Pahlavi state had relied on attire to forge a new culture of consumption and modernity for its citizens. This essay differs from previous studies on the anti-veiling/veiling movement by expanding the analytical framework to consider the economic and consumer possibilities that these dictates created and to understand the ways in which consumers maneuvered around the top-down directives on clothing.

Qajar textiles and fashions

Historically, Iran had developed a sophisticated trade in both wool and silk, used in the production of Persian dress.[1] The production of silk was apparently "so considerable," that even after significant quantities of silk had been used to make shawls, belts, ribbons, and other objects a surplus remained and was exported.[2] Silk and wool had also been key exports, but by the end of the eighteenth century Iran's textiles had lost their competitive edge and become indiscernible from rival products. Trade on the Silk Road and manifold invasions had introduced new tastes to the Persian wardrobe.[3] Sir John Malcolm

150   *Firoozeh Kashani-Sabet*

remarked on these changes during his travels to Iran at the dawn of Qajar rule. He noted that Persian men no longer wore turbans, but "a long cap covered with lamb's wool," and that city dwellers enjoyed "dressing richly." Malcolm described men's garments as made up of "chintz, silk, or cloth, and are often trimmed with gold or silver lace." None other than the king customarily wore jewels, whose resplendence, according to Malcolm, the shah's subjects appreciated.[4] Women wore "pantaloons of enormous width, hanging down to their heels, and a short dress, reaching to the knee; their whole figure is shrouded in a black veil, and their faces are thickly bedaubed in paint."[5]

Another traveler observed that the rich often wore shirts of red silk, and some also opted for wearing vests of different textures during the winter and summer months. Women leaving their homes often appeared in public draped in a long robe of either cotton or muslin. They benefited from a variety of headdresses, as compared to some European women, and the shawls used for adorning the head took "a thousand different forms."[6] Women in tribes who lived in tents were "seldom veiled" and viewed as industrious as compared with urban women.[7]

Iranians of the Qajar era used various rich fabrics to produce their dress. The wealthy frequently opted for silk, while the majority of the population also used cotton, which was largely imported into the country by the end of the nineteenth century. James Justinian Morier reported that Persians he had encountered preferred dark hues, including "[b]rowns, dark olives, bottle greens, and dark blues."[8] Foreign producers, such as the Russians, for example, often relied upon a cadre of "Russo-Persian" subjects from the Caucasus to report on Persian tastes and fashion needs. Such products then flooded Iran's northern markets, which were dominated by Russian goods. Iranians showed a desire for foreign products. The rich apparently had agents in England and France, while others managed to find European merchandise in Istanbul's markets.[9] One writer even reported that Iranian women had originated high heels, invented to protect their feet from the hot sand.[10]

Isabella Bird, who traveled with the Bakhtiyari tribe for a time, reported that Bakhtiyari women dressed themselves in "loose blue cotton trousers drawn in at the ankles, short open chemises, and short open jackets." In addition, they used a "black or coloured kerchief," drawn either in the front or behind to cover the head.[11] She also noted that tribeswomen produced basic outfits for themselves and other family members "except the felt coats, sewing with needles like skewers and very coarse loosely-twisted cotton thread. They sew backwards, i.e. from left to right, and seem to use none but a running stitch. Everywhere they have been delighted with gifts of English needles and thread, steel thimbles, and scissors."[12] Travelers to Iran brought with them new possibilities for the fashion industry. For example, Charles Wills, a physician connected to the British telegraph service in Iran, reported that a "sewing-machine company has set up a dépôt with many machines."[13] An American physician in Iran, James Bassett, citing an annual report from 1884 on the American Presbyterian mission's work with girls in Iran, wrote that several "of the girls were taught to cut and fit and to sew on the sewing-machine."[14] Jacob Baba Yohannan reported that women in Iran not only collected cotton and wool, but they spun and wove it into clothing as well. Although the sewing machine had made its way into Iran, it had not, by 1901, been "domesticated."[15]

Iran imported a significant amount of British cotton cloth to meet the sartorial needs of its inhabitants.[16] Although Iran produced domestic cotton cloth, most notably in Isfahan, such fabrics were made by hand and cost consumers more money to purchase than British cloth. This competition undermined the Persian domestic industry as foreign goods, even if of inferior quality, became accessible to a wide population. Foreign producers of various fabrics paid attention to Persian tastes: cotton fabrics had "strong colors"; cretonne fabrics displayed "birds or soldiers." Iranians also used sheets in their daily consumption, much of which was imported from Austria. Sheets tended to be in solid color, and coarse to endure regular usage. They were used even as nightclothes, given that Iranians did not have separate night-time outfits.[17]

Other commodities upon which Iranians depended to produce clothing included silk and wool principally manufactured in Khorasan and Kerman. For centuries, Iranian silk had been one of the country's main export commodities, but a silkworm disease all but destroyed Iran's silk industry in the nineteenth century.[18] In the early nineteenth century, Antoine Guillaume Olivier observed that, after silk, Iranians consumed wool in large quantities and used wool from sheep and lambs to make headgear or to drape themselves with it.[19] Wool from Khorasan was exported to Russia and the Caucasus, while Kerman wool made its way to Bombay and also to the merchants of Basra. In Isfahan, the weaving industry suffered a blow as European imports entered the market.[20] To compete with foreign products, which had different designs, Iranian weavers altered their patterns and produced inferior goods that ultimately hurt their industry.[21]

As the Iranian economy faced pressure from foreign goods, Iranian writers and merchants increasingly urged both the elite and the masses to consume Persian manufactured products, especially in meeting their daily fashion needs. Khan-i Khanan, a Qajar courtier who had written a reformist treatise, noted in his work that promotion of local industries remained a key to securing the country's economic independence.[22] Building factories for cotton production ranked high among industries that supported Iranian self-sufficiency.[23] The attention to cotton production was significant, as a French analysis of Iranian trade with Great Britain and India found that key Persian imports from those regions included tea, cotton products, spices, and indigo.[24]

Consumer tastes and women's attire, 1906–21

The constitutional revolution, although known for ushering in a different political framework for the country, also unleashed some of the tensions between the forces of tradition and modernity in its depiction of women's attire. Most historians have considered women's activism during the

152 *Firoozeh Kashani-Sabet*

constitutional period.[25] To complement their studies, a brief look at women's fashion and consumer tastes can map out another dimension of women's lives during these turbulent years.

While the cartoon journalists of the era frequently depicted ordinary women in veils, they experimented with new and revealing fashions for women through their portrayal of the Iranian homeland as a young and unveiled woman.[26] The depiction of women, whether veiled or otherwise, in the constitutional press showed the various styles and patterns of veiling. While some cartoonists depicted women in black veils, others showed some variety in the selection of fabrics for women's *chadors*.[27]

The forces of tradition and modernity battled one another not only in the context of dress, but also in the sphere of female education, which included instruction of skills in knitting and sewing. In 1907, one female writer lamented that traditionally female crafts such as sewing had its limitations as women were not being allowed to learn how to stitch with sewing machines.[28] Iranian women had few opportunities for schooling during the constitutional years, despite the opening of several schools for girls.[29] However, many Iranians found ways to express and meet their fashion needs. The burgeoning print culture of constitutional Iran gave rise to a new form of consumerism through advertisements. One women's journal, for example, contained a notice that a clothing store housed "all sorts of modern stylish outfits for women and men." The advertiser even offered to sew custom-made outfits from illustrations in books at a reasonable price.[30] Another announcement in the same issue advertised the services of a women's clothing factory that also promised to produce fashionable garments.[31] Elements of good housekeeping for Iranian women included sewing.[32]

The reliance on advertisements in the periodical press signaled a novel approach to entrepreneurship in Iran. Announcements for books had previously appeared in early Qajar newspapers. For example, the newspaper, *Vaqa'ih Ittifaqiyyah*, carried several notices between 1268 A.H./1851 and 1270 A.H./1853 that the *Shahnamah* had been reproduced and put on sale at a local printer's.[33] By the turn of the century, ads for public services such as tailoring also appeared in Persian newspapers, though still relatively few in number. Print ads attempted to persuade potential shoppers and to shape their consumer habits. They also played a role in popularizing "modern" fashions for Iranian women and men of the era, whose attire became targets of these early advertising efforts. Published notices for goods and services also reflected editors' choices and preferences. Iranian fashion announcements from the constitutional era typically lacked illustrations, unlike Ottoman ones, though they appeared with regularity in specific journals.[34]

However, women's journals contained other images that warned women against buying goods from peddlers. One cartoon depicts a female peddler carrying her child on her back. She claimed to be a fortune-teller promising talismans to women seeking good luck for marriage and otherwise. At the same time, she offered drugs purporting to relieve infertility, toothaches, and

Dressing up (or down) in interwar Iran 153

eye ailments, as well as hair dye, creams, dried fruits, and nuts. One of the women engaged in conversation is warning her friend not to be swayed by the spurious promises of the peddler.[35] The absence of a robust advertising culture did not prohibit peddlers and other vendors from bartering their goods in creative ways.

After the Russian ultimatum of 1911 brought an end to constitutional rule, Iran braced for the Great War. While several newspapers existed during this interval, we have few accounts of women's activities. However, the American Presbyterian Board of missions reported in its annual report that the wife of the governor of Urumiyah had attended the commencement ceremonies of the Fiske Seminary "with uncovered head and European dress and several others followed her example." Of the Muslims attending the ceremony, "only one" wore the chador and Islamic dress.[36] A few years later, in 1922, American missionary Robert Elliott Speer reported that "the old limitations of woman's dress have not been thrown aside, but they have greatly relaxed, and the women are increasingly careless in covering their faces."[37] Speer further speculated that the unveiling of women in Constantinople would likely have a "great effect" on Muslim women in Iran.[38] Whatever the impact of unveiling paradigms elsewhere in the Middle East, Iran would try out novel styles of dress in the ensuing years.

Fashion and social order, 1921–41

Iran emerged from the war years bruised but eager to pay attention to setting cultural norms, including the regulation of its citizens' outward appearance, as well as to articulating economic priorities. In September 1923, the city of Tehran hosted an exposition to promote indigenous goods. Vendors and participants were asked to submit samples of products to be displayed to the appropriate authorities. Domestic textiles products approved for the exposition included footwear (boots, galoshes, and the like), as well as silk and wool cloths, embroideries such as golduzi from Rasht, shawls from Kerman, *zaris*, and other delicate fabrics. In addition, items of clothing such as robes, jackets, *abas* (religious robes), furs, and ties were also to be displayed at the show.[39] The exposition was convened in the "vicinity of the bazaar and which had been tented over." Approximately 40 to 50 booths had been assembled to promote the industries of various Iranian provinces.[40] Local merchants continued to echo this call for the promotion of indigenous goods. In 1926, for example, the union of guilds in Isfahan issued an announcement entitled, "The Homeland is in Danger," and criticized Iranians' reliance on imports for meeting their day-to-day nutrition and clothing needs.[41] Another similar notice was issued with the title, "Islam is in danger." The demand for the consumption of domestic goods had acquired a patriotic, and anti-foreign, dimension that seemed somewhat incongruous when juxtaposed against the backdrop of the increasingly accepting attitude that Iranian literati had taken toward the blending of Western and Persian sartorial tastes. The arrival of

154 *Firoozeh Kashani-Sabet*

European tailors in Tehran had influenced Persian designs as Western tailors introduced new fashion styles to Iranians.[42]

Like other institutions of social indoctrination in interwar Iran, schools played a crucial role in executing some of the cultural objectives of the state, including its emphasis on the homogeneity of citizenship and secularism in public life. Modern girls' schools reinforced traditional crafts such as sewing and housekeeping.[43] One schoolbook approved for use in girls' schools taught students the differences between pins and needles needed for tailoring.[44] Another schoolbook for girls in the 1920s offered insights on attire. This source recommended that clothing be comfortable and loose enough to allow for easy blood flow. Public attire also needed to conform to a country's norms of dress in order not to make one an object of ridicule.[45]

In 1929, the committee on education approved a set of regulations for elementary and middle schools. Recommendations included the use of simple outfits by all students. Beauty products and other expensive accessories were forbidden to students at such educational facilities. At girls' schools all employees were prohibited from wearing "open" and sleeveless ("décolleté") outfits.[46] Despite such regulations, some Iranian women took risks with their public appearances and experimented with unveiling. In 1929, Jane Doolittle, principal of the American Girls' School in Tehran, reported that, for graduation ceremonies that year, which included two Persian girls and one Turkish girl, the graduates "appeared on the commencement platform without their customary veils." Although the girls "feared the result for us," there was apparently no noticeable backlash from this decision.[47]

Iran lacked a consistent and rational policy toward attire in the early Pahlavi period, though it chose to enforce secularism in part through a public embrace of Western-influenced modes of dress. From military outfits for the army to mandating headgear for men, Iranian policymakers relied on international fashion to make domestic cultural and political statements. Given the dearth of precedence, Iranian officials dictated dress codes for many of the country's newly established institutions. Such policies not only effaced individuality, they reduced the possibility of social revolt through uniformity of dress. As a result, men and schoolboys also had to abide by comparable dress codes.[48]

Historical accounts and scholarly analyses have persuasively demonstrated that the unveiling of Iranian women occurred through a gradual process. Even before the unveiling campaign of 1936 had been launched, travelers and other observers, as noted above, had recorded episodes of unveiling by individual Persian women. However, after 1926, the state took specific legal measures directed at defining the public appearance of women and men— steps that ultimately culminated in the unveiling law of 1936. Beginning in 1928, a uniform dress code was authorized for Iranian men, who were also ordered to wear the Pahlavi hat.[49] That same year, revised police regulations allowed Persian women to be admitted to "cinemas, restaurants and other public places," and these policies also

Dressing up (or down) in interwar Iran 155

granted them the right to speak to men in the streets, to ride with men in carriages (with the top down), and, more important than all, authorized police protection for those Moslem women who might choose to appear unveiled in public.[50]

Even military men were enjoined to comply with the new regulations concerning their outfits. In 1931, the shah "ordered all employees of the Ministry of War ... to put on homespun clothing."[51]

Other measures included the abolition of the Pahlavi hat and its replacement with an international hat, for which new regulations were created. The "casque colonial" would be available in the two colors of black and white and could only be worn during the summer months from sunrise to sunset. Straw hats were also permissible during the summer months. These changes in men's headgear generated some confusion and became the topic of debate in the daily newspaper, *Ittila'at*. One reader had applauded the paper's editorial office for clarifying some of the ambiguity surrounding the hats.[52] Because the public lacked familiarity with these new-fangled fashion norms, the state had to instruct men in proper hat decorum. For example, hats needed to be removed promptly upon entry into indoor spaces, and, when greeting someone in the streets, gentlemen needed to doff their headgear out of courtesy.[53] In other words, Iranian men were taught to imitate their European counterparts, not only in attire, but also in etiquette.

For women, scouting provided another opportunity to experiment with the state's social and fashion directives.[54] In 1935, Iran launched a girl scouts' movement with 12 participants.[55] Shortly thereafter, several girls' schools enrolled representatives in the scouting program, eventually expanding membership to several hundred individuals. Girl scouts, like other participants in Iran's cultural programs, abided by specific dress codes, in this case, an attire approved by the international scouting organization. Scouting, though not always popular, became another way for the Pahlavi state to nudge women into trying out different female fashions.[56]

Similarly, on February 24 1936 the education ministry issued regulations for formal regalia to be worn at specified social functions convened by the newly founded University of Tehran. Each school of the university had a different color: The schools of medicine and dentistry, for example, sported an orange ceremonial dress, while the school of literature had a bluish-green robe.[57]

The interwar years proved a time of fashion experimentation for Iran – a social process that unfolded in people's wardrobes. Countless government memos dealt with seemingly petty matters of public attire such as the legality of wearing a hat without rims in the evening.[58] When assessing the unveiling campaign of 1936, it is important to consider this movement as part of the Pahlavi regime's pervasive interest in mandating appropriate modes of public attire and appearance. While unveiling became the most bitter and contested manifestation of the controversy over the state's efforts to dictate dress codes,

156 *Firoozeh Kashani-Sabet*

it was certainly not the only realm in which such indoctrination and control had taken place.

On January 7 1936, when the unveiling campaign began, official ceremonies marked the momentous occasion with platitudes to Reza Shah, while in the provinces and parts of the capital people protested the order. The manifestation of dissent, particularly religious opposition to the unveiling campaign, has been amply documented in studies of modern Iran and remains a hot-button topic.[59] Despite the ways in which the unveiling campaign divided Iran, the movement leading up to its promulgation had also created new commercial opportunities. These economic openings offered women and men a degree of choice and ownership of the top-down cultural processes that had seemingly all but stifled their individualism and capacity for entrepreneurship.

From fashion community to industry, 1925–45

It is perhaps imprecise to mention the existence of a "fashion industry" in Iran as the century turned. Iranian fashions originated and existed within the textile and manufacturing industries. Clothing was both decorative and utilitarian, but there were few opportunities during the Qajar era for the mass production and advertisement of fashions. The interwar years, by contrast, witnessed the development of a burgeoning fashion community in Iran, supported by the creation of vocational and crafts schools and popularized through the expanding print medium. In particular, ads appeared with frequency in journals and in the daily newspaper, *Ittila'at*. Women became icons in advertisements for the sale of products such as fabrics or sewing machines as patterns of consumption in Iran became increasingly gendered.[60]

As the state mandated different modes of dress, tailors and fashion designers were quick to jump on these opportunities to market their goods and services. In 1928, for example, when the men were ordered to don the Pahlavi hat, one shopkeeper tried to entice men into the store by urging them to refurbish their wardrobe to complement the Pahlavi hat. As its caption read: "An Attractive Hat Requires an Attractive Outfit."[61] Notices for retail goods geared toward men and women appeared as well.[62]

The apparent rise in the number of tailors and fashion retailers during interwar Iran, as gauged by printed advertisements and assorted announcements in newspapers and journals, had something to do with the content of women's education and the opening of industrial schools that supported, first, the creation of a fashion community and, eventually, the emergence of a fashion industry. By "fashion community," I mean the collective involvement of various entities that generated a fashion-conscious society by mid-century. Participants of the fashion community included industries that facilitated textile production (cloth, dyeing) related to fashion in Iran, as well as advertisers, small retailers, and consumers.

Women became early targets of the fashion industry as the curriculum in girls' schools contained a unit on attire (*libas*), while boys' schools lacked

Dressing up (or down) in interwar Iran 157

instruction in such areas. As part of a young girl's training, she was instructed to understand the differences among various fabrics and furs; to recognize clothing appropriate to various seasons; and the maintenance of clothes, hats, and shoes.[63] In the middle schools girls received a three-year course of study in tailoring (*khayyati*) that taught them to sew a range of appropriate outfits for newborns and for preschoolers, differentiating their needs by gender, as well as instruction in the preparation of workout clothes for exercise. The third-year sewing class was more sophisticated, as young girls had to design and cut samples based on patterns. The samples were then tested on mannequins. Attention was paid to the design of sleeves and shirt collars, in part based on the type of fabric used.[64]

Adult education allowed Iranians to gain proficiency in opening and managing factories, and the state regulated the content of industrial education by offering instruction in basic engineering skills such as the building of factories, electrical work, arithmetic, and physics.[65] Fields that dovetailed with fashion included centers that taught dyeing techniques (*rang-razi*). The Learning Institute for Dyeing (*amuzishgah-i rang-razi*) held classes that educated students not only about the techniques and chemistry of dyeing, but also about wool and silk cultivation and production in preparation for dyeing.[66] In addition, the program for the Art Institute of Weaving (*hunaristan-i nassaji*), which was approved in 1939, offered training in spinning thread, as well as in silk and cotton knitting and production. These independent, yet broadly interrelated, educational facilities brought clothing and textile production to the fore and helped to create a fashion community in Iran.[67]

Women remained targets of crafts related to fashion such as knitting and sewing. To provide assistance to indigent girls, and to make them more marriageable, a boarding institute for the arts was inaugurated in 1938. The boarding Arts Institute trained young girls in housekeeping and offered courses in sewing, hat-making, knitting, and the like. The Arts Institute aimed not only at preparing women for vocations specific to fashion, but also at making them appear industrious and eventually worthy of marriage. As it argued, "If a woman does not know housekeeping, she will not be able to dominate her life and home and will end up with a dark future."[68] A woman's knowledge of sewing, knitting, and the like apparently enabled her to make a positive impression before a suitor and ultimately acquire a better life partner.

At the same time that fashion-related learning centers opened up in Tehran and elsewhere, numerous factories began operations throughout the country. In 1938, an exhibit showcased the products of two fabric and weaving industries of Isfahan from the Vatan and Zayandeh Rud factories, which highlighted the recent progress made in these areas. The exhibit displayed a range of clothes for purchase, an exchange made possible because women, through schools and other media, had become fashion-savvy and better informed consumers of fashion. In fact, the advertisement for the exhibit specifically addressed women. It read: "All of the women of Iran can become chic." The factory owners had put on sale numerous products including spools of thread

158   *Firoozeh Kashani-Sabet*

and fabric, claiming that their products surpassed all others in terms of style and endurance. Factory owners saw ample opportunities for profit through the state's emphasis on modern fashions and showed marketing know-how in packaging their goods.[69] Another entrepreneur announced the opening of a joint-stock silk company (*shirkat-i sahami-yi harir*), inviting Iranians to buy shares worth up to 1 million rials of the business.[70] One writer noted the popularity of silk with female consumers and lauded the opening of silk factories as a way of improving the country's economic conditions. According to this source, consumers not only expected to eat well, they also strove "to dress well."[71] Another observer remarked that "day after day the amount of factories operational throughout different regions of the country increased," enabling bazaars and stores to stock up with attractive products.[72] Occasionally, though, factories lacked necessary personnel to provide key services. One factory for spinning and knitting fabric in Bushehr had reportedly needed a manager to oversee its dyeing machinery.[73]

Iran imported commodities related to fashion such as shoe polish, threads, and indigo during these years.[74] Advertisements for unconventional fashion needs, like girdles, also appeared in print and likely in response to women's demands.[75] As before, seamstresses and retailers publicized their services in the printed medium for widespread consumption, reaching more audiences than ever before. Tailors increasingly competed for their share of the burgeoning fashion industry and relied upon school certification to tout their special abilities and to assert market dominance, as well as to convince consumers of the superiority of their products and services. Khanbaba Khan Darvish and his brother, for example, noted in their announcement that they had received their diploma in design and cutting (*boresh*) from Paris.[76] In 1938, another resourceful clothier, Mohammad Darab, marketed his modern sewing arts institute (*hunaristan-i khayyati*) by featuring his qualifications as a tailor and his certification from a Paris fashion institute. Darab tried to entice customers to his studio by also making available a copy of his book on the fundamentals of sewing. As Darab recognized, fashion had created new commercial partnerships. Consumers had a choice of stores, goods, and services available to them as they satisfied their personal tastes and complied with the changing public expectations of etiquette and attire. While interwar Iran did not regulate fraudulent advertising, women could rely in part on their schooling and common sense to make their way through the treacherous quarters of Iran's complex and expanding fashion industry.

Conclusion

Iran's fascination with attire and public appearances generated a culture of fashion consciousness and consumption. Even in the absence of state-regulated sartorial prerogatives, Iranians of the Qajar era had developed simple patterns of attire that emphasized modesty, comfort, and practicality. The constitutional revolution triggered a *kulturkampf* between the forces of tradition and

Dressing up (or down) in interwar Iran 159

modernity that eventually played out in the politics of dress. The Pahlavi regime took this battle to a new level as it dictated dress codes for individuals partaking of the many new state-sponsored institutions of learning, communications, and social services. The unveiling campaign of 1936 was the culmination of a decade-long process of top-down cultural change that viewed attire as an instrument of public manipulation and control.

Despite the rigid and sometimes confusing dress codes that emerged during the interwar years, Iranians managed to show resourcefulness in finding commercial opportunities and expanding personal choice through fashion. Some even saw the humor in the obsession that the politics of dress had created.[77] Scholars have rightly criticized the mandatory unveiling of women and the other fashion regulations of the early Pahlavi years for their shortsightedness and unnecessary intrusion into people's personal lives. Perhaps unwittingly, the obsession with attire also gave rise to new industries, modes of economic production, and commercial ingenuity that defied Iran's controlled political climate and subtly expanded consumers' choices in the marketplace of fashion and ideas.

Notes

1 For a history of Persian silk (though not attire) in the Safavid era, see Rudi Matthee, *The Politics of Trade in Safavid Iran: Silk for Silver, 1600–1730* (1999).
2 Guillaume-Antoine Olivier, *Voyage dans l'Empire Othoman, l'Egypte et la Perse, fait par ordre du gouvernement, pendant les six premières années de la République* (1807), p. 182.
3 Jill Condra, *The Greenwood Encyclopedia of Clothing Through World History*, Volume 1 (2008), pp. 67–68.
4 Sir John Malcolm, *The History of Persia, from the Most Early Period to the Present Time*, Vol. 2, (1815), p. 549.
5 Moritz von Kotzebue, *Narrative of a Journey into Persia, in the Suite of the Imperial Russian Embassy, in the year 1817*, (1819), p. 181.
6 Guillaume-Antoine Olivier, *Voyage dans l'Empire Othoman, l'Egypte et la Perse, fait par ordre du gouvernement, pendant les six premières années de la république*, vol. 5, p. 262.
7 For a sophisticated and fascinating discussion of Persian women's attire during various epochs, see Jennifer Scarce, *Women's Costumes of the Near and Middle East* (2003), pp. 132–81.
8 James Justinian Morier, *A Journey Through Persia, Armenia, and Asia Minor to Constantinople, in the Years 1808 and 1809* (1816), p. 242.
9 Belgique. Ministère des Affaires Etrangères. *Recueil Consulaire Contenant les Rapports Commerciaux des Agents*, vol. 72, (1891), p. 355.
10 "Origin of High Heels: They Were First Made of Wood and were Invented in Persia," *Los Angeles Times (1886–1922)*, 23 April 1891, p. 4.
11 Isabella Bird, *Travels in Persian and Koordistan* (2004), p. 107.
12 Isabella Bird, *Travels*, op. cit., p. 112.
13 Charles Wills, *Persia as It Is* (1886), p. 310. The journal, *Echo de Perse,* also contained references to the Singer sewing machine for Iranian consumption.
14 James Bassett, *Persia: Eastern Mission, a Narrative of the Founding and Fortunes of the Eastern Persia Mission* (1890), p. 280.
15 Jacob Baba Yohannan, *Woman in the Orient* (1901), pp. 106–07.

160 *Firoozeh Kashani-Sabet*

16 Willem Floor, *Textile Imports into Qajar Iran: Russia Versus Great Britain, The Battle for Market Domination* (2009); ibid., *The Persian Textile Industry in Historical Perspective, 1500–1925 (Moyen Orient et Ocean Indien XVIe–XIXe s)* (1999).

17 *Recueil Consulaire* (1891), p. 356.

18 *Recueil Consulaire* (1891), p. 364.

19 Olivier, *Voyage dans l'Empire Othoman, l'Egypte et la Perse*, op. cit., p. 183.

20 Robert Chenciner and Magomedkhan Magomedkhanov, "Persian Exports to Russia from the Sixteenth to the Nineteenth Century," *Iran*, Vol. 30 (1992), pp. 123–30.

21 Thomas Phillip, "Isfahan 1881–91: A Close-up View of Guilds and Production," *Iranian Studies*, Vol. 17, No. 4 (Autumn 1984), p. 402.

22 Khan-i Khanan, "Risalah-i dar siyasat," (Manuscript, Kitabkhanah-i Milli, no. RF 385), p. 147.

23 *Subh-i Sadiq*, No. 37, 20 May 1907.

24 *Bulletin du Comité de l'Asie Française*, Vol. 7 (1907), p. 454.

25 For studies of women in the constitutional period, see Mangol Bayat-Philipp, "Women and Revolution in Iran, 1905–11," in Lois Beck and Nikki Keddie, eds., *Women in the Muslim World* (1978); Janet Afary, "On the Origins of Feminism in Early 20th-Century Iran," *Journal of Women's History*, 1 (Fall 1989), pp. 65–87; Eliz Sanasarian, *The Women's Rights Movement in Iran* (New York: Praeger, 1982); Afsaneh Najmabadi, "Women or Wives of the Nation?" *Iranian Studies*, 26 (1993); Huma Natiq, "Nigahi bih barkhi nivishtiha va mubarizat-i zanan dar dawran-i mashrutiyat, *Kitab-i Jum'a* 30 (1979), pp. 45–54; Abdul Husayn Nahid, *Zanan-i Iran dar junbish-i mashrutiyat* (Saarbrucken: Nuvid, 1989). For an excellent article on women under the Qajars, see Mansoureh Ettehadieh, "Zan dar jami'ah-i qajar," *Kilk*, 55–56 (Fall 1373/1994), pp. 27–50. Also, F. Kashani-Sabet, *Conceiving Citizens: Women and the Politics of Motherhood in Iran* (2011).

26 For example, *Tanbih*, Nos. 18 and 19, 1329/1911, p. 2. Also, F. Kashani-Sabet, *Frontier Fiction: Shaping the Iranian Nation, 1804–1946* (1999), chap 4; and A. Najmabadi, *Women with Mustaches and Men without Beards: Gender and Sexual Anxieties of Iranian Modernity*, (2005).

27 See *Shikufah bih Inzimam-i Danish: Nakhustin Nashriyah'hayah Zanan-i Iran* (Tehran: Kitabkhanah-i Milli-yi Jumhuri-yi Islami-yi Iran, 1377/1999). Numerous depictions of women in this edited collection of Persian women's newspapers show them in chadors of various styles. My references to *Shikufah* and *Danish* in this essay are taken from this important edited volume.

28 *Tamaddun*, No. 15, 27 Rabi' al-Avval 1325/10 May 1907, p. 3.

29 Parvin Paidar, *Women and the Political Process in Twentieth-Century Iran* (1995); Camron Amin, *The Making of the Modern Iranian Woman: Gender, State Policy, and Popular Culture, 1865–1946* (2002); Afsaneh Najmabadi, *Women With Mustaches,* op.cit.; Hamideh Sedghi, *Veiling, Unveiling, and Reveiling* (2006); Nikki Keddie, *Women in the Middle East: Past and Present* (2007); Janet Afary, *Sexual Politics in Modern Iran* (2009); Rostam-Kolayi, Jasamin, "Expanding Agendas for the 'New' Iranian Woman: Family Law, Work, and Unveiling," in Stephanie Cronin, ed., *The Making of Modern Iran: State and Society under Riza Shah, 1921–1941* (2003), pp. 164–89; Kashani-Sabet, *Conceiving Citizens*, op. cit.; and ibid., "Patriotic Womanhood: The Culture of Feminism in Modern Iran, 1900–941," *British Journal of Middle Eastern Studies* 32, no. 1 (2005), pp. 29–46. All these works have addressed veiling and other discourses on women during this era.

30 *Danish*, No. 3, 9 Shavval 1328, p. 8.

31 *Danish*, No. 3, 9 Shavval 1328, p. 2.

32 *Danish*, No. 6, 7 Dhulqa'da 1328, p. 4.

Dressing up (or down) in interwar Iran 161

33 Firoozeh Kashani-Sabet, *Frontier Fictions*, op. cit., p. 36.
34 Elizabeth Frierson, "Cheap and Easy: The Creation of Consumer Culture in Late Ottoman Society," in Donald Quataert, ed., *Consumption Studies and the History of the Ottoman Empire, 1550–1922: An Introduction* (2000), pp. 243–61.
35 *Shikufah*, 1st year, No. 9, p. 4.
36 *Annual Report of the Board of Home Missions of the Presbyterian Church in the USA* (1917), pp. 305–6.
37 Robert Elliott Speer and Russell Carter, *Report on India and Persia of the Deputation: Sent by the Board of Foreign Missions of the Presbyterian Church in the U. S.A. to Visit These Fields in 1921–22* (1922), p. 374.
38 Ibid., p. 375.
39 US Department of State, American Consular Service, Tehran, March 14 1923, enclosure, "Ville de Téhéran, Exposition des produits nationaux, réglement fundamental," p. 5.
40 US Department of State, from consul, Tehran, Iran, March 4 1924, "Persian Commercial and Industrial Exhibition," p. 1.
41 National Archives, Iran, File 21000053, 11 Azar, 1305/1926, "Vatan dar khatar ast." Also, same file, same date for the second announcement, "Islam dar khatar ast."
42 Yahya Zuka', *Libas-i Zanan-i Iran* (Tehran, 1947), p. 40.
43 For discussion of women's education and girls' schools, see Jasamin Rostam-Kolayi, "Origins of Iran's Modern Girls' Schools: From Private/National to Public/State," *Journal of Middle East Women's Studies*, vol. 4, no. 3, (Fall 2008), pp. 58–88. Also, Afsaneh Najmabadi, "Crafting an Educated Housewife in Iran," in Lila Abu-Lughod, ed., *Remaking Women: Feminism and Modernity in the Middle East* (1998), pp. 91–125; Camron Amin, *The Making of the Modern Iranian Woman*, op. cit.; and F. Kashani-Sabet, *Frontier Fictions*, op. cit., chapter 6.
44 Aqa Sayyid Mirza Ali Khan, *Hunar amuz-i dushizigan* (Tehran, 1924), p. 27.
45 Ahmad Sa'adat, *Rahnima-yi Sa'adat* (Tehran, 1923), p. 88.
46 National Archives, Iran, Ma'arif "Beh," Tashkilat, Series 51005, Folder 17, File 364, "Nizamnamah-i madaris-i ibtida'i va mutavassitah-i zukur va anas-i dowlati," p. 10.
47 Presbyterian Historical Society (PHS), Jane. E. Doolittle to the Board of Foreign Missions, January 3 1929, p.3.
48 Vizarat-i Ma'arif va Awqaf va Sanayi'-i Mustazrafah, *Salnamah va Ihsa'iyah* 1312/1313 and 1313/1314, illustration between pp. 56–57.
49 Houchang Chehabi, "Staging the Emperor's New Clothes: Dress Codes and Nation-Building under Reza Shah," *Iranian Studies*, Volume 26: 3–4 (Spring/Fall 1993), pp. 209–29. For a copy of the Law of Dress Uniformity, see National Archives, Ma'arif "Beh," Series 51006, File 324, "Qanun: Muttahid al-Shikl Nimudan-i Albasah-i Atba'-i Iran dar Dakhil-i Mamlikat," 10 Dey 1307/31 December 1928.
50 US Department of State, October 18 1934, J. Rives Childs, "The March of Modernism in Persia," p. 12.
51 US Department of State Records, No. 384, Tehran, February 19 1931, Charles C. Hart to Secretary of State, p. 1.
52 *Ittila'at*, 9 Tir 1315/July 1 1935, "Tabdil-i Kolah."
53 National Archives, Iran, Ma'arif "Beh," Series 51006, File 324, 7 Tir 1315/June 29 1935.
54 *Ittila'at*, 26 Mehr 1317/18 October 1938, "Tarbiyat-o pish ahangi-yi dukhtaran."
55 Mahmud Delfani (ed.), Šazmān-i Pīshāhangī-i Īrān dar dawrah-i Riz̤ā Shāh (Tehran, 2003).
56 Vizarat-i Ma'arif va Awqaf va Sanayi'-i Mustazrafah, *Salnamah va Ihsa'iyah* 1312/1313 and 1313/1314, pp. 12–13. For more on scouting see F. Kashani-Sabet,

162 *Firoozeh Kashani-Sabet*

"Cultures of Iranianness: The Evolving Polemic of Iranian Nationalism," in Nikki R. Keddie and Rudolph P. Matthee, eds., *Iran and the Surrounding World: Interactions in Culture and Cultural Politics* (2002), 162–81. Also, *Ittila'at*, 27 Mehr 1317/October 19 1938, for a picture of the new scouting hat for girls.

57 National Archives, Iran, Ma'arif "Alif," Series 51006, File 449.

58 National Archives, Iran, Ma'arif "Beh," Series 51006, Folder 17, File 367.

59 *Khushunat va Farhang: Asnad-i Mahramanah-i Kashf-i Hijab* (Tehran: Intisharat-i Sazman-i Asnad-i Milli-yi Iran, 1371/1992) and *Vaqa'ih-i Kashf-i Hijab* (Tehran: Mu'assassah-i Mutali'at-i Farhangi, 1371/1992) are important sources on this subject. Also, Sina Vahid, *Qiyam-i Gawharshad* (Tehran: Vizarat-i Farhang va Irshad-i Islami,1366/1987). Some of the key English-language scholarly sources have already been cited above.

60 For relevant theoretical works, see Victoria de Grazia, "Introduction," in Victoria de Grazia with Ellen Furlough, eds., *The Sex of Things: Gender and Consumption in Historical Perspective* (1996), p. 5; also the review essay by Mary Louise Roberts, "Gender, Consumption, and Commodity Culture," *American Historical Review*, vol. 103, no. 3 (June 1998). For comparative studies in the Arab world, see Mona Russell, *Creating the New Egyptian Woman: Consumerism, Education, and National Identity, 1863–1922* (2004); Nancy Reynolds, *A City Consumed: Urban Commerce, the Cairo Fire, and the Politics of Decolonization in Egypt* (2012).

61 *Ittila'at*, No. 621, November 4 1928, p. 3.

62 *Ittila'at*, No. 630, November 14 1928, p.4.

63 Vizarat-i Farhang, *Salnamah va Amar, 1315/136* and *1316/1317*, p. 715.

64 Vizarat-i Farhang, *Salnamah va Amar, 1315/136* and *1316/1317*, p. 716.

65 Vizarat-i Farhang, *Salnamah va Amar, 1315/136* and *1316/1317*, pp. 819–39.

66 Vizarat-i Farhang, *Salnamah va Amar, 1315/136* and *1316/1317*, pp. 870–73.

67 Vizarat-i Farhang, *Salnamah va Amar, 1315/136* and *1316/1317*, pp.853–58.

68 *Ittila'at*, 8 Mordad 1317/30 July 1938, "Hunaristan-i shabanah-ruziyeh dukhtaran."

69 *Ittila'at*,12 Azar 1317/December 3 1938, "Tamam-i Banuvan-i Iran Mitavanand Shik Bashand."

70 *Ittila'at*, 6 Mordad 1317/28 July 1938.

71 *Ittila'at*, 9 Mordad 1317/July 31 1938, "Shirkat-i Furush-i Parchah-hayeh Abrishami."

72 *Ittila'at*, 19 Mordad 1317/10 August 1938, "Karkhanah-i Risandegi va Bafandegiyeh I'timadiyah dar Bushehr."

73 *Ittila'at*, 19 Mordad 1317/August 10 1938, "Karkhanah-i Risandegi va Bafandegi."

74 *Ittila'at*, 9 Tir 1314/1 July 1935. Also, *Ittila'at*, 7 Tir 1315/June 28 1936.

75 *Ittila'at*, 15 Mordad 1314/7 August 1935.

76 *Ittila'at*, 13 November 1928.

77 *Banu*, No. 2, January 1944, p. 32: "Libas-i naw-i Mullah." These series of cartoons show a mullah who has put on a new outfit and thus attracted public attention. He is surrounded by villagers who notice his new clothes and ask him a lot of questions, eventually exasperating him. The mullah then runs home and asks his wife to go outside and to tell the people where he bought the fabric from, who sewed it for him, how much it cost and then to leave him alone! The cartoon is mocking the disproportionate attention his outfit generated as much as it pokes fun at the intrusive habits of his neighbors.

6 Astrakhan, Borqa', Chadari, Dreshi

The economy of dress in early-twentieth-century Afghanistan

Thomas Wide

Introduction

Despite an upsurge of popular and academic interest in Afghanistan, largely driven by over a decade of Western military involvement in the country, our view of Afghan women remains essentially talibanized: the iconic image is still that of ghostly blue shadows in dusty streets, a picture which creates the impression of women as oppressed and voiceless, prisoners in their own society. The role and status of women in Afghan society has become a central lens for analysing and measuring the US-led intervention, as well as one of the main justifications for staying. 'What about the women?', has become a familiar refrain.[1]

This is not the first time that women, and veiling, have been at the centre of political debate in Afghanistan, however. In the 1920s, the Afghan king Amanullah Khan (r.1919–29) embarked upon an ambitious and wide-ranging reform project with which he hoped to transform his country. At the heart of this project were proposed reforms pertaining to women, including the discouragement of practices such as polygamy, child marriage, forced marriage, and the promotion of women's education and health. The reform project was a controversial one, and Amanullah's ten-year period of rule was beset by intrigue and unease, as well as occasional outbreaks of outright rebellion, which eventually led to his downfall in 1929. During this period of self-conscious state-backed 'renaissance' (*nahza*), increasingly polarized positions on the role of women and 'the veil' emerged. By 1928, statements about the covering, or uncovering, of woman's bodies had become one of the central means by which people expressed their support for, or opposition to, Amanullah's government. Just how crucial this issue had become is clear from the aftermath of the uprisings of 1928–29 that toppled Amanullah. Of all the policies that the new government of Habibullah Kalakani (*c.*1890–1929) could have started with, its very first concerned veiling: 'The unveiling of women which had been allowed is now cancelled. Instead, it is decreed that no woman may leave the house without an escort (*mahram*).'[2]

The chapter returns to this pivotal moment in Afghan history in order to reappraise the role of 'the veil' in the transformations of the 1920s and the uprisings of 1928–29. It uses an interpretive model that one might call Afghanistan's 'economy of dress', which provides a means to analyse holistically interactions between the 'production' and 'consumption' of forms of dress amongst Afghans from different socio-economic backgrounds. Such an interpretive model stems from sociological rather than economic thought; it does not reduce choices of dress to material and financial factors, but rather creates a field of analysis broad enough to investigate 'the social life of dress' in all its complexity in Afghanistan. This has three main benefits for the historian of veiling practices in Afghanistan. First, such an approach stresses that issues of veiling cannot be divorced from other changes in dress and bodily comportment during the period, changes which affected men as much as women. This avoids fetishizing 'the veil' as somehow unique and apart from other forms of dress, subject to 'its' own laws and strictures. By focusing on men as well as women this approach also overcomes a common tendency to see questions of 'gender' in Afghanistan as questions primarily about 'women'.[3] Second, a focus on Afghanistan's economy of dress draws out the practical as well as ideological investments made by Afghans in their choice of clothing. It uses the metaphor of a 'marketplace' of goods and ideas, with consumers of dress weighing up the different practical, financial, and ideological investments they wished to make. This interpretive model helps rescue 'the veil' from the abstracted form it increasingly took in contemporary debates and subsequent historical analysis, and encourages one to see veiling as a lived practice with practical as well as symbolic considerations. This is not in any way to ignore the symbolic dimensions of 'the veil', but rather to pull practical and symbolic factors together into a single interpretive framework.[4] This in turn offers the historian new ways to understand the desire for change, and resistance to change, amongst Afghans of the period beyond the standard dichotomies of modernism vs traditionalism/tribalism, Westernization vs nativism, reform vs conservatism, etc. Third, such a field of analysis is broad enough to allow for an understanding of the way shifting economic conditions and the introduction of new technologies, activities and public/private spaces influenced what people did, and what they wore while doing it, thus providing a means for bridging the divide between structural-materialist and culturalist approaches to understanding historical change in Afghanistan.[5]

Such an approach encourages a shift of focus from previous interpretations of the period. While it has become commonplace to view the 1920s as marking a radical break with Afghanistan's past, this chapter emphasizes the continuities. First of all, women were never the voiceless, choiceless and powerless prisoners in their own society that they have so often been portrayed as. Moreover, changes in women's status and dress must be seen in the context of larger-scale material and cultural changes in the late nineteenth century and early twentieth century, rather than as the product of the radical intervention of a few Afghan pioneers. At the same time, while the Ottoman Empire has traditionally been seen as the inspiration for many of the transformations in early-twentieth-century Afghanistan, a study of the Afghan economy of dress

Economy of dress in early-20th-century Afghanistan   165

instead emphasizes the overwhelming centrality of British India in supplying physical, cultural and intellectual material for the 'manufacturing' of modern Afghanistan.[6] When the chapter turns to the 1920s and the period leading up to the uprisings of 1928–29, its approach again encourages some shifts of emphasis. While there is no doubt that Amanullah did push for an increasingly ideologically driven and unrealistic reform programme covering many aspects of Afghan life, there was in fact never an implemented 'anti-veiling campaign'. Even if Amanullah had wanted there to be, his government did not possess the resources to fund or police such a campaign. At the same time, however, there *really was* a significant campaign of dress reforms aimed at men in Kabul, which became the source of more practical and less ideological concerns to an increasingly beleaguered population. The chapter ends with a reappraisal of opposition to Amanullah's regime, attempting to solve the riddle of why Amanullah's promotion of 'unveiling' (*raf'-e hejab*) became one of, perhaps *the*, most vociferously protested against of all Amanullah's reforms. And this despite the fact that no actual law about 'unveiling' was ever implemented.

Veils are not discourses: some preliminary remarks

With the framework of an 'economy of dress' in mind, it is worth some preliminary remarks on 'the veil'. First, a note on terminology: this chapter has thus far placed 'the veil' in speech-marks in order to distinguish the discourse of 'the veil' from various types of veil that women actually wore. Veils are not discourses, they are pieces of clothing. 'The veil', however, is a discourse. As a discourse, the usual term for 'the veil' in Afghanistan was the Arabic word *hejab*. This term was frequently elided with the term *purda*, the more usual term for the seclusion of females from men outside the immediate family. Unfortunately for the researcher, historical actors frequently used these terms interchangeably. For the actual physical veils, again a number of terms were used. Although the Arabic term *borqa'* has become an increasingly well-known and freighted term in the English-speaking world, the more usual term amongst Afghans for the long full-length veil in Afghanistan was, and remains, *chadari*. This *chadari* must be distinguished from the *chadar*, which refers to a variety of headscarves and head coverings used across the country. It is not just the terminology for veils and veiling that can be incorrigibly plural, but also the forms of veil themselves. Thus the second preliminary remark: women's dress in Afghanistan, of which various forms of veiling are a part, has always been highly varied. Afghanistan is made up of a great range of ethnic groups, all with their different codes of dress and veiling practices. Moreover, these veiling practices have always been fluid, dictated by status, socio-economic background, fashion, age, geographic location, and personal and familial preference – and all subject to change over time. As a very general rule, while women of higher-status families lived under strict social conditions in rural areas, conditions were markedly less strict for families

166 *Thomas Wide*

from lower socio-economic backgrounds. In these communities, women played a major role in textile production, fruit picking, livestock rearing and harvesting, alongside the arduous domestic tasks of collecting water (often from many miles away),[7] cooking, clothing (often making the clothes themselves),[8] and raising and feeding the family. While they worked, these women would not veil their faces, although their hair would usually be covered. So, too, with nomadic communities, where women wore various types of head covering, and sometimes no head covering at all.[9] This should make us wary of reformist and historical interpretations that have stressed the 'tribal', 'traditional' or 'religious' hostility to the 'unveiling of women' in Afghanistan. Such readings merely provoke further questions: 'Which women are being referred to? What type of veil (if any) were these women wearing before? Where was this taking place?' In regard to this last question, it should be remembered that in the early twentieth century at least 90 per cent of the Afghan population was rural. Its direct contact with Kabul life, the royal court and the official class was minimal. Not only were veiling practices and forms of dress quite different in these rural areas, but the reach of the government to enforce any such top-down 'sartorial social engineering' was almost non-existent.[10] Any account of changes in veiling practices in Afghanistan must take into account the fact that the scope of such changes was in fact extremely limited: most of the country went on exactly as it had done before.[11] In the same way, while reformers of the 1920s, and subsequent historians, have been quick to valorize the period of Amanullah's rule as the moment of *nahza* in which Afghan women first obtained a voice in their own society, this is to overstate the scale of the break with the past. A study of the chronicles of nineteenth and early-twentieth-century Afghan history reflect a society in which women played active roles in various areas of public and private life. Economically, as has been mentioned, women were essential participants in agriculture and cottage industries, both of which were at the heart of the Afghan economy and remain so up to this day. Politically, Afghan histories mark numerous times when women played key roles in entreating, advocating and mediating.[12] Unsurprisingly, such influential women were most visible amongst the royal family, where characters such as Halima, the wife of the Amir Abdur Rahman Khan (r.1880–1901) held great influence.[13] High-status women could carve a role for themselves as businesswomen too, and could work in cooperation with other women: in the late nineteenth century, the mother of Prince Gholam 'Ali Khan, acted as investor to a female broker (*dalala*) called Khanom Jan whose business was the buying and selling of clothes to rich Kabuli families.[14] Another powerful businesswoman was Seraj al-Khawatin, one of the wives of Amir Habibullah Khan (r.1901–19), who dealt in opium between Herat and British India.[15] Women's role in government could also extend to intelligence work, the British Agent at Kabul remarking on the hiring of large numbers of female informants by Habibullah Khan's brother, Nasrullah, in 1912.[16] Militarily, too, women had long been noted for supplying food and aid to those fighting, as well as on

Economy of dress in early-20th-century Afghanistan 167

occasion taking part in the fighting themselves.[17] It was perhaps in the cultural sphere of artistic production, however, where Afghan women were most prominent in the nineteenth and early twentieth centuries. Historically, several of the most famous of all Afghan poets had been women, including the semi-legendary medieval poet Rabe'a Balkhi and the early-nineteenth-century poet Ayesha Durrani (d.1820). Indeed one of the first books ever printed in Afghanistan was the collected works of Ayesha Durrani, published by lithograph during the reign of Abdur Rahman.[18] Such a proud Persian poetic tradition was continued by poets of the late nineteenth century such as Gowhar Kabuli, Mahjuba Herawi and Makhfi Badakhshi. These last two poets, despite living on opposite sides of the country, struck up a correspondence with each other in which they reflected upon the difficulties of being women – and women poets – in Afghanistan.[19] Their correspondence illustrates the fact that the prestige of Persian poetry allowed these women a certain freedom and contact with men; Herawi writes in one letter of receiving admiring letters from male poets, including one, a certain Habib Nawabi, who asked her to send him a photo of herself.[20] Herawi was flattered by the attention, but had to refuse: 'he [i.e. the poet Nawabi] does not realize that no-one has even seen the edge of my headscarf (*chadar*) outdoors. How then is a photo of myself possible?'[21] The two poets followed this exchange with letters about the strict rules imposed on women in different parts of the country, and the 'unhelpful' (*namasa'ed*) nature of such restrictions.[22] This need to remain veiled, if not necessarily silenced, was symbolically enshrined in the pen names they took: Makhfi, meaning 'hidden' and Mahjuba meaning 'veiled'.

All these literate female poets were home-schooled, a form of education known as *maktab-e khanegi*. This should warn us away from thinking that all Afghan women from the period were illiterate and banned from learning. Learning for women *could* take place, although it was almost always an elite practice and always in informal, private settings. However, it should be remembered that the literary education of men also took place in similarly informal settings, if not necessarily in private. Outside the elite circles of Persian poetic production, women also played central roles in popular, mostly oral, poetry, especially certain genres of Pashto poetry.[23] Of particular note in this regard is the most famous of all Pashto poetic genres, the *landey*, a two-line poem expressing a single emotion or idea, usually with a strong visual image, and frequently composed from the perspective of a woman addressing a man.[24] Even prior to the so-called *nahza* of 1919–29, Afghan women found ways to discuss their situation and express their hopes, fears, joys and sorrows.

Afghan ornamentalism: British India and the Afghan economy of dress

At the same time as Ayesha Durrani's poetry was being published in Kabul in the late nineteenth century, shifts in fashion were starting to be discerned

168   *Thomas Wide*

amongst royal elites in Kabul. These changes largely reflected the influence of currents stemming from British India during a period of increased circulation and exchange of peoples, goods and ideas between the two countries.[25] These shifts in fashion were also part of larger transformations as Afghanistan became a clearly bounded nation-state with some form of centralized government for the first time. Along with the rise of a strong ruler in the form of Abdur Rahman, emerged a new and powerful mode of rule that one might call 'Afghan ornamentalism'. The term 'ornamentalism' was originally coined by David Cannadine to stress the role of hierarchy and class in Britain's mode of imperial rule, and the expression of such hierarchies through displays of pomp and pageantry.[26] Afghanistan seems an interesting case study in this respect, a country whose borders, economy and ruling family were forged in close relations with the British and yet which was never a formal part of the British Empire.[27] Despite not being under direct British control, the Afghan court seems nevertheless to have been heavily influenced by the representations of hierarchy, ceremonialism and spectacle of the British in India and drew on it for the development of its own expressions of dynastic power.

The term 'ornamentalism' points to the visual nature of Abdur Rahman's rule; as the art historian Holly Edwards puts it: 'He [Abdur Rahman] incrementally envisioned and actively sponsored a more visually 'marked' Afghanistan, one in which public spaces began to reflect aspiration and manifest change rather than simply to reify the familiar.' Abdur Rahman erected freestanding, outward-looking palaces, full of the 'Victorian clutter' of fireplaces and crystal chandeliers, and which were imported from British India.[28] At the same time, forms of dress bolstered this new 'visually "marked" Afghanistan': finding the baggy and loose-fitting Afghan clothes 'extravagant' and 'hideous', Abdur Rahman employed Indian tailors to teach Afghan tailors how to make British-style trousers.[29] Establishing a pattern which would continue with his son and grandson, he fined his officials six months' pay if they did not wear this new style of clothes.[30] Abdur Rahman even employed a British tailor, Mr Walter, who wrote a tailoring manual, which was translated into Dari and published in Kabul in the early 1890s.[31] Abdur Rahman also allowed the women of the royal court, while remaining highly secluded, to wear dresses based on designs stemming from British India, a style that Dupree describes as 'Victoriana'.[32] Amongst his court and in the military, Abdur Rahman also promoted the wearing of European-style uniforms, designed to bolster an image of well ordered and somehow abstract coercive power. Due to the lack of native clothes manufacturers in Afghanistan, however, these uniforms were largely imported second-hand from British India. The unintended consequence of Abdur Rahman's desire for uniforms was the development of a thriving industry between Afghanistan and British India in which second-hand or condemned stores from frontier stations of British India would be bought at auction and then sold on by Afghan traders moving between the two countries.[33] This led to a situation whereby Afghan government employees could be seen 'in every imaginable British habiliment, from a

Economy of dress in early-20th-century Afghanistan 169

naval jacket to a whipper's-in (*sic*) hunting coat'.[34] Afghanistan may never have been a colony of British India, but its new forms of dress clearly bore the label, 'Made in Britain'.

The influences of British India on the Afghan economy of dress were to continue and develop in the reign of Abdur Rahman's son Habibullah Khan, and now were augmented and quickened by transformations in technologies, transport and public spaces. Economically, Habibullah inherited a country whose finances were in robust health; the parsimonious Abdur Rahman had built up a large treasury, which Habibullah went about spending with gusto. At the same time, Habibullah benefitted from the large British subsidy that his father had negotiated in exchange for Britain's control of Afghanistan's foreign affairs. Such financial plenty stimulated a court-sponsored 'building boom' in Kabul and several other cities.[35] While Abdur Rahman's reign saw the first flourishings of the 'ornamentalist' mode of rule, it was in Habibullah's reign that this became increasingly coherent and prominent. As has been seen in the time of Abdur Rahman, much of the cultural and material influences for this new visual vocabulary came from British India: the architecture of the period was an essentially Anglo-Indian style, designed largely by British engineers, built with iron girders imported from British India, and dragged from the border by elephants, themselves imported from British India.[36] Along with imported British Indian girders and elephants, came imported loanwords like 'veranda' (*baranda*) and 'corridor' (*kuridur*) which were used to describe these new courtly spaces in the Afghan press.[37] Habibullah's brother, Nasrullah Khan (1874–1920), even built himself a European-influenced house inspired by the Dorchester Hotel, which he had visited on his trip to London in 1895,[38] naming it *Koti Landani* in memoriam.[39]

This new built environment had concomitant impacts on dress and bodily comportment, forging a style of life that emphasized hierarchy and difference between the court and the rest of the country, at the same time as it offered new opportunities for courtly women. Along with new buildings came new European-style gardens, including the *Arambagh* designed as a public space exclusively for women.[40] These new buildings and gardens not only acted as projections of the new visual vocabulary of royal power, but also provided locations for new forms of assembly and sociability for men and women, as well as the settings for the increasingly lavish and lengthy state ceremonies instituted by Habibullah. The most prominent of these was the *jashn-e melli* (national day), in remembrance of Abdur Rahman, a ceremony notable for the participation of women.[41] The public involvement of women at these events was to become an increasingly prominent, and controversial, feature of Afghan public life.

Afghan ornamentalism involved not just British Indian architectural and clothing designs, but also a burgeoning interest in ceremonialism and protocol. The royal tours made by Habibullah's son Enayatullah and Habibullah himself, in 1905 and 1907, clearly played an important role in drawing the Afghan royals towards the style, if not the form and content, of British

170   *Thomas Wide*

imperial rule. The Afghan accounts of these tours, written by the court historian Fayz Mohammad Kateb, paint a landscape of official encounters, codified etiquette, state protocol and lavish ceremony, all captured in minute detail from the number of cannon fired in salute at each stage of each trip to the precise manner in which the Viceroy, Lord Curzon, greeted the Afghan royals.[42] On his return, Habibullah's obsession with court etiquette extended to the royal *harem*; Habibullah ordered the writing of a handbook which set out the exact manner in which servants should carry out their work, be it serving tea or helping with the royal ablutions.[43] In order to keep up with what he saw as international standards of royal protocol, Habibullah also gave his wives official names; a royal decree sent to the governor of the districts of Bulaghin and Dornama stated that new official titles (*alqab*) for royal women had been determined 'according to rank', as was the custom amongst the other 'kings of the world' (*padshahan-e 'alam*), and that these names should be published in all the villages of the province.[44] Part of these ever more systematized codes of courtly behaviour was an increasing focus on the clothes of those at court. Members of Habibullah's court were now made to wear a uniform of black coat and an Astrakhan hat.[45] Different outfits were stipulated for different activities: in one court decree, Habibullah ordered that, if the proper clothes were not worn for prayers, a third of the offender's salary would be docked.[46] Habibullah's desire for new military uniforms, however, ran up against the limited capabilities of the Afghan native clothing industry. Demand outweighed supply and Habibullah was eventually forced to look abroad for uniforms, ordering 100,000 khaki suits from England through his trade agent in Bombay.[47]

The influence of British India extended beyond clothes to incorporate new forms of bodily culture too, which brought with them their own modifications in dress. In the early 1900s, Habibullah took a shine to gymnastics and, soon, through the agency of previously exiled Afghans in Dehra Dun, Indian instructors were summoned and began teaching calisthenics in the recently founded Habibia College.[48] Gymnastics courses were also introduced to the Afghan army by the Turkish military instructor, Mahmud Sami, a man described by the Kabul-based leather-worker Ernest Thornton, with typical British admiration, as 'a firm believer in physical training'.[49] The crown prince Enayatullah, who had visited British India in 1905, introduced the game of football, with replicas of footballs manufactured in British India made in the Kabul leather-factories by Thornton.[50] Such sports encouraged the introduction of shorts, or at least different forms of trousers and boots to play in. Habibullah also became an avid golfer, convinced as he had become, on the advice of his British doctor, that it would be good for his chronic gout.[51] Gardening, using seeds imported from British India, also became a popular form of gentle exercise and relaxation for the king, and drove him to take on the fashion mores of an English country squire, all tweed suits and shooting breeches.[52] At the same time, this new culture of organized sports and training had an impact on the bodily comportment of royal women too,

Economy of dress in early-20th-century Afghanistan 171

Habibullah encouraging them to take up horse-riding practice, which they did, although out of sight in the privacy of the *harem*.[53]

All these new spaces, ceremonies and activities were also now increasingly recorded by photography, a technology again imported from British India. The Afghan courtly elites took to this new medium immediately. While the female poet Mahjuba Herawi had been unable to be photographed for fear of upsetting her husband, the women of the Kabul court seemed delighted to be photographed, unveiled, and almost always in Western dresses, by other members of the royal family.[54] These photos were even put on display during parties and sold to aristocrats to raise funds for an orphanage.[55] Not only did the Afghan court thus sanction the photographing of Afghans in Western dress, but it also used photography to signal the court's adoption of such clothing, and perhaps to promote these forms of dress amongst the populace more widely. Considering that the ladies of the royal harem should by traditional standards have been protected from the public gaze, this was a striking innovation.

While technologies like photography were aimed at capturing and fixing people in time, other technologies were encouraging mobility and movement, which in turn required new forms of dress. Nile Green has charted the development of motorized transport and road infrastructure in early-twentieth-century Afghanistan, while also noting the role of such new technologies in fuelling a 'state-sponsored aestheticization of industrial travel', in which travel emerged as the 'transformative act of modernity'.[56] The motorcar became the ultimate marker of aristocratic internationalism, Habibullah importing several British-built Rolls-Royces from British India. These motorcars and roads now bound together the newly built pleasure palaces, gardens and golf courses of Kabul, Paghman and Jalalabad, creating a small network of courtly spaces for the expression of progressive sensibilities and dress. Certain aristocratic women now had separate 'touring' clothes of long dark dresses and wide-brimmed hat tied around their chin with ribbons, and were even photographed at the wheel of these new cars.[57] Such clothes combined an expression of conspicuous luxury with the practical considerations of not wanting one's hat to blow off while driving at speed on bumpy roads.[58] Technology requires technicians as well as suitable clothing, and these Rolls-Royces demanded experienced mechanics and chauffeurs to look after them. Soon a number of British Indian mechanics arrived, along with a British chauffeur who drove the Amir around, dressed in smart livery.[59] At the same time, the newly founded printing press, minting works and gunpowder factory were managed by a small group of Ottoman technocrats who set up home in Kabul, bringing the *efendi* fashions of fez and Western suit to the streets of Kabul, something which made quite a stir amongst the court elites.[60]

With transport links improving between Kabul and Peshawar, new designs and fashions were not only increasingly popular, but also increasingly available to the idle rich, as British Indian tailors found it easier to make trips to Kabul to do business. In 1915, a representative from one of Bombay's

172   *Thomas Wide*

tailoring houses visited Kabul and sold '$30,000 worth of high-class apparel ... to both gentlemen and ladies of the court'.[61] The women of the royal *harem* selected their new clothes from pictures of 'the latest Parisian fashions'.[62] Such new fashions did not, however, mark a decisive break with old traditions of *purda* – the ladies of the court were not permitted to be seen or measured for their clothes and all measurements had to be sent to the representative.[63] New fashion technologies, particularly the importation and use of sewing machines (often American made) also facilitated the development of new styles and fashions in Kabul.[64] The government even acted as state sponsors of these new technologies and fashions, providing classes on mechanical methods and appliances to Kabul tailors, and even fostering creativity and design with prizes for 'the best or most original work produced'.[65]

It was not just foreign tailors, however, that brought new fashions with them, but also prominent Afghan exiles who took advantage of the amnesty declared by Habibullah on his accession in 1901 to return to their homeland. These exiles had found themselves scattered across Asia, with prominent families ending up in Karachi, Lahore, Bombay, Dehra Dun, Tehran, Damascus, Istanbul, Samarkand.[66] The central role of these returning men in bringing new ideas and trends to Afghanistan has long been noted.[67] Just as important, however, was the role played by returning Afghan women. One such character was Olya Janab, a wife of Habibullah Khan who had been brought up and schooled in Dehra Dun in British India. An accomplished Urdu speaker and poet, she translated the poetry of Indian scholars such as Shebli No'mani into Persian, foreshadowing the large-scale intellectual exchanges between Afghans and Indian Muslims of the 1920s and 30s.[68] At the same time as such Indo-Afghan literary endeavours, she also followed British Indian fashions.[69]

These exiles and foreigners, both men and women, brought new ideologies to Afghanistan too, forged in the cosmopolitan environments of the port-cities and capitals of Asia. A form of Afghan dandyism emerged in aristocratic circles, which combined an internationalism of outlook with suitably cosmopolitan attire. The ultimate exemplar of this new Afghan dandy was Mahmud Tarzi, the editor of Afghanistan's first regular newspaper and later Afghanistan's first Foreign Minister, who had spent his formative years in Damascus as a young *efendi* and had travelled extensively in the Ottoman Empire.[70] Photographs of the period show him dressed in bow tie and fez, and sporting a neat moustache.[71] As Ryzova has recently argued, the Ottoman *efendi* was marked out not just by what he wore, however, but by a whole set of practices, poses and attitudes – what she calls a 'stance towards modernity'.[72] Such a framework seems apt for Tarzi, a man whose 'stance' may have been all the more accentuated by the fact that, on his return to Kabul, he found himself at first the only *efendi* in town. To encourage such efendification, Tarzi was given £200 by the Afghan government to spend on fezes to bring back with him while on a trip to the Ottoman empire in 1904.[73] Along with the physical importing of headgear, photographs also suggest that there were

Economy of dress in early-20th-century Afghanistan   173

even new poses and mannerisms that Tarzi brought with him from the Ottoman empire: a famous photo of him at the helm of the newspaper he edited, *Siraj al-akhbar*, leaning sideways with head resting on his hands in dreamy contemplation, is almost exactly the pose struck by a young consort of Habibullah's, as if in imitation of Tarzi, in a photograph of the period.[74] In 1923, Tarzi's daughter, now Queen Soraya, was photographed holding an identical pose, although this time while awkwardly standing and resting her arm on a flower pot, in the royal palace's conservatory.[75]

Tarzi married a Syrian woman, Asma Rasmiya (1887–1945), and had several daughters, all of whom returned to Kabul in 1905.[76] The Tarzi women played just as influential a role as Mahmud in promoting new fashions and attitudes in Kabul. Asma Rasmiya acted as director of Afghanistan's first girls' school and editor of Afghanistan's first newspaper for women, all the while dressing in Western fashions. Two of her daughters married into the royal family, Soraya (1899–1968) marrying the future king, Amanullah, and Khayriya, known as Khanom Efendi (1893–1981), marrying Amanullah's brother, Enayatullah Khan (1888–1946). Since Enayatullah was Afghanistan's foremost connoisseur of photography, it is no surprise that the Tarzi daughters became perhaps the most photographed of all women during the period. Together they acted as arbiters of taste, wearing the bustles and drawn-in waists of Edwardian Britain, as well as make-up.[77] As Dupree has noted, such fashions required concomitant changes in residential furnishing and bodily comportment. No longer able to sit with ease on the ground, chairs and tables became essential items of furnishing for such families' houses, rather than merely novelties as they had been in the time of Abdur Rahman.[78]

The Tarzis were not just translators of fashion, however, but also translators (in the Latin sense of *trans + latus*, 'carrying across') of new ideologies stemming from the Ottoman Empire and beyond, which themselves bolstered changed attitudes towards women and forms of dress amongst elites. 'Progress' (*taraqqi*) and 'love of homeland' (*hobb al-watan*) became the watchwords of the day amongst intellectuals.[79] A key component of this new ideology of patriotism and progress was the issue of women. In the new Afghanistan that Tarzi envisaged, women were crucial to the development of the whole society – for were they not the other half of man?[80] In order to 'wake up' (*bedar shodan*) Afghan men and women, Tarzi wrote a series of biographical accounts of women in history, which were published in his newspaper, *Siraj al-akhbar*.[81] These articles were directed specifically at women, hoping to explain how women could be an active force in the service of the Afghan nation.[82] Tarzi clearly had an awareness of similar intellectual debates taking place in the Ottoman Empire and Iran at the time and flagged his support with the promotion of such pioneering Muslim women as the Ottoman *litterateur* Khalida Adib, printing one of her speeches in the pages of his newspaper.[83] All these efforts illustrate the intertwined relation of the ideological, the cultural and the material in the changing role of women in Afghanistan – Tarzi's articles used print and photographic technologies to

174   *Thomas Wide*

make women more 'visible' in public life: a visibility already encouraged by transformations in the built environment, social landscape, and transport infrastructure of the Afghan capital.

While this ideology of elite cosmopolitanism and progress manifested itself in new fashions, poses, and practices amongst high-status Afghans, further down the economic scale, the old second-hand clothes market that had risen to prominence in Abdur Rahman's day continued to flourish in the Afghan bazaars. In 1915, the very year that Mahmud Tarzi was publishing a paean to Afghan dandyism in the form of a travel-diary of a trip he made through the cafes, theatres and barbershops of the Ottoman Empire, the Afghan government's special trade agent in Bombay was noting that 'cast-off or second-hand uniforms from other countries meet with a remarkably good demand in Afghanistan'.[84] At the same time as elites were being fitted by Bombay tailors for tweed shooting suits and broad-brimmed hats decked with ribbons, non-elites were also staking their own claim as consumers in the transnational economy of dress. The sheer scale of this second-hand clothes market is clear from the trade agent's remark that 'of all cast-off clothes imported into India, about 80 per cent go to Afghanistan'.[85] To try and promote indigenous industries in the face of this onslaught of cheap imported clothes, Habibullah invested in the wool-factory and government leather-works, which specialized in making boots.[86] Even here, however, there was a need for foreign steel to be imported to make hobnails for the soles.[87] Unfortunately, such local-made boots could not compete with the quality or price of imported ones, and there were periods in Habibullah's reign when the factory stopped production altogether.[88] The sums simply did not add up: while the Afghan nobility could afford to pay $50 for a pair of high quality foreign boots, poorer Afghans could pick up Russian- and Indian-made mass-produced boots (largely from Cawnpore) in the Afghan bazaars for less than Afghan-made ones.[89] The Afghan boot industry, it seems, could not find a firm footing for itself in the Afghan economy of dress.

Even the English leather-worker and boot-maker Thornton had to admit the overwhelming volume of trade in foreign second-hand clothes and boots in Afghanistan, and furnished this fact with an anecdote about an Afghan he saw dressed in an old coat 'that once adorned a Cockney, for it yet bears upon its collar the words "Empire Theatre".'[90] Another British writer, Angus Hamilton, mentions the entire staff of an Afghan regiment stationed on the Russian border 'appearing in all the full-dress grandeur of second-hand railway uniforms'.[91] While the American Consul at Bombay put the reason for the appeal of imported military uniforms down to 'the general military ardor of the people',[92] this is clearly inadequate. Using the model of a dress economy, it seems more plausible that there were both practical and ideological investments made by Afghan citizens in wearing such clothes. Practically speaking, such manufactured uniforms would have been hard-wearing, functional, warm and cheap – the American Consul noted that a second-hand regimental coat with brass buttons might cost $0.40 in a frontier bazaar, while a second-hand uniform would cost from $1 to $1.50.[93] For the military, this would certainly have been cheaper than their official uniforms, which had to be ordered from Karachi and then transported at some cost by government agents to Afghanistan, the cost of which was often levied from soldiers' salaries.[94] At the same time, might such second-hand clothing represent a cheap means by which everyday Afghans could signal their awareness of foreign fashions and technologies of design? While the burgeoning traffic of expensive foreign couture into Afghanistan suggests an increased form of elite cosmopolitanism amongst the rich, it seems there were other forms of cosmopolitanism – everyday forms of cosmopolitanism – which existed amongst consumers from lower socio-economic backgrounds.[95] Traditional forms of headwear, for example, which were to be valorized by Afghan nationalists in the 1920s as examples of distinctly native dress,[96] circulated in the bazaars of Kabul, British India and Central Asia, and were made from materials from across the region. Ranging in price from five cents to $5, caps embroidered with gold thread from Benares vied for attention in the frontier markets with Afghan-made indigo-dyed blue turbans; Peshawar-made turbans embroidered with Russian gold thread sat alongside Austrian-made caps, priced at $1.80 each, and competed with silk versions manufactured at Meshed, which found a market amongst the wealthier rural Afghans.[97] At the same time, the raw materials for such headwear also reflected the transnational nature of textile circulation – Russian gold thread, Indian beads and manufactured silk, and Bukharan lace were all used in various forms of headwear.[98] While increasingly signified as 'native'/ 'traditional' dress by Afghan reformist elites, such headgear bears the influence of international trade and circulation as much as the imported sewing-machine-manufactured *haute couture* of the tailors of Bombay.

A floating signifier: views of 'the veil' in early-twentieth-century Afghanistan

As the section above has made clear, many of the important economic and socio-cultural changes of early-twentieth-century Afghanistan had a concomitant impact on patterns of dress and bodily comportment. New ideologies emerged alongside these changes, which in turn drove further developments in dress. With regard to women's dress, changes were most visible amongst the court elites, where a new aesthetic of dress was bolstered by a mode of rule characterized by 'ornamentalism' and an ideology of aristocratic internationalism. However, there had not yet developed the kind of polarized discourse over dress, and particularly veiling practices, which was to develop in the late 1920s.

'The veil' was still very much a floating signifier which could be freighted with varied, even contradictory, meanings depending on who was doing the wearing and who was doing the watching.[99] Outside the capital, Afghan women continued to wear a wide variety of head coverings across the country,

176   *Thomas Wide*

coverings which reflected both various ideological and practical considerations as part of the clothing economy of the time. In Kabul, the most common form of veiling amongst the 'middling sorts of people'[100] remained the *chadari delaq*, similar to the present-day *borqa'*. Even this one piece of clothing could carry a variety of meanings, however. For the wearer it could act as a sign of: urbanity, in opposition to rustics who went without full face coverings, or any covering at all; social status, in that it implied that the women did not work;[101] being upwardly mobile, particularly if one's family had recently moved to Kabul from the provinces; a sign of wealth, particularly the white *borqa'* which was easily dirtied and thus needed constant cleaning after journeys through Kabul's dusty streets (a clear example of Veblen's 'conspicuous consumption');[102] religious observance, as illustrated in Habibullah's *firman* requesting that all good Muslim women wear a khaki-coloured *chadari* which was modest and unobtrusive.[103] This type of khaki veil could also have practical applications in providing a means of hiding shabby clothes. Veils also played a social role, in preventing the free mingling of unrelated men and women. Veils then also had a further practical application in allowing women the ability to travel amongst unknown men in the streets – a kind of 'portable *purdah*' which might thus facilitate mobility, not restrict it.[104]

Aside from the *chadari*, other forms of veiling and covering were also prevalent in Kabul which carried their own meaning and practical purpose for the wearer and observer: the various forms of headscarves of *kuchi* nomadic groups moving through the streets which were a marker of ethnicity;[105] the elaborate and brightly coloured head coverings that signified the professional class of dancing girls;[106] the black hats rimmed with fur worn by Jewish residents; the yellow hats and *chadaris* which Hindus living in Kabul were forced to wear after a decree from Habibullah to mark their religious difference.[107] Simple *chadars* and turbans with long hanging tails also had practical roles for women and men in acting as a 'dust veil' during the frequent dust-storms, particularly during the spring months.[108] Quite apart from the meaning that the wearer hoped to express through her/his clothes, these veils and head coverings could also be read in a variety of different ways by the observer/ analyst. For example, they might signify ethnic boundaries (as they invariably did for colonial observers trying to systematize and codify Afghan dress),[109] national allegiance, conservatism, progressiveness, modesty, chastity, coquettishness, backwardness. At one and the same time, the wearing of various forms of veil and head covering could thus signify opposite things, depending on who was doing the wearing, how they were wearing, and who was watching. With these thoughts in mind, it is now time to turn to the transformations of the 1920s and the changing nature and discourse of dress during the period.

The emir's new clothes: the reign of Amanullah 1919–29

The reign of Amanullah has been largely characterized as one of idealism driving radical reform, with Amanullah playing the role either of visionary

Economy of dress in early-20th-century Afghanistan 177

reformer overcome by the forces of tribalism/religious reaction or 'irresponsible, hot-headed young man', overcome by his own folly, depending on the analyst's point of view.[110] On both readings, Amanullah's mode of rule has been seen as largely imitative – an idealistic/naïve king attempting to emulate those dynamic leaders, especially Ataturk, who were pushing through radical reform programmes in various new nations across Asia. On this reading, Amanullah was inspired by a 'foreign' ideology and attempted to graft reforms onto a country that was not ready or willing to accept them. As has thus far been argued, this chapter attempts to move away from such purely 'ideological' explanations of change, and resistance to change, during the period. Indeed, it was not until the last year of Amanullah's reign that an ideologically driven top-down attempt at 'sartorial social engineering' of the population took place. However, even here the reforms that were actually implemented were almost solely focused on men's, not women's, dress, and were solely confined to the capital of Kabul. This section thus discusses the various material and cultural factors driving changes in dress during the 1920s, and then turns to a reappraisal of the role of dress in the uprisings that overthrew Amanullah in 1928–29.

With regard to Afghanistan's economy, Amanullah took over a country quite different from that of his father, Habibullah. Whereas Habibullah had inherited a state whose finances had never been in ruder health, the financial capital that had been built up by Abdur Rahman was largely squandered over 20 years of government expenditure and mismanagement. Not only did Amanullah thus start off with an empty treasury, but he also almost immediately sacrificed the one consistent form of income that the government could count on – Afghanistan's annual subsidy from the British Government – in exchange for the complete independence of his country.[111] At the same time, Amanullah put great strain on state finances by expanding the size of his government's administration, taking on many more state employees in Kabul and the provinces, all of whom required salaries. The country could scarcely support such state expenditure, and in the very first year of his rule he was forced to default on salaries to government employees and the military, something that was to become a recurring pattern.[112] In order to make up for the loss of the British subsidy and the increase of government expenses, Amanullah attempted to draw in more revenue through taxes. He tightened revenue measures, thus increasing the tax burden on the people, at the same time as he cancelled former subsidies to tribal *khans*.[113] Unsurprisingly, this did little for his popularity. The importance of these developments for our purposes is two-fold: first, the extremely weak economic situation of both the government and the country at large forms the essential background to any discussion of the 1920s, and has been consistently underplayed in historical accounts of the period. Second, the vastly increased government administration under Amanullah created a new official class in Kabul. It was this class which was to be the most visible manifestation of transformations in Kabul society, as well as almost the only sector of Afghan society whose dress,

178   Thomas Wide

including forms of veil, could be dictated and enforced by the Afghan state. It is to this official class, and their forms of dress, which the chapter now turns.

Kabul cosmopolitan: changing forms of dress in the 1920s

During the 1920s, the role of various veils as a form of 'portable *purdah*' was put to the test as increasing numbers of Afghan women from the official class moved outside the narrow confines of the *haremseray* and Kabul townhouse and took part in new activities that formerly would have taken place at home.[114] Often the recipients of large grants of previously government-owned land, members of the official class possessed both significant economic and social capital, which they could use to promote their ideological aims of an increased role for women in public life. Large numbers of schools and charitable bodies were set up during the period, often with gifts of money (*e'ana*) from these wealthy men and women. Amongst these was the first girls' school, *Maktab-e Masturat*, in 1921, located in the house of Abdur Rahman's wife, the old queen Halima.[115] The importance of the financial support of such men and women for these institutions is illustrated in an article in the women's newspaper, *Ershad al-Neswan*, asking for donations from its female readers for the installation of a telephone line in the school.[116] So it was, too, with the newly founded women's hospital, located in the old home of Amanullah's aunt Okht al-Seraj, and to which Soraya personally donated medical equipment.[117] In terms of administration, the school was a family affair; Tarzi's wife, Asma Rasmiya, was director (*modira*), while her daughters, Khayriya and Soraya, were deputy (*nayeb-e modira*) and inspector (*mofatesha*), respectively. Such new facilities created new challenges for traditional gender relations: were male teachers allowed to teach girls in public schools?[118] How were male (frequently foreign) doctors to examine female patients? At the same time, such new public facilities encouraged new forms of dress. The girls' school had its own uniform created with the advice of Queen Soraya herself, and soon these girls were seen on the streets of Kabul on their way to and from school.[119] Even medical accessories could also double as fashion accessories: a Turkish doctor, Fuad Beg, carried out in-house eye-tests and made spectacles that were increasingly worn by the rich as markers of difference.[120]

Although Amanullah did not have the kind of money that Habibullah had had to spend on construction, this did not stop him from embarking on two ambitious building projects on the edge of Kabul, the new administrative centre of Daralaman and the pleasure gardens of Paghman, complete with its own arch *à la* L'Arc de Triomphe in Paris.[121] These new locations provided new entertainments and spaces for the performing of self-consciously progressive activities. A cinema was founded in the centre of town (until it burnt down), and films and theatre performances were put on by a new institution known as the *Namayeshat-e Erfani* in the new theatre buildings in Paghman and in Kabul. Inheriting his father's love of a good party, Amanullah inaugurated new government holidays and festivals, creating increasing opportunities for public spectacle – preparations for such ceremonies revolved around such new concerns as making sure the publicity for the events was published by the state presses rather than just spread by word of mouth, or ensuring that there was a qualified Afghan electrical engineer on hand to keep the whole event suitably electrified.[122] New forms of sociability emerged amongst women of the official class who wanted to take part in these public events; a special group was set up to welcome the King and Queen on their return from abroad, and royal women even lobbied the king, asking for permission to take part in the Independence Day celebrations.[123] Official-class women were becoming increasingly visible in Kabul's burgeoning public spaces.

Foreign sports such as tennis and football, whose introduction into Afghanistan has been traced above, were now increasingly played by the official class and scions of that class at the various high schools that had sprung up around the city. These were often exhibition matches in which everyday Kabulis could come and watch the spectacle of these new sophisticated forms of exercise. At the same time, spectators could admire the locally produced flannels in which Prince Enayatullah played tennis matches. Such sports fashions extended to the young ladies in school, who wore special outfits to play volleyball.[124] These new forms of bodily culture and comportment were then recorded by the increasingly widespread technology of photography.[125] Whereas in Habibullah's day photography had been the preserve of a handful of royal amateur enthusiasts, there were now Indian and Afghan professional photographers making a living out of taking pictures around Kabul.[126] The audience, too, for such photographs expanded: photographs of women in Western-style dress were even published in a government-sponsored publication, 'Souvenir d'Afghanistan', which was printed in Paris and then shipped back home for distribution.[127] As will be seen, such photographs of Western-dressed Afghan women could prove dangerous ammunition for those who would oppose the Afghan state.

Alongside this increasing availability of photographic technology, travel technologies continued to encourage a questioning of traditional dress and seclusion practices. While the motorcars of Habibullah's day had been almost exclusively for royal use, motorcars and motorcycles now became increasingly available to the official class in Kabul, either borrowed from the government or bought outright. The touring dresses which had previously been the reserve of court women were now increasingly taken up by official-class women whose husbands had invested in motorcars imported from British India. Forward-looking women in forward-moving cars were soon a daily sight whizzing up and down the newly built boulevard linking Kabul with Daralaman. For the first time, too, regular public transport in the form of American-made buses started to ply the road between Kabul and British India. This development of public motorized transport forced men and women to come into close contact as they travelled, and tested the efficacy of the veil's social role of ensuring that *purdah* was always maintained.[128] Alongside the

180 *Thomas Wide*

development of motor transport, a small railway was built to connect those two poles of Afghan cosmopolitanism, the Lab-e Darya and Daralaman.[129] This form of transport proved a big hit with Kabulis, and on holidays the four carriages would be packed with men and women, again raising the question of women's seclusion and the efficacy of the veil. The ramifications of new forms of transport for traditional gender relations had international as well as intra-national dimensions, with the sending of boys and girls abroad to Europe and Turkey for education.[130] This new form of transcontinental travel also drove new forms of dress: the girls were seen off by the King and Queen wearing 'Egyptian-style veils' more suitable to their destination in Istanbul than their point of departure.[131] Queen Soraya had also had a separate set of head coverings made for the girls to wear while in class abroad. These were styled on French berets, expressing Afghanistan's 'keeping up' with fashions origi-nating in the Middle East and Europe.[132] Like the photographs of Afghan women during the period, such clothing and travels were to become important points of contention at the end of Amanullah's reign.

All these new activities, spaces and technologies also provided opportu-nities for men to mix more freely with women, raising the question of *purdah* once more. While Mahmud Tarzi had written of the pleasures of the café cultures of Beirut and Istanbul, where one could sit and talk with a whole host of women late into the night,[133] Kabul now had its own cafés in which men and women could converse relatively freely and – if you were lucky – there was always the chance that the king or queen themselves might sit down next to you. This cultural shift in which elite men and women were able to mingle together, in increasingly visible locations, was bolstered by the arrival of large numbers of foreign men and women into Kabul after 1919. The new schools were soon populated by a combination of British Indian and Eur-opean staff, creating a whole new class of transnational educationalists.[134] Alongside these largely foreign-run schools, Kabul now saw the first foreign embassies arrive on its soil, as well. These foreign embassies encouraged whole new codes of behaviour and dress, as afternoon tea became a key fix-ture of the Kabul official-class social scene. Afghan invitations to such events now stipulated that all Afghan guests be dressed in black formal-wear.[135] These diplomats also brought their wives, who became key objects of emula-tion and fashion for the Afghan official class, bringing their ball gowns and flapper-dresses with them from Europe.[136] The new embassies, as well as newly built hotels, also provided a place for intrepid foreign tourists to come and stay, and the 1920s can be marked as the decade when Afghanistan first became a viable tourist destination. Amongst these pioneering tourists were society beauties, like the Italian princess Donna Nives, who stayed with the Italian Ambassador for nine months in 1922–23,[137] honeymooning couples traversing Asia,[138] and intrepid female American journalists in big hats, sen-sible shoes and with 11 pieces of hand luggage.[139] These women recorded their interactions and impressions of the transformations taking place in Kabul. It was not only European and North American women who made the

Economy of dress in early-20th-century Afghanistan 181

journey to the 'fairytale city', however.[140] In 1928, the female Muslim writer Hanifa Khouri travelled by sea and motorcar from Egypt to Kabul at the invitation of Queen Soraya. She later wrote an article in the Egyptian newspaper *al-Lata'if al-Musawara* on the experience, describing the 'women's renaissance' (*al-nahda al-naswiya*) that she saw taking place in Afghanistan and praising Soraya for her ceaseless work on behalf of Afghan women.[141] These foreigners acted as inspirations and arbiters of new fashions amongst the Afghan official class. At parties at the houses of ministers and diplomats these women were seen, and photographed, without face or head coverings of any sort.[142]

It was not just in the houses and on the streets of Kabul that these progressive Afghan and foreign women were increasingly visible: the expansion of state-backed newspaper printing in the regional centres of the country meant that their activities and speeches were increasingly recorded and disseminated amongst the population.[143] Groups of women still assembled in picturesque locations like the *Bagh-e Babur*, as they had done since the nineteenth century,[144] only this time the festivities and speeches were recorded and publicized in the Afghan press.[145] Queen Soraya became a particular fixture of the press, and was described in detail engaging in a variety of public acts, be it speaking at the girls' school or issuing an invitation to a female Indian teacher to visit Afghanistan.[146] Not to be outdone by her technologically minded husband, Soraya now joined Amanullah in sending telegrams abroad, which were then published in the Afghan newspapers.[147] Alongside accounts of Soraya, there were also articles by educated women like the director of the girls' school and a female *monshi* (clerk), who wrote on subjects such as the need for women to go to school or 'the concept of freedom'.[148] Collective articles praising Amanullah and written by all the female students of the girls' school were also published in the new cultural magazine *Anis*.[149] The condition of women's bodies became a topic of discussion in print too, *Anis* including articles on such questions as whether 'thinness' was a good or bad thing for women.[150] These newspapers also bore witness to new clothes companies opening in Kabul, such as the *Sherkat-e Semin* in Murad Khane district, which provided clothing to men and women of the official class.[151] These newspapers were not wholly Kabul-centric either: the Qandahar-based *Tulu'-e Afghan* discussed women and women's issues, printing speeches by prominent women,[152] articles on such themes as the role of women in society[153] and poetry denouncing polygamy.[154] There was even the first newspaper specifically for women, *Ershad al-Neswan*, mentioned above, which began publication in Kabul in 1921. An extant copy of this newspaper illustrates the symbiotic link between women reformers and the Afghan state: the front-page article explained the benefits of Amanullah's administrative reforms, and half of the inside page was taken up with a poem celebrating the birth of Amanullah's son, Prince Rahmatullah Khan.[155]

These socio-cultural shifts amongst the official class in Kabul, fed by transformations in material culture and the influx of ideas and peoples from elsewhere, were matched by a new ideology that both reflected these transformations and advocated further change. A discourse emerged which increasingly identified Afghan women with the Afghan nation and thus bound the *nahza* of Afghan women and the Afghan nation together. This process bears the influence of similar nationalist ideologies elsewhere in the Middle East and Asia, especially that of Iran.[156] Of particular note, exhortations to the Afghan army increasingly bound ideas of military service to the protection of Afghanistan's *namus* ('honour'), a concept closely connected to that of women in Afghan society.[157] This connection was made explicit when Soraya was described as the 'mother of the army' (*mader-e ordu*),[158] and she in turn described the Afghan Army as 'my children' (*awlad-ha-yom*).[159] Letters were also published in which regional military units pledged their support not to the Afghan king, but to Queen Soraya instead.[160] As in Iran, a discourse combining issues of women's health and education and the nurturing of the 'homeland' (*watan*) developed as well.[161] In one speech, Amanullah described the Afghan nation (*mellat*) as sick and relying on the government to be its doctor.[162] This new conceptual framing was expressed discursively in articles on women's health, and more practically in the development of health education and facilities for women.[163] When it came to dress, this gave fuel to arguments that the full-scale *chadari* was not only old-fashioned, but also unhealthy and even unsafe for women.[164] The identifying of women's bodies with the homeland extended to matters of dress too. While Amanullah would often don 'native' (*watani*) dress of *pirahan-tomban*, turban and locally made boots, prominent women also encouraged Afghan women to wear indigenously manufactured clothing.[165] The motive for promoting locally made clothes was primarily economic – a means to stimulate nascent native industries and challenge the import of cheap foreign clothes that continued to flood the country – but there was also the ideological dimension of promoting pride in 'national' manufacture and design. This state-endorsed encouragement had little success, however; official-class women in Kabul had too much invested, economically and ideologically, in the foreign-imported fashions and fabrics that signalled their internationalism in politics and dress.

This attention to international trends in fashion mirrored other forms of women's internationalism during the period. This chapter has already mentioned how increasing numbers of foreign women came to Afghanistan, sometimes at the invitation of Queen Soraya, and forged bonds of solidarity and friendship with their Afghan sisters. Such interest in the status of women throughout the world extended to the press and educational establishments. Girls' school textbooks published in Kabul during the 1920s encouraged Afghan girls to take an interest in women abroad: the introduction to one textbook stressed that its purpose was to inform its female readers about the conditions of Muslim women throughout the world, as well as the conditions of non-Muslim women 'as a point of comparison'.[166] Sections then followed on such powerful non-Muslim women as the Amazons,[167] whose martial qualities and valour were set against the bravery of Muslim women in times

Economy of dress in early-20th-century Afghanistan   183

of fighting (*ghazawat*).[168] This internationalism of outlook amongst women's rights advocates was extended to the justifications that they provided for their actions; in 1924, Amanullah defended female education with the argument that the ulema in many other countries of the Islamic world did not protest at the education of women.[169] These justifications, made using the example of practices taking place in other parts of the Muslim world, were used for issues of dress too. In 1923, the Afghan press discussed the early clothing reforms of the Shah of Iran, praising the policy of encouraging the wearing of indigenously produced fabrics in clothes' production.[170] As has been noted above, however, despite its foreign precedents and justifications, the state-backed promotion of indigenous textiles was fatally flawed. In terms of production, indigenous producers could not compete in terms of cost, quality or quantity with those of cheap imports. In terms of consumption, the strength of nationalist sentiment was not enough to make up for the symbolic cost that consumers would pay in giving up those foreign clothes which acted as markers of sophistication, status and progress.

'The flappers of Paghman': fusion dressing in the 1920s

While these transformations in material and intellectual life encouraged modifications to high-status women's clothing, they did not lead to the abolition or obsolescence of veiling *per se*. The cultural climate amongst the official class, fuelled by the increasing availability of goods, people and ideas from outside the country, led to the piecemeal adoption of elements of new styles of dress. Combinations of Western dress with traditional elements abounded, creating a form of 'fusion dressing'. The Bengali teacher Syed Mujtaba Ali described these 'flappers', as one American journalist called them, thus:

> Upper-class women … in high-heels, knee-length frock, full-sleeve tight blouse, gloves and hat. The faces were not fully visible as they were covered by a thin net veil hanging from their hats. The bolder the woman, the thinner the net.[171]

As Micklewright has noted, 'the last indigenous elements to disappear are the ones most heavily invested with social or symbolic importance: headgear, or garments worn in a ritual context'[172] and this was certainly the case with forms of veil in Kabul. High-status women certainly used new forms of veil, particularly the thin tulle veil popular at that time in Egypt and Istanbul (known as *çarşaf* in Turkish), but did not do away with them altogether in public. These new forms of veil acted as suitable symbols of these Afghan women's progressive values, their socio-economic status and their place in the expanding official class in Kabul. Their veils were designed to signify a form of cosmopolitan modesty, comfortable in public spaces, and yet still in line with religious precepts. Similar processes were at work too with men's

184 *Thomas Wide*

clothing, where the full Western-style suit (*dreshi*) could be offset with a traditional turban.[173] The wearing of head and face coverings by reformists, in whatever modified form, thus reveals the Islamic nature of this progressive vision. Certainly for almost all of Amanullah's reign, Afghan women were not prepared to remove their face veils. On the contrary, they were keen to use their veils to stress their Islamic credentials.[174] Scholars have noted that the discourse on 'the veil' amongst urban intellectuals in Egypt and Iran had two main strands, one secular and anti-Islamic, the other reformist Islamic.[175] While these intellectual and social developments elsewhere in the Islamic world were noted by social reformers in Afghanistan, no secular and anti-Islamic approach ever surfaced. Official-class Afghan women did not advocate an abolition of all forms of veil, just the adoption of a modified version.

It must be remembered, however, that this official class made up a miniscule part of the Afghan population, and were almost completely confined to Kabul. The rapid influx of new ideas, technologies, and foreign people into the newly-constructed spaces of Kabul, combined with an improved road infrastructure binding Kabul to British India, had created a situation whereby Kabul was increasingly wired in to international trends, fashions and tastes. The rest of the country, on the other hand, relied on quite different forms of circulation and transnational exchange: the informal information networks of traders, religious students, nomadic pastoralists; the local communal spaces of guest-house (*hujra*) and mosque; and the more traditional transport means of horse, camel or donkey. The trends of a 'globalizing' Kabul thus became increasingly detached from the rest of the country, which viewed the performances of conspicuous consumption and the activities of internationalized elites – tennis, afternoon tea, fancy-dress parties – with increasing bemusement and hostility.[176] And it was the involvement of elite women in these new activities towards which opposition seemed to gravitate. This is perhaps no surprise, considering how visible such women were; the fact that these individuals were predominantly from the royal family or the official class meant that they were frequently seen at official and state functions. These functions were both heavily attended and more importantly *talked about* by Afghans in Kabul and beyond. Moreover, the regime's state-endorsed ideology, which bound the issues of women's rights into its own brand of nationalism and internationalism, meant that these prominent women and Amanullah's government were increasingly identified together. Anger at these women's seeming lack of modesty could thus be directed towards the government, and anger at the government was directed towards them as the most visible manifestation of the regime's controversial reforms. Thus, when opposition flared up into a serious rebellion in Khost in the east of the country in 1924, it was the reforms with regard to women that were focused upon.[177] And this despite the fact that there were many other reasons for opposition to Amanullah's regime at that time, most particularly the increasingly heavy tax burden and the encroaching of centralized government into rural areas.[178] With a poorly maintained army and extremely limited coercive power, Amanullah found himself having to back down on many of his reforms, and was forced to close down the girls' school in Kabul.[179] It was a humbling experience and, for the next four years, the Afghan government did not introduce any radical reforms at all. Until, that is, a new energy and appetite for reform was spurred by Amanullah and Soraya's 'world tour'.

Embodying the new Afghanistan: the 'world tour' of 1928

Alongside Amanullah's desire to see the world (the trip was compared in the Western press to Peter the Great's journey to Western Europe),[180] and encourage trade links and foreign investment in his country, the world tour acted as a way of 'putting Afghanistan on the map'. Afghanistan had only achieved independence nine years previously, and the Afghan royal couple were keen to present Afghanistan as a progressive Islamic nation arriving onto the world stage.[181] The tour was thus a continual performance in which the royal couple attempted to play out the roles of enlightened, self-possessed Muslim rulers. Soraya's dress was pure theatre, and the European and Middle Eastern press fell over themselves to describe in minute detail what she wore for each official function. Mussolini, quoted in the British press, stated, 'Queen Souriya [*sic*] travelled from one end of Europe to the other fascinating sovereigns and statesmen with her beauty and charm, and no one could find one flaw in her entire conduct.'[182] But the tour was also of great interest to Afghans back home, with each stage recorded in detail in the state press.[183] Soraya was seemingly aware of her own symbolic status as the most visible Afghan woman of all and knew how to use the language of dress to articulate this vision of a new Afghanistan. She thus adapted her dress according to each country she visited; in Paris she went with head completely uncovered; in England, she wore a hat almost identical in style to that of the English monarch, Queen Mary; in Egypt she wore a half-sized *ruband* (a form of cloth face-covering). The European press wrote about the couple in raptures, the Islamic press less so. In Egypt, Amanullah's wearing of a top hat on his visit to al-Azhar and Soraya's appearances without her face veiled caused ripples of discontent amongst both ulema and intellectuals.[184] The Syrian intellectual Rashid Rida made it clear that anger at the royal couple was solely a matter of dress:

> Were it not for the fact that the king wore the European hat, and Her Majesty the Queen went unveiled – something which has not yet been broadly accepted in Egypt where Her Majesty the Queen of Egypt still wears the veil – no-one in Egypt would have made the slightest criticism of him. Rather, he would have met with general approval and unmixed praise.[185]

In Iran, too, Soraya caused disapproval from Iranian religious leaders when she and several other women entered the shrine in Mashhad without wearing

186   *Thomas Wide*

a *chadar*.[186] On her return to Qandahar, she put a thin *chadar* over her head, combined with a European hat; a technique which offended some viewers more than if she had been uncovered – as if the diaphanous veil was in some way mocking tradition, 'a fraudulent pretension to *hejab*'.[187]

In spite of criticisms from various quarters, the royal couple's trip abroad strengthened their resolve to push for further reform. Their experiences in Europe seemed to spur them to view all forms of veiling as essentially backward; no longer could forms of veil be used to express sophistication or progressive sentiments. 'The veil' had now become abstracted and essentialized, a symbol of 'backwardness' (*aqabmandagi*) and ignorance (*jahalat*) in contrast to everything that the self-conscious reformers stood for: educational development, technical and scientific progress, women's rights. Aware of the ability of Soraya's person to literally 'embody' ideals, which had the power to persuade both inside and outside Afghanistan, reformers prepared to 'unveil' her in the most public way possible. The occasion was a set of lectures at the Estur Palace in Kabul in October 1928, following on the back of a whole raft of radical new reforms proposed by Amanullah. At the end of his final lecture, Amanullah stressed the backwardness of 'the veil', declared that Islam did not demand that women cover their faces, hands and feet and called on Afghan women to unveil. At that moment, Soraya stood up and, in front of a large crowd, tore off the transparent veil she had been wearing since her return from Europe. Several women followed her.[188] As with the royal couple's performance on the world tour, it was an act of pure theatre. And yet, however much Amanullah might have wanted it to, this act of unveiling could never step outside the symbolic realm into that of national policy or law. Unlike Ataturk's or Reza Shah's 'authoritarian modernization', where cultural reforms can be read as assertions of state power, Amanullah's exhortation to unveil only stressed the limitations of that power.[189] The Afghan state had simply not developed a strong or loyal army or coercive powers that could force or discipline its female citizens to the extent of controlling what they wore. The only women whose dress could be controlled by the state were a handful of royals. Amanullah's unveiling of Soraya could thus only be a symbolic gesture, a mark of intent, an example to inspire.[190]

Western suits and cardboard hats: the male dress reforms of 1928

While the campaign to 'unveil' the women of Afghanistan was thus nothing but a symbolic act of showmanship, Amanullah *was* able to put into action reforms regarding men's dress that did carry real force in Kabul. Pre-1928, Amanullah had instituted certain rules determining the clothes worn by male government officials. This essentially amounted to the wearing of a Western suit while at work or on the street.[191] Soon after his return, he held a *loya jerga* ('grand assembly') for Afghan notables in the theatre of Paghman. These men were provided with black morning coats, trousers, a white shirt and tie, and a Western-style hat by the Afghan government, and compelled to wear this outfit at all times while in Paghman. Following this assembly, an order was made that anyone not wearing a European-style hat and suit on the streets of Kabul would be fined. These reforms have been treated perfunctorily at best by most historians of the period, but they deserve serious attention. A look at the list of demands of the opposition to Amanullah, and the list of Amanullah's reforms which were cancelled by Habibullah Kalakani in 1929, show that male dress was indeed an important issue, with Kalakani making the cancellation of the wearing of the 'European hat and suit' (*kolah-e ferengi wa dreshi*) one of his first decrees.[192] Using the model of the Afghan 'economy of dress', it is clear that there were very practical reasons, as well as symbolic, for opposition to these male dress reforms. First, Amanullah's law ordering the wearing of Western suits and hats in Kabul meant that there was suddenly an unprecedented demand for such clothes, a demand which simply could not be met by the suppliers of clothing in the city. Although there were Western-style hats and suits made in Kabul during the period, their numbers were limited.[193] Kabul still relied largely on imports, mostly second-hand, from British India. Accounts of the period just after the introduction of the dress reforms testify to the scarcity of such hats and suits, and the increasingly frantic behaviour of Kabulis as they searched for these clothes, and the money to pay for them. The Bengali teacher Mujtaba Ali describes the clothes his servant Abdur Rahman came to work in the day after the reform was announced:

> No shalwar, he was wearing trousers. Like those of prisoners, they only covered three quarters of his legs. They were so tight on his thigh that they looked like satin breeches of French gentlemen from the seventeenth century. His shirt was without a collar. There was a tie on his open neck. The jacket was so small that there was no question of buttoning it – the shirt and tie could be seen through it. The hat came down to his eyebrows as if it were on display in a shop.[194]

Mujtaba Ali goes on to recount Abdur Rahman's ordeal as he tried to get to work in the morning, dodging marauding bands of police who were fining on sight anyone they found not in Western suit and hat.[195] In this situation, the second-hand clothes market could not keep up, Mujtaba Ali noting: 'I was incapable of describing the *dreshis* worn by the people on the streets. The Kabul city was displaying all sorts of torn, dirty, oversized and small jackets, trousers, plus-fours and breeches.'[196] The special correspondent of the Civil and Military Gazette, commenting on the dearth of European headgear, mentioned that he had had his own *topee* stolen and had been forced to buy another one which had been made out of cardboard.[197] On the edge of town, Mujtaba Ali found the city virtually cut off to outsiders:

> The village woodcutters, poultry-men, vegetable vendors were being fined by hoards of policemen the moment they were setting their foot into the

188   Thomas Wide

city limits. No one gave them any receipt, so within a few yards another group of policemen were stopping them and extorting fines.

With the Afghan government's finances in perilous straits, and many of its officials not having been paid for months, it was perhaps unsurprising that the police took advantage of the opportunity to make some money.[198] This only fostered the already widespread resentment, however. When allied with the symbolic cost of being forced to wear such Western dress – particularly for those for whom traditional headwear held particularly strong honorific connotations, such as members of the ulema or important tribal or political figures[199] – one can well see how male dress reforms in Kabul fuelled hostility to Amanullah, even amongst those urbanites in Kabul who would have been considered his natural supporters.

This section has attempted to draw out the heavy practical costs to men in the dress reforms of 1928, and the concomitant lack of any actual reforms with regard to women's dress. And yet, opponents of Amanullah (as well as subsequent analyses of the period) focused, and continue to focus, heavily on the issue of 'unveiling' (*raf' hejab*). How is this to be explained? To answer this question, the chapter now turns to the role of rumour and hearsay in creating this 'misinterpretation' of Amanullah's actions and intent.

An official unveiling campaign? The role of rumour in the uprisings of 1928–29

This chapter has already touched upon the increasing divergence between the different means of circulation of goods and information in the main cities and rural areas. With regard to the spread of information, while state-endorsed newspapers multiplied in the main urban areas of Afghanistan during the 1920s, oral transmission remained the key means of spreading news and information amongst the largely illiterate population both inside and outside the cities. In such a context, it is no surprise that there was a large market for rumours and hearsay in Afghanistan. As the historian Luise White puts it, in the context of colonial Africa, 'experience was true but not as reliable as hearsay'.[200] During Habibullah's reign, rumours had done the rounds about the behaviour of the women at court,[201] and throughout the 1920s *bazargap* ('market chatter') continued to circulate: that the royal women travelled around almost naked, with skirts above the knees and no sleeves.[202] These rumours were fuelled during the royal couple's world tour, when photographs showing the Queen wearing a sleeveless ball-gown with plunging neckline, unveiled and with a short European-style haircut, were circulated widely throughout the tribal areas and sent to Kabul. In September 1928, the British Viceroy noted the hostility to Amanullah that had emerged in the tribal areas:

> Khyber reports Afridis discussing situation freely, and openly expressing opinion that Amir is mad. They greatly resent his purdah reforms and

Economy of dress in early-20th-century Afghanistan 189

female education measures. Kurram similarly reports that reforms, especially those connected with polygamy and purdah, are becoming increasingly unpopular, and are likely to lead to disturbances.[203]

All of these rumours and images were driven by a misinterpretation of what Amanullah and Soraya were asking for. Ever since this period, commentators have suggested that Amanullah decreed the 'unveiling' of women.[204] This is a mistake; nowhere in the historical records does Amanullah make any such official government 'decree'. The closest Amanullah seems to come to making such a decree is an announcement in the official newspaper that

> the use of the *borqa'* is prohibited as it is both expensive and unhygienic. In future women will wear the Syrian style of veil, with overcoat and hat. They will be given two months in which to obtain these articles of dress. Any disobedience of this order will incur a fine of twenty Afghanis.[205]

No source from the time suggests that this was ever implemented. Certainly such a decree would have been completely unenforceable, even in Kabul. It is true that both Amanullah and Soraya made speeches stressing the benefits of unveiling, but these were a) exhortations, and frequently rhetorical in tone and b) qualified by saying that it was a choice for individual families to make and would not be enforced by law. With extremely limited state power, all that could be aimed at was a public campaign that aimed at changing social mores through example. And yet, what is so striking in the reports of the uprisings in 1928–29 is how often those who opposed Amanullah demanded that Amanullah end the 'unveiling' (*raf' hejab*) – something Amanullah never encouraged or implemented beyond a symbolic gesture and the occasional rhetorical exhortation.[206] How are the demands of those who opposed Amanullah to be interpreted? Were they an intentional misinterpretation of Amanullah's position, as a means to foment resistance to his rule? Or merely a case of Chinese whispers whereby Soraya's manner of dress, and her very public and symbolic act of unveiling, had been transformed into a decree banning the veil? The answer is almost certainly 'a bit of both'. Either way, the effect was disastrous for Amanullah's regime. In the debates that followed the initial uprisings, Amanullah attempted to persuade the rebels that he had never had any plan to get rid of veiling, and acknowledged that it would never have been enforceable outside of Kabul anyway – but it was too late.[207] By this stage, the rumour had become so entrenched that it could not be dispelled. To compound the trouble, further rumours then circulated in the eastern tribal regions that the government required citizens to send their daughters to Turkey for education, or be forced to pay a fine.[208] This rumour seemed to have been proved when Afghans in the east of the country saw the first deputation of female students destined for Turkey drive through their areas on their way to British India.[209] It was in this climate of wild hearsay and intrigue that various sections of the Shinwari tribe revolted and took the

190   *Thomas Wide*

eastern city of Jalalabad in November 1928. At the same time, displeasure in Kabul at the actually enforced reforms to male dress was expressed in the burning of European hats on the streets of Kabul.[210] After a separate uprising to the north of Kabul broke out, men in Kabul took off the Western clothes they had been forced to wear and went back to their traditional *pirahan-tomban* and turban. The Bengali Mujtaba Ali recorded in his memoirs how he now found himself the only man in Kabul left wearing full suit and hat.[211] With an army that had not been paid and a population in Kabul that had been financially put upon, harassed and humiliated, it was little surprise that there was neither much military or popular support left for Amanullah in Kabul. Within three months his regime had fallen.

Conclusion

While it is tempting to see changes in the status of women and developments in dress during the 1920s as a radical break with Afghanistan's past, this chapter has emphasized the continuities and longer-term gradual drivers of change. It has argued that, contrary to the writings of reformist-minded activists and historians, Afghanistan's women played a far more active role in Afghan social, cultural and economic life pre-Amanullah than is often recognized. At the same time, changes in dress in the 1920s largely built on, rather than broke with, changes already under way in the early twentieth century. The model of an Afghan 'economy of dress' has helped situate changing veiling practices in a larger story of shifts in dress which affected not only women but men, and not only elites but other sectors of the population too.

This chapter has argued that all these changes in dress had practical and symbolic dimensions. On the practical level, high-status Afghans' clothing adapted to a new set of public spaces, new objects of circulation and new technologies of travel and manufacturing. For high-status men, this meant primarily an increasing adoption of Western-style clothes, as well as a new-found interest in ceremonialism. For high-status women, this meant the gradual introduction of Western fashions and new forms of veiling practices. For individuals further down the economic ladder this translated into a consumption of second-hand clothes and materials circulating between Russia, Afghanistan and British India.

These material and cultural changes continued to affect and influence choices of dress into the 1920s. However, such clothing took on a more purely symbolic dimension during Amanullah's reign, powered predominantly by prominent self-conscious reformers allied to the state. During this period dress became a clear marker of allegiance to the grand project of national renewal and reform, and a key target of criticism from those who would oppose it. Official-class women, in particular, used their high visibility to 'perform' these ideals, stepping out into a variety of new roles in public life and attempting to act as examples to be followed. At first, these women modified and adapted their head coverings as a means to articulate this

Economy of dress in early-20th-century Afghanistan 191

vision. As the 1920s progressed, however, reformers, of whom the most visible was Queen Soraya, increasingly viewed head coverings as representing the country's 'backwardness' – a form of dress not just to be modified but to be eradicated. By 1928, royal women's clothes, and the bodies that those clothes covered or did not cover, had increasingly become the central symbolic sites of debate and opposition. A whole raft of grievances and complaints against the state became channelled and expressed through these most visible of clothes and persons. At the same time, however, men's clothing became the source of more practical and less symbolic concerns, as laws enforcing the wearing of Western-style hats and suits in Kabul proved increasingly wearisome to a population who had neither the funds nor the access to such forms of clothing. Through such a reading, this chapter has stressed the value of the interpretive model of an 'economy of dress', which offers a fruitful means for understanding historical change and motivation in Afghanistan. A 'marketplace' of goods and ideas has helped connect the economic to the intellectual, the material to the cultural, and move discussions of the period beyond all-too-prevalent oppositions of 'tribalism', 'conservatism', 'religiosity' 'xenophobia' on the one hand, and 'modernization', 'Westernization', 'secularization' and 'globalization' on the other. It is not that these terms have no explanatory force. But dress is a lived practice that cannot be reduced to such abstractions. A material and cultural artefact, with practical and symbolic dimensions, dress in Afghanistan thus offers a window onto the complex and variegated ways that Afghans have made sense of, and given purpose to, their lives in times of profound change.

Notes

1 For a useful discussion of the ethical status of such justifications, see Lila Abu-Lughod, 'Do Muslim Women Really Need Saving? Anthropological Reflections on Cultural Relativism and Its Others', *American Anthropologist*, Vol.104, No.3 (2002), pp.783–90.

2 This decree was printed in Habibullah Kalakani's newspaper, *Habib al-Islam*, Vol.1, No.1, p.3. I am very grateful to Mustafa Khan for assistance in tracking down original copies of this extremely rare newspaper in the Shomali plains, and to Robert McChesney for sharing typed copies from his own collection.

3 I am influenced here by the work of Rosalind O'Hanlon; see, for example, 'Manliness and Imperial Service in Mughal North India', *Journal of the Economic and Social History of the Orient*, Vol.42, No.1 (1999), pp.47–93.

4 For such an approach, in the context of early-twentieth-century Egypt, see Beth Baron, 'Unveiling in Early Twentieth Century Egypt: Practical and Symbolic Considerations', *Middle Eastern Studies*, Vol.25, No.3 (July 1989), pp.370–86.

5 For a useful discussion of these different approaches, see Manu Goswami, 'Rethinking the Modular Nation Form: Toward a Sociohistorical Conception of Nationalism', *Comparative Studies in Society and History*, Vol.44 (2002), pp.770–99.

6 The classic articulation of the role of Ottoman ideas on 'Afghan modernism' is Vartan Gregorian, *The Emergence of Modern Afghanistan* (Stanford, CA: Stanford University Press, 1969).

192   *Thomas Wide*

7 For contemporary accounts of women's roles in such tasks see T.L. Pennell, *Among the Wild Tribes of the Afghan Frontier* (London: Seeley and Co., 1909), p.99; George Macmunn, *Afghanistan From Darius to Amanullah* (London: G. Bell and Sons, 1929), p.296.

8 Henry D. Baker, *British India with Notes on Ceylon, Afghanistan and Tibet* (Washington, DC: US Department of Commerce, Consular Report 72, 1915), p.550.

9 E. Akbar, 'An Analysis of Afghan Women's Social Status and A Perspective of the (*sic*) Rights' in *Proceedings of the Seminar: Women's Human Rights in Afghanistan 15th–19th October 1994 Mazar, Afghanistan* (n.p., 1994), pp.34–35. Even in urban areas these nomadic women would frequently be unveiled, see. J. Fleming, 'Clouds Above Festival Kabul', *Asia*, Vol.29, No.4 (1929) p.286; on unveiled women amongst the Ghilzai, see Macmunn, op. cit., p.297; for unveiled Waziri and Marwat women, see S.S. Thorburn, *Bannu: Or Our Afghan Frontier* (London: Trubner, 1876), p.351. For a photograph of nomadic women without face veils in Afghanistan, see photo taken by Major Charles Harvey-Kelley in 1925, Eur. Mss. D1218/11, No.13.

10 The term is from Houchang Chehabi, 'Staging the Emperor's New Clothes: Dress Codes and Nation-Building under Reza Shah', *Iranian Studies*, Vol.26, No.3–4 (1993), p.222.

11 This point was made by foreign observers in Kabul even at the time, the Military Attache in Kabul noting that, despite the ambitions of Amanullah's purported reforms, 'these ideas, however, have not so far interfered in any way with the normal existence of 9/10th of the people'. British Military Attache in Kabul to Humphrys, 24th September 1928, IOR/L/P/L&P/1285.

12 For examples of entreating, see Fayz Mohammad Kateb, *Seraj al-tawarikh* (Kabul: 1913–15), Vol.1, pp.51, 54, 72–73; for mediation see, amongst others, ibid., Vol.2, p.199, 238; for such mediating roles in the early twentieth century, see Fayz Mohammad Kateb, *Seraj al-tawarikh jeld-e chaharom* (Kabul: Entisharat-e Amiri, 2011), Part 2, p.532.

13 A detailed personal account of Halima, or 'Bobo Jan' as she was often known, can be found in Sardar Abdul Ghafoor Seraj, *Az Yaddasht-ha-ye Maderam*, (unpublished mss, n.d.) I am grateful to Ali Seraj for sharing this work with me in Kabul. For a British perspective on this remarkable woman, see George Nathaniel Curzon's account from November 1894, *Short Memo of Visit to Kabul*, British Library, Mss Eur F111/56, pp.10–11. See also, Hasan Kawun Kakar, *Government and Society in Afghanistan: The Reign of Amir Abd al-Rahman Khan* (Austin: University of Texas Press, 1979), pp.17–18.

14 Fayz Mohammad Kateb, *Seraj al-tawarikh* (Qum? Organ-e Nashriyat-e Sayyed 'Amal al-din Hosayni, 1993–94), pp.624–25.

15 See British Newswriter at Herat's diary, period ending 2nd October 1913, which notes that 'twenty-two *kharwars* of opium have been handed over to Seraj-ul-Khawatin's servants and is to be sent to Kabul', L/P&S/10/200.

16 Kabul Agent's Diary, week ending 7th May 1912, IOR/L/P&S/10/200.

17 See, for example, Kateb, *Seraj al-tawarikh*, Vol.2, p.358. For the most famous of all female fighters, the semi-legendary Malalai, see Mohammad Halim Tanwir, *Zanan-e sokhanwar wa namwar-e Afghanistan* (Peshawar: Saboor Publishing Centre, 2001), pp.210–11.

18 Ayesha Durrani, *Qasayed-e hamdiya wa na'tiya wa mahdiya* (Kabul, n.p. 1888). For an account of Ayesha Durrani's life, and the publication of her *diwan*, see Maga Rahmani, *Parda neshinan-e sokhanguy* (Kabul: Matba'-ye Umumi, 1953/4), pp.53–55; also, Mo'addeb al-Soltan Esfahani, *Aman al-tawarikh* (unpublished mss, New York University Fales Collection), Part 7, pp.4–5.

Economy of dress in early-20th-century Afghanistan 193

19 For an account of Badakhshi's relation with Mahjubah Herawi, see Sayyid Akram al-Din Hasariyan, *Sayyidah Makhfi Badakhshi* (Kabul: Bonyad-e Entisharat-e Nashr-e Jawan, 2005/6).

20 This letter is quoted in ibid., p.25.

21 Ibid., pp.25–26.

22 Ibid.

23 For an overview of Pashto oral and written literature during the period, and the role of women in poetic production, see Thomas Wide, 'Demarcating Pashto' in Nile Green and Nushin Arbabzadeh (eds), *Afghanistan In Ink* (London: Hurst, 2012).

24 For the *landay*, see Benedicte Grima, *The Performance of Emotion among Paxtun Women*, (Austin: University of Texas Press, 1992), p.147.

25 For a study of the economic relations between British India and Afghanistan in the nineteenth century, see Shah Mahmoud Hanifi, *Connecting Histories in Afghanistan: Market Relations and State Formation on a Colonial Frontier* (New York: Columbia University Press, 2008).

26 David Cannadine, *Ornamentalism: How the British Saw Their Empire* (Oxford: OUP, 2001).

27 For a study of Afghanistan and British India in the nineteenth century, see B.D. Hopkins, *The Making of Modern Afghanistan* (London: Palgrave Macmillan, 2008).

28 The phrase is from Holly Edwards, 'Unruly Images: Photography In and Out of Afghanistan', *Artibus Asiae*, Vol.66, No.2 (2006), p.116.

29 Abdur Rahman, quoted in Dupree, 'Behind the Veil in Afghanistan', *Asia*, (July/August 1978), p.11.

30 Ibid.

31 Gol Mohammad Khan Mohammadzai and Monshi Soltan Mohammad, *Ta'limnamah-e khayati* (Kabul: Dar al-Saltanah, 1892).

32 N.H. Dupree, 'Victoriana comes to the Haremserai in Afghanistan' in Paul Bucherer-Dietschi (ed.), *Bauen und Wohnen am Hindukush* (Liestal: Stiftung Bibliotheca Afghanica, 1988).

33 Angus Hamilton, *Afghanistan* (London: W. Heinemann, 1906), p.268.

34 Ibid., p.268.

35 Dupree uses the term to refer to the Amanullah period, but it seems just as apt for Habibullah's reign. N.H. Dupree, 'A Building Boom in the Hindukush. Afghanistan 1921–28', *Lotus International*, No.26 (1980).

36 For a description of the construction of one such 'Indo-Afghan' collaboration, the *Qasr-e delkusha*, see Kateb, *Seraj al-tawarikh jeld-e chaharom*, Part 2, p.363, 418; Part 3, p.176. The exact origin of the elephants of the early twentieth century is unknown, although the Bengali teacher Syed Mujtaba Ali notes that the elephants in Kabul in the 1920s had come from the state of Tripura in north eastern India, see Syed Mujtaba Ali, *Deshe bideshe*, unpublished translation by Nazes Afroz, Ch.40, p.4. My sincere thanks to Nazes Afroz for sharing his translation of this very important Bengali source with me.

37 *Seraj al-akhbar*, Vol.1, No.19, p.2 quoted in M. Schinasi, *Kaboul 1773–1948* (Naples: Universita degli Studi di Napoli L'Orientale, Dipartimento di Studi Asiatici, 2008), p.108.

38 For a detailed Afghan description of Nasrullah's trip to London, see Kateb, *Seraj al-tawarikh*, Vol.3, pp.1064–1163.

39 For an account of this building, see Schinasi, *Kaboul*, op. cit., pp.91–93.

40 Kateb, *Seraj al-tawarikh jeld-e chaharom*, Part 3, p.97.

41 For the involvement of women in the *Jashn* of 1902, see ibid., Part 2, p.268.

42 For Enayatullah's trip, see ibid., Part 2, pp.675–702; for Habibullah's trip, see ibid., Part 3, pp.227–51. For Indian accounts of Habibullah's trip, see Nile Green,

194   *Thomas Wide*

'The Afghan Afterlife of Phileas Fogg: Space and Time in the Literature of Afghan Travel' in Nile Green and Nushin Arbabzadeh (eds), *Afghanistan In Ink* (London: Hurst, 2012).

43 Habibullah Khan, *Dastur al-'amal-ha-ye harem* (n.p. n.d.).

44 *Firman* of Habibullah Khan to Amir Mohammad Khan, Governor of Bulaghin and Dornama, dated 15th Shawwal, 1321 (3rd January 1904). My thanks to May Schinasi for sharing the collection of *firmans* between Habibullah and the Governor of Bulaghin and Dornama with me.

45 Schinasi, *Kaboul*, op. cit., p.110.

46 Kateb, *Seraj al-tawarikh jeld-e chaharom*, Part 2, p.537.

47 Baker, op. cit., p.536.

48 Kateb, *Seraj al-tawarikh jeld-e chaharom*, Part 2, p.427; Thornton, op. cit., p.11.

49 Thornton, op. cit., p.161–62.

50 Thornton, op. cit., p.158.

51 NWFP diary, week ending 9th August 1913, IOR L/P&S/10/200.

52 See the *firman* of Habibullah Khan to Mirza Mohammad Husseyn Khan, Mustowfi al-Mamalik, dated 4th Muharram 1336 (20th October 1917), concerning the suitability of his seeds recently purchased from India in the Afghan climate, Afghan National Archive (ANA), *Faramin-e Habibullah*, No.249.

53 Kabul Agent's diary, week ending 15th January 1917, IOR L/P&S/10/200.

54 See the Khalilullah Enayat Seraj Collection (KES), digitized by Williams College and available at http://contentdm.williams.edu/wamp; for the importing of photography equipment from British India, see Kateb, *Seraj al-tawarikh jeld-e chaharom*, Part 3, p.468. For accounts of the development of photography in Afghanistan, see May Schinasi, 'La Photographie en Afghanistan', *Annali*, Vol.56, Fascicolo 2 (1996), pp.194–214; Holly Edwards, op. cit., pp.111–36.

55 For the displays of photos, see Mehmet Fazli, *Resimli Afghan siahatı* (Istanbul: Matba'-yi Ahmed Ihsan, 1909), p.102. For Habibullah's charitable photography sales, see Kateb, *Seraj al-tawarikh jeld-e chaharom*, Part 3, p.468.

56 For the role of road-building and motorized transport, see Nile Green, 'The Road to Kabul: Automobiles and Afghan Internationalism, 1900–1940', in Magnus Marsden and Benjamin Hopkins (eds), *Beyond Swat: History, Society and Economy along the Afghanistan-Pakistan Frontier* (New York: Columbia University Press, 2012). For his study of the 'state-sponsored aestheticization of industrial travel', see Nile Green, 'The Trans-Border Traffic of Afghan Modernism: Afghanistan and the Indian 'Urdusphere'', *Comparative Studies in Society and History*, 53, 3 (2011), p.7.

57 See, for example, KES 228-H-139.

58 For a photograph of such 'touring' women, see KES, H-420–509.

59 The man's name was Fennell, see NWFP diary, week ending 16th March 1912, IOR L/P&S/10/200.

60 Fazlı, op. cit., p.105.

61 Baker, op. cit., p.548.

62 Ibid.

63 Ibid.

64 Ibid., p.540.

65 Ibid., p.546.

66 For many references to returning exiles in Habibullah's time, see throughout Kateb, *Seraj al-tawarikh jeld-e chaharom*.

67 See, for example, Gregorian, op. cit., Ch.7.

68 Shebli No'mani trans. Olya Janab, *al-Faruq* (Lahore, n.p., 1932) For Indo-Afghan interactions during the period, see Green, 'The Trans-Border Traffic of Afghan Modernism', op. cit.

69 Thornton, op. cit., 71.

Economy of dress in early-20th-century Afghanistan   195

70 For Tarzi's own account of these formative travels, see Mahmud Tarzi, *Seya-ḥatnamah-ye seh qeṭ'a-ye ru'ye zamin dar bist o no ruz: Aseya, Urup, Afriqa*, 3 vols. (Kabul: Enayat Press, 1915). For an analysis of this work, see T.N.B. Wide, 'Around the World in 29 Days: The Travels, Translations, and Temptations of an Afghan Dragoman' in Roberta Micallef and Sunil Sharma (eds), *On the Wonders of Land and Sea* (Boston: Ilex, distributed by Havard University Press, 2013).

71 Mahmud Tarzi, *Seyahatnamah*, p.15.

72 See Lucie Ryzova, *Efendification: The Rise of the Middle Class Culture in Modern Egypt*, (DPhil diss. Oxford University, 2009). I am also influenced here by the work of Wilson Chacko Jacob, *Working Out Egypt: Effendi Masculinity and Subject Formation in Colonial Modernity, 1870–1940* (Duke University Press, 2011).

73 For Tarzi's importing of these fezes see the letter dated 19th November 1903, from the British Consul in Damascus W.S. Richards to Sir Nicholas R. O'Conor, British Ambassador in Constantinople L/P&S/10/22, p.135.

74 For Tarzi, see the photo reproduced in Rawan Farhadi (ed.), *Khaterat-e Mahmud Tarzi* (Kabul: Nasharat-e Enstitut-e Deplomasi-ye Wezarat-e Umur-e Kharijah, 2011), p.10; for the young consort, see KES HH-67-1–156.

75 See KES 662.

76 For the return of the Tarzis back to Kabul, see Kateb, *Seraj al-tawarikh jeld-e chaharom*, Part 2, p.707–8.

77 Mujtaba Ali, op. cit., p.2.

78 See Dupree, op. cit. p.138.

79 For articles on 'progress' (*taraqqi*), see, for example, *Seraj al-akhbar*, Vol.6, No.14, pp.2–3, serialized over following seven issues. For 'love of homeland' (*hobb al-watan*), see *Seraj al-akhbar*, Vol.1, No.7, p.6.

80 See Tarzi's introduction to his first article in the series '*Namwaran-e zanan-e 'alem*', ibid., pp.8–10.

81 These articles were later collected and edited by Ma'suma 'Esmati as *Namwaran-e zanan-e jahan* (Kabul: Matbu'-ye Dawlati, 1997). The best general account of *Seraj al-akhbar* remains May Schinasi, *Afghanistan at the Beginning of the Twentieth Century*' (Naples: Istituto Universitario Orientale, 1979).

82 For a fuller discussion of Tarzi's writing on women, see Senzil Nawid, 'The Feminine and Feminism in Tarzi's Work', *Annali*, Vol.55, No.3 (1995), pp.358–66.

83 *Seraj al-akhbar*, Vol.2, No.23, pp.13–14.

84 H.D. Baker, op. cit., p.535.

85 Ibid. The authors of a National Geographic article suggested that 'Second-hand uniforms are among the principal articles of import into the land of the Amir', Frederick Simpich and 'Haji Mirza Hussein' (a.k.a. Oscar Von Niedermayer), 'Every-Day Life in Afghanistan', *National Geographic*, June 1921, p.96.

86 For an account of this factory by the man who was tasked to run it, see Thornton, op. cit. Habibullah's desire to stem the flow of foreign imports is clear from a conversation he had with the English geologist Walter Saise: 'my wool ... goes to India, and comes back cloth. I shall save that expense. I want to be able to clothe as well as feed my people.' Walter Saise, 'A Visit to Afghanistan', *Proceedings of the Central Asian Society* (12th April 1911), p.10.

87 Baker, op. cit., p.535.

88 See Kateb, *Seraj al-tawarikh jeld-e chaharom*, Part 2, p.514.

89 Baker, op. cit., p.545, 551. For the success of Russian boots in the Afghan market, see A.H. Grant, 'A Winter at the Court of an Absolute Monarch', *Blackwood's Magazine*, Vol.180, No.1093 (November 1906), p.600. Russian galoshes also seem to have found a market in Afghanistan, see Saise, 'A Visit to Afghanistan', op. cit., p.16.

90 Thornton, op. cit., p.52. Saise also testified to this second-hand trade, noting that 'the country people keep to the national dress; but on cold days you see even them in overcoats with 'Sussex', or 'Guard', or 'Ticket-Collector', on the collars.

196 *Thomas Wide*

They are discarded clothes, imported into the country, and sold at low prices.' Saise, op. cit., p.13.

91 Hamilton, op. cit., p.112.

92 Baker, op. cit., p.551.

93 Ibid.

94 For one such shipment of uniforms from Karachi, see Kateb, *Seraj al-tawarikh, jeld-e chaharom*, Part 2, p.603.

95 For a useful discussion of different forms of 'cosmopolitanism' see W. Hanley, 'Grieving Cosmopolitanism in Middle East Studies' in *History Compass* 6/5 (2008), pp.1346–67.

96 Amanullah was frequently photographed in such 'local' or 'peasant' dress in the 1920s, see, for example, KES A-11-642; KES A-8-639.

97 Baker, op. cit., p.549–50.

98 Ibid; for the use of Russian gold thread, see ibid., p.543.

99 I am influenced here by Nancy Tapper's arguments concerning veiling practices in N. Lindisfarne-Tapper and B. Ingham, 'Approaches to the Study of Dress in the Middle East' in *Languages of Dress in the Middle East* (Richmond: Curzon 1997), pp.1–39.

100 I take the term from Jonathan Brooks and C.W. Brooks (eds), *The Middling Sort of People: Culture, Society, and Politics in England, 1550–1800* (London: St Martin's Press, 1994).

101 The Indian revolutionary Zafar Hasan Aibek's Urdu memoirs describe the great pomp with which Habibullah's wives were driven through the city wearing *borqas* of delicate white cloth. The status of these royal women was such that horsemen rode alongside ordering onlookers to shut their eyes, Zafar Hasan Aibek, *Khaterat (Ap Biti)*, (Lahore: Rafa'e Printers, 1990), p.84.

102 Ghobar mentions this white *borqa'*, which was banned early on in Habibullah's reign, in Ghulam Mohammad Ghobar, *Afghanistan dar masir tarikh* (Kabul: Entisharat-e Maiwand, 2009), p.700. For Veblen's analysis of 'conspicuous consumption' see Thorsten Veblen, *A Theory of the Leisure Class: An Economic Study of Institutions* (New York: Macmillan,1899), Ch.4, pp.49–70.

103 Ghobar, op. cit., p.700.

104 This point is made by N.H. Dupree in her article, 'Behind the Veil in Afghanistan', op. cit., p.11.

105 See, for example, Pennell, op. cit., p.104.

106 See, for example, the photos taken by John Burke in Kabul in 1879 of the 'nautch girls' (professional dancing girls), original in the British Library, Photos 430/3(59) and 430/3(60).

107 A *firman* commanding the wearing of yellow turbans, can be found in the ANA in Kabul, on display in the exhibition room. See also Kateb, *Seraj al-tawarikh jeld-e chaharom*, Part 2, p.596. For a reference to the yellow *chadaris* worn by Hindu women in Kabul, see Fleming, *Clouds Above Festival Kabul*, op. cit., p.280–88.

108 Baker, op. cit., p.549.

109 See, for example, the descriptions of different forms of dress amongst the frontier tribes in Pennell, op. cit., p.104.

110 For the first view, see Leon Poullada, *Reform and Rebellion in Afghanistan, 1919–1929* (Ithaca, NY: Cornell University Pres, 1973.) The subtitle, 'King Amanullah's Failure to Modernize a Tribal Society', makes clear the book's approach. For the second reading, see, for example, William Kerr Fraser-Tytler, *Afghanistan: A Study of Political Developments in Central Asia* (London: Oxford University Press, 1950), from which the quote is taken p.196.

111 For an account of Afghanistan's gaining of independence, see Ludwig Adamec, 'Afghanistan 1900–1923: A Diplomatic History' (Berkeley: University of California Press, 1967).

Economy of dress in early-20th-century Afghanistan   197

112 Amalendu Guha, 'The Economy of Afghanistan During Amanullah's Reign, 1919–29', *International Studies* 9, 1967–68, pp.182.

113 Ibid., p.172.

114 For an in-depth discussion of these reform-minded women, see M. Schinasi, 'Femmes afghans: instruction et activités publiques pendant le règne amâniya (1919–29)', *Annali dell'Istituto Universitario Orientale di Napoli* 55/4, 1995, pp.446–62; also, N. H. Dupree, 'Revolutionary Rhetoric and Afghan Women' *Afghanistan Council Occasional Paper No.23* (New York City: The Asia Society, 1981).

115 Notices announcing the school's inauguration were published in the newspaper *Aman-e Afghan* Year 1, No.32, p.6. This newspaper, along with that of *Tulu'-e Afghan* and *Anis* used in this paper, can be viewed at the Kabul Public Library. The letter on the use of Halima's house for the school, from the Education Superintendent (*nazir-e mu'aref*) to the Ministry of Interior, dated 25 Hut 1299, can be found at ANA, Letters from the Amani Period, No.1115.

116 *Ershad al-Neswan*, Vol.1, No.12, pp.1–2. This issue of this extremely rare newspaper is held at the ANA. Although Rahin (2007) mentions three copies of *Ershad al-Neswan* in Kabul University Library, I was unable to locate these on a recent visit (21st April 2012).

117 For a contemporary report on this hospital, by Okht al-Seraj, see *Aman-e Afghan*, Vol.7, No.33, p.3. For an overview of its administration, see Schinasi, *Femmes Afghanes*, op. cit., p.455.

118 Although the school had mostly women teachers, several male teachers did teach there, including the Afghan artist Gholam Mohammad Maymanagi, the poet Betab, the Indian maths and science teacher Jamal ud-Din, and even the Minister of Education Fayz Mohammad, see Schinasi, *Femmes Afghanes*, op. cit., p.451.

119 Sohrab Katrak, *Through Amanullah's Afghanistan* (Karachi: 'Sind Observer' & Mercantile Steam Press Limited, 1929), p.27.

120 See the photo of Afaq Sultan having her eyes examined by Fuad Beg, KES A-1022-1653.

121 For the design and construction of Daralaman, see Schinasi, *Kaboul*, op. cit., pp.151–60.

122 Letter from Amanullah Khan concerning printing of publicity for the Jashn, dated 3rd Asad 1301, ANA uncatalogued; letter of Amanullah's secretary to Minister of Interior on the sending of an electrical engineer to Paghman, ANA No.433.

123 The welcoming group was known as the *hay'at-e esteqbal*; it set about re-decorating the palace for Soraya on her return from her royal tour and then participating in the Independence Day celebrations, see Schinasi *Femmes Afghanes*, op. cit., p.457. A letter from the *Shah Aghasi* to the Minister of Justice, dated 7th Haut 1303, asking for permission for a group of women to take part in the independence-day celebrations can be found at ANA, No.68.

124 On the volleyball players, see May Mott-Smith, 'Behind the Purdah in Afghanistan', *Asia*, No.54 (16th December1929), p.16.

125 For the development of photography during the Amani period, see Habibullah Rafi', *Armaghan-e Tamaddon: Tarikhcha-ye Wurud-e Wasa'i-e 'Asri beh Afghanistan*, (Peshawar: Siyar Arik, 1999), pp.27–31.

126 Schinasi, *La Photographie*, op. cit., pp.197–200.

127 *Souvenir D'Afghanistan* (Paris: Etablissements Papeghin, 1924).

128 For an account of one such bus journey, see Mujtaba Ali, op. cit., chs.7–12.

129 For an account of a journey on the train, see Jackson, 'Clouds over Festive Kabul', op. cit., p.325.

130 Schinasi, *Femmes Afghanes*, op. cit., p.456.

131 Descriptions can be found in the Afghan newspaper *Aman-e Afghan*, Vol.9, No.38, p.1, 2, 3.

132 For a photo of these girls and their berets, see KES 906-A-275.

198   *Thomas Wide*

133 See, for example, Tarzi's account of a trip to a Beiruti nightspot in Tarzi, *Seyahatnama*, pp.56–57.
134 Schinasi, *Femmes Afghanes*, op. cit., p.450. A sign of these educationalists' internationalist outlook was that four of them – two Bengalis, a Frenchman and a Russian, had all studied under Rabindranath Tagore's university of Shantiniketan. See Mujtaba Ali, op. cit., Ch.27.
135 For one such tea invitation, see Fayz Mohammad, Minister of Education, to the Minister of Justice, 16 Mizan 1302, ANA No.283.
136 For Afghan photographs of such women, see, for example, KES A-506–1137.
137 Maria della Neve Ruffo della Scaletta, *Diario (1922–23)*, (private collection). I am grateful to May Schinasi for showing me a copy of this handwritten diary.
138 For one such intrepid couple, see *Daily Mail* (29th December 1928).
139 May Mott-Smith, 'On through the Khyber to Kabul', *Asia*, No.29 (1929), pp.396–401.
140 The term comes from an article by Roland Wild, 'Amanullah's Fairy-Tale City' in the *Daily Mail* (28th September 1928).
141 This article was reprinted in Mazhar Ali, *Afghanistan* (Cairo: Mat?ba'at al-Sunnah al-Muhammadiyah, 1950), pp.92–95.
142 See, for example, the photo of a party at the home of the Minister Mohammad Hashim, Paghman, 1928 KES A391–1022.
143 For an account of the newspapers of the Amani period, see Abdul Rasul Rahin, *Tarikh-e matbu'at-e Afghanistan* (Skärholmen: *Shura-ye Farhangi Afghanistan*, 2007), pp.225–87.
144 Charles Masson, *Narrative of Various Journeys in Balochistan, Afghanistan, the Panjab and Kalat* (London, Richard Bentley, 1844), p.241, quoted in Schinasi, *Femmes Afghanes*, op. cit., p.454.
145 See, for example, *Aman-e Afghan*, Vol.5, No.44, p.3; *Ershad al-Neswan*, Vol.1, No.3, p.1.
146 *Aman-e Afghan*, Vol.6, No.40, p.6.
147 For one such telegram, see *Aman-e Afghan*, Vol.3/4, No.7, p.10.
148 For the article by the director of *Maktab-e Masturat* see *Aman-e Afghan*, Year x, No.22, p.x; for the female *monshi's* article see *Tulu'-e Afghan*, Vol.3, No.11, p.1.
149 *Anis*, Vol.6, No.96, p.3.
150 *Anis*, Vol.1, No.16, p.6.
151 *Anis*, Vol.1, No.27, p.10.
152 *Tulu'-e Afghan*, Vol.2, No.49, p.3.
153 *Tulu'-e Afghan*, Vol.6, No.56, p.2.
154 *Anis*, Vol.6, No.59, p.1.
155 *Ershad al-Neswan*, Vol.1, No.12, pp.1–2.
156 For useful discussions of the place of women in the discourse of Iranian nationalism, see Afsaneh Najmabadi, *Women with Mustaches and Men without Beards* (Berkeley: University of California Press, 2005); Muhamad Tavakoli-Targhi, *Refashioning Iran* (New York: Palgrave, 2001), Firoozeh Kashani Sabet, *Frontier Fictions* (Princeton: Princeton University Press, 1999), esp. Ch.6.
157 See, for example, *Aman-e Afghan*, Vol.6, No.4, p.4.
158 *Aman-e Afghan*, Vol.6, No.3, p.3.
159 *Aman-e Afghan*, Vol.6, No.2, p.7.
160 *Aman-e Afghan*, Vol.5, No.50, p.3.
161 For a discussion of the discourse of women, hygiene and patriotism in Iran, see Firoozeh Kashani-Sabet, 'Hallmarks of Humanism: Hygiene and Love of Homeland in Qajar Iran', *The American Historical Review*, Vol.105, No.4 (2000), pp.1171–1203; also Firoozeh Kashani-Sabet, 'The Politics of Reproduction: Maternalism and Women's Hygiene in Iran, 1896–1941, *IJMES*, Vol.38 (2006), pp.1–29.

Economy of dress in early-20th-century Afghanistan 199

162 This speech can be found in Nasrullah Sowiman ed., *Notoqha-ye a'lihazrat Amanullah Khan ghazi, qesmat-e awwal* (Kabul Akademi-ye 'Olum, 1989–90), p.14.

163 The Afghan newspapers, especially *Anis*, carried articles on the importance of health and hygiene. For a book on household management, designed for women, and co-written by a woman, see Mohammadi Begum and Husayn Mohammad, *Idarah-ye al-dar raje' beh eqtes?ad wa akhlaq-e baytī* (Matba'ye Sherkat-e Rafiq, 1928).

164 See, for example, Amanullah's speech in October 1928, Adamec (1974), *Afghanistan's Foreign Affairs*, p.137. Also, Ali Ahmad, *The Fall of Amanullah*, p.18. Translation of this manuscript can be found at IOR/L/P&S/10/1285.

165 For Amanullah's dress, see KES A-11-642; A-8–639. 'Watani' dress, as long as it was neat (*munazam*), was also allowed for his ministers, see letter from the Ministry of Interior to Mirza Qutb al-Din Khan, 1301/1922 (no further date specified), ANA, Letters from the Amani period, No.92. For a woman's exhortation to wear locally made clothes, see *Tulu'-e Afghan*, Vol.2, No.49, p.3. This encouragement of native industries was not a new phenomenon, and Habibullah had made similar exhortations during his reign, see Kateb, *Seraj al-Tawarikh, jeld-e chaharom*, Part 2, p.495.

166 *Aman al-neswan baroye senf-e awwal rushdiya-ye onasiya* (Kabul: Matba'a-ye Wezarat-e Mo'arref 1925), p.1.

167 Ibid. p.9.

168 Ibid. pp.88–89.

169 Quoted in *Roydad-e loya jerga-ye dar al-soltana-ye Kabul* 1303 (Kabul: Dar al-Saltanah, 1925), p.332.

170 *Aman-e Afghan* Vol.4, No.4, p.7.

171 Mujtaba Ali, op. cit., Ch.25, p.3. The phrase 'flappers of Paghman' which heads this section is Fleming's, 'Troubles of an Afghan King', *Asia* (1929) p.412.

172 Nancy Micklewright, 'Women's Dress in 19th Century Istanbul: Mirror of a Changing Society' (PhD. diss., University of Pennsylvania, 1986), quoted in Baron, *Unveiling in Early Twentieth Century Egypt*, op. cit., p.375.

173 See, for example, the photograph of Abdul Majid, KES A-999-1630.

174 It was telling that the first girls' school was named *Maktab-e Masturat*, meaning 'School of the veiled ones' (*mastura* pl. *masturat*, the Arabic for 'veiled').

175 With regard to Egypt, see Leila Ahmed, *Women and Gender in Islam* (New Haven, CT: Yale University Press, 1992), esp. Ch.8; for the case in Iran, see Najmabadi, op. cit. Ch.5.

176 For an interesting discussion, and photograph, of one such fancy-dress party, see David B. Edwards, *Before Taliban: Genealogies of the Afghan Jihad* (Berkeley: University of California Press, 2001), pp.8–10.

177 Nawid, *Religious Response to Social Change, 1919–1929: King Aman-Allah and the Afghan Ulama* (Costa Mesa, CA: Mazda Publishers, 1999) pp.95–98.

178 See Poullada, *Reform and Rebellion in Afghanistan*, op. cit., pp.94–95.

179 The school reopened again several months later, although it was now housed in the royal palace, see Schinasi, *Femmes Afghanes*, op. cit., pp.451–52.

180 Nawid (1999), op. cit., p.137. Amanullah's Private Secretary, Ali Ahmad, even quoted Amanullah as saying of the inspiration for his trip, 'it was all due to the efforts of Peter the Great that Russia freed herself of foreign needs. It is, therefore, necessary for me to tread the same path.' Ali Ahmad, op. cit., p.12.

181 In this way comparisons can be drawn with a similar tour made in 1934 by Iran's Reza Shah, see A. Marashi, 'Performing the Nation: The Shah's Official State Visit to Kemalist Turkey, June to July 1934' in S. Cronin (ed.), *The Making of Modern Iran: State and Society Under Riza Shah 1921–41* (London: Routledge 2003).

200   *Thomas Wide*

182 Daily Express 13th February 1929, quoted in L/P&S/10/1290.

183 *Anis*, for example, devoted large parts of its content to the tour, and even used the tour as an excuse to write short histories of the countries the royal couple travelled to, see, for example, *Anis*, Vol.1, No.16, p.3.

184 For an account of the impact of the world tour on Egyptian discussions of national identity, see Usman Ahmedani, 'L'Orient par L'Islam et L'Islam pour L'Orient? Ideas of Eastern and Islamic Unity in Inter-War Egypt' (MA thesis, Oxford University 2012).

185 *Al-Manar*, Vol.28, No.10, p.784. I am grateful to Usman Ahmedani for pointing me towards this article and sharing his translation.

186 Kazem, op. cit. p.169.

187 Nawid (1999), op. cit., p.143.

188 Nawid (1999), op. cit., p.142.

189 For such a reading, see Touraj Atabaki and Erik Jan Zürcher, *Men of Order: Authoritarian Modernization under Atatürk and Reza Shah* (London: I.B. Tauris, 2004).

190 A telegram dated 14th July 1928 from the British Representative in Kabul, Sir Francis Humphrys, makes clear the fact that there was not to be any compulsion in the matter of women's dress: 'Queen Souriya recently gave an address to the Kabul Girls' School, in which she emphasized that the wearing of veils was out of date. She urged the girls to work for the abolition of the Purdah system, which would have to be achieved without compulsion,' IOR/L/P&S/10/1285.

191 A letter from the Minister of Justice to the Eshik Aghasi dated 30 Jawza 1302 states that Amanullah had ordered 'via telephone' the banning of 'the travelling of officials in the street without western suits (*dreshi*)' ANA, Letters from the Amani period, No.258.

192 *Habib al-Islam*, Vol.I, No.1, p.4.

193 See, for example, a photo of a man in a Kabul-manufactured hat KES A-1119–1830.

194 Mujtaba Ali, op. cit., Ch.33, p.1.

195 Ibid., pp.1–2.

196 Ibid., p.2.

197 Article from *The Times* 22nd November 1928, extracted in IOR/L/PS/1285.

198 For the perilous state of Afghanistan's finances, see the report of the British Military Attache in Kabul to Humphrys, 24th September 1928, IOR/L/P/P&S/1285.

199 One such notable was the ex-Amir of Bukhara, living in exile in Kabul. As the British Minister Humphrys described it: 'the first victim of the new rule was the ex-Amir of Bokhara who, while driving down 'the Mall' with an Aide-de-Camp was asked by a policeman to remove his silk turban and was then fined a shilling for not wearing a Homburg hat. Since receiving this attention the ex-Amir has not again ventured to take the road.' Humphrys' report to Secretary of State for Foreign Affairs, 31st October 1928, IOR L/P&S/10/1285.

200 Luise White, *Speaking with Vampires: Rumor and History in Colonial Africa* (Berkeley: University of California Press, 2000), p.31.

201 See, for example, the rumour that Nasrullah Khan was angered at the Amir over the fact that the ladies of the court travelled around with only thin veils over their faces, NWFP diary, week ending 19th July 1913, L/PS/10/200.

202 Mujtaba Ali writes about the role of *bazaargap* in Kabul, op. cit., Ch.17, pp.1–2.

203 Viceroy's letter from Simla, 13th September 1928, IOR/L/P&S/1285.

204 See, for example, F. Raskolnikov's account, 'Civil War in Afghanistan', *The Living Age*, May 1929, p.210.

205 Quoted in NWFP diary for the period ending 19th October 1928, IOR L/P&S/10/1285.

Economy of dress in early-20th-century Afghanistan   201

206 For the central importance of 'unveiling' to the opponents' of Amanullah, see the fifth demand made by Sirdar Shir Ahmad Khan on 14th November 1928 at Jalalabad, quoted in Fazl Ghani Mogaddedi, *Afghanistan dar 'ahd-i a'lihazrat amanullah khan 1919–1929* (California: Folgergraphics Inc, 1997), p.260; also the list of demands quoted in IOR/L/PS/10/1285, No.52; a separate list of demands made by the Shinwari Mohammad Alam can be found in L. Adamec, *Afghanistan's Foreign Affairs to the Mid-Twentieth Century* (Tucson: University of Arizona Press, 1974), p.140–41.

207 A *firman* of 18 points, supposedly sent by Amanullah refuting the rumours that he ever intended to try and force through an unveiling campaign, can be found in Kazem op. cit., pp.162–64, although Kazem does not mention a source for this.

208 Ali Ahmad, op. cit., IOR/L/PS/10/1285 p.18, 25.

209 Mujtaba Ali, op. cit., Ch.33, p.7.

210 Ghulam Nabi Khan, quoted in the *Daily Express* (7th March 1929), extracted in IOR L/PS/10/1290.

211 Syed Mujtaba Ali, op. cit., Ch.34, p.5.

Part III

Soviet Central Asia and the Caucasus

7 Women-initiated unveiling

State-led campaigns in Uzbekistan and Azerbaijan

Marianne Kamp

When and why the veils came off Muslim women in the Soviet Union is a story that moves from initiatives among urban Muslim women activists in Uzbekistan and Azerbaijan in the early 1920s, to full-blown Communist Party efforts in the late 1920s. In the 1920s, the Soviet Union was just one among several states where leaders embraced the idea that Muslim women's forms of face and body covering were objectionable, and that removing those veils would modernize the nation's image and, beyond that, might bring about some essential, desirable transformation. In the Soviet Union, unveiling was far from a cosmetic change: its sponsors believed that, if veiled Muslim women would unveil and thus end the practice of women's seclusion, they would themselves become vectors of social, cultural, and economic change. However, long before the Communist Party embraced this position, Muslim women in the Russian Empire, and then in its newly formed Socialist Republics, had been debating and challenging hijab in both of its forms: veiling and seclusion.

Historians often juxtapose state and society, as though there is some coherence to "society" and as though it is separated from "the state." This perspective dominates studies of Soviet Central Asia, where "the state" is frequently presented as an outsider, a colonial entity that was made up of Russians, while "society" is seen as Muslim objects of colonialism who played no role in determining their own lives and who are assumed to share common characteristics and attitudes. If instead we examine the unveiling campaign through a woman-centered lens, we raise other questions: are women a category? If Muslims are not a single group, but rather a diversity of people with differing experiences shaped by gender, class, culture, and nationality, then we may disaggregate what Muslim women experienced in the unveiling campaigns, from what men experienced as an attack on "society." And if we do not assume that "the state" constructed by Communists in Central Asia was alien to Central Asian society, but rather ask about who was constructing the state, and why those actors imagined that unveiling might be useful, we will begin to question the framework that Northrop articulates in *Veiled Empire*, that the unveiling campaign in Uzbekistan was primarily a colonial import, and that this explains why "society" (i.e. male society) rejected it violently. Similarly, this paper challenges Gülzar İbrahimova's judgment that every

206 *Marianne Kamp*

aspect of Soviet policy on women in Azerbaijan, including unveiling, was an expression of Communist totalitarianism, and was forced on Azerbaijani women and men against their own desires.[1]

Muslim women in Azerbaijan and Uzbekistan had their own ways of thinking about veiling and unveiling in the 1920s; those who participated in Party-sponsored clubs, or who wrote for the native-language press, interacted with Party organizations to shape the state's unveiling campaign. This chapter draws on my earlier research, which focused on finding Uzbek women's experiences by examining archival documents, personal narratives, newspaper articles, and other publications from the late 1920s, and through oral histories, in order to see the unveiling campaign through the lenses of those veiled women who unveiled, whether by choice or under duress.[2] This chapter relies on published scholarship for evidence regarding Azerbaijan, but also on women activists' discussions that were published in the Communist Party Women's Division (*Zhenotdel*) journal, *Kommunistka*, in the 1920s. Sequentially, this chapter deals first with Muslim women's discourses about veiling and unveiling from the late Russian imperial period through the 1920s. Those discourses shaped actions—women's unveilings—and then, through the Women's Division, influenced Communist Party understandings of the veil. Second, the chapter turns toward state-led unveiling. In 1926, pressure from women activists in Uzbekistan prompted the Communist Party to embrace unveiling as the key to revolutionary change in culture, economy, society, and family, through its Hujum ("Attack") campaign. In Azerbaijan, a similar debate among activists led, in 1928, to the Party's decision to promote mass unveiling. When unveiling changed from a women's movement to a state and party-promoted initiative, its meaning changed, and the final section of this chapter explores that shift from feminist meanings to state patriarchal meanings.

State-led, top-down campaigns against women's face-covering (veiling) in interwar Soviet republics, Iran, Turkey, and Afghanistan may appear to have some similar impetus, and to share some goals, but "the state" varied so much that similarities in state actions may be superficial. Ideas about unveiling in each of these states had roots in colonial discourses, transnational intellectual exchanges among Muslims, and indigenous debates. The presence or absence of colonial power in the interwar years factored in the ways that elites and state actors conceived of unveiling campaigns: the unveiling campaign led by Atatürk as president of an independent Turkish republic was a very different political expression than the Egyptian elite-led unveiling campaign in British-dominated Egypt, and neither of those conditions was identical to the odd, new configuration of Communist dominance in Central Asia and the Caucasus.[3] Giving too much attention to the state and to colonialism, however important they were, shuts out a women-centered perspective. Women were the objects of unveiling campaigns, but they were also subjects in these campaigns: veiled women either unveiled, or did not, and in order to understand how women responded to unveiling campaigns, we might want first to examine the ways that women shaped those campaigns.

Women-initiated unveiling 207

Although we can discuss "woman" as a category, the experiences of women in any society vary widely. Only a few of the Muslim women who participated actively in debates about veiling and unveiling put their thoughts or words into writing: we are limited to accessing the writings of the few that did think it worthwhile to put their own words on paper, or who are represented by others, whether those others are men or women, "native" or outsiders. The Soviet government did not carry out opinion surveys: the available opinions of veiled women, whether they represent the masses well or not, are found in publications from the 1920s, newspapers, tracts and booklets, works of fiction, and, to some extent, in complaint letters and court documents. The views of Communist Party activists, men and women, local and outsider, are far more abundant and easy to find than those of veiled Muslim women; but, of course, the categories are not so easily delineated, as some Uzbek and Azerbaijani women were also Communist Party activists, and they contributed their voices and actions to the official unveiling campaign. The views of people who had no connection to the Party, and those who vociferously supported veiling, are harder to find, and come filtered through Party lenses. By 1928, Party representatives wanted to find mass support for unveiling, and characterized supporters of veiling as either unenlightened or as enemies.

Why veil? Why unveil?

The idea that to unveil women would bring about positive social consequences traveled across the Islamic world in the late nineteenth century. Tracts and newspapers, as well as individuals who crossed borders, carried the debate between critics and advocates of unveiling, such that arguments for or against tended to rely on common tropes, theories, and understandings of Islamic texts, regardless where they were published.[4] Turkic-speaking Muslims in the Russian Empire and Ottomans shared particularly strong intellectual networks and readily exchanged publications. They produced many tracts about girls' upbringing, linking questions about educating daughters (to what extent was education proper, should girls be taught to write, and so on) with larger issues of women's social roles: to what extent should any female be involved in choosing her mate? Should she have a voice outside the home? Occasionally, these writers also discussed dress, entering the debate over veiling. Women who presented themselves as religious teachers contributed to tract literature and, among Muslims in the Russian Empire, women who had gained access to modern education began to voice their opinions in the Russian Empire's Turkic-language press, which flourished after the 1905 Revolution.[5]

Studies of women's dress among the larger Muslim populations of the Russian Empire—Volga Tatars, Crimean Tatars, Azerbaijanis, and Central Asians—indicate some commonalities in veiling practices and some significant changes in the late nineteenth and early twentieth centuries. The forms of and names for covering garments were quite varied, and they did not always include face coverings. Until the 1920s, veiling was practiced by many,

208 Marianne Kamp

but not all, Muslim women. Women from sedentary Uzbek and Tajik societies who lived in cities or farming communities veiled, or at least were told they should veil. Bukharan Jewish women veiled, and many Tatar women who moved to Central Asia veiled, though they seem to have been abandoning veiling in the early twentieth century. Uzbeks and Tajiks usually wore a head- and body-covering robe called the *paranji*, and a thick net of woven horsehair, the *chachvon*, that covered the entire face and chest. Many Turkmen women covered the lower half of their faces with a *yashmak*, which could also be found among some nomadic Uzbek groups. Generally, Kyrgyz and Kazakh women did not cover their faces. Azerbaijani women, whom sources from the 1910s and 1920s refer to either as Muslims or Turks, wore a body-covering robe, the *chador*.[6] In the Caucasus, veiling was common to many Dagestani women, and to Ajars, but was not universal to all Muslim women, and was not practiced by Georgians or Armenians, or among Russians or others who moved there as colonists.

Observers often noted stricter face covering among urban Muslim women, and an absence among rural women. In Central Asia, evidence indicates change over time; regarding Tashkent, observers reported that women did not all cover their faces at the time of the Russian conquest (1865) but, by 30 years later, veiling in the *paranji* and *chachvon* seemed universal among women in the native districts of the city. This evidence led Northrop to posit that increased veiling was a cultural response to the Russian colonial presence.[7] By contrast, Russian colonists did not live in the city of Bukhara; they established a colonial city a few miles away at Kagan. Both before and after the Russian conquest, visitors recorded that all Bukharan women, including Jewish women, veiled in the *paranji* and *chachvon*; thus, it would seem Bukharan women's veiling was not a response to, or altered by, the Russian colonial presence. Crimean Tatar women's forms of body and face covering changed substantially in the nineteenth century. Historian L. I. Roslavtseva writes that, in the second half of the nineteenth century, the *feraje*, a robe like the *paranji* with false sleeves, went from being a shoulder-worn garment to one that was draped from the head. Crimean Tatar women sometimes used the sleeves of the *feraje* or *paranji* to cover part of their faces; others used scarves or an Ottoman-style *yashmak* to veil their faces below the eyes.[8] Azerbaijani women and some Volga Tatar women wore large, flowing chadors, drawing them in to cover their faces.[9] Uzbek and Tatar women whom I interviewed gave the impression that Tatar women in Turkestan, Bukhara, and Khiva did not cover their faces in the 1920s; this contrasts with Vorob'ev's evidence that Tatar women who lived in rural areas near Kazan did continue to cover their faces into the late 1920s.[10] Perhaps Tatar women's early-twentieth-century unveiling was a trend found more among urban and intelligentsia women (including those who moved to Central Asia) than among rural women.

Descriptions of veiling and seclusion often mentioned class differences. The Nalivkins, based on their research in the Fergana valley in the 1870s and

Women-initiated unveiling 209

1880s, connected rural veiling and seclusion with wealth, a relationship found in many other descriptions from both the Russian colonial period and the early Soviet period. Generally, rural women who were wealthy and did not work in their family's fields wore full body and face veils, and those women who did work in the fields (the majority) did not, but might put some other kind of robe or scarf on their heads without any face covering.[11] Among urban women, class or wealth distinctions were evident in the quality of the veiling robe.

Debating veiling and seclusion

For educated Muslims who contributed to the *Jadid* (Muslim reformist or progressive) press in the Russian Empire before the 1917 Revolution, women's veiling was a subject of debate, though other issues, such as polygyny, were given more attention. *Suyum Bike*, a Tatar women's journal published in Kazan from 1913 to 1917, carried articles written by women and by men, by Tatars and other Turkic-speakers, who described women's lives in order to make the case for expanding women's rights among Russia's Muslims. Authors wrote from Samarkand, Bukhara, Tashkent, and other Central Asian cities to compare the relative freedoms and restrictions in the lives of Kazakh, Turkestani, and Sart women.[12] After a certain Qayum Qulanqi hailed Kazakh women as far more free than any other Muslim women, and gave as evidence their lack of hijab, another contributor, "F.H." laid out multiple illustrations of Kazakh women's lack of rights. F.H. wrote:

> Qayum Effendi explains rights and equality as if it only is found in walking openly and not veiling the face ... he seems to think that at some time in the past Kazakh women used to be veiled and then threw it off. This is totally mistaken. They never have been veiled, and Qayum Effendi thinks that this lack of veiling shows such great freedom that he ignores all of the other ways that they lack rights.[13]

A contributor from Samarkand, A. Azmet, argued that "it would be no mistake to say that the Sart people preserve hijab the most among Muslims." Azmet described in great detail the *paranji* and *chachvon*, and the circumstances under which Sart women wore them, expressing his understanding that veiling was an extension of seclusion, designed to separate women from non-family men, and from public spaces and participation in public life.[14] To demonstrate that the Muslims in other parts of the world were also discussing hijab, *Suyum Bike* published a translation of a discussion of veiling from an Arabic publication. The discussion elucidated two Qur'anic meanings of hijab: first, the covering of body parts that should not be shown; and second, seclusion. The discussion historicized veiling, noting its connections to culture and custom, and remarking that the question of hijab had recently become heated in Istanbul and Egypt. Ultimately, the author concluded that hijab is

210   *Marianne Kamp*

harmful, but there is no need to oppose it: veiling is not a necessity but a custom, and customs do change.[15]

Suyum Bike's readers exchanged opinions about women's rights: whether, where, when, and why women were treated as unequal to men; what the Qur'an and Sharia said on this topic; whether Islamic laws could be changed; whether women were fair in arguing that men imprisoned them and treated them like slaves; how to increase women's education; whether veiling was harmful; and to what extent women's veiling was connected to women's lack of rights. Women authors frequently quoted and then attacked men authors whom they regarded as naive or unaware of inequalities, or, worse still, advocates of inequality between women and men.

Like others in the Jadid movement, these Tatar women regarded bringing modern education to Muslim girls as their most important task. Their ways of depicting Turkestani, Sart, and Kazakh women were sympathetic, but also critical. After lengthy descriptions of all of the family-based injustices that Central Asian women might experience, writers for *Suyum Bike* called on those very women to speak up for themselves. Authors appealed for expanding Central Asian girls' education in new institutions that taught a modern educational curriculum, precisely because the writers saw these two concepts— voice and modern education—as linked. In *Suyum Bike's* pages, Muslim feminists viewed veiling not as the cause of women's inequality with men, but as an extension of seclusion and hence a symptom of women's inequality with men; seclusion could be overcome by guaranteeing modern schooling to all girls.

Many of these published debates were repeated at the Muslim Women's Association conferences in 1917. Immediately following the February Revolution of 1917, citizens' organizations throughout the Russian Empire called congresses to discuss rights and formulate demands. Among many such organizations, Muslims in Russia gathered across party lines in groups of ulama, teachers, and women. The women, like their counterpart women in Russia's women's suffrage associations, drew up lists of demands, presented them to the men's assemblies, and wrote petitions to Muslim Duma members and members of the provisional government. The April Muslim Women's Conference in Kazan focused on formulating legal demands, such as for equality with men in marriage, divorce, and inheritance. Following discussions where most participants rejected both veiling and seclusion, participants declared that "in the Qur'an, there is no hijab for women."[16]

Veiling as anti-colonialism?

Long before Bolsheviks even thought about unveiling Muslim women, Muslims in the Russian Empire began their own discussion of the veil. When we as historians view Muslim discussions of unveiling as responses to colonialism, that is, I think, a reflection of our limited research.[17] Russians talked about and disparaged veiled Muslim women, but hardly any of them spoke or

Women-initiated unveiling 211

read Turco-Tatar, or had any awareness at all of the discussion that Muslims were having amongst themselves. Articles in *Suyum Bike* were strongly linked to Muslims' international discourses, and paid very little heed to Russian views or opinions, or, at least, if authors were concerned about what Russians thought, they did not bother to mention it. To imagine that Muslims in the Russian Empire spent this much time and energy arguing about women's rights and veils because Russians thought ill of veiled women is once again to imagine that "Europeans" are at the center of everyone's worlds, i.e. to adopt a Eurocentric perspective that marginalizes the voices and views of the debate's central participants, who were Muslim women.

Early-twentieth-century discourses about veiling and unveiling among Muslims in the Russian Empire share little with post-1970s discourses about veiling and unveiling among the world's Muslims. In those early-twentieth-century debates, we do not find piety-based testimonies, where Muslim women describe their own subjectivity as constructed through an expression of individual, personal submission to Allah that is manifested outwardly in a religious form of covering; nor do we find the widely spread meme that declares punishment will be double for the woman who dons hijab and then removes it.[18] In the early-twentieth-century discourses, there is no mention of individual faith at all, nor of faith (*iman*) bearing any relationship to covering the face or to hijab.

In the early twentieth century, when Muslims in Russia made religious arguments in support of hijab, they expressed the idea that the Qur'an, or Sharia, mandated hijab, both as seclusion and as dress, for the good of society and for the maintaining of moral behavior. They usually used the term *fitna* to express the chaos that would result if women acted against traditions like veiling, or if women learned to write and thus used communication to break seclusion. The early-twentieth-century defenses of veiling drew on concepts of tradition and community, but not of individual *iman*. Women religious teachers who wrote tracts on this topic tended to support veiling of women as important to social order, but they vociferously rejected the position that teaching girls to write would cause *fitna*. Theirs was an inconsistent position that endorsed women's individual right to full education, and also defended the (male) community against the actions of women as individuals, by arguing that women should not leave the home without men's permission and should continue to cover their heads, faces, and bodies.[19]

Veiling's opponents also made arguments based on community, for example, that veiling harmed women's health and their development as mothers and, hence, harmed the future of the nation. But veiling's opponents tended to conceive of women, as well as men, as individuals, rather than emphasizing their roles as community members. By 1917, veiling's opponents established their arguments firmly on the idea of *huquqi insaniya*, or human rights. The feminists who wrote for *Suyum Bike* defined "human rights" as individual liberties, the freedom (a much used word in their articles) to go outside at one's own decision, to gain an education, to be able to state one's agreement

212 *Marianne Kamp*

to or disagreement with a marriage proposal, as well as the right to vote, and be elected, to break seclusion, and to unveil.[20] No participant in this debate ever suggested that women should not wear scarves over their hair. Rather, the hijab discussion was a debate between those who thought that wearing full-body and face coverings protected society from *fitna*, and those who viewed wearing such coverings as keeping women separated from men and preventing them from contributing to the life of the nation.

Women's activism in the Caucasus and Central Asia, 1917–29

The Bolshevik Revolution, civil war, and Central Asian attempts to throw off Russian rule in the basmachi–Red Army conflict combined to make Central Asia a fragmented and unstable region. The Reds held Tashkent, but most other parts of Turkestan, as well as Bukhara and Khiva, were contested zones for several years. By 1924, the Bolsheviks had established control firmly enough that they could carry out the remapping and political reorganization that created the modern Central Asian republics, including Uzbekistan.

In the Caucasus, the Bolshevik road to domination was more challenging. Ottoman forces took advantage of Russia's military weakness after the February Revolution and supported the Turks of the trans-Caucasus, the Azerbaijanis, in their struggle to gain freedom or at least autonomy from the Russian Empire. In the spring of 1918, Azerbaijani and Ottoman Turkish forces gained the upper hand, forcing the first Bolshevik government (the 26 Commissars) out of Baku in July. Azerbaijani politicians declared the "Azerbaijan People's Republic" on May 28, 1918, creating an independent state with a very unstable government made up of nationalists, socialists, and Islamic parties, that lasted for almost two years, until the Bolsheviks reconquered Baku in April 1920.[21] Azerbaijani historian Gülzar İbrahimova argues that this was a period of liberal, democratic policies that favored women's rights, though the evidence that she presents says almost nothing about women's rights. Instead, it shows continuity with Muslim agendas for women's reform in the Tsarist period: Muslim women's groups and some progressive men opened modern schools and charitable associations for Muslim girls.[22]

It is hardly surprising that women's rights were not at the top of political agendas for either the Communists or their opponents while they were competing for power in Azerbaijan and Central Asia. Interestingly, though, some Turkistani women were concerned to promote their own rights. Women's rights, including discussion of unveiling, became an important theme in the new publications of male Uzbek authors, poets, and novelists. The Communist Party's Women's Division quickly formed branches in Turkistan's cities (1919), and then in Azerbaijan (1920), and this brought Russian and other outsider women into direct interaction with Azerbaijani and Turkistani women, and into the already ongoing debates among Muslims about women's rights and veiling. This intervention, the establishment of the Communist

Party's Women's Division, changed the terrain. No longer were Muslim discussions about women's rights and veils taking place in the sphere of "civil society"; instead, the Party, the only party, became the main organizer of women's activism.

Party control of women's issues was not unified or clearly directed. The Women's Division of the Communist Party took on a life of its own, relying both on its outsider leadership (Russians and other non-natives) and its local cadres (Uzbek or Azerbaijani women) to pursue its goals. Those goals were to teach women about their rights under Soviet law; to promote schools for girls, and literacy and professional training for women; to involve women in political life through meetings and elections; and to provide women with means to earn a living by creating work and craft collectives (*artels*). Because the Women's Division was part of the Communist Party, it was supposed to explain to women their role in the building of a socialist society. Records of Women's Division activities in the Soviet "East" suggest that explaining communism never completely left the agenda, but that it was not the main message that women participants would have gained from participation in Women's Division activities. In Azerbaijan and Central Asia, the Women's Division formed women's clubs and "red corners" featuring literacy classes and handcrafts. They also pursued the strategy that was more widely applied in Russia, calling *delegatka* (women delegate) gatherings, directed at bringing women from the working classes together for short conferences to learn about their rights and building socialism. The leadership of the Women's Division divided over the correct methods for carrying out Party work among women in Azerbaijan and Central Asia: those whose experience was based in Russia argued that to organize women separately from men was inherently a deviation from the Party line and a turn toward feminism. Activists in Azerbaijan and Central Asia countered that organizing women separately, through such non-political modes as women's clubs, was the only effective way to counter the seclusion of women; they tried to defend themselves against the charge of being "Muslim feminists."[23] In Azerbaijan, activists drew the line between the Party's policy and feminist deviation by preventing non-Muslim women from participating in the women's clubs: "It goes without say that this is wrong: Armenian and Russian women freely go to general meetings and so it follows that they should not gather separately from men. In clubs for Muslim women workers, women of other nationalities may enter only in the role of helper in the initial organizational work."[24] Women's Division activists in Azerbaijan and Uzbekistan continually had to defend their unorthodox methods for organizing and politicizing women.

Both indigenous and outsider activists in the Women's Division discussed and criticized veiling as an extension of women's seclusion, which they saw as the underlying obstacle to women's equality with men. In the early 1920s, some activist Uzbek women decided to stop wearing the *paranji* and *chachvon*, and there are records of a few small-scale public meetings where Uzbek women unveiled. These records appeared in the Uzbek language press; they

214   *Marianne Kamp*

did not appear in the Russian language press, or in publications by Russian Women's Division activists.[25] These records, and evidence from oral history interviews, are the basis of my contention that the movement for unveiling in Uzbekistan first came from Uzbek women activists; it was not, originally, a Party idea imposed from outside. While contending that Uzbek women themselves began removing the *paranji* and *chachvon*, I acknowledge that this was a small movement that emerged among urban women, often women who were associated with the Uzbek intelligentsia (the *ziyollilar*).

In Azerbaijan, records of Muslim women unveiling were more abundant, and better known to Russians. Azerbaijani women's post-revolutionary activism drew on pre-revolutionary roots: before 1917, some women (usually from the elite or intelligentsia) had been involved in Muslim Women's Associations, in reformed Islamic schooling, and had attended Russian *gymansiia* (this later facilitated communication between them and newly arrived Russian activists); and Azerbaijani women, supported by the wealthy Baku oilman, Zaynalabdin Tagiyev, established *Ishig*, a women's journal.[26] The historian Almas Muradova quotes Azerbaijani activist Ayna Sultanova's account of events that took place in 1917, at a Congress of Muslim clergy of the Transcaucasus:

> However progressive women came to the congress. There were several teachers, including Shafiga Efendieva, and Adilia Shakhtakhtinskaia, who made speeches. The appearance of Azerbaijani women without chador, with uncovered faces, had the impact of an exploding bomb on the clergy representatives. Interrupting the speech of a woman teacher, the representative of the clergy Mir Mamed Kerim-ogly stood up demonstrating all of his own saintliness, and walked out of the congress. The congress was interrupted, Ayna Sultanova wrote, and it stopped its work for several days. In a spontaneous movement, the persecuted lead-ing Azerbaijani women flowed out into a movement on the street, resulting in helpless confusion even among the congress's own leadership. Dark forces in the city used this movement toward their own selfish ends. The panic spread among Azerbaijani women who hurried to buy them-selves new slippers and to don their chadors so that they would have the opportunity to go onto the street, go to work and to school, and so forth.[27]

Sultanova, who became a leading Bolshevik activist and the editor of the Azerbaijani women's journal *Shərq Qadını*, recalled this 1917 unveiling both as something that Azerbaijani women teachers thought of as their right, and as a trigger for social turmoil.

The Bolsheviks' 1920 appropriation of power in Azerbaijan divided women; many of the elite activists went into exile, while the socialist activists stayed and gained opportunities. Immediately, Azerbaijani socialist activist Ceyran Bayramova initiated the Baku Muslim women's club, an organization that the Women's Division came to regard as the exemplary club, a model to be emulated across the Caucasus and Central Asia.[28] At clubs and women's meetings, women unveiled. Ishkova, the Russian director of the Women's Division in Azerbaijan, reported that, on International Women's Day, March 8, 1923, "in several districts [of Baku] at general gatherings Muslim women pulled off their own chadors and trampled them below their feet."[29]

In 1926, reports of Uzbek women unveiling publically were becoming more frequent, and one activist with the Women's Division, Bashorat Jalilova, tried to spark mass unveiling. At the International Women's Day (March 8) celebrations in Tashkent, she stood up in front of the crowd of women, called for "an end to slavery," and threw off her *paranji*.[30] Clearly, she was hoping that others would follow her example, but they did not do so, at least not at that demonstration. But small-scale events where Uzbek women publicly removed their *paranjis* were spreading outside of intelligentsia circles; a silk factory in Kokand held such a demonstration in the spring of 1926, and some Uzbek women workers chose to unveil themselves.

Throughout the 1920s, there was violence against unveiled and politically active women in Azerbaijan.[31] Party initiatives among women were already drawing violent responses. In a 1926 report on the growth of *delegatka* meetings, N. Zavarian mentioned this violence, blaming Party activists for their inadequate work in preparing and supporting such gatherings of women: "There were a lot of such things that were ill thought out in Azerbaidzhan, Turkmenistan and Uzbekistan, the result of which has been more than a few cases of stalking, assault, and even murder of women delegates."[32]

The Party and unveiling in Uzbekistan

In May 1926, the Women's Division activists gathering in Moscow discussed a new, more aggressive campaign to bring change to Central Asia's women. They formulated their initial ideas for the "Hujum," or "Assault," which was to be an all-out attack (though a non-violent one) on traditions that prevented Central Asian women from enjoying equal rights. Women's Division activists regarded these traditions as keeping Central Asian women "backward," or "fallen behind," rather than allowing them to experience the progress that the Soviet experiment promised. The campaign was multifaceted: there were to be serious prosecutions of offenders against women's rights; education of women concerning their rights, such as their right to be of age for, present at, and to give their own consent to marriage; and efforts to get more girls into schools and more women into social and political activities. Unveiling had little to do with the Hujum until political leaders in Uzbekistan made it the campaign's centerpiece. By the fall of 1926, the idea of the Hujum garnered approval as the official policy of the Party's Central Asian Bureau, which tasked the Uzbekistan Communist Party with forming a commission to carry out the campaign.[33] In February 1927, the Hujum Commission made

216 *Marianne Kamp*

plans for mass unveilings of women, to begin on International Women's Day, March 8, 1927. Schools, Women's Division organizations, the Communist Party, and the Komsomol (Communist Youth League) were all to play active roles in getting women to remove their *paranjis*.

This shift from women's own activism to Party-led policy had enormous significance. Although the Women's Division played a strong role in shaping the campaign, the Uzbekistan Communist Party and the Komsomol were charged with making the Hujum's goals their own. This promised broader and deeper results, if men in positions of authority would support efforts to make women's rights into reality. But this shift took a movement for unveiling that had been voluntary, small-scale and quite unthreatening, led by women with the support of some like-minded men, and turned it into a Party-led project that told both men and women what they needed to do, bringing unveiling into communities where the idea had never been discussed at all and had no proponents.

Local cells of the Party instructed their Uzbek members, who were almost all male, to unveil their wives. As Northrop argues, Uzbek male Party members' ability to force their wives to unveil became an indication of their loyalty to the Party.[34] Although it began as a women's movement that grew out of debate, used persuasion, and spoke to some Uzbek women's desire to stop wearing an uncomfortable and bothersome garment, unveiling became a policy that the Party could enforce on women through men, the opposite of anything that a feminist would want.

Uzbek women activists of the late 1920s would not have agreed with the liberal feminist about the importance of free choice, though. In fact, their activism was not eclipsed or erased by the Party's declaration of the Hujum. To the contrary, many Uzbek women activists seized the moment and took Party authorization as support for organizing much bigger unveiling demonstrations than in the past, pressing other women to unveil and lobbying for a legal ban on the *paranji*. This produced a complicated situation: male Uzbek Party members, often against their own wishes, pushed or ordered their wives to throw off their *paranjis*, at the same time that Uzbek women activists were trying to persuade women to do the same thing. There were huge unveiling meetings on all of the major state holidays in 1927, 1928, and 1929, and these unveiling actions varied in meaning for their women participants. Some women threw off their *paranjis* because they wanted to, while others did so because they were forced to.[35]

Many male Uzbek Party members resisted the Party's directive. Moreover, much of Uzbek society, both male and female, was shocked at the unveiling campaign, rejecting the whole concept for a host of interrelated reasons: it was a radical change; it looked to many like a form of Russification; it challenged religious leaders who said that hijab in the form of the *paranji* was mandatory; it allowed young women to challenge all of those who had personal authority over them, but especially fathers, in-laws, and husbands. Furthermore, this promotion of unveiling took place at the same time that the

Women-initiated unveiling 217

government was closing Islamic religious institutions, arresting imams, and initiating land reforms that divided up large estates, dispossessing the wealthy. The rapid effort to convince and force women to unveil split Uzbek society into supporters and opponents. Supporters of unveiling, mainly women activists along with some male Party and Komsomol members, pushed the campaign aggressively, putting pressure on women to come out and unveil, and trying to use men's authority over women to make women unveil, by threatening those men with loss of Party affiliation or, worse still, arrest for violation of women's rights in everyday life. The contradiction here between an effort to open the possibilities for women's agency and the reinforcement of male authority over women is striking.[36]

While unveiling's supporters both convinced and coerced women to unveil, unveiling's opponents used physical violence and terror to convince women not to unveil, and to punish those who did unveil. The cost to women for unveiling during the Hujum was sometimes life. Uzbeks who resisted women's unveiling did not do so subtly: they threatened unveiled women with murder and, frequently, they carried out those threats.[37] This did not change activists' minds about the wisdom of unveiling; rather, Women's Division activists and their supporters began to view Uzbek women who were murdered by men in their families and communities as martyrs whose cause must not be abandoned. Advocates of unveiling responded to violence with determination to persuade more women to unveil, and with an effort to create a legal ban on *paranji* wearing. While some Party members were disgruntled over the Hujum, others took the outcome as evidence that their interpretation of society was correct: the Hujum had revealed the true enemies of the Party and its plans for progress.

The Party-led campaign, the Hujum, continued for three years, from 1927 through 1929. Violent resistance to women's unveiling also continued; records suggest that at least 2,000 women were murdered by unveiling's opponents. The campaign did accomplish some of its goals, beyond producing thousands of women who stopped wearing the *paranji* and clarifying who could be seen as an enemy. The Hujum was a multifaceted campaign, and its more significant accomplishments were in changing law and increasing enforcement of some laws, such as prohibitions on the marriage of minors and punishing those who attacked unveiled women. Those accomplishments notwithstanding, public meetings for throwing off the *paranji* were by far the most visible aspect of this campaign and drew a tight association between the slogan "Hujum" and unveiling. The All-Union Women's Division director, A. Artiukhina, after her Moscow office gathered reports on the murders of unveiled women, tried to distance the Women's Division from the Hujum by declaring that it had been initiated by Party organizations in Uzbekistan, who had approached their task as though changing women's lives could be accomplished through a temporary campaign about the veil, rather than through sustained efforts focused on turning women into builders of socialism.[38]

218   *Marianne Kamp*

The Party and unveiling in Azerbaijan

As was the case in Uzbekistan, unveiling in Azerbaijan until 1928 was small scale and voluntary. Ishkova, the Women's Division director there, noted that in 1926 a debate about unveiling suddenly began, inspired, she said, by the movement in Turkey; the Party's Central Committee and the Commissariat of Justice both discussed a legal ban on wearing the chador.[39] The debate continued in the Azerbaijani press and was re-energized by reports of the Hujum in Uzbekistan. Party members and women activists began holding meetings to discuss whether to ban the chador, and the Women's Division journal *Kommunistka* devoted pages in issue after issue to presenting stenographic records of some of these debates.

The following excerpt of a discussion among Women's Division workers exemplifies some of the arguments for and against a ban:

> Tagiyeva (territorial division of Transcaucasus): It is unnecessary to discuss the chador. The chador itself has absolutely no authority, no meaning, and it will fall off by itself.
>
> Tagiyev (Transcaucasus Central Committee): On the question of the chador I think that I disagree with you, because I have long already stood for the necessity of removing the chador by means of a decree … . Is it really a simpler thing to struggle against "*shakhsei-vakhsei*"[40] by a decree than it is to struggle against the chador? The Central Committee already made a decree that anyone going out and beating themselves for "*shakhsei-vakhsei*" will be fined 300 rubles. By means of a decree we have stopped teaching divine law in schools, we are bringing in the latin alphabet, and so on.
>
> Those are three examples where by decree we have laid to rest, finally, much more serious remnants of the past than the wearing of chador, and these have had only positive results. That is why I say that it is possible to carry out removal of the chador by decree …
>
> Lomtitadze (Georgia): We consider that decreeing the removal of chador is untimely and it will be necessary to be very careful about such an issue.
>
> Akhundova (Azerbaijan): We should remove the chador not by means of a decree, but rather first remove it from wives of Communists and responsible workers, and then go to the masses.[41]

Activists who supported a decree against the chador in Azerbaijan, or against the *paranji* in Uzbekistan, argued that a decree would protect already unveiled women from threats, assaults, and murder, by making unveiling universal rather than an individual act. Communist Party opponents of a decree saw it as a threat to women; if their husbands objected, the unveiled women might wind up divorced and without support. Supporters of the ban thought it would enable women to come out of their homes, go to school, and join the workforce. Activist opponents thought that the Party should work on attracting girls to schools and women to the workforce instead of putting its effort into a decree against veiling. Supporters of a decree responded that veiling is seclusion, and that seclusion must be broken before girls can go to school or women to work. The debate over the ban was lively, but it did not include the voices of those who supported veiling; it was merely a debate over the timing and methods of unveiling.[42]

Ayna Sultanova, an Azerbaijani activist, reported to a conference on activities to bring an end to the chador in Baku region in 1928:

> This year the Central Committee of the Party of Azerbaijan was given the task of deploying a wide campaign, first of all among Party members, on the removal of the chador, and this campaign is considered not a Women's Division campaign, but a matter among all Party organisations. The question was discussed among us, and placed before the [Central Committee]. At first a plan for the campaign was accepted, and then it was discussed in the [local and district committees], in the presidium, in the plenums, and it was discussed at the gathering of cell secretaries, the question of the necessity of removing the chador was placed before individual cells. At last the activists of the Party gathered, and Party members were invited with their wives. Then the leading Party members removed chadors from their wives, and others followed their example … . After that we turned toward general gatherings of party and non-party, and we turned to organisations of family evenings, where wives of our party members demonstratively removed their own chadors, and after them the non-party followed. The campaign went on in the whole Baku region, in nearby villages and several of the [rural districts]; and until now the campaign continued quite well, with great accomplishments.[43]

Although there was no "decree" to prohibit wearing the chador, various Party and state organizations in Azerbaijan did issue "directives" to prevent women from wearing the chador in public places. Azerbaijani historian Almas Muradova judges the People's Commissariat of Enlightenment's February 1929 "directive" forbidding men from wearing religious dress and women from wearing chador at movie theaters to have been "a direct violation of human rights."[44] More broadly, chadors were forbidden to school teachers and students; Party members were told to unveil their female relatives or face penalties; and male workers were sometimes told to unveil their wives or lose their positions.

Unveiling became popular among young Azeri women, but the unveiled faced opposition. One of ethnographer Faride Hayat's subjects told her that "unveiled women would face assault in the streets; children would throw stones at them, and men would shout abuse." Hayat writes:

> Inevitably, throughout the 1920s the struggle against the veil and women's entry into the public arena led to a great deal of social upheaval which

220 Marianne Kamp

was reflected most dramatically in acts of violence against women. Regular accounts of beatings, divorces, and even murder of unveiled women appeared in the newspapers. In one year, 1924, for example, 1388 such cases were reported.[45]

Violence did not deter activists in Azerbaijan from promoting unveiling. To the contrary, in 1930, the popular response to a heavily publicized incident when an Azerbaijani father murdered his unveiled daughter was for women to "denounce the veil and pledge commitment" to unveiling.[46] However, scholarship and memoir writing from Azerbaijan has not focused on accounts of violence. If anything, the substantial recent historiography on women in Azerbaijan has completely elided this topic, discussing the unveiling campaign only briefly, and making no mention at all of violence against unveiled women.

The historian Ivan Gussaev noted that across the whole republic in 1929, "269,870 women threw off the chador."[47] This would have been more than 10 percent of Azerbaijan's total population.[48] At the time, Women's Division leaders commended Azerbaijan for taking the right approach to unveiling, by working through Party and Komsomol organizations to persuade men to allow women to unveil, rather than using excessive "administrative measures" or relying on force or decree.

Decades later, and without any evidence of re-examining primary sources, Azerbaijani historians have reversed that appraisal of unveiling, deeming it to have been totalitarian, an example of administrative pressure, and a violation of human rights. İbragimova and others argue that the Party forced this approach on Azerbaijan due to its interest in pushing Azerbaijani women into the labour force.[49]

In Uzbekistan, other aspects of the Hujum, such as its focus on enforcing laws designed to enhance women's rights, have been subsumed under a more general memory of the Soviet project, while the word Hujum always conjures memories of women unveiling, with either positive or negative associations. During the late-Soviet period, those who viewed an end to the *paranji* as a good thing remembered the Hujum as a heroic time, when women bravely stood up for their own rights. By contrast, post-Soviet understandings of the Hujum tend to regard it as an attack on Uzbek culture and sometimes as an attack on Islam.

The Hujum among non-veiled Eastern women

In the Soviet Union's late 1920s atmosphere of cultural revolution, Party members from "Eastern nationalities" throughout the USSR changed laws in an effort to liberate women not only from traditional forms of dress, but also from "crimes of custom," meaning payment of bride price, arranged marriages of minor girls, polygyny, male-controlled divorce, and prevention of girls' education. Uzbekistan's Hujum methods were shared by women activists in southern Kazakhstan: Party members in the cities of Turkistan and Shymkent, where there were large Uzbek populations, held large unveiling meetings. Women's division activists in Fergana valley cities that were home to Uzbeks and Tajiks, like Osh, Jalalabad, Khujand, and Kanibadom, held the same kinds of unveiling meetings as activists within Uzbekistan held.[50]

Turkmen women did not cover their whole faces, but they did use a scarf to cover their mouths when in the presence of their in-laws. Adrienne Edgar writes that, in 1927, when the Party's slogans about "liberation" became symbolized by unveiling, "the campaign for women's emancipation in Turkmenistan was hindered by the lack of a potent symbol around which to rally women's activists. ... The response ... was to seek a local substitute for the veil." Efforts to get rid of the yashmak did not catch on, and there were no dramatic burnings of the yashmak. Edgar examines Turkmen resistance to the more substantive changes that the Party promoted, concerning young marriage, bridewealth, and other "crimes of custom." She notes that many of these customs remained, but that, as education became more available to them, Turkmen girls' experiences of childhood changed and their adult opportunities expanded.[51]

Activists among some other ethnic groups also tried turning a change of dress into a symbol of emancipation: activists among Kalmyks tried to get them to abandon their tightly bound vests (kamzol), for example. In general, though, when the Communist Party and its Women's Division decided on an all-out "attack" to emancipate the "women of the East," they focused on more substantive issues connected with individual rights. At the time of the Hujum, in the late 1920s, rural Tatar women were still covering their faces, but women's activism was not focused on veils; instead, activists sought to draw more classes of women into activism, and to turn from agitation about rights to practical issues such as livelihoods and land distribution.[52]

Soviet state-led unveiling in regional comparison

The Communist Party was the leading entity in the Soviet state, and the Hujum, or attack against traditions, was a Party-led effort, especially in its symbolic dimensions and in its propaganda. The state was responsible for the substantive changes: stiffening legal penalties against men who "sold" daughters for bride price, prosecuting men who took a second or third wife, or jailing those who murdered a daughter for unveiling. The Party was responsible for the widespread public effort to get women in Uzbekistan to throw off their *paranjis*, using propaganda, public demonstrations, and pressure on Party members. In Azerbaijan, activists agitated for unveiling through an extensive press campaign, and through public meetings and demonstrations. In both Uzbekistan and Azerbaijan, the campaign against veiling was a matter of agitation and propaganda; it was not a matter of law. When Uzbek women activists pressed for a legal ban against the veil, the highest level of the Women's Division of the Communist Party balked, and ultimately refused

222   *Marianne Kamp*

to support this request. Azerbaijan's Communist Party pushed even harder for a decree against veiling, but ultimately settled for directives within public institutions, such as the Commissariat of Enlightenment (Education), which issued a directive against veiling in schools—a regulation that had ever broader impact as public schooling extended to reach all girls. Neither the USSR nor its constituent republics passed any laws to impose a general unveiling on all women.

The campaign to unveil women in Uzbekistan and surrounding republics had no corollary among men. In Jadid writings there had been a debate about men's dress: wearing a European-style suit was associated with modernity and progress, but also was criticized as Russification. In the 1920s, there was no state or Party discourse about men's dress at all. Some Uzbek Party leaders, like Xo'jaev and Ikramov, preferred to present themselves clean-shaven and in European-style suits, while for the President of Uzbekistan's Soviets, Oxunboboev, and for the leading literateur Xamza, wearing traditional long shirts, loose pants, a robe, a round cap and a beard was a way of identifying as "a man of the people." There was no generalized agitation against turbans, even though there was a vicious effort to arrest Muslim clerics.

Muslims in Azerbaijan and the Caucasus were aware of Turkey's reform of men's clothing. Orexalashvili, an activist from Ajaria, a Muslim autonomous region in Georgia that bordered on Turkey, referred to those changes in advancing an argument for a decree against the chador, but made no corresponding call for limitations on men's clothing:

> Permit me to say that in Turkey in this regard the matter has become much more productive than among us in Ajaristan. Permit me to say that mullahs who at home among themselves in Turkey do not have the right to wear special clothing and who do not have the right to preach there, illegally cross the border into Ajaristan and here they dress in their special clothing. So that such disorder does not prevail, we need to be not on Turkey's tail; we need to take the most heroic measures in relation to the chador. Why does it need to be removed? Because it is a hindrance not only to the one who is under the chador, for her to participate in society's life, but it also hinders those women who already removed the chador. We know examples when an Ajaristan man says to his wife, "If you remove the chador, I will marry another who goes about in the chador."[53]

In Turkey and Iran, women's and men's dress reforms were part of a project of modernizing the look of the people. In Uzbekistan and Azerbaijan, there was no campaign directed at changing men's clothing, and no one cared what a woman wore after she took off her *paranji* and *chachvon*, or her chador. She could wear a large scarf and cover her mouth with it, but she was still considered "unveiled." She could and probably did wear a traditional loose dress and pants and robe; changing her into Russian-style clothing was not the point of the campaign.

Women-initiated unveiling 223

Unveiling was a symbol of the Hujum in the USSR, but the campaign was really about women's emancipation. Edgar writes: "the Soviets sought to mobilize Muslim women to pursue education, careers, and political activism … communists sought to emancipate all Soviet women, including those of the Russian heartland."[54] In this sense, it bore some similarities to the state-led unveiling campaign in Turkey, which was concomitant with legal changes to promote women's rights.[55]

Both Uzbek and Azerbaijani women began their own unveiling before the Party created its unveiling campaign. Likewise, women in Turkey had an unveiling movement before Kemal Atatürk proclaimed a state demand for women to unveil. When states co-opt women's movements, the movement itself and its symbols change their meaning. In Uzbekistan, what had been a case of women thinking about and deciding whether to veil, and thus demonstrating their agency, instead became a campaign where the Party told everyone what to do, with contradictory messages: men should tell women to unveil (in other words, unveiling is men's business, and under men's authority), and women should unveil (in other words, women should decide to support the Party's agenda). Similarly, in Turkey, Iran, and Afghanistan the state asserted its influence on women through men: men were expected to unveil their wives. Some of the logic articulated by Soviet unveiling activists may have been at play in these other contexts as well: men were actively to consent to the state's new vision of women; pragmatically, unveiling would be more thorough and rapid if men became its active agents; and women themselves were more willing to unveil if men in their families allowed or encouraged them to do so.

Did the state's appropriation of unveiling result in physical violence against the unveiled in countries outside of the Soviet Union? Within the Soviet Union, the Party's takeover of this movement meant that unveiling became much more widespread, but also that unveiling acquired many new meanings, becoming a site of violent conflict. In both Uzbekistan and Azerbaijan, men murdered women for unveiling, expressing the belief that both women and their dress should indeed remain under men's control, and not under the Party's control. A liberal perspective on veiling and unveiling asserts that dress should be a matter of personal choice, but choice is never absolutely free. When Uzbek women chose to continue veiling during the Hujum, they limited their own opportunities, and they put in jeopardy the livelihood and the ambitions of men in their families, but they protected themselves from harassment and assault. When women chose to unveil, they faced physical attacks and threats, and hundreds were murdered by family or community members. Whether this aspect of the state-led unveiling campaign was unique to the Soviet Union or was a response to such campaigns elsewhere remains an open question.

Notes

1 Douglas Northrop, *Veiled Empire: Gender and Power in Stalinist Central Asia* (Ithaca, NY: Cornell University Press 2004). Gülzar İbrahimova, *Azərbaycan*

224 *Marianne Kamp*

Qadini: Tarix və gerçəklik (Bakı: Elm 2009). My approach regards "colonialism" as not irrelevant, but not an especially helpful analytic frame, either; it is perhaps close to the position that Bhava Dave explains in the introduction and first chapter of *Kazakhstan: Ethnicity, Language, and Power*. Routledge, 2007.

2 Marianne Kamp, *The New Woman in Uzbekistan: Islam, Modernity, and Unveiling under Communism* (Seattle: University of Washington Press 2006). Kamp, "Unveiling Uzbek Women: Liberation, Representation, and Discourse, 1906 to 1929," PhD dissertation (University of Chicago 1998). In 1992 and 1993, I carried out 32 oral history interviews with elderly women in several cities in Uzbekistan: Tashkent, Bukhara, Namangan, and Kokand. I conducted the interviews, transcribed, and translated them; the research was underwritten by IREX. Most of the women identified themselves as Uzbek, three were Tatar, and several were Tajik. I also refer to some interviews from a later project, "Oral Histories of Collectivization in Uzbekistan," undertaken in Uzbekistan from 2001 to 2004, in numerous rural districts of seven provinces of Uzbekistan. This project, created by co-primary investigators Russell Zanca, Elyor Karimov, and Marianne Kamp, and sponsored by NCEEER, the University of Wyoming, and IREX, involved cooperation with the Yosh Olimlar Jamiyati of the Academy of Sciences of Uzbekistan. Yosh Olimlar associates carried out most of the 120 interviews and transcribed them; I translated them.

3 For Uzbekistan and Azerbaijan, the Russian Empire was clearly a colonial power. The Soviet state continued many of the forms of Russian imperial control, but in other ways tried to reduce the asymmetries of colonialism by treating all subjects of the state as equal and by trying to make similar economic investments across the USSR. Those who study the Soviet peripheries have a lively debate as to whether to consider Central Asia during the Soviet period in a colonial/post-colonial framework. See Bhavna Dave's useful summary and critique of the various positions in this debate, in *Kazakhstan*, op. cit.; see also Adeeb Khalid, "Introduction: Locating the (Post)-colonial in Soviet History," *Central Asian Survey* 2007 (26, no. 4): 465–73.

4 Examples of these shared themes are in: Qassim Amin's well-known works, *The Liberation of Women, and The New Woman: Two Documents in Egyptian Feminism*, trans. Samiha Sidhom Peterson (Cairo: American University of Cairo Press 2000 [1898 and 1900]); Bahithat al-Badiya's work, translated and excerpted in *Opening the Gates: A Century of Arab Feminist Writing*, eds. Margot Badran and Miriam Cooke (Bloomington: Indiana University Press 1990); Taj al-Saltana, *Crowning Anguish: Memoirs of a Persian Princess from the Harem to Modernity, 1884–1914*, ed. Abbas Amanat (Washington, DC: Mage 2003); Fakhr ul-Banat Sibghatulla qizi, *Aila Sabaqlari*, ed. Teshaboi Ziyoyev (Toshkent: Yozuvchi 1992 [1913]); Hanifa Khanim bint Ismatulla, *Targhib mu'allimalarga maktab ravshanda yazilmishdir* (Kazan: Dombrovskii 1898).

5 The most thorough works on Tatar women's intellectual and political formation in this period are T. A. Bektimirova, *Stupeni obrazovaniia do sorbonny* (Kazan: Alma-Lit 2003); Sagit Faizov, *Dvizhenie Musul'manok Rossii za prava zhenshin v 1917 g stranitsy istorii* (Nizhnii Novgorod: NIM Makhinur 2005). See also Kamp, *New Woman*, op.cit.

6 A note on transliteration: Uzbekistan adopted a Latin alphabet in 1996, and I use it for transliterating words from Uzbek and from early-twentieth-century Turkic texts as well. For Azerbaijani names and words I follow the post-1992 Azerbaijani Latin script. Chador (Az: çadr) is an exception; I am using the spelling that has been generally adopted in English.

7 Northrop, *Veiled Empire*, op. cit., 19. Tashkent's population became proportionately less Kazakh during the Russian colonial period or, at any rate, the proportion of the native population that seemed to identify with Kazakh ways of life

Women-initiated unveiling 225

did not increase, while the proportion that identified with "Sart" norms did; increased women's veiling may be related to migration-based growth of Tashkent's population and to changes in the dominant ethnic identification.

8 L. I. Roslavtseva, *Odezhda krymskikh tatar: kontsa XVIII-nachala XX v. Istoriko-etnograficheskoe issledovanie* (Moskva: Nauka, 2000), 31–35, and 38–40. Roslavtseva explains that Crimean Tatar fashions showed strong influence both from the Ottoman Empire and from Central Asia.

9 M. Dzhebrailova writes concerning Azerbaijanis: "The chador was primarily characteristic for urban women and those living near cities." *Azerbaidzhanskaia Natsional'naia Odezhda: pamiatniki material'noi kul'tury Azerbaidzhana* 4, ed. P. A. Azizbekova (Ak. Nauk Az. SSR. no date) 2.

10 Kamp, oral history interviews: Sara G., b. 1916, Tashkent, interviewed 1993; Sofia M., b. 1920 Kokand, interviewed 1993. Writers for the journal *Kommunistka* frequently repeated that Tatar women had widely unveiled by 1905. Historian Azade Ayse Rorlich noted that Tatar religious thinkers debated the necessity of the veil starting in the 1890s. Rorlich, *The Volga Tatars: A Profile in National Resilience* (Stanford, CA: Hoover Institution Press 1986), 62–63. N. I. Vorob'ev. *Kazanskie Tatary: opyt putevoditelia po etnograficheskomu otdelu Tsentral'nogo Muzei T.S.S.R.* (Kazan: Biblioteka ekspiditsionnoi bazy T.S.S.R., vyp. VI, 1927), 25, 28–29

11 Nalivkin, V. and M. Nalivkina, *Ocherk byta zhenshchiny osedlago tuzemnago naseleniia fergany,* (Kazan: Tipografia Imperatorskago Universiteta 1886), 96–97.

12 Kazakhs were traditionally nomadic peoples of the Central Asian steppes. Authors used the terms "Turkestani" and "Sart" to refer to women of sedentary agricultural and urban communities in Central Asia. Neither term differentiates by language; Turkestani and Sart included speakers of Uzbek (a Turkic language) and Tajik (a Persian language).

13 F. H. "Qazaq Xatun-qizlari," *Suyum Bike* 1914 (no. 22): 19–20. The present-day Tatar rendering of the journal's name is *Söyem Bikë*. I have arbitrarily chosen to transliterate almost all Turkic texts according to twenty-first-century Uzbek latin norms.

14 'A. 'Azmet, "Hijab. Sart xatunlari 'alemindan." *Suyum Bike* 1915: 21, 12–15. Azmet's comparison between his own background (presumably Russian Tatar) and what he saw in Turkistan led to his claim that Sarts practiced hijab more thoroughly than anyone else. Azmet clearly had never encountered strict purdah in its South Asian context.

15 Jemaleddin Validov, "Hijab Masalasi: al-Hilal majlisinden qisqartirib terjima etildi." *Suyum Bike* 1914, 8, 4–6.

16 *Suyum Bike* published a series of articles about Muslim Women's Association conferences. The Muslim Women's Association used the same strategies as other feminist organizations in Russia; Faizov, *Dvizhenie Musul'manok Rossii*, op. cit., is a thorough presentation of these congresses. On feminist organizing in Russia, see Rochelle Goldberg Ruthchild, *Equality & Revolution: Women's Rights in the Russian Empire, 1905–1917* (Pittsburgh: University of Pittsburgh Press 2010). Azade-Ayşe Rorlich provides a much fuller context for changing thought and activism among Russia's Volga Tatars, in *The Volga Tatars*, op. cit. I Halili, "Qazondag'i 'umumi Muslimalar isiiezdi," *Suyum Bike* May 10, 1917 (11): 166–74.

17 This is the central argument to Leila Ahmed's discussion of discourses on veiling in Egypt, and it has shaped all scholarship on women and Islam since she articulated this point. Ahmed, *Women and Gender in Islam: Historic Roots of a Modern Debate* (New Haven, CT: Yale University Press 1992). I would argue that this gives insight to some aspects of the debate about veiling, but obscures others.

226 Marianne Kamp

18 These discourses are now so pervasive as to be almost inescapable in any discussion of veiling. See for example their deployment in Noor O'Neill Borbieva, "Empowering Muslim Women: Independent Religious Fellowships in the Kyrgyz Republic," *Slavic Review* 2012 (71, no. 2): 288–307. A fairly early documenting of the double punishment meme is found in the film, *Veiled Revolution*, by Elizabeth Fernea and Marilyn Gaunt (Icarus/First Run 1982).

19 Labiba Husseniya's remarks at the May 1917 Kazan Muslim Women's Congress encapsulate this view. Halili, *Suyum Bike* May 10, 1917, op. cit., 166–74. The argument over whether girls should learn to write is discussed in Kamp, *New Woman*, op. cit., 40–43.

20 Halili, *Suyum Bike* May 10, 1917, op. cit., 166–74.

21 Azerbaijan's declaration of independence, in *Azerbaidzhanskaia Respublika: doumenty i materialy 1918–1920 gg.* Ed. Dzh. B. Guliev (Baku: Elm 1998), 12 (Azeri version) and 13–14 (Russian version). The Azerbaijani and Russian versions of this declaration differ in countless ways. On this period in Azerbaijan's history, Bolukbasi, Suha, *Azerbaijan: A Political History* (London: I.B. Tauris 2011); Hasanli, Jamil, *Russkaia Revoliutsiia i Azerbaidzhan: trudnyi put' k nezavisimosti, 1917–1920* (Moskva: Izd "Flinta" 2011); Balaev, Aidyn. *Azerbaidzhanskoe nat'ional'noe dvizhenie v 1917–1918* (Baku: Elm 1998).

22 Gülzar İbrahimova, *Azərbaycan Qadini*, op. cit. On Tsarist period education for Muslim girls, 111–27; on Azerbaijani Democratic Republic actions on women, 172–75; on education in that period, 175–94.

23 The Communist Party Women's Division changed its name to the Division of Women Workers and Peasants in order to express clearly the understanding that class is the most important social divide, and to affirm that it was not trying to represent all women. Since the founding of the Russian Social Democratic Party, its members accused Russian feminists of blindness to class, of creating an artificial cross-class solidarity among women, and of making men into women's enemies. Ruthchild, *Equality & Revolution*, op. cit., explains this well. It is an argument that recurs in worldwide discourses about feminism to this day. Examples of articles supporting use of women's clubs include: Vikt. Tseitlin. "God raboty sredi zhenshchin Azerbaidzhana" *Kommunistka* 1922 (1): 29–30. E. Ralli, "Zhenskie musul'manskie kluby," *Kommunistka* 1922 (6–7): 30–32. K. Ishchova (*sic.*), "Rabota sredi zhenshchin musul'manok v Azerbeidzhane," *Kommunistka* 1923 (5): 34–36.

24 K. Ishkova, "4-e soveshchanie zavzhenotdelami Azerbeidzhanskoi kommunisticheskoi partii," *Kommunistka* 1923 (10): 45–47. Ishkova, the ethnically Russian director of the Women's Division in Azerbaijan who had been involved in founding Baku's Ali Bayramov club, clearly thought of herself as one of these exceptions.

25 Kamp, *The New Woman*, op. cit., 138–44.

26 Farideh Heyat, *Azeri Women in Transition: Women in Soviet and post-Soviet Azerbaijan*. Routledge, 2002, p 69.

27 Almas Muradova, *Vovlechenie zhenshchin Azerbaidzhanskoi SSR v organy gosudarstvennoi vlasti 20–30 ie gody XX veka* (Baku: Nurlan 2007), 13.

28 Most famous among the exiles was Shefika Gaspirali, daughter of the Tatar reformer Ismail Bey Gaspirali (Gasprinski). Shefika Hanum had established *Alem-i Nisvan* (1905–6), the first journal for Turk/Tatar women in the Russian Empire, and she moved to Azerbaijan after the creation of the Azerbaijan People's Republic. She was married to a nationalist politician, Nasib Yusifbeyli. Şengül Hablemitoğlu and Necip Hablemitoğlu, *Şefika Gaspirali ve Rusya'da Türk Kadın Hareketi (1893–1920)* (Ankara: Ajans-Turk 1998). Azade-Ayşe Rorlich, "The Äli Bayrmov" Club, the Journal *Shärg Gadïnï* and the Socialization of Azeri women 1920–30," *Central Asian Survey* 1986 (3–4): 221–39.

Women-initiated unveiling 227

29 Ishkova, "4–3 soveshchaniia," 46.
30 Kamp, *The New Woman*, op. cit., 146.
31 Hayat, *Azeri Women*, op. cit., 98. Interestingly, post-Soviet histories by Azerbaijani scholars assiduously avoid this topic.
32 N. Zavar'ian, "Delegatskie sobraniia na vostoke." *Kommunistka* 1927 (7): 40.
33 Kamp, *New Woman*, op. cit., 162–64. The commission was led by the highest ranking Uzbek men and women in the Party including Fayzulla Xo'aev, Akmal Ikromov, and Tojixon Shodieva.
34 Douglas Northrop, "Languages of Loyalty: Gender, Politics, and Party Supervision in Uzbekistan, 1927–41," *Russian Review* 2000 (59, no. 2): 179–299.
35 Kamp, *New Woman*, op. cit., 165–85.
36 This is a summary of Kamp, *New Woman*, op. cit., 186–214.
37 Kamp, *The New Woman*, op. cit., chapters 7 and 8. Kamp, "Femicide as Terrorism: The Case of Uzbekistan's Unveiling Murders" in *Sexual Violence in Conflict Zones: from the Ancient World to the Era of Human Rights*, ed. Elizabeth Heineman (Philadelphia: University of Pennsylvania Press, 2011), 56–70.
38 A. Artiukhina, " Ot 'nastupleniia' k sistematicheskoi rabote (k obsledovaniiu raboty Srednei Azii)," *Kommunistka* 1928 (1): 57–63.
39 "Nuzho li izdat' dekret, zapreshchaiushchii noshenie chadry (iz stenogrammy Zakavkazskogo soveshchaniie rabotnikov sredi zhenshchin 16 Iulia 1928)" *Kommunistka*, 1928 (8): 79.
40 By "Shakhsei-vakhsei" Tagiyev referred to the Shia ritual of publically mourning the death of Husayn in the month of Ashura; rituals traditionally include self-flagellation. Azerbaijan's Muslim population included a predominantly Shia south and mainly Sunni north. See Bolukbasi, *Azerbaijan*, op. cit., chapter 1.
41 "Nuzhno li izdat' dekret" *Kommunistka* 1928 (8): 81.
42 This discussion is found in the following articles in *Kommunistka*. Nukhrat, "Ostnovnye voprosy soveshchaniia," 1928 (6): 77–79; S. Liubimova "Dekret o chadre i obshchestvo 'doloi kalym i mnogozhenstvo'" 1928 (8): 73–78; A. Nukhrat, "Itogi Diskussii" 1928 (11): 57–59; K. Ishkova, "Nuzhen li dekret, zapreshchaiushchii noshenie chadry" 1928 (11): 59–62; A. Nukhrat "Ot zatvornichestva k proizvodstvu" 1929 (1): 24–27; " Mestnye rabotniki ob izdanii dekreta" 1929 (1): 32–35; Osman Dzhuma Zade "Shire razvernut' raz'iasnitel'nuyu kampaniiu" 1929 (7): 48–49; M. Amosov "Shire organizuite massy" 1929 (14): 23–30.
43 " Mestnye rabotniki ob izdanii dekreta" *Kommunistka* 1929 (1): 33.
44 Muradova, op. cit., 23.
45 Heyat. *Azeri Women in Transition*, op. cit., 92, 98. I question whether this was or is "inevitable." Heyat notes that at the time there were political explanations for the violence: Communists charged nationalists with attacking activist women. In addition, much of the violence was in Baku, where tension between Azerbaijanis and Armenians allowed some linkage between anti-unveiling violence and ethnic antagonisms.
46 Heyat, op. cit.,99.
47 Gussaev, 2005, cited in Muradova, op. cit., 23.
48 According to the All Union Census of 1926, Azerbaijan's population was about 2.3 million. Of these, 1.4 million were Azerbaijanis. Thus another way to look at the figure would be that 270,000 out of about 700,000 Azerbaijani females (a number that included girls too young to veil) unveiled in 1929, or nearly half of all adult Azerbaijani women.
49 Muradova, op. cit.; Gülzar İbrahimova, *Azərbaycan Qadini*, op. cit.
50 In fact, Khujand was part of Uzbekistan's Fergana province until 1929, when Tajikistan's status changed from Autonomous province within Uzbekistan to Union Republic, and the border was redrawn to add Khujand to the new Tajik SSR.

228   *Marianne Kamp*

51 Adrienne Edgar. *Tribal Nation: The Making of Soviet Turkmenistan* (Princeton, NJ: Princeton University Press, 2004), 221–60, quotations 235.
52 S. Liubimova, "Rabota sredi zhenshchin v Tatarii" *Kommunistka* 1927 (7): 73–76.
53 "Mestnye rabotniki ob izdanii dekreta" *Kommunistka* 1929 (1): 32–33.
54 Edgar, op. cit., 260.
55 More detailed comparison appears in Kamp, *The New Woman*, op. cit., 67–75, and in Adrienne Edgar, "Bolshevism, Patriarchy, and the Nation: the Soviet Emancipation of Women in Pan-Islamic Perspective," *Slavic Review* 2006 65 (2): 252–72.

Part IV
The Balkans

8 Behind the veil

The reform of Islam in interwar Albania or the search for a "modern" and "European" Islam

Nathalie Clayer

The Albanian case is unique. When the independence of this young European country was again recognized by the international community in 1920,[1] Islam was the religion of the majority of the population (around 70 per cent of an estimated 800,000 inhabitants). Albania was thus the only predominantly Muslim European state. Unlike the majority of Muslims in Western Europe, Albanian Muslims were neither immigrants nor recent converts to Islam. Nor did they form a "surviving minority,"[2] as was the case with Muslim groups living in other Balkan countries; rather we could say that they made up a "surviving majority." One of the components of the national identity-building process had been to legitimize the existence of a sovereign nation, even if predominantly Muslim, in Europe, in the case of the collapse of the Ottoman Empire.[3]

Despite this Muslim majority, from 1920 onwards the Albanian state was immediately defined by its political leaders as *afetar* ("without religion"), that is to say "without any official religion." The aim was to strengthen national feeling among a population divided between different denominations, Muslims, Catholic Christians, and Orthodox Christians.[4] In fact, the state was multi-denominational rather than a-denominational. The a-denominational character of the state also fitted the wishes of secularist intellectuals and civil servants, who were non-Muslims as well as Muslims—Sunnis or members of the heterodox Islamic brotherhood of the Bektashis. These secularists dominated the country's intellectual life and the state apparatus, and were working for what they called the "modernization" and the "Europeanization" of the country.

The dominant role of secularist elites paved the way for the "reform of Islam." This process was made easier by the nationalization of Islamic religious institutions and by the progressive control exerted over them by the state. Indeed, the Albanian state played an important role in the organization and reform of official religious institutions. For example, it interfered in the organization of the first national Islamic Congress which took place in 1923, issuing orders concerning the choice of the delegates. It was not essential that they were clerics, but above all they had to be "patriots," and "more or less liberal." The civil authorities themselves even chose some of the delegates,

232 Nathalie Clayer

who were supposed to represent one province or another.[5] Government representatives were also present during the meetings. Apart from the congresses, the attitude of clerics was closely controlled. Their nomination had to be accepted, and was sometimes even decided by the civil authorities who also dismissed some clerics. Finally, with the further reform and centralization of religious institutions in 1929, the state came to provide a substantial part of the Islamic Community's budget.[6]

The "reform of Islam" was also facilitated by the fact that the authority of the official religious leaders was sometimes even imposed through the intervention of the civil authorities. For instance, in 1926 the head of the Islamic Community informed the Ministry of the Interior that propaganda had been launched in Shkodër against the new Madrasa established in that city, as well as against the new organization of the Jemaat (Islamic Community) and the collection of money that it implied. The Ministry therefore ordered the head of the Community not to allow sermons to be delivered in mosques without the authorization of the Community, and promised that the civil authorities would take action against offenders.[7]

The links between the political authorities and the Islamic Community were especially close since Islam and the Islamic religious institutions were also used by the government for social control. As early as 1922, sermons (*vaz*) were used to persuade parents to send their children to school, and to strengthen national fraternity and loyalty to the government. Even in 1936, the official aim of the Islamic Community was to contribute by means of sermons and lectures to the strengthening of national fraternity and national feeling, as well as to advise Muslims to conform to progress and "true civilization." Islam was also particularly used in the context of the economic crisis. During Ramadan in 1931, for example, preachers had to address this problem, and Islamic charity was encouraged in order to help solve the social crisis. In 1937, the leaders of the Islamic Community called upon wealthy Muslims to give to the poor who were suffering from unemployment in order to show that there was no need for socialism and Bolshevism. Indeed, Islam was certainly considered by the Albanian political authorities as a tool against the diffusion of Communist ideas, which, at that time, were attractive especially for young people.[8] The "harmful nature" of Communism was denounced by Muslim clerics in numerous articles and booklets.[9]

Among the "reforms of Islam" that were introduced in this context, we should mention first the autonomy granted to the Sufi brotherhoods, in particular to the Bektashiyya, which had already been promoted by some Albanian nationalists at the end of the Ottoman period as a liberal form of Islam. These changes, imposed by the political power against the wishes of the leaders of the Islamic Community, were quite different from developments taking place in Turkey, where Sufi orders were banned. Nevertheless, from 1936 onwards, four Sufi networks—the Qadiriyya, the Rifaiyya, the Sadiyya, and the Tijaniyya—were grouped within a special organization, under the umbrella of the Islamic Community.[10]

Another important reform was the suppression of the Sharia courts, following the adoption of the Civil Code in 1928–29. Their abolition was only reluctantly accepted by the leaders of the Islamic Community because it erased the religious character of marriages and introduced some provisions concerning inheritance and divorce that were contrary to the Sacred Law. On the other hand, other reforms proposed by the political authorities were well accepted, because they were in accordance with the ideas promoted by reformist ulama.[11] Thus, in 1929, all the provincial *madrasas* were closed down and a new General Madrasa was set up in the capital, in order to train a new staff of religious officials, in a "modern" spirit.[12]

However, by using the example of another reform, the ban on the veil, I want to highlight the mechanisms of such reforms and the relations between the various actors involved. More generally, I want to show how these mechanisms reveal the place of Islam within Albanian society during the interwar period.

The progressive lifting of the veil

The ban on the veil only occurred step by step.[13] Between 1920 and 1928, only some actors—intellectuals and politicians—called or asked for such a reform in the press or in parliament, particularly when important political decisions were to be taken. This occurred between 1920 and 1923, a period which represents the beginning of a difficult state-building process.[14] It also occurred in 1924, during the short government of Fan Noli, established after the so-called "June Revolution." The question was again debated in 1928, when the Civil Code was introduced and when the political system was transformed from a republic to a monarchy. But, during this first phase, no action was actually taken, either by the political authorities or by religious leaders.

In 1929, however, at a time of political change and of religious reorganization under state control, the ban on the veil became part of the radical measures requested by Behxhet Shapati, the new head of the Islamic Community, elected at the close of the national Islamic Congress. Indeed, it has been suggested that Shapati asked the Minister of Justice to ban the *perçe* (veil) and requested that, through the police, he should advise the population to abandon the veil by prohibiting husbands and fathers to go in the company of veiled women.[15] However, it seems doubtful that the new head of the Islamic Community would have taken this initiative, which was probably the work of the political authorities. Indeed, the Ministerial Council banned not only the *perçe* (veil), but also the *ferexhe* (*fereje*), a dustcoat worn by women when they went out. The Minister of Justice nevertheless recommended to police stations that they should be very careful not to offend the people, and try to convince them by working together with the district councils responsible for explaining to women why the ban was necessary.[16]

At the same time, during the following years, the political authorities used various means in order to impose this decision: propaganda in newspapers,

234 *Nathalie Clayer*

lectures and, above all, insistence that women working for the state, such as midwives and teachers, must comply. In fact, at least in 1935, punitive measures were taken against those women who did not respect the ban.[17] In addition, initiatives were sometimes taken by local authorities, such as the mayors of Gjirokastër and Tirana.[18]

But the question of the ban on the veil gained new impetus in 1936–37, during a new period of political crisis. At that time, the country's sovereignty was more and more openly challenged by Italy. A liberal government had been set up in October 1935, but lasted only until November 1936. During this "liberal government" led by Mehdi Frashëri, the debate on the veil was relaunched in the press, especially in the Islamic Community's journal and the newspapers of some young intellectuals. Then, in 1937, when an important set of reforms was launched by the Albanian authorities to assert the country's sovereignty, the ban on the veil became the subject of a law.

Here again, the initiative was supposed to have been taken by the official religious authorities. According to this version, the two muftis of the southern provinces asked the General Council of the Islamic Community to ban the veil. Following this request, the head of the Islamic Community, Shapati, wrote a report, containing a *fatwa* by him stating that it was not *haram* (forbidden by religion) for a woman to show her face. On 1 March 1937, the General Council of the Community agreed with this report and the *fatwa*, and decided to make the decision known on the one hand to the population by means of sermons, and on the other to the government. The latter immediately presented a draft law to parliament that was approved on 8 March 1937. Under the title "Law on the ban on face covering," it stipulated that it was forbidden for a woman to cover her face, totally or partially, with any kind of veil. Offenders, as well as the husbands, fathers, or guardians who had not exerted their authority and those who were making propaganda in favor of the veil, incurred a fine.[19]

In reality, this initiative probably originated in political circles, and it seems that a kind of compromise was achieved between the political and the religious authorities. Indeed, the law concerned only the covering of the face and remained silent about the wearing of the *fereje*, a garment that the police were supposed to have banned since 1929.

What is important to note is that this law had a strong echo abroad, and this had certainly been the true aim of the political authority. In fact, the ban on the veil aimed to symbolize the Westernization of the country, by making it possible for women to have a place in economic and social life. As a Western country, Albania should be a sovereign country among the other Western countries.[20]

However, in the country itself, the veil did not totally disappear for two reasons. On one hand, there was popular opposition and, on the other, the government remained very cautious. Resistance developed especially in Shkodër, the stronghold of Islam in northern Albania, and in small cities of central Albania, such as Tirana, Kavajë, Elbasan, and Durrës. Despite the example given by high religious officials and the order given to civil servants concerning their wives, the veil reappeared after a short period. In some places, women began to wear a *xhari*, a piece of material which allowed them to uncover their faces when meeting a policeman, and quickly to cover them again afterwards. Even in 1940, problems were still noticed in Kavajë by the civil authorities.[21] In fact, these authorities had received instructions that when applying the law they should not act brutally. Politically, it was better to convince than to forbid. At the beginning of the campaign, King Zog had sent his three sisters unveiled to Shkodër, along with the Minister of the Interior and other officials, in order to convince the population.[22] Persuasion was also part of the programme of the Albanian Women's Association's local groups which were in charge of the organization of conferences.[23]

The debate and its actors

A multiplicity of actors, with various positions and interests, were involved in this reform, as well as in the debate that surrounded it. There were three categories of actors, all of whom had to take into account the fact that the population was severely affected by the economic and social crisis and that religion was still an important reference for the people. These categories, which were not always very clearly separated, were: state representatives, secularist intellectuals and Muslim clerics. In fact, these different actors together represented only a tiny proportion of the population. As with the question of the Civil Code, some non-Muslims participated in the debate, while they interfered to a lesser extent in other reforms of Islam. Nevertheless, the main actors remained Muslims. This reveals that the social division implied by the multi-denominational character of the population was still very important, except for a section of the younger generation.[24]

The state representatives

The state representatives did not intervene much in the debate, but they played an important role in the field, because they were responsible for enforcement of the ban at different levels.

In general, the policy they had to implement was dictated by a desire for reform. The aim was to "modernize" the country, but above all to build a "faithful nation" and to assert the sovereignty of the country. However, in concrete terms, the implementation of this policy was changing with time and circumstances. Furthermore, the civil servants in charge of its implementation had their own views that could have an impact upon their actions. Mayors, officials, teachers, and policemen could act locally according to their own feeling, either enforcing or not enforcing the orders received from above.

Some of the state representatives were Muslim conservatives who were against the ban. In this case they could be still "more cautious" vis-à-vis the population in implementing the ban. But it seems that, as officials, they

236 *Nathalie Clayer*

were often obliged to set an example. It also seems that, in fact, most of the civil servants even anticipated the government initiatives; I have already referred to the local initiatives in favor of the ban taken in 1929 by the mayor of Gjirokastër. He asked the city's population to abandon the veil, because it was the cause of women's isolation.[25] Teachers, especially those belonging to the younger generation, were often more eager for reforms than the government itself. In particular, some of them seem to have called for a clearer and quicker disappearance of religion, and especially of Islam, from the public sphere.[26] This was the case for non-Muslims, but also for young Muslims trained in Western countries or in new schools in Albania. Their attitude reflects both the social competition in which they were involved vis-à-vis the older elites and especially the clerics who had previously exerted a monopoly over education, and the effects of ideas developed by secularist intellectuals.[27]

The secularist intellectuals

The secularist intellectuals, who voiced opposition to the veil in the press (or in the parliament) from 1920 onwards, were often guided by a European-centered vision of Islam. They used the question of the veil as a component of the debate on "modernization," "Westernization," "secularization," and the strengthening of the state. They generally belonged to the younger generation. Most of them were of Muslim origin, but others were Christians. However, as they were all secularist, their religious origin did not matter so much. Among non-Muslims, there was no specific discourse, even if for them secularization meant not only the separation of state and religion, but also the end of the hegemony of Islam in society.[28] The young Albanians of Muslim origin who took the floor had a different profile. Some were born to important notable families, such as Ali Këlcyra and Namik Delvina. They had studied in the West or in Istanbul, in modern schools where Positivism was quite widespread. Other secularist intellectuals were of more modest social origin. They had studied in Western Europe or in Albania. Some of them were attracted by Communism, such as Halim Xhelo and Selim Shpuza.[29]

However, they all were fighting against the "Eastern mentality and habits," and wanted their country to turn to the West, even though they were debating how to do this and some of them were trying to build a specifically Albanian way to "Westernization."[30]

For the secularist intellectuals, the veil (as well as the *fereje*) was linked with notions of seclusion, servitude, and slavery of women. It was associated, not with the outside Muslim world as in the current debate concerning the veil in Western Europe, but with the Ottoman past, seen as synonymous with "yoke," "barbarism," "backwardness," "fanaticism," and "Asia." It was also closely associated with the socio-political decline of the Islamic community and the backwardness of the nation. Indeed the veil was described by such intellectuals as the cause of the backwardness of the whole nation, because Muslims were the majority of the population, and because girls were not educated and did not participate sufficiently in economic life. But, for them, the question was not only intrinsic. There was also the problem of foreign perceptions, and concern that the first impression gained by "European tourists" (as they wrote) would be to see veiled women in all Albanian cities.

These intellectuals considered that the ban on the veil was necessary in order to make Albania a European country or at least to portray it as such. It could lead Albania towards progress and show that Albanians deserved to live as a free people in the middle of Europe. They considered that the geographical location of Albania in Europe, as well as the fact that the country was living in the twentieth century, were two reasons for the ban on the veil.

Last, they used the example given by Kemalist Turkey, or by other Muslim countries (like Iran and Afghanistan), which had made similar reforms. For instance, in 1923, the deputy Ali Këlcyra declared in the middle of the Albanian parliament that Mustafa Kemal went to the Turkish parliament with his unveiled fiancée and that newspaper photographs showed the faces of Mustafa Kemal and "his wife."[31]

The case of Mehdi Frashëri

Among this group of secularist intellectuals, the figure of Mehdi Frashëri occupied a specific place. Deputy, civil servant, minister, president of the Council of State, and intellectual, he was one of the main officials responsible for the autonomy of the Bektashi Community, which he represented in 1943–44 on the Regency Council, being himself a Bektashi Muslim. He was also one of the main architects of the Civil Code introduced in 1928–29 in Albania.[32]

In 1928, the question of the veil enabled him to contrast Bektashism, portrayed as "liberal," with Sunnism, presented as "fanatical" and the enemy of progress. Indeed, in the introduction of his book about the *Ancient History of Albania*, he tackled the question of religion. He depicted Sunnism as a fanatical form of Islam, which considered every type of progress and every change as a threat to religion, while presenting Bektashism as a "protest" against this type of Islam. According to Mehdi Frashëri, Bektashism prohibited polygamy and, whereas Sunni Islam required women to be veiled, Bektashis considered that women had to be veiled only with the "veil of honour," which was not a material veil. Women therefore were only required to be honourable, and were not required to cover their face.[33]

In a long text published the same year as a serial in a newspaper aimed at "intellectuals and patriots," Mehdi Frashëri explained his ideas about "Muslim reforms."[34] He presented the position of women and the question of the veil, as well as the perception of Christians by Muslims, as the two revealing factors of the evolution of Islam. The veil appeared with the decline of Islam. Therefore, the most radical reform required was the one concerning the position of women.[35] He claimed that such a reform was necessary in order for Albanians to be included among "European people." Since Albanians wanted to live free, independent, and advanced lives, Mehdi Frashëri

238 *Nathalie Clayer*

saw only two solutions for Albanian Muslims who represented the part of the Muslim world that was face to face with Christian people: either make reforms or Islam would have to disappear from the face of Albania.[36] Only radical reforms like those of Mustafa Kemal in Turkey could bring civilization and independence, as the Christian people had experienced four centuries before, with the Protestant reform.

At that time, Mehdi Frashëri was preparing new legislation covering all fields, including family law, previously covered by the Sharia courts. Thus, his approach to the reform of Islam had another important aspect: that of religious authority. In fact, in the same article,[37] he advocated returning to the sources without the intermediary of an authority, in accordance with Luther's principle. Moreover, he claimed that even some features of the Islamic religion urged him to follow this line. Indeed, in Mehdi Frashëri's view, the Prophet himself did not assume authority, and Islam, as a general principle, opted to have no clergy. Because the educational level of the clerics was too low, and until the arrival of a new educated generation, clerics should confine themselves to the practice of religion, whereas the Muslim councils established all over the country should be made up of educated people, doctors, lawyers, agronomists, professors, etc. Mehdi Frashëri went so far in this direction that he proposed totally new training for muftis. He stated that all the country's *madrasas* however, should be closed, and replaced by the establishment of two colleges (one in the south, the other in the north), with a new educational system where Arabic should be taught according to the American Berlitz method. The best students should be sent to Europe to study philosophy, as well as the Arabic language in the departments of foreign languages. On their return, they should be appointed muftis, since, in Islam, those who are more learned are in a better position to interpret the texts and since muftis do not need to wear turbans and *jubes* (robe worn by imams and ulama with full sleeves and long skirts).

The ulama

It is easy to understand that people holding religious authority reacted to a debate in which Islam was often disparaged and their authority challenged. They were also reacting to the measures taken by the state and its representatives to ban the veil. However the reactions were expressed in various ways, often depending on the social position of those concerned.

A first group of Muslim clerics was made up of the leaders of the Islamic Community, i.e. of the official religious institutions. These people were themselves reformists. For instance, in 1925, when a national Islamic Congress was convened in Tirana, they declared that Albania was taking part in the "revival" of Islamic civilization inaugurated by Muhammad Abduh. They wanted to introduce reforms in order to achieve culture, civilization and progress. As a result, the political authorities looked favorably on them. Nevertheless they only had a limited room to maneuvre vis-à-vis these political authorities and,

Behind the veil: interwar Albania 239

when they had differences of opinion with them, especially when reforms implied restrictions to their own authority, they had great difficulty imposing their view.[38] They themselves did not form a totally homogeneous group. For instance, in 1926, when the students of Tirana's *madrasa* asked for authorization to create a sports association, only one member of the High Council of the Sharia was in favour of this idea.[39]

The attitude of the leaders of the Islamic Community concerning the veil had fluctuated according to their place in the debate and in the process. Until 1929, they generally defended the veil, or at least opposed criticism of it using two arguments—a woman's honour and religious authority.[40] In 1929 and in 1937, when official measures were taken concerning the ban on the veil, the leaders of the Islamic Community were supposed to have taken the initiative, but, as I have argued, this does not seem very plausible. In 1929, the argument they used to justify the measures taken by the civil authorities was that wearing the veil was not a Qur'anic prescription and that the Islamic religion did not insist on covering the face. Some months later, the Islamic Community published in its journal the translation of a lecture given in the Berlin Mosque on a woman's position in Islam. Here again the interpretation of the Qur'an, inspired by the leader of the Lahori Ahmadiyya, Muhammad Ali, led to the conclusion that uncovering of a woman's face and hands was lawful.[41]

When the veil debate livened up again in the press in 1936, these leaders, as representatives of the Islamic Community, chose above all to defend the Islamic religion and, for that purpose, to denounce the criticisms made against the veil, since it was associated by their adversaries with Islam. In the Community's journal, they denounced the idea that the veil—and the Islamic religion—was the cause of the lack of progress of the Albanian nation and accused their adversaries of wanting to force Albanian women to live in excessive luxury. In doing so, they inevitably appeared all the more as the champions of the veil. Yet, relying on the Qur'an, the article concluded that a woman could go out with her face unveiled, but without any make-up, and with a cloak (*jilbab*) leaving only the face and the hands uncovered.[42] It shows the ambiguity of their discourse.

With the decision of the political authorities to impose the ban on the veil at the beginning of 1937, the leaders of the Islamic Community were placed in a different position. Again they had to justify such a decision at the religious level, and even to appear to promote it. The arguments presented in these new circumstances were in fact of various types.[43] Some were of course religious. Shapati explained that, according to verses 31–32 of Surat XXIV of the Qur'an, a woman had to be covered in front of strangers. But according to Imam Azam, this prescription excluded the face and hands. All the Hanafi ulama preached this interpretation. Later on, they argued, because of the problems that had appeared in Muslim societies, Muslim jurists had prohibited women from showing their face.[44] According to *fiqh* books, a Muslim woman had the right to work outside the home, to trade, to be a witness at the court, etc. Then Shapati wrote:

240 *Nathalie Clayer*

"Ibn Abidin said that the fact that a free woman shows her face is not *haram* [unlawful], but it is not necessary, it is *meqruh* [not forbidden by God, but looked upon by Muslim teachers with disgust]. According to this prescription, we issue the following *fatwa*: The stranger, Zeyd, when he sees the face of a foreign woman, Hindi, is it *haram* ? Answer: it is not *haram*."[45]

Apart from the religious justification, the leaders of the Islamic Community also used the rhetoric of the civil authorities, and eventually that of the secularist intellectuals whom they had opposed. They presented abandoning the veil as a "social measure." They explained that its main aim was to improve the position of Muslim women within Albanian society, because the country needed such an investment of women in social life in order to achieve, as soon as possible, the level of cultural progress and economic development of a civilized country. Moreover, they did not forget to mention that the measure was taken just at the time when the King promised a set of reforms.

Like the secularist intellectuals, they also structured their arguments round the question of perception. The veil had become a problem because it was misused by some people and, because it was considered as a prescription of the Islamic religion, the result was a criticism of the Islamic religion itself. Abandoning the veil was therefore necessary to highlight the true nature of Islam in the mind of public opinion. The fact that the Albanians, particularly Muslims, wore different clothes made others laugh at them. Every day, "foreign tourists" were taking photographs of Muslim women, showing them to the rest of the world as testimony to the barbarian nature of the Muslim religion. Just like the secularist intellectuals, the leaders of the Islamic Community declared lastly that, in the twentieth century and in the middle of Europe, Albanians had to adapt themselves to all the "good customs" of the civilized nations.

In this way, urged on by the political authorities, the leaders of the Islamic Community henceforth seemed to agree with the young religious Muslims sent to Lahore in India, who had expressed a different position during the debate in 1936. This small group of future ulama, who were not yet involved in the leadership of religious affairs, had published at that time an article about the veil in their small journal—a supplement to the journal of the Lahori Ahmadiyya, *The Light*.[46] Like the leaders of the Islamic Community, the authors criticized those who wanted unlimited freedom for women to mix with any foreigner. They also drew the same conclusions from the analysis of the Qur'an, which they considered as giving the principles of religion and civilization: there was no prescription concerning the covering of the face and the hands. However, they seemed to hold an opposite position in the debate. Indeed, they were convinced that the progress of Muslims was closely related to "solving the problem of the veil." Like the secularist intellectuals, they even declared that the veil was responsible for the educational backwardness of Muslim women.

But the real difference was between the leaders of the Islamic Community and other ulama who were against lifting the veil. These people did not use the press or any printed matter to express themselves in public space. Nevertheless, we know that the leaders of the Islamic Community had to face opposition from such ulama, which they tried to hide.[47] In fact, a blurred frontier existed between these ulama and those belonging to the official Community who only reluctantly accepted the lifting of the veil. But the ulama who opposed the ban on the veil had been against both the other reforms (introduction of the Civil Code and closing down of Sharia courts and local *madrasas*) and the new religious hierarchy close to the political power. Apart from their real opinion concerning the veil, it provided a good opportunity to oppose the *fatwa* and the law.

It would have been interesting to know how a reformist member of the ulama like Hafiz Abdullah Zëmblaku, who chose to have no relations with the authorities and who remained outside the new religious institutions, reacted in the 1937 debate. A former reader of the Turkish Islamist journals *Beyanülhak* and *Sebilürreşad*, in the 1920s he took as a model the missionaries of the Lahori Ahmadiyya, with whom he was in contact. He claimed to have the same objectives as this network: to make the religious prescriptions and texts accessible to everybody in vernacular languages, to work against the superstitions that entered into religion, to defend the Sharia, and to reinforce the bonds between Muslims, to show that Islam was a modern religion and that the clerics were also acting on the path to civilization, as well as to oppose the intense activity of Christian missionaries. That is why he worked for the teaching of religion and true beliefs in the Albanian language, through courses, preaching, and a set of booklets. He even invented a transcription of the Arabic language into Latin script in order to make it more accessible.[48]

We know that at the beginning of 1938 Hafiz Abdullah Zëmblaku was confined by the political authorities to the city of Vlorë, but we do not know the reason for this.[49] Some years before, however, he seems to have had an intermediary position on the question of the veil, between the young students in Lahore and the leaders of the Islamic Community. He criticized those who were against the veil, as well as those who were in favour of it for the wrong reasons. He considered that religious prescriptions obliged a woman to wear a complete veil, but that the old *fereje* was not necessary; a modern thick coat was much better, with a headscarf (*shami*) on the head and a kind of shawl.[50] Three years later, like the leaders of the Islamic Community, he appeared to deny the right of newspapers to address the question of the veil, which he saw as an issue that concerned only the ulama, thus reducing the debate to the question of religious authority.[51]

Therefore, we can see that multiple issues appeared throughout the debate and how the question was tackled by the different categories of actors.

The stakes behind the veil

In the first place, it is clear that the debate and the measures concerning the veil had their climax when political and social events or crisis occurred: at key

242   *Nathalie Clayer*

moments in the state-building process, at times when the country's sovereignty was questioned, and during economic and social crises. Whereas Islam was a means of social control for the political authorities against the spread of Communist ideology in society, notably among young people, the question of the veil had a particular meaning. In 1937 it became a tool of foreign policy deployed to assert Albania's sovereignty. However, because it symbolized the "modernization" and "Europeanization" of the country for secularist intellectuals and civil servants, the ban was also a sign given to these groups and to the rest of society that the state-building process was progressing. So they had to be faithful to the country and the government. More generally, the problem of the relations between religion and state was crucial.

State and religion

Throughout these debates and measures, the relationship between state and religion was involved repeatedly. In 1923, when the ban on the veil was discussed in parliament along with the prohibition of polygamy, some deputies reacted by saying that such decisions could not be taken by the Assembly and that the government had no right to intervene in religious affairs; time and education would resolve the problem. Others believed in the duty of the parliament and the state to take care of the cultural and social development of the nation and thus to solve this kind of question. Using a juridical approach, Mehdi Frashëri sided with the former (claiming that parliament had no authority in religious matters), but explained that other questions, such as the equality between women and men before the courts, and inheritance and divorce, could be debated by the Assembly.[52] In the following years, the Albanian government in fact adopted the second position and often interfered in religious affairs, by directing, controlling, or using the religious scene, as illustrated by the question of the veil. That is why we can say that the Albanian state was multi-denominational rather than a-denominational. There was no separation of state and church as there was, at least theoretically, in France. But, as in Turkey, only the government could combine religion with politics.[53] The difference with Turkey was that, despite Albania's Muslim majority in demographic terms, the state did not give the nation a Muslim character, which means that the question of the plurality of confessional groups arose.

The problem of building a nation out of several denominational groups appears clearly in the arguments put forward by Mehdi Frashëri in his famous article of 1928 on the reforms of Islam. For him, Albania's fate was linked to the progress of the Muslim community since it formed the majority of the population. In order to achieve a true and non-superficial union of the different parts of the nation, which was a question of survival for a small nation like Albania, the Muslim majority had to be liberal. At the same time Mehdi Frashëri thought that abandoning Sharia-based jurisprudence was necessary not only because this was "old-fashioned" legislation and because religion concerned the consciousness and legislation of the state, but also because the

Behind the veil: interwar Albania 243

Albanian people was made up of non-Muslims as well as Muslims.[54] Like Mehdi Frashëri himself, people who were not Sunni Muslims (e.g. Bektashis or Christians) had of course a specific position towards the former dominant religion. They wanted it to lose its hegemonic status, and demanded more rights for other denominational groups.[55]

In the course of the debate, the question of the secularization of public space also arose, since the veil was generally considered as a mark of the Islamic religion. Secularist intellectuals, as well as many officials and political leaders, seem to have been extremely sensitive to this, because for them "secularization" was synonymous with "de-Ottomanization" and "modernization." All marks of Ottoman domination, often mistaken for marks of Islam, were to be banned, which led to a certain depreciation of Islam. Public space was partially de-Islamized, especially in schools and in the administration, but also in urban space, even if the state itself contributed to the building of some mosques during the interwar period.[56] Consequently, the context was not that of the re-Islamization of the public sphere and disillusionment with secularism that characterize Western Europe today.[57]

Another difference from the current situation in some European countries is that the education system was not the main theater of the public sphere involved in the debate on the veil. In Albania at that time, the percentage of girls attending school was rather low; veiled girls were simply not sent to school.[58] However, apart from the veil, the separation of religion and education was an important facet of state politics, notably where religious teaching became a subject of polemics. Hafiz Abdullah Zëmblaku, for instance, saw the state, and particularly the Ministry of Education, as enemies of religion and promoters of unbelief. He considered them as "Young Turks" and "Freemasons." He himself had a lot of trouble with the authorities who banned him from teaching the Albanian language, because he taught it together with religion.[59] Here we can perceive of course the problem of the loss of legitimacy for clerics in the educational sphere, mentioned above. As a result, the journal of the Islamic Community strongly denounced the role of teachers in propagating atheism and Bolshevism.[60] But, for Hafiz Abdullah Zëmblaku, even the head of the Islamic Community, who sided with the political authorities, was an enemy of religion and a promoter of unbelief. Religious authority was thus also questioned in itself.

Religious authority

The question of religious authority came up in the debate on the veil first because the ban on the veil was considered as one of the key reforms of Islam to be implemented and because some of the actors raised the following questions: Who is able to debate about Islam? Who can decide on reforms? And who can lead them ?

I have already pointed out that the leaders of the Islamic Community very often used the argument of religious authority to answer opponents of the

244 *Nathalie Clayer*

veil. In 1928, when one of the leaders of the Islamic Community, Hafiz Ismet Dibra, had to answer the long article by Mehdi Frashëri, he gave his answer not directly to him, but to "the Muslims who wonder after reading Mehdi's Frashëri on the reforms of Islam." Moreover, instead of criticizing the point of view of his adversary, Dibra first denied his authority in the field of religion, pointing out all his "mistakes" as proof of his incompetence. In particular, Mehdi Frashëri's tendency to imagine *ijtihad* (interpretation) out of the context of the Sharia, as well as his failure to show signs of respect towards the Prophet, were considered unacceptable.[61] Such an answer, in fact, followed the same lines as that of Mehdi Frashëri, since the latter had advocated returning to the sources without the intermediary of an authority, proposing to establish Islamic councils composed of laymen and to train new muftis using modern educational methods, as we have seen.[62] In the same way, in 1935, Hafiz Abdullah Zëmblaku explained that, since the Kingdom had no official religion, religion was free, and nobody had the right to meddle with religious matters, except the religious scholars. Thus, he urged the journalists to speak about the economy rather than religion.[63]

The secularist intellectuals were really challenging the religious authority because of their direct access to the Qur'an through translations[64] and their constant attacks on Islam, but also because of widespread ignorance among Muslim clerics. This led some Muslims to react by proposing a plan to train clerics capable of guiding people with an Eastern as well as a Western culture, and more generally to launch reforms based on *ijtihad*.[65]

Furthermore, the question of the veil reveals that the authority of the leaders of the Islamic Community was not only challenged by secularist intellectuals but also by some religious entrepreneurs. The new religious hierarchy had difficulty gaining recognition from all the country's Muslims. Some ulama were unwilling to accept the reforms which the Community had agreed to implement in close collaboration with the civil authorities, or to accept the new hierarchy and the centralization of the religious authorities. Hafiz Abdullah Zëmblaku, for example, had refused a position of mufti. Many ulama in Shkodër went on teaching in a traditional way, without any contact with the new Tirana Madrasa. Most of them considered the introduction of the Civil Code and the ban on the veil as being in conflict with the Sharia.[66]

Europe as reference or towards a "European Islam"

Despite the opposition, if we analyze the content of the whole debate, it is striking to see "Europe" appearing as a common reference for all the actors, whatever their position concerning the veil.[67] In fact, the relationship between Islam and Europe was at the heart of the debate. The Islam shaped by all the actors was not only an Islam in Europe. At the Paris mosque, in 1930, Ilyas Vrioni, the Albanian Ambassador, presented his country as "a fortress of the Islamic traditions in Europe."[68] But it was also a "European Islam." For the secularists, as we have seen, the reform of Islam had to be carried out precisely because the country was situated in Europe. On the other side, Hafiz Ismet Dibra, one of the leading ulama of the official Community, agreed with Mehdi Frashëri that Muslims, although a majority in Albania, would not be able to live and to retain their faith, without accepting the principles of "modern" and "European" life. In particular, in order to live in the middle of Europe it was necessary for them to make their own all kind of sciences that were the product of progress. Consequently the reform of Islam was essential.[69]

Nevertheless, it seems that the position of the various actors was not exactly the same on the European modernization reference. For the secularist intellectuals or state representatives, the reference was always positive, whereas for the ulama, it could be positive or negative. The ulama used it when they wanted something from the government, when they answered the secularists, or when they wanted to convince Muslims about the need for reforms. Thus, they often mentioned that European states had realized again the importance of religion, had strengthened the teaching of religion at school, or hosted religious congresses. They pointed to the fact that even developed countries did not prevent their people from being "fervent believers." Even Abdullah Zëmblaku, when he was criticized for using too many Arabic words, argued that, in Europe too, Arabic words had been incorporated into the languages.[70] In this way they were highlighting European realities to which the secularists and Westernists did not refer. However, when the ulama tried to reassert the importance of Islam, they could place "Europe" in opposition to "Islam" in a negative way for the former and a positive way for the latter. In this case, Europe became "materialist," the seat of unbelief, of women's dishonour, of luxury and frivolity.[71] The official Islamic hierarchy, through its journal, denounced the "new trends with a European influence," the "*Oksidentalofilë*" (those who loved the West).[72]

Another important reference in the debate was Turkey, as was the case throughout the Muslim world at that time.[73] The reforms of Mustafa Kemal were quoted as an example by the secularists and the state representatives.[74] On the one hand, the leaders of the Islamic Community, probably with the aim of convincing the political authorities, explained that Mustafa Kemal was not against Islam.[75] But someone like Hafiz Abdullah Zëmblaku could criticize the "Young Turks" and the "masons" of Turkey as bad examples for the Muslim world, while criticizing the state representatives as well as the leaders of the Islamic Community.[76]

On the other hand, references to the Arab World (or to India) posed problems, and arguments based on such references were violently rejected by secularist intellectuals.[77] Even the Arabic script and the Arabic language were stigmatized by the secularists as well as by the state representatives. The political authorities tried to ban prayers (*dua*) in Arabic from the public sphere, arguing that it could make a bad impression on foreigners; that the people had to understand what they were hearing; and finally, that it was contrary to the independence of the Albanian Islamic Community.[78] This last

246 *Nathalie Clayer*

point shows that the authorities, as in France today, were faced with the problem of "domestication in a global religious field."[79]

Albanian Islam and external networks

During the interwar period, many Albanian entrepreneurs were in contact with the outside Muslim world: with Turkey, Egypt, and India, and with Muslims in the Balkans and in the rest of Europe.[80] These contacts were used in the local field in different ways and for different purposes: to train students, to obtain Islamic literature, to benefit from various debates, etc. Apart from their relations with Egypt, the leaders of the Islamic Community, in particular, made extensive use of their relations with the Lahori-Ahmadi network based in India, as well as in Berlin, Vienna, and London. From 1927 onwards, they sent students to Lahore and ordered the translation of many articles and booklets developing the idea of compatibility between Islam and modernity in order to reply to the arguments of those who downgraded Islam and to stress the compatibility of Islam and Europe embodied by the activities of the Lahori missions in England or Germany.[81] Hafiz Abdullah Zëmblaku, although opposed to the Community, also justified his "missionary action" in highlighting the work of the Lahori-Ahmadi in the Western world and his own contacts with them. He also used their networks to disseminate his method of transcription of Arabic.[82]

However, it seems that official networking was not possible because of the principle of nationalization imposed by the state. As early as 1923, the decision to break with the Caliphate had been of specific political importance with the aim of setting up an independent Islamic Community. Eight years later, when the leaders of the Albanian Islamic Community received an invitation to attend the Jerusalem Congress, they declined it on the pretext that their treasury did not have sufficient funds to send a representative.[83] There was also no delegate from Albania at the Geneva Congress of European Muslims held in 1935.[84] We have to point out that, according to the law, religious communities in Albania could not be financed from abroad and could only have spiritual and cultural relations with foreign individuals or institutions; correspondence with religious centers situated abroad had to be authorized.[85]

Thus the progressive ban on the veil that occurred in Albania in the interwar years reveals different phenomena. In order to build and to gain recognition for their state in the "middle of Europe," and despite—or because of—the Muslim majority in the country, Albanian political authorities and secularist intellectuals wanted to build a "modern" and "European" Islam. Their action was also dictated by a wish for secularization in order to set up a multidenominational nation, but also by the lower value attached to Islam among the elites. Some leaders of the Islamic Community were also convinced of the need to build a "European Islam," but not exactly in the same way, and not at the expense of a loss of power. The most significant result of their action

Behind the veil: interwar Albania 247

was the appearance of a new religious elite promoting an Islam of the Qur'an and of progress, such as that presented by the Lahori Ahmadiyya working at that time in the heart of Europe for the promotion of Islam. However, the process of banning the veil shows the complexity of building a European Islam *"à l'albanaise,"*—a specific approach to secularization, the submission of the upper levels of the Islamic official hierarchy to the political authorities, the difficulty that this hierarchy had in imposing itself on all Muslims in the country, and the limited impact of the reforms within Albanian society.

Notes

1 Albania was first recognized by the European powers as an independent principality in 1913, but it was occupied by different countries during the First World War.
2 The expression is from Xavier Bougarel.
3 See my book, Clayer, *Aux origines du nationalisme albanais. La naissance d'une nation majoritairement musulmane en Europe*, Paris: Karthala 2007.
4 Approximately 20 percent of the population were Orthodox Christians, mainly in the south of the country, and 10 percent Catholic Christians, mainly in the northern part.
5 Arkivi Qendror i Shtetit (AQSh), Tirana, Fondi 152 (Ministri e puneve të Brendshme), Viti 1923, Dosja 31, fl. 1–3.
6 See for example AQSh F. 152, V. 1925, D. 623; F. 882 (Komuniteti Mysliman), V. 1929, D. 3; *Statuti i Komunitetit Mysliman Shqipëtar*, Tiranë, 1929. In this text, "Community" with a capital letter refers to an institution and not to a group of people.
7 AQSh, F. 882, V. 1926, D. 90, fl. 17–26.
8 AQSH, F. 882, V. 1922, D. 10, fl. 26; V. 1931, D. 106, fl. 3–4; V. 1936, D. 53, fl. 1; *Zani i naltë* (Tirana), XII/2, February 1937, p. 34. In 1937, measures were taken by the political authorities against Communist groups (cf. Michael Schmidt-Neke, *Entstehung und Ausbau der Königsdiktatur in Albanien (1912–1939)*, Munich: Oldenbourg 1987, p. 262).
9 The most significant work in this respect was that of Hafiz Ali Korça (*Bolshevizma. Çkatërimi i njerëzimit*, Tirana 1925). From 1933–34 on, atheism was one of the main targets of the Islamic Community in its journal. See also the booklet of Hafiz Ali Kraja (*A duhet feja. A e pengon bashkimin kombëtar*, Shkodër 1934).
10 Nathalie Clayer, *L'Albanie, pays des derviches*, Berlin: Otto Harrassowitz 1990. For the reactions of the Muslim religious leaders, see for example AQSh, F. 882, V. 1923, D. 1.
11 As in Turkey, religious reformists and political reformers had a common goal, to elaborate a "true spiritual Islam," cleansed of its impurities.
12 See Alexandre Popovic, *L'islam balkanique*, Berlin: Otto Harrassowitz 1986, pp. 27 ff.
13 Here the discussion will be on the veil (*perçe* in Albanian), covering the face, and not on the headscarf. At that time, in Albania, the veil was worn by urban women, whereas in the countryside it was quite rare.
14 In 1923, following a proposal by Ali Këlcyra, a deputy from southern Albania, the President of the Albanian parliament proposed a vote on a recommendation to the government to make propaganda through the Islamic Congress in order to improve the social life of women, taking Turkey as an example. But the proposal

248   *Nathalie Clayer*

was never put to the vote (*Bisedimet e këshillit Kombtar*, III/no.4, Tirana, 1923, pp. 49–57).

15 Fatmira Musaj, *Gruaja në Shqipëri* [The Woman in Albania] *(1912–1939)*, Tirana:Akademia e Shkencave 2002, pp. 306–7.

16 Ibid., pp. 309–10.

17 Ibid., p. 311.

18 Ibid.

19 *Zani i naltë*, XII/3, March 1937, pp. 65–73. The law was published in the Official Journal (*Fletorja Zyrtare*, Tiranë, XVI/15, 10/3/1937, p. 1).

20 A special file in the archives of the Albanian Ministry of Foreign Affairs is devoted to the articles collected in the press of various countries on that reform launched in Albania (AQSh, F. 151, V. 1937, D. 75). See F. Musaj, *Gruaja*, op. cit., pp. 319–21.

21 F. Musaj, *Gruaja*, op. cit., pp. 316–19; AQSh, F. 882, V. 1937, D. 88, fl.1; F. 152, V. 1940, D. 86.

22 Bernard Fischer, *King Zog and the Struggle for Stability in Albania*, New York: Columbia Univ. Press 1984, p. 249.

23 F. Musaj, *Gruaja*, op. cit., p. 302.

24 On the political level too, religious diversity was marked. Members of parliament represented proportionally the denominational composition of the population.

25 F. Musaj, *Gruaja*, op. cit., pp. 308–9.

26 In April 1928, the cadi of Delvinë (in the south-west of the country) complained that the director of a primary school was opposing the teaching of religion at school (AQSh, F. 882, V. 1928, D. 95).

27 See, for example the case of Safet Butka (1901–43), trained in Austria (Uran Butka, *Safet Butka*, Tirana, Maluka, 2003, cf. pp. 31–34 and 98).

28 In September 1924, the editors of a Catholic newspaper in Shkodër asked the Democratic government to ban the veil in the name of democracy, politics, and morality (*Ora e maleve*, II, 37, 6 September 1924, p. 3).

29 The set of articles which I took into consideration is that used by F. Musaj for the period 1922–23, with articles from the journal *Drita* (Gjirokastër, edited by a Muslim), *Agimi* (Shkodër, edited by a Catholic), *Mbrojtja kombtare* (Halim Xhelo) and *Kombi në rrezik* (Musaj, *Gruaja*, pp. 140–43). Among the most important texts I used are also those published in the newspaper *Zëri i popullit*, from Korçë in March 1923 (no. 28) and March–April 1924 (29 March and 6 April), articles published in *Shqipëria e re*, in Romania, in April 1925; various articles from Namik Delvina published in his newspaper *Ora* in 1932 (see nos. 541, 544, 561); articles written by Mehdi Frashëri quoted below, as well as some of his texts published in the journals *Illyria* in 1934 and *Minerva* in 1935; two articles published in *Arbënia* (no. 209 and no. 256 of 1936); and the article of Selim Shpuza published in 1936 in the journal *Bota e re*, under the title "*Modernism and çarçaf*" (no. 7).

30 In 1934, the journal *Illyria* (no. 38, 11 January 1936, p. 1) explained that it was necessary to form a front against Eastern influences, and to assimilate the Western mentality, not by importing it, but by creating an Albanian culture.

31 *Bisedimet e këshillit Kombtar*, III, no. 3, Tirana 1923, p. 48.

32 M. Schmidt-Neke, *Entstehung.*, pp. 335–36.

33 Mehdi Frashëri, *Historia e lashtë e Shqipërisë dhe e Shqipëtarëve*, Tirana, Phoenix, 2000 (1st ed. 1928), pp. 44–45 and 46–47.

34 "Reformat Myslimane në Shqipëri," in *Gazeta e re* (Tiranë), no. 17, 20/11/1928, p. 1; no. 26, 1/12/1928, p. 2; no. 27, 2/12/1928, p. 4; no. 30, 6/12/1928, p. 2; no. 31, 7/12/1936, p. 3; no. 35, 12/12/1928, p. 2; no. 36, 13/12/1929, p. 2; no. 37, 14/12/1937, p. 2; no. 39, 16/12/1928, p. 2.

Behind the veil: interwar Albania 249

35 Mehdi Frashëri also suggested making other reforms concerning the way of performing prayers and the diffusion of knowledge. In a later article, published in 1931, concerning the economic situation of the country and the lack of development of agriculture, he suggested that one of the factors was that the Islamic religion was humiliating women in numerous ways ("Aveniri i Shqipërisë në pikpamje bujqësore," *Bujqsija*, III/1–2, January–February 1931, p. 17).

36 Mehdi Frashëri considered that the other Balkan Muslims, who were under the domination of the Balkan states, were condemned to emigrate to Anatolia.

37 See footnote 34.

38 It was particularly the case when the jurisdiction of Sharia judges was limited in 1919 and when the Civil Code was introduced in 1928–29.

39 AQSH, F. 882, V. 1926, D. 71, fl. 1–2. This member was Salih Vuçitërn, a person who belonged both to the religious and to the political field.

40 In 1924, the Mufti of Shkodër criticized the idea put forward in a Catholic newspaper of banning the veil (see footnote 28), because it undermined Islam, and stated that if the Catholics committed a second offence, there would be a quarrel between the two "elements" (*Zani i naltë*, I/11, August 1924, p. 348). Reacting to the same affair, the Muslim editors of the newspaper *Dajti* in Tirana explained that the veil was one of the fundamental means of preserving a woman's honour (*Dajti*, no. 45 (17 September 1924), p. 3). As we will see below, in 1928, the answer of Hafiz Ismet Dibra to Mehdi Frashëri mainly concerned the question of religious authority.

41 "Gjendja e Grues n'Islamizmë," *Zani i naltë*, VI/4 (March 1930), pp. 966–76.

42 "Zbulimi i Grues Muslimane," *Zani i naltë*, XI/5 (May 1936), pp. 142–49. One of the arguments used against their adversaries was also that the latter wanted unveiling only because of shame in the face of foreigners. So they accused the secularist intellectuals of wanting "to destroy the country in order to please the foreigners."

43 *Zani i naltë*, XII/3 (March 1937), pp. 65–77.

44 Shapati argued that some regions, in particular mountainous areas, continued to observe the true prescriptions of the Prophet and did not veil women. Thus, for nationalists, mountainous areas appeared as the bastion of tradition.

45 Ibid.

46 Sherif Putra, "Moda e mbulesës dhe veçimi i grave," *Drita* (Lahore), 6–8 (June–July–August 1936), pp. 6–19. In fact, this text was a translation of an article written by the future head of the Lahori Ahmadiyya, Muhammad Ali, and published in 1905 in *The Review of Religions* (Lahore). This appears in the second part of the text which was published in the journal of the Albanian Islamic Community in 1937, after the ban on the veil (*Zani i naltë*, XII, 5 (May 1937), pp. 202–13).

47 Whereas a report from Elbasan shows that there were opponents (AQSh, F. 882, V. 1937, D. 88, fl.1), the journal of the Islamic Community published a false report showing that there was no opposition to unveiling (*Zani i naltë*, XII, 3 (March 1937), p. 96).

48 See, for example, H.A. Sëmlaku, *Bilbil i gjashtë. Kanarja*, Korçë, 1930, p. 41–43, *Bilbil i shtatë*, Korçë, 1931, p. 15, 24–26, and *Bilbil i tetë*, Korçë, 1931, p. 15–21.

49 H.A. Sëmlaku, *Kanar i ri dhe bilbili faqe bardhë*, Korçë, 1938, p. 5.

50 So it is unclear whether he considered that the face had to be covered or not. H. A. Sëmlaku, *Trëndafil i 1*, Korçë, 1932, pp. 169–70.

51 See below.

52 *Bisedimet e këshillit Kombtar*, viti III, 4, Tirana 1923, pp. 49–57.

53 See Hamit Bozarslan, "Islam, laïcité et la question d'autorité de l'Empire ottoman à la Turquie kémaliste," *Archives de Sciences Sociales des Religions*, 125, Paris (January–March 2004), pp. 99–112.

54 See reference in footnote 34. Here the difference between the Albanian and the Turkish case has to be stressed. In Albania, the non-Muslim minorities were

250   *Nathalie Clayer*

larger (approximately 30 percent of the population), and most of the non-Muslims were also ethnic Albanians.

55 In 1923, as well as in 1929, the question of relations between the Islamic Community and the Bektashis was at the heart of the question of religion and state.

56 Nathalie Clayer, "Construction de mosquées en Albanie, 1920–39," *Archives de Sciences Sociales des Religions*, 151 (July–September 2010), p. 91–105.

57 The expression is from Jocelyne Césari and Jean Baubérot ("Laïcité, communautarisme et foulard: vrais et faux débats," http://lmsi.net).

58 Musaj, *Gruaja*, op. cit., p. 142.

59 See, for example, H.A. Sëmlaku, *Bibil i Fesë. Sheri-ati Muhamedija*, Korçë, 1930, pp. 77–79 and *Trëndafil i 1*, Korçë, 1932, pp. 83 and 96 ff.

60 See, for example, "Kundër Ateizmit," *Zani i naltë*, XI/8–9 (August–September 1936), pp. 287–90.

61 *Zani i naltë*, V, 10–11 (August–September [November] 1928), pp. 678–90; V, 12 (December 1928), pp. 726–34. H.I. Dibra even pointed out incompetence on the part of his adversary in his own field, diplomacy.

62 Later on, in July 1938, Mehdi Frashëri gathered Muslim intellectuals in the Albanian capital in order to help the cultural development of the "Muslim element" (*Zani i naltë*, 8 (August 1938), p. 255).

63 *Bilbili besëtar*, Korçë (28 September 1935), pp. 51–52.

64 A first partial translation of the Qur'an had been made by a Christian Albanian (first fascicle, Bucharest, 1921; 2d fascicle, Korçë, 1928). In addition, an English translation and commentary by Muhammad Ali, from the Ahmadiyya, was circulating in the country.

65 "Persri mbi fonksionarët t'onë fetarë," *Zani i naltë* (August–September 1930), pp. 1121–26.

66 See, for example, the great debate about the required reforms which started in 1927, whose echoes are to be found in the journal of the Islamic Community (*Zani i naltë*). After this period, the only criticism of the leaders of the Islamic Community that appeared in print was that by Hafiz Abdullah Zëmblaku, but it certainly points to a broader opposition.

67 Here, of course, I cannot take into account the adversaries of the ban on the veil who did not take part in the debate in print.

68 AQSh, F. 882, V. 1930, D. 114.

69 See reference in footnote 60. There was never a debate about *dar al-Harb* and *dar al-Islam*.

70 See, for example, "Veprimet e Këshillit të Naltë të Sheriatit dhe nevojat e trupit musliman," *Zani i naltë*, II, 3 (Maj 1925), pp. 459–64; "Bisedimet e Kongresit Muslyman," *Zani i naltë*, II, 4–5 (June–July 1925), p. 502; Hafiz Ali Kraja, *A duhet feja*; H.A. Sëmlaku, *Trëndafil i 1*, Korçë, 1932, p. 154.

71 See, for example, "Zbulimi i Grues Muslimane," *Zani i naltë*, XI, 5 (May 1936), pp. 142–49.

72 Ibid.

73 See Catherine Mayeur-Jaouen and Anne-Laure Dupont (eds.), *Débats intellectuels au Moyen-Orient dans l'entre-deux-guerres*, *REMMM*, no. 95-96-97-98, 2002.

74 In the religious field, the Turkish model could even be followed very concretely. Thus, in 1928, the Albanian ambassador in Ankara sent a collection of *khutbas* (Friday sermons) for translation into Albanian because, "it fitted with the religious principles and to the need of the time." The book was translated as *Këshillet e së premtes* (Shkodër, 1928).

75 See, for example, "Vepra e Gazi Qemal Ataturkut," *Zani i naltë*, X, 3 (March 1935), pp. 81–84; "Përsëri Mustafa Kemali flet mbi maltësinë e Islamizmës ... ," *Zani i naltë*, X, 9–10 (September–October 1935), pp. 319–20.

76 *Trëndafil i 1*, Korçë, 1932, p. 120.

Behind the veil: interwar Albania 251

77 See, for example, the article "Zani i naltë kundra Qytetnimit," published in *Bota e re*, 20 (30 January 1937), where the author, Selim Shpuza, criticized the journal of the Islamic Community for having quoted the discourse of an Arab *shaikh* of Al-Azhar (Selim Shpuza, *Vitet '20–'30*, Tirana, Toena, 1999, pp. 146–51).
78 AQSh, F. 882, V. 1926, D. 90, fl. 1–2.
79 John R. Bowen, "Does French Islam Have Borders ? Dilemmas of Domestication in a Global Religious Field," *American Anthropologist*, 106(1) 2004, pp. 43–55.
80 A lot of them corresponded with different persons from abroad, the Hajj was performed, and students were sent to Egypt or even to Lahore.
81 Nathalie Clayer, "La Ahmadiyya Lahori et la réforme de l'islam albanais dans l'entre-deux-guerres," in V. Bouillier and C. Servan-Schreiber (eds.), *De l'Arabie à l'Himalaya. Chemins croisés en hommage à Marc Gaborieau* Paris: 2004, pp. 211–28.
82 See note 48.
83 AQSh, F. 882, V. 1931, D. 116.
84 The Albanian participants to these congresses came from Macedonia, i.e. from Yugoslavia.
85 See the text of 1923 on the status of the religious Community (AQSh, F. 152, V. 1923, D. 855, fl. 15) and Roberto Morozzo della Rocca, *Nazione e religione in Albania (1920–1944)*, Bologna: Il Mulino, 1990, p. 32.

9 Difference unveiled

Bulgarian national imperatives and the re-dressing of Muslim women, 1878–1989

Mary Neuburger

Recent scholarship has poignantly argued that the founding of modern "Western" nation-states is to a large degree a product of their drawn-out colonial encounters with "the East." It is convincingly argued that "the West" constructed its own self-assured, national, and supra-national identities in the process of "discovering" and "inventing" the exotic yet inferior "East."[1] Furthermore, a diverse body of scholarship has delineated the central role of discourses on gender and sexuality in the development of Western societies and, in particular, nation-states.[2] If the image of "pious mother" became key to Western national self-images, it was the counter-image of the women of the harem—veiled, oppressed, and mysterious—that typified representations of Eastern barbarism.[3] Furthermore, Western economic and political penetration of its colonies was to a large degree justified by the "gendering" of the "irrational Orient" versus the "rational Occident." The "liberation" of Islamic women from their "oppression" as typified by the veil became central to Western "civilizing" missions, which had far-reaching echoes on the frontiers of European society.

In Russia and the Balkans, frontier encounters with Islam—replete with both intimacy and violence—were in many ways more direct and protracted than Western European experiences. Significantly, both Russia and the Balkans had been "discovered" and "Orientalized" in Western European travelogues and other writings of the eighteenth and nineteenth centuries.[4] Many Russian and Balkan intellectuals had internalized these characterizations of their regions as chronically "backwards" because of purported cultural contamination by the neighboring East. This most certainly provoked their growing tendency to re-think local, national, and international encounters with Islam and assert their own "Europeanness." Moreover, such Western European formulations had catalyzed the growing penchant among Eastern European scholarship and politics to designate more backwards "others" in their midst: what Bakic-Hayden calls "nesting Orientalisms."[5] Frequently, Muslim women, and in particular the meaning-laden practice of veiling, became a target in the projects to define and reshape the "barbarity within" and, in so doing, regarb the nation itself in the cloak of newly discovered "progress."

Re-dressing of Bulgarian Muslim women, 1878–1989   253

For both Russia and the Balkans, campaigns aimed at unveiling Islamic women became an important part of the processes of "national" and later "socialist" development. In the communist period, both Yugoslav and Soviet modernizing policies were fettered to some degree by their federal structures, which recognized autonomies and even stimulated separate national identities for their Islamic peoples.[6] In contrast, for "uni-national" Bulgaria, the de-veiling of Muslim women became a critical part of a constellation of concerted modernization efforts aimed at consolidating the Bulgarian nation.

The modernization of Bulgarian society reached its apogee in the theory and practices of the communist period, as the road to socialism was paved over labyrinths of local difference. Bulgaria—often wrongly touted as Eastern Europe's most homogeneous state—was home to a spectrum of cultural variants in the beginning of this period. Although Bulgarian-speaking Orthodox Christian and Turkish-speaking Muslims were the most numerous groups—albeit with multiple dialects—there were also Pomaks (Bulgarian-speaking Muslims), Sephardic Jews, Armenians, Gagauz (Turkish-speaking Christians), Vlachs and others. In the name of progress, the Bulgarian Communist regime embarked on a project of sorting and defining its own population, a campaign of eradicating or domesticating local differences. In general, regional differences among the Christian Slavic population, as long as they were Bulgarian, were exalted, and Bulgarian women were praised as "preservers" of "progressive" folk culture. In contrast, cultural development for Muslims had very narrowly defined parameters, and the accoutrements of most of the population, in particular of women, were defined as "backward." This created a milieu in which the garment choices of Islamic women became a litmus for the measure of success of state modernization projects and, in response, a mode of everyday resistance to Communist directives.

Meanings behind the veil

Historically, the concept of the "veil" has been and remains the quintessential metaphor for all that the "East" purportedly represents in contrast to a "Western" norm. But both the term and the concept of the "veil" have been highly problematic from the outset. First of all, "the veil" can denote a variety of head coverings for the hair, face, and body or signify the general practice of seclusion of women from the public sphere.[7] Historically, veiling has been an urban, elite phenomenon and, thus, was not practiced by a large percentage of the population of most Islamic societies. Furthermore, historical inquiry has revealed that the practice of veiling has pre-Islamic and, significantly, Byzantine Christian roots.[8] In fact, it is notable that in the Near and Middle East the presence of the veil might have actually grown to be a noteworthy phenomenon only in the colonial period because of the intrusive presence of Westerners.[9] Therefore, "veiling" as an intellectual construct of Orientalist literature, as the essential symbol of Islam, is most probably at odds with a diversity of local traditions. Therefore, the more recent resurgence of veiling, or reveiling, in the Middle East and elsewhere is not a return to tradition but a modem phenomenon, in many cases, a sign of resistance to the penetration of Western influence. Thus, the history of both the concept and the practices of veiling, later de-veiling, and, most recently, reveiling have less to do with local tradition and its continuity or "reform," and more to do with changing relationships between East and West.[10]

By the nineteenth and early twentieth centuries, the Western discourse on "veiling" had made strong inroads into reformist movements within various Islamic communities and nascent nation-states. In the Ottoman Empire the veil had become one of the central subjects of debates between so-called modernists and traditionalists, particularly in Egypt but also in the Empire's capital and the Balkans.[11] These scholars had a degree of contact with reformist and "traditionalist" Islamic movements within the Russian Empire, spawned by Turks, Tatars, and other Turkic peoples.[12] Similarly, these debates devoted considerable attention to "the veil" as a central measure of progress or as a mode of resistance to "Westernization."[13] As Kadioglu points out, "Women were burdened with the difficult task of defining the boundaries between tradition and modernity since the initiation of modernization projects from above."[14] By the twentieth century, de-veiling campaigns in Egypt, Iran, Turkey, and elsewhere would reveal the forms and functions that women were expected to assume within nation-state building projects; women were slated to perform as producers, reproducers, and visible symbols of national progress. The"colonial feminism" of the West had made a smooth transition into what Kadioglu labeled the "state feminism" of Ataturk, Reza Shah, as well as of Soviet, and later Bulgarian, leaders in the Balkans.[15] In the modernizing Middle East as well as the Eastern Bloc, the "emancipation" of women through de-veiling had less to do with their individual rights and more to do with women's potential contribution to "national development."[16]

Yet, in Russia and the Balkans, where Islamic peoples were in the minority, these "revolutions from above" were loaded with added ambiguities. In the Russian Imperial era, Russian women and minority women had been part of the so-called "Woman Question." Because of their presumed conservatism, women's issues had been lumped in with questions of the "backward nations" of the Empire as anathema to state reform efforts.[17] In contrast, after 1917 the "Russian woman" was the progressive archetype for the new "Soviet woman." Russian *Zhenotdeli* (Women's Departments) descended on the Islamic regions of the Soviet Union as de-veiling missionaries in communist campaigns.[18]

Islamic women played a dual role within the greater Soviet experiment as the "ultimate proletariat" whose liberation would be both a signifier of Soviet achievement and a tool in the global spread of communism. Within the gradation of "nesting yokes of oppression," the women of the Soviet East occupied the core. According to one Soviet source:

> Inequality of women was one of the defining features of pre-Revolutionary Russia. The situation of women in the Tsarist frontiers, in Central Asia

Re-dressing of Bulgarian Muslim women, 1878–1989   255

and especially in Turkmenistan, was the most humiliating and unequal. The patriarchal way of life and the ways of Islam held sway; the woman was enslaved in the literal meaning of the word ... . Darkness, ignorance, domestic slavery; slave-subordination to men was the fundamental characteristic of life ...[19]

In response to this inherited state of affairs, the Soviets sought to change the material situation of women by bringing them into "Socialist production," presumably their most important task.[20] In drawing women into the public sphere of Soviet collective farms and industry, the Soviets deemed it important to free them of their "enslaving clothes" which "cripple them and undermine their health."[21] In renouncing the "black partition of the *parandja* (veil) which separates women from the white light of all life,"[22] the women of the Soviet East would set an example for the women of Asia and Africa, who could potentially benefit from Soviet "colonial feminism." The "Muslim woman question," like other "questions" in Soviet society, was considered "solved" after the first 20 years of Soviet power, and so the *zhenotdeli* were disbanded.[23] The Soviet blueprint, as other models of modernity in the Middle East, was held up as a model not so much to Islamic women but to modernizing states which were intent on consolidating power.

The nation unveiled

The Bulgarians ultimately were the most attentive students of Soviet, Turkish, and other experiments of "liberating" the women of Islam from the veil of tradition. But in the Bulgarian case, the de-veiling crusade took on a novel intensity as a campaign against both the "backwardness" and the "foreignness" that the veil and other "Islamic" accoutrements came to represent. Perched on the arbitrary boundary between East and West, the burden of geography on Bulgarians had fierce repercussions. As in other cases, of course, the concept of "veiling" was laden with difficulties when applied to the Bulgaria of the twentieth century. The Muslim population of Ottoman Bulgaria had been both urban and rural in nature, yet, after the gaining of autonomy from the Empire in 1878, much of the urban elite Muslim population migrated back into the new confines of the Empire. What remained of the Turkic and Pomak population inhabited primarily rural areas and were largely peasants by the end of the World Wars.[24] Thus, discussions of "throwing off the veil" among Bulgarian reformers in the 1930s and 1940s may have referred to little more than a peasant head-scarf tied across the chin instead of in the back of the neck. Nevertheless, head scarves tied in this fashion and other garments perceived as "veiling" female bodies had become the mark of "backwardness" and, even more, of "non-Europeanness," a "foreign" remnant of the humiliation of five centuries of Ottoman rule.

State-inspired de-veiling campaigns in Bulgaria, as other colonial and post-colonial policies, emerged as part of a constellation of ambitious

256 *Mary Neuburger*

modernization efforts that, ideologically, required a homogeneous, loyal, modern, "native" population. In fact, to a large degree, it was through the discovery and construction of this "difference within" that Bulgarian intellectuals and bureaucrats began to define what was "native," thereby setting the parameters of the incipient Bulgarian nation. From the 1930s through the 1980s, Bulgarian state policies on the "Muslim woman question" increasingly defined the "veil" as fundamentally "foreign" to Bulgaria, to Europe, to progress, and later to communism. Bulgarian national discourse from its inception in the nineteenth century had been intertwined with the enlightenment discourse of "progress" and European superiority. This melded well, and made an easy transition to the neo-social Darwinism of Marxism-Leninism that justified a penetration and leveling of "backwardness within"; any "foreignness" in the labyrinths of its mountainous Balkan terrain had to be rooted out.

The "liberation" of Bulgaria from Ottoman rule by Russian forces in the 1877–78 Russo–Turkish War had ushered in a period of ethnographic exploration and "discovery" within the newly autonomous Bulgaria and the surrounding Ottoman provinces. In the late nineteenth and early twentieth centuries these highly politicized ethnographic projects drew "scientific" conclusions about the indigenous "Bulgarianness" of the ethnoscape or, alternatively, the grafted-on Islamo-Turkic "foreignness" of the populations within and outside its borders. These projects, although they revelled in the diversity of so-defined "Bulgarian" regional dialects, national costumes, and traditions, decried the foreignness of the "veil" worn by the Pomaks, linguistically the purest of Bulgarians, as not *narodno* (native), but *chuzhdo* (foreign).[25]

Supported by the Imperial Russian Academy of Sciences, Stoyu Shishkov embarked on an in-depth study of the Pomaks, Slavic-speaking Muslims, of Southern Bulgaria. Shishkov, in his pioneering ethnographic study of the scattered Pomak villages in the western Rhodopes, posited and scientifically "proved" the "Bulgarianness" of this purportedly "Turkified" and "Islamicized" group. According to Shishkov, the geographically contiguous "Turks" were also the product of "Ottoman assimilation politics" but had perhaps irretrievably lost their Bulgarian heritage. In contrast, the Pomaks "who spoke the most pure dialect of old-Slavic" were Bulgarians in the "purest" sense and, therefore, were more correctly called "Bulgaro-Mohamedans." Because they were scattered throughout Macedonia and Thrace, his conclusions bolstered Bulgarian claims to these territories.[26] Pomaks, although relatively small in number, became key to Bulgarian aspirations for expansion and consolidation of power within. The wearing of "the veil" by Pomak women was, accordingly, the ultimate affront, a sign of rejection and betrayal of the Bulgarian "nation."

The ethnographic mapping of Bulgaro-Mohamedans and the Bulgarian inscription of meaning on local veiling intensified in the interwar period. The "national catastrophes" of territorial losses in both the Second Balkan War and World War I had sparked an intensified drive for scientific proof of the

Re-dressing of Bulgarian Muslim women, 1878–1989 257

"Bulgarianness" of the Bulgaro-Mohammedan population, as well as a drive to "convert" them to a Bulgarian national consciousness.[27] According to Bulgarian ethnographers the pure Bulgarian character of the region had been polluted in the Ottoman period via the bodies of Bulgarian women. Bulgarian men had been killed wholesale and Bulgarian women taken into the "harems" of the Ottoman soldiers, some "Turkified," others only "Islamicized." According to Shishkov, the further from the Ottoman garrisons, the "purer" and more "virginal" the Bulgarian—and the Bulgaro-Mohammedan— population.[28] Branchev points out the fact that Bulgaro-Mohammedan women, in many villages, wore a preponderance of red garments, as was the old-Slavic custom. He further points out that "only *feredzhe* (veil), a long black garment, taints their beautiful clothing."[29] These seekers of "ethnographic truths" seemed to seek Bulgarian clarity in the contours of the bodies of these Islamic women, hidden under the folds of baggy pants and draping scarves.

By the 1930s, the Bulgarian government took an active interest in the controlling and directing of the reformers' de-veiling impetus that had arisen within various Islamic communities in Bulgaria. Within the Islamic community, which increasingly defined itself as Turkish, a Kemalist movement grew in strength. The new, de-veiled Turkish woman of Atatürk's Turkish republic offered a new model for reform-minded Turks in Bulgaria. Yet, far from supporting Kemalism as a movement, the Bulgarian government and local officials observed and rooted out Kemalist Turks from positions of local responsibility.[30] Instead, as policy, the administration supported the "Old-Turkish" line of the Islamic hierarchy within Bulgaria—the *Glavnoto Muftistvo* (the Grand Muftiship)—and its local supporters, muftis, imams, teachers, and anti-Kemalist emigrants from Turkey. Although the Muftiship was under increasing fiscal and administrative control by the Bulgarian Ministry of Foreign affairs, it still had a modicum of autonomy including the employment of Sheriat courts to settle matters within the Islamic community and the possession of vakf properties. It seems that the Bulgarian state was willing to allow, and even supported, the policies of the "Old Turks" on veiling and other issues because this cut off the local Turkish population from political and cultural influence from Turkey.

Significantly, at the same time, the state financially and administratively supported a modernization drive among intellectuals from within the Bulgaro-Mohammedan or Pomak population. In an effort to cut off this population from its historical affinities to local Turks, financial support and encouragement was provided to the *Rodina* (homeland) movement which began in Smolyan in 1937. A handful of Bulgaro-Mohammedan intellectuals founded the *Rodina* society and located it in Smolyan, the regional center for the Bulgaro-Mohammedan population in the western Rhodopes. Its goal was to diffuse "Bulgarianness" to their "misguided brothers," a campaign largely centered on "de-veiling."[31] The archives of the *Rodina* society are filled with ample appeals to the Bulgaro-Mohamedans which demand that:

258 *Mary Neuburger*

> The women shall cast aside once and for all the *feredzhe, bula, yashamak* [all three considered to be veils], and other such reshaping articles as these. They shall exchange them with Bulgarian costumes—a regular dress, and scarves which are tied behind the head.[32]

Evidently the changes in costume were as inconsequential as tying a scarf behind instead of in front of the head, although any article that obscured "the shape" of women was deforming to their "Bulgarian" essence. The Smolyan archives attest to the fact that even the Islamic institution—the Muslim Confessional Organization of Smolyan and its surrounding area—had been staffed with pro-*Rodina* officials by the late 1930s.[33] Thus the society expressed surprise when one of its "appeals to Bulgaro-Mohammedan women" was ripped down off the walls of the Muftiship, whose own printed order had also commanded the shedding of the garments of "black slavery."[34]

In the pre-communist period, Bulgarian governmental policies towards the veil were an integral part of the ongoing "scientific" project of defining, ordering and often eradicating the difference within. The state sought to nurture a loyal and "domesticated" foreign element in its local Turks, inert, mostly illiterate, and still governed in part by Islamic law. In this way, this population would be cut off from the burgeoning Turkish nationalist identity to the southeast. At the same time, de-veiling Pomak women became the objective of the state-inspired program of Rodina, which sought to "uproot all that is un-Bulgarian and foreign in Bulgaro-Mohammedan clothes."[35] In the wake of World War II these frameworks for dealing with the "barbarity within" would fuse with the imperatives of Socialist development and the Soviet model of modernity.

Newly veiled threats

In the Communist period, the presence of "veiling" in the Bulgarian countryside became even more laden with meaning, in light of the ever intensifying modernization drive. Marxist internationalism, ironically, mingled well with the rhetoric of Bulgarian nationalism into practices of national development. In theory and practice the "veil," and a number of other Balkan Muslim articles of clothing, became defined as both "foreign" and "backward," pressing the weight of history on the body coverings of Muslim women. Initially there was a degree of continuity with the pre-communist period. Pomaks were administered as part of the Bulgarian population without question, while Turks were given a degree of superficial administrative autonomy under the slogan of "friendship of peoples between Bulgarians and Turks." But the consolidation of power by the Bulgarian Communist Party was followed by an ever intensifying assimilation campaign. At every stage, Islamic women—Turks and Pomaks—were an important part of a Bulgarian drive to modernize and put a European veneer on every surface of Balkan diversity. De-veiling became the measure of success in the path to progress, the drive towards socialism, and the building of a homogeneous nation. At the same time, veiling, by definition, became a mode of resistance to communist directives on the local level.

In the years of Communist consolidation of power, 1945–47, the issue of the "veil" was not broached, as political support for the Communist-led *Otechestven Front* (OF—"Fatherland Front") was sought among the Muslim masses. During preparations for the 1946 elections, numerous Party agitators reported that the local Muslim population feared anti-Islamic policies on the part of a Fatherland Front coalition. De-veiling was reportedly central to then concerns, as one agitator from Dobrich in north-east Bulgaria reports, "One part of the Turkish population is worried that veils will be stripped off and that women will be made *obshti* (common property) if the Communists win."[36] According to one report in the same year, the Commissar of Provisions of the Fatherland Front requested from the local Muftiship exact specifications on how many meters of cloth were needed in the city of Haskovo for the making of *feredzhe* (veils) for local women.[37] It seems that the message of de-veiling was temporarily subordinated to the gaining of political power, though election results ultimately had little importance for the Communist take-over.

Even after communist rule was assured, de-veiling was initially subordinated to the drawing of women into the political sphere—the administrative dimension of building socialism. Initially, Bulgarian cadres had been the vanguard of economic, social, and cultural change in the Bulgarian hinterland. Discussions of early OF strategy for mass organization in the provinces lament the paucity of cadres, particularly Turks and, more specifically, Turkish and Pomak women, for the task of gaining local support. The inability to mobilize Islamic women to participate in the new socialist economy of political orientation provoked compromises:

> In villages with numerous minorities—Turks or significant numbers of Bulgaro-Mohamedans—as in villages with the most backwards Bulgarians, organizational meetings may be called for women members of the Fatherland Front separate from men.[38]

Here, the party seemed ready to accommodate a measure of presumably "backward" behavior, even among Bulgarians, as a way of pulling women out of the home arid into their political and "educational" meetings.

In the 1940s and 1950s the Bulgarian Communist Party (BCP) began to bring Muslims into the party apparatus and into the Bulgarian economy and society. The drive to activate Muslims, and, particularly, their "most backward" element—women—to fulfill the first five-year plans and to be productive on the new collective farms was coupled with a literacy drive, in Turkish and/ or Bulgarian; this, to propagate the tenets of the new state ideology. The OF sent its *zhenaktiv*—part of the *zhenotdeli* or women's sections—into Turkish regions to give lectures such as "The Turkish Woman—an Active Builder of

260 *Mary Neuburger*

Socialism," "Islam—The Reactionary Enemy of Women," and to teach courses, hold meetings, and organize committees to bring Muslim women into the work of the party.[39] Women were actively recruited into "socialist competition," and were incited, for example, into an erroneous rivalry to produce the most tobacco per *dekar* of land.[40] Muslim women outside the collective farms were particularly targeted as the "most backward" element of Bulgarian society.[41] The BCP assumed that collectivization and party training of local cadres would automatically precipitate the levelling of any backward features on the Bulgarian landscape.

Yet, throughout the 1950s the dreaded practice of "veiling" persisted, as did the wearing of other accoutrements considered "non-European" by the Bulgarian communist spin-doctors. In particular the *shalvari*—baggy Turkish style pants—were considered inappropriate attire for "builders of socialism," as was an entire list of folk garments. In fact, local reports on the "Turkish question" tended to designate de-veiling and the shedding of the *shalvari*— that is, the re-dressing of Muslim women—as the ultimate measure of Communist success in the provinces.[42] OF representatives from the provinces duly presented facts and figures on de-veiling and discussed the continued wearing of *shalvari* for describing both the difficulties and "achievements" in the ongoing "cultural revolution."[43] They also delineated the reasons for specific difficulties: that women themselves did not want to de-veil, that their husbands had forbidden it, or that isolated de-veiled women had to bear ridicule from their villages and censure from their *hojas*.[44]

The biggest sacrilege by Turkish cadres against the BCP party line was the continued veiling by the wives, sisters, and daughters of Turkish Communist Party members themselves. Numerous reports lamented the fact that local cadres "haven't broken with the old ways," as evidenced by the veils worn by the women in their families.[45] In Razgrad, for example, it was reported that "many of our Turkish leaders say they are for de-veiling but don't set an example ... their female comrades (*drugarki*), mothers, sisters and neighbors do not follow the example of de-veiling." In the same town, the president of the cooperative, reportedly, "didn't convince his wife to wear a dress," posing the question of "how to liquidate the *shalvari* which remain in their dressers."[46]

A variety of "rational" reasons were given by the Communist Party for its need to root out such "backward" articles from the Muslim woman's wardrobe. De-veiling as a "dialectical jump" in the "cultural revolution" required the modernization, rationalization, and Europeanization of women's dress on the Bulgarian frontier. Pomak and Turkish women were presented with lectures and presentations on the need to discard "out of date, expensive, old clothes—the veil," for "cheaper, more hygienic and practical dresses."[47] By the late 1950s, collectivization and de-veiling were intensified and carried out throughout the country as standard BCP policy. Whereas, in the past, the economic and cultural campaigns had relied on intensive persuasion, by 1960, reports from the provinces tout the de-veiling of women in certain locales as "achieved in one week" or in a matter of months.[48] In Kolarovgrad (now

Re-dressing of Bulgarian Muslim women, 1878–1989   261

Shumen) it was reported in 1960 that, because of the work of the regional committee of the OF, the cultural revolution had been achieved, and "they [Muslim women] have broken the shackles of religious fanaticism and are almost all wearing beautiful, light, comfortable, European clothes."[49]

Women's committees and even Muslim religious teachers were employed in this cultural revolution; yet it was the direct intervention of the cooperatives that played a definitive role. The work of these *zhenotdeli* (women's committees), included the recruitment of Turkish women to its ranks whenever possible, intensive "explanation sessions" for Islamic women, and even door-to-door visits by female cadres. The rewards were high for Islamic women who became part of these brigades and, thereby, so proved their loyalty to the Bulgarian state project. Propaganda sessions were often flavored with the testimonials of de-veiled Muslim women. As one recently "de-veiled" Turkish woman stated, "I've begun to feel like a person ... in nothing do I differ from my Bulgarian female comrades (*drugarki*)."[50] In addition, the OF called local meetings of *hojas* and convinced them to go from village to village preaching the gospel of de-veiling to their flocks.[51] One of the most decisive measures, however, associated with the completion of the "cultural revolution" was the move by cooperative farms to "advance" dresses against the salaries of Muslims, men and women, who had purportedly claimed that a lack of money had inhibited their re-dressing, or the re-dressing of their wives. In multiple locales, this action was reported as having a direct effect on the achievement of nearly 100 percent de-veiling by the end of the 1950s.[52] In this same period, sewing brigades were sent into Islamic regions to liquidate the problems of veils and *shalvari*. For example, with the sewing of 900 dresses in 11 days, in Razgrad, the "great leap forward" was achieved.[53]

In the late 1950s, veiling—in whatever form—and the wearing of *shalvari* seems to have persisted on the local level in spite of BCP pronouncements about their high level of success in these matters. OF members from the provinces periodically complained of the persistence of veiling, and particularly *shalvari*. In many cases, when the transition to dresses was made, *shalvari* were still worn under dresses in the villages.[54] The persistence of traditional dress, and even what was called "reveiling" after de-veiling had been achieved, was seen by OF cadres as a form of protest by the local population.[55] Although "reveiling" was noted as early as 1951 in the case of Haskovo, in Varna the "anti-government" action immediately followed the heavy-handed "leap forward" of 1959. In both cases "reveiling," as in later movements in the 1970s in the Middle East, might have been a reaction to the penetration of Bulgarianizing, modernizing BCP influence in the countryside, and, notably, their heavy-handed collectivization and de-veiling campaigns that marked the late 1950s.

In the 1960s the methods of the BCP and the "socialist achievements" in the realm of the "Turkish women question" continued and intensified. A 1962 party functionary "exchange of experiences" session on work with local Muslim populations boasted of the successes of the *zhenotdeli* and the

262   *Mary Neuburger*

massive recruiting of Turks into collective farms. Reports were ripe with facts and figures about the over-fulfilling of the "plan" by Muslim women, noting that there were even 12 pig farmers among Turkish women in the Zlatovgrad region.[56] Delegate pronouncements boasted of accomplishments in de-veiling in various regions and the achievements of door-to-door campaigns in various spheres of cultural "progress." Even a conference of Imams and Muftis called by the Grand Muftiship in 1965 declared, "Now wherever you go there is no difference, and you can't even tell who is a Turk and who is a Bulgarian ... . The Turkish woman is freed from her century-old black veil."[57]

Reports of questioning or ignoring party directives continued and even seemed to increase in this period when the "cultural revolution" had presumably eradicated the "backwardness" of Muslim women. One delegate to the 1962 conference session on work with the Turkish population noted that the following question had been asked in his provincial home: "Why are you running after the *feredzhe* (veil) when the Shoppes [Bulgarian from the Sofia region] aren't taking off their *kozhuti* (sheepskin hats) and in the Rhodopes Bulgarians aren't taking off their *kalnatsite* (fur caps)."[58] This local Turk very pointedly questioned the campaign against the Islamic form of headdress when other headgear, part of the regional variation of Slavic costume, were left untouched. Furthermore, "reveiling" and the wearing or even the "redonning" of *shalvari* were widely noted, as were other manifestations of Islamic sentiment, again in connection with "resistance" to the Party program.[59] In Razgrad, for example, it was noted that, "women are going to mosque *en masse* as a protest and taking an active part in Ramadan, with the character of a demonstration."[60] In Chernik, it was noted that women were meeting independently to read the Koran. Furthermore, they were known to support local dervishes, who "carried out their work through women," and who were considered even more suspect than mainstream Islam because they were outside the jurisdiction of the Muslim hierarchy.[61] Because BCP success was measured by the presence of "the veil" and other expressions of Islamic sentiments, these practices also became a means of everyday resistance at the local level.

The campaign of re-dressing Muslim women continued into the 1970s, indicating that this question had not been "solved" to the satisfaction of the BCP. In *Yeni Isik* ("New Light"), the Turkish language organ of the Party, strategies of attempted "Europeanization" of Turkish dress were evident. Conferences in Kirdjali in 1971 on the following topics, "The Way of Life and Culture of the Modern Woman" and "The Culture and Behavior of the Modern Person," demonstrated the continued campaign to modernize Turkish women's dress.[62] In the same publication, a Turkish woman was pictured as *"güzel ve modern"* (beautiful and modern) in dental hygienist garb. Furthermore, a "fashion review" was organized in the Kirdjali region with the sewing cooperative *"Druzhba"* (Friendship), that displayed "clothes throughout the centuries," which presented *shalvari* as belonging to a past epoch. In contrast, the fashion show asserted: "In our time clothes are light, comfortable, hygienic, and beautiful."[63] The BCP's attempt to bring "hygiene" to the Muslim regions of the Bulgarian countryside continued throughout the communist period, as the question apparently never was "solved."

The dramatic culmination of efforts to Bulgarianize Muslim minorities led to the well-known assimilation campaign of 1984–89, euphemistically referred to as the "rebirth process" (*vuzroditelskiat protses*).[64] The cornerstone of this process was the forcible change of Turkish names from Arabo-Turkic to Slavic-Christian forms, accompanied by the prohibition of the majority of Islamic religious rites. In 1985, Zhivkov made his famous statement marking the "final solution" to the Turkish Question; "There are no Turks in Bulgaria." For Islamic women this meant the wholesale illegalization of *feredzhe*, *shalvari*, and a plethora of other "Turkic" articles of clothing. It seems that, by 1984, the Bulgarian state was ready to take dramatic action to re-dress the "Bulgarian nation" in European clothes.

After the fall of communism in 1989, Muslim minorities enjoyed new possibilities for expressing themselves culturally and politically. Of course, Bulgarians also have more opportunity to express heightened nationalist tendencies, often anti-Turkish, anti-Islamic in character—somewhat inhibiting open manifestations of Turkishness. Nevertheless, a political party, the Movement for Rights and Freedoms (MRF), emerged in 1990 as the champion of minority rights—specifically Turkish and Islamic. At the same time, there has been a vigorous movement of reform and renewal within the Grand Muftiship itself. While the MRF is decidedly secularist in tone it also supports and enjoys reciprocal support from the reformed Muftiship.

The Muftiship, in its new, post-1989 newspaper, *Muslims* (*Musulmani* in Bulgarian or *Muslumanlar* in Turkish), provides no women represented without veiled hair and necks.[65] Although there is no polemic on veils or the need to reveil, veiling seems to have re-emerged as a political statement against the heavy handed "Bulgarianizing" of the communist period. As in Iran in the 1970s and across the Middle East today, it seems that emergent veiling is far from a return to past traditions. The "veils" shown in *Muslumanlar* resemble those worn in Modern Turkey and other Middle Eastern countries and most assuredly are not from a local Muslim, Turkic past. Instead, they have emerged as a reaction, albeit a fairly isolated one, to the efforts to control Muslim women and their practices of dress and hygiene, to modernize and Europeanize them and, thereby, to build socialism in the reflections of their images.

Conclusion

Bulgarian nation-state building imperatives from the 1930s to the 1980s required the recasting of Muslim women on the Bulgarian periphery into the image of the modern "Bulgarian woman." Nationalism and socialism readily and pragmatically intertwined and sought out deviants among the unwitting

264 *Mary Neuburger*

members of the modern nation, later, national in form but socialist in content. Hidden behind a veil of difference, Muslim women bore a unique burden as indicators of state success and symbols of local resistance. Today, they may play an important role in the post-communist Bulgarian relationship to its Muslim minorities in a time of rapid change and painful transition. In the Bulgarian case, it becomes clear that the greater processes of the relationships and discourses of history can have intense repercussions for everyday encounters and practices. No doubt, the protracted engagement of East and West may continue to hold such importance for the daily lives of Muslim women deep in the Rhodope mountains.

Notes

1 Edward Said, *Orientalism* (New York: Pantheon Books, 1978).
2 Michel Foucault, *History of Sexuality*, Vol. 1 (London: Penguin, 1990); and George Mosse, *Nationalism and Sexuality: Middle Class Morality and Sexual Norms in Modern Europe* (Madison, WI: Univeristy of Wisconsin Press, 1985).
3 See Mosse, op. cit., p. 23; Julie Marcus, *A World of Difference: Islam and Gender Hierarchy in Turkey* (London: Allen and Unwin, 1992), p. 32; and Maureen Molloy, "Imagining (the) Difference: Gender, Ethnicity and Metaphors of Nation," *Feminist Review*, No. 51, 1995, pp. 94–112, 105.
4 On the Balkans see Maria Todorova, "The Balkans: From Discovery to Invention," *Slavic Review*, Vol. 52, No. 2, 1992, pp. 453–82. On Russia see Francesca Wilson, *Muscovy: Russia Through Foreign Eyes 1553–1900* (London: Allen and Unwin, 1970), p. 218; and Tibor Szamuely, *The Russian Tradition* (New York: McGraw Hill, 1974), p. 83.
5 Milica Bakic-Hayden, "Nesting Orientalisms: The Case of Former Yugoslavia," *Slavic Review*, Vol. 54, No. 5, 1995, pp. 917–31, 917.
6 See Yuri Slezkine, "The USSR as a Communal Apartment, or How a Socialist State Promoted Ethnic Particularism," *Slavic Review*, Vol. 53, No. 2, 1994, pp. 414–55.
7 Beth Baron, "Unveiling in Early Twentieth Century Egypt: Practical and Symbolic Considerations," *Middle Eastern Studies*, Vol. 25, No. 3, 1989, pp. 370–86, 370.
8 Juan Cole, "Gender, Tradition, and History," in Fatma Göcek, M. and Shiva Balaghi, eds., *Reconstructing Gender in the Middle East: Tradition, Identity, Power* (New York: Columbia University Press, 1994), pp. 23–29, 26.
9 Ibid., p. 24.
10 For discussion of veiling, de-veiling and reveiling in Iran, see Nahid Yeganeh, "Women, Nationalism, and Islam in Contemporary Political Discourse in Iran," *Feminist Review*, Vol. 44, 1993, pp. 3–18; for a discussion of the same issue in Turkey, see Ayse Kadioglu, "Women's Subordination in Turkey: Is Islam Really the Villain?" *Middle East Journal*, Vol. 48, No. 4, 1994, pp. 645–60.
11 Kadioglu, op. cit., pp. 646–47; and Nermin Abadan-Unat, *Women in the Developing World: Evidence From Turkey* (Denver, CO: University of Denver Monograph Series in World Affairs, 1986), p. 28.
12 Massami Arai, *Turkish Nationalism in the Young Turk Era* (New York: E. J. Brill, 1992), pp. 65–68.
13 Arai, op. cit., p. 92; and Edward Lazzerini, *Ismail Bey Gaprinskii and Muslim Modernism in Russia, 1878–1914* (Seattle: University of Washington, 1974), pp. 237–51.

Re-dressing of Bulgarian Muslim women, 1878–1989 265

14 Kadioglu, op. cit., p. 646.
15 Ibid., p. 651.
16 Abadan-Unat, op. cit., p. 23; and Nayereh Tohidi, "Soviet in Public, Azeri in Private: Gender, Islam, and Nationality in Soviet and Post-Soviet Azerbaijan," *Women's Studies International Forum*, Vol. 19, Nos 1/2, 1996, pp. 111–23.
17 Catherine Clay, "Russian Ethnographers in the Service of the Empire," *Slavic Review*, Spring 1995, pp. 45–62, 58.
18 Tohidi, op. cit., p. 133.
19 Shakher Nuriev, *Zhenskii Vopros: Problemi i Resheniya* (Ashkhabad: Izdatelstvo "Turkmenistan," 1991), p. 3.
20 Ibid., p. 6; Bibi Palívanova, E*mansipatsiya Musulmanki: Opit Paskreposhcheniya Zhenshchini Sovetskovo Vostoka* (Moskva: Izdatelstvo "Nauka," 1982), p. 15; and Dilorom Alimova, *Resheniye Zhenskovo Voprosa v Uzbekistanye (1917–1941 gg.)* (Tashkent: Izdatelstvo "FAN," 1987), p. 12.
21 Vera Bilíshai, *Resheniye Zhenskovo Voprosa v SSSR* (Moskva: Gosudarstvennoe Izdatestvo Politicheskoi Literaturi, 1956), p. 146.
22 Ibid., p. 146.
23 Palivanova, op. cit., p. 279; and Tohidi, op. cit., p. 113.
24 The Muslim Gypsy population, although significant, is a separate case and, therefore, will be omitted from this study. The increasingly rural character of the Turkish population was in direct contrast to the Bulgarian population, which was primarily rural into the nineteenth century and became increasingly urban after independence.
25 Stoyu Shishkov, *Bulgaro-Mozhamedanite (Pomatsi): Istoriko-Zemepisen I Narodoychen Pregled c Obrazi* (Plovdiv: Turgovska Pechatinitsa, 1936).
26 See Ibid.; and Stoyu Shishkov, *Pomatsi v Trite Bulgarski Oblasti: Trakia, Makedonia i Mizia* (Plovdiv: Pechatnitsa "Makedonia," 1914).
27 See Khristo Khristov, *Iz Minaloto na Bulgarite Mozhamedani v Rodopite* (Sofia: Izdatelsvo na Bulgarskata Akademia na Naukite, 1958).
28 Shishkov, 1936, op. cit., p. 64.
29 Nikolai Branchev, *Bulgari-Mokhamedani (Pomatsi): Zemepisnite Predeli* (Sofia: Izdaniya na Bulgarsko Narodnoychno Druzhestvo, 1948), p. 32.
30 Kirdjail ODA, 14K-1-96 (1934–47), pp. 1–599.
31 Ibid., p. 55.
32 Smolyan ODA (Okruzhen Durzhaven Arkhiv, Smolyan Regional Government Archive Smolyan, Bulgaria),26K-1-2 (1939), p. 7.
33 Smolyan ODA, 42k-15-2 (1938), p. 142.
34 Smolyan ODA, 42k-15-10 (1942), p. 142.
35 Petur Marinov, ed., *Sbornik Rodina*, Book 1 (Smolyan: Izdaniye na "Rodina," 1939), p. 34.
36 Sofia, TsDA (Tsentralel Durzhven Arhkiv, Central Government Archive, Sofia, Bulgaria), 1B-15-222 (1946), p. 3.
37 Haskovo ODA (Okruzhen Durzhaven Arkhiv, Haskovo Regional Government Archive Haskovo, Bulgaria), 182K-1-92 (1946), p. 20.
38 Haskovo ODA, 675-1-66 (1950), p. 6.
39 Haskovo ODA, 675-1-62 (1953), p. 31.
40 Kirdjali ODA (Okrzhen Durzhaven Arkhiv, Kirdzhali Regional Government Archive Kirdjali, Bulgaria), 44-2-24 (1951), p. 77.
41 Sofia, TsDA, 1B-26-29 (1952), p. 1.
42 Sofia, TsDA, 28-16-49 (1960), p. 1.
43 Sofia, TsDA, 28-16-49 (1960), p. 1.
44 Haskovo ODA, 675-1-113 (1958), p. 16.
45 Haskovo ODA, 675-1-112 (1951), p. 71.
46 Sofia, TsDA, 28-16-49 (1960), p. 21.

266　*Mary Neuburger*

47　Sofia, TsDA, 28-16–49 (1960), p. 36.
48　Sofia, TsDA, 28–16–49 (1960), p. 23 and p. 16.
49　Sofia, TsDA, 28-16–49 (1960), p. 10.
50　Sofia, TsDA, 28–16–49 (1960), p. 106.
51　Sofia, TsDA, 28–16–49 (I960), p. 15.
52　Sofia, TsDA, 28–16–49 (1960), p. 125 and p. 51.
53　Sofia, TsDA, 28–16–49 (1960), p. 21.
54　Sofia, TsDA, 28–16–49 (1960), p. 16.
55　Haskovo ODA, 675-1–112 (1951), p. 73; and Sofia, TsDA, 28-16–49 (1955), p. 23.
56　Sofia, TsDA, 1B-5-509 (1962), p. 27.
57　Sofia, TsDA, 747–1-19 (1965), p. 165.
58　Sofia, TsDA, 1B-5–509 (1962), p. 94.
59　Sofia, TsDA, 1B-5–509 (1962), p. 90.
60　Sofia, TsDA, 1B-5–509 (1962), p. 127.
61　Sofia, TsDA, 1B-5–509 (1962), p. 37.
62　Yeni Isik, 13 December 1971, p. 3.
63　Ibid., p. 3.
64　For complete discussion see Kemal Karpat, ed., *The Turks of Bulgaria: The History, Culture, and Political Fate of a Minority* (Istanbul: The ISIS Press, 1990); and Kemal Karpat, "Bulgaria's Methods of Nation Building—The Annihilation of Minorities," *International Journal of Turkish Studies*, Vol. 4, No. 2, Fall/Winter 1989, pp. 1–23.
65　See *Muslulamlar*, April 1993, p. 2.

Bibliography

Abadan-Unat, Nermin. *Women in the Developing World: Evidence from Turkey* (Denver, CO: University of Denver Monograph Series in World Affairs, 1986).

Abu-Lughod, Lila. "Do Muslim Women Really Need Saving? Anthropological Reflections on Cultural Relativism and Its Others," *American Anthropologist*, Vol. 104, No. 3, 2002, pp. 783–90.

Adak, Sevgi. "Women in the Post-Ottoman Public Sphere: Anti-Veiling Campaigns and the Gendered Reshaping of Urban Space in Early RepublicanTurkey," in Nazan Maksudyan (ed.), *Women and the City, Women in the City: A Gendered Perspective to Ottoman Urban History*, Berghahn Books, forthcoming (September 2014).

Adamec, Ludwig. *Afghanistan 1900–1923: A Diplomatic History* (Berkeley: University of California Press, 1967).

——*Afghanistan's Foreign Affairs to the Mid-Twentieth Century* (Tucson: University of Arizona Press, 1974).

Afary, Janet. "On the Origins of Feminism in Early 20th-Century Iran," *Journal of Women's History*, 1 (Fall 1989): 65–87.

——*Sexual Politics in Modern Iran* (Cambridge: Cambridge University Press, 2009).

Ahmad, Ali, *The Fall of Amanullah*, trans. from the Persian of Shaikh Ali Mahboub by Maj. Robert Noel Girling Scott, Foreign & Political Department, March 1930 (Delhi: Government of India Press, 1930).

Ahmed, Leila. *Women and Gender in Islam: Historic Roots of a Modern Debate* (New Haven, CT: Yale University Press, 1992).

——*A Quiet Revolution: The Veil's Resurgence, from the Middle East to America* (New Haven, CT: Yale University Press, 2011).

Ahmedani, Usman. "L'Orient par L'Islam et L'Islam pour L'Orient? Ideas of Eastern and Islamic Unity in Inter-War Egypt" (MA thesis, Oxford University, 2012).

Akbar, E. "An Analysis of Afghan Women's Social Status and a Perspective of the (*sic*) Rights" in *Proceedings of the Seminar: Women's Human Rights in Afghanistan 15th–19th October 1994* (n.p: Mazar, Afghanistan, 1994).

Amin, Camron. *The Making of the Modern Iranian Woman: Gender, State Policy, and Popular Culture, 1865–1946* (Gainesville: University Press of Florida, 2002).

Amin, Qassim. *The Liberation of Women, and The New Woman: Two Documents in Egyptian Feminism*, trans. Samiha Sidhom Peterson (Cairo: American University of Cairo Press, 2000 [1898 and 1900]).

Arai, Massami. *Turkish Nationalism in the Young Turk Era* (New York: E. J. Brill, 1992).

268 Bibliography

Arat, Yeşim. "The Project of Modernity and Women in Turkey," in Sibel Bozdoğan and Reşat Kasaba (eds.), *Rethinking Modernity and National Identity in Turkey* (Seattle: University of Washington Press, 1997).

Armstrong, Harold. *Turkey and Syria Reborn: A Record of Two Years of Travel* (London: J. Lane, 1930).

Atabaki, Touraj (ed.). *The State and the Subaltern: Modernization, Society, and the State in Turkey and Iran* (New York: I.B. Tauris, 2007).

Atabaki, Touraj and Zürcher, Erik Jan (eds.). *Men of Order: Authoritarian Modernization under Atatürk and Reza Shah* (London: I. B. Tauris, 2004).

Aydın, Senem. "Everyday Forms of State Power and the Kurds in the Early Turkish Republic," *International Journal of Middle East Studies*, Vol. 43, No. 1, February 2011, pp. 75–93.

Azak, Umut. "A Reaction to Authoritarian Modernization in Turkey: The Menemen Incident and the Creation and Contestation of a Myth, 1930–31," in Touraj Atabaki (ed.), *The State and the Subaltern: Modernization, Society and the State in Turkey and Iran* (New York: I.B. Tauris, 2007).

Badran, Margot. *Feminists, Islam and Nation: Gender and the Making of Modern Egypt* (Princeton, NJ: Princeton University Press, 1995).

Badran, Margot and Cooke, Miriam (eds.). *Opening the Gates: A Century of Arab Feminist Writing* (Bloomington: Indiana University Press, 1990).

Bahithat al-Badiya. Translated and excerpted in *Opening the Gates: A Century of Arab Feminist Writing*, eds. Margot Badran and Miriam Cooke (Bloomington: Indiana University Press, 1990).

Baker, Henry D. *British India with Notes on Ceylon, Afghanistan and Tibet* (Washington, DC: US Department of Commerce, Consular Report 72, 1915).

Baker, Patricia L. "Politics of Dress: The Dress Reform Laws of 1920–30s Iran," in Nancy Lindisfarne-Tapper and Bruce Ingham (eds.), *Languages of Dress in the Middle East* (Richmond: Curzon Press, 1997), pp. 178–92.

Bakic-Hayden, Milica. "Nesting Orientalisms: The Case of Former Yugoslavia," *Slavic Review*, Vol. 54, No. 5, 1995, pp. 917–31.

Baron, Beth. "Unveiling in Early Twentieth Century Egypt: Practical and Symbolic Considerations," *Middle Eastern Studies*, Vol. 25, No. 3, 1989, pp. 370–86.

Bassett, James. *Persia: Eastern Mission, a Narrative of the Founding and Fortunes of the Eastern Persia Mission* (1890) (Ulan Press, 2012).

Bayat-Philipp, Mangol. "Women and Revolution in Iran, 1905–11," in Lois Beck and Nikki Keddie (eds.), *Women in the Muslim World* (Cambridge, MA: Harvard University Press, 1978).

Berkes, Niyazi. *The Development of Secularism in Turkey* (Montreal: McGill University Press, 1964).

Bird, Isabella. *Travels in Persia and Koordistan*, (London: The Long Riders' Guild Press, 2004).

Blaut, J. M. *The Colonizer's Model of the World: Geographical Diffusionism and Eurocentric History* (New York: The Guilford Press, 1993).

Bolukbasi, Suha. *Azerbaijan: A Political History* (London: I.B. Tauris, 2011).

Bowen, John R. "Does French Islam Have Borders? Dilemmas of Domestication in a Global Religious Field," *American Anthropologist*, Vol. 106, No. 1, 2004, pp. 43–55.

Bozarslan, Hamit. "Islam, laïcité et la question d'autorité de l'Empire ottoman à la Turquie kémaliste," *Archives de Sciences Sociales des Religions*, 125, Paris (January–March 2004), pp. 99–112.

Bibliography 269

Brockett, Gavin. D. "Revisiting the Turkish Revolution, 1923–38, Secular Reform and Religious 'Reaction'," *History Compass*, 4 (2006), pp. 1060–72.

Brooks, Jonathan and Brooks, C.W. (eds.). *The Middling Sort of People: Culture, Society, and Politics in England, 1550–1800* (London: St Martin's Press, 1994).

Canefe, Nergis. "Sovereign Utopias: Civilisational Boundaries of Greek and Turkish Nationhood (1821–1923)," unpublished PhD dissertation, York University, North York, Ontario, 1998.

Cannadine, David. *Ornamentalism: How the British Saw Their Empire* (Oxford: OUP, 2001).

Chehabi, Houchang. "Staging the Emperor's New Clothes: Dress Codes and Nation-Building under Reza Shah," *Iranian Studies*, Vol. 26, Nos. 3–4 (Summer/Fall 1993), pp. 209–29.

——"The Banning of the Veil and Its Consequences," in Stephanie Cronin (ed.), *The Making of Modern Iran: State and Society under Riza Shah, 1921–1941* (New York and London: RoutledgeCurzon, 2003).

——"The Westernization of Iranian Culinary Culture", *Iranian Studies*, Vol. 36, No. 1 (March 2003).

——"Dress Codes for Men in Turkey and Iran," in Touraj Atabaki and Erik Jan Zürcher (eds.), *Men of Order: Authoritarian Modernization under Atatürk and Reza Shah* (London/New York: I. B. Tauris, 2004).

Chenciner, Robert and Magomedkhanov, Magomedkhan. "Persian Exports to Russia from the Sixteenth to the Nineteenth Century," *Iran*, Vol. 30 (1992).

Çınar, Alev. *Modernity, Islam, and Secularism in Turkey* (Minneapolis: University of Minnesota Press, 2006).

Clay, Catherine. "Russian Ethnographers in the Service of the Empire," *Slavic Review*, Spring 1995, pp. 45–62.

Clayer, Nathalie. *L'Albanie, pays des derviches* (Berlin: Otto Harrassowitz, 1990).

——"La Ahmadiyya Lahori et la réforme de l'islam albanais dans l'entre-deux-guerres," in V. Bouillier and C. Servan-Schreiber (eds.), *De l'Arabie à l'Himalaya. Chemins croisés en hommage à Marc Gaborieau* (Paris: 2004), pp. 211–28.

——*Aux origines du nationalisme albanais. La naissance d'une nation majoritairement musulmane en Europe* (Paris: Karthala, 2007).

——"Construction de mosquées en Albanie, 1920–39," *Archives de Sciences Sociales des Religions*, 151 (July–September 2010), pp. 91–105.

Cole, Juan. "Gender, Tradition, and History," in Fatma Göcek, M. and Shiva Balaghi (eds.), *Reconstructing Gender in the Middle East: Tradition, Identity, Power* (New York: Columbia University Press, 1994), pp. 23–29.

Condra, Jill. *The Greenwood Encyclopedia of Clothing Through World History*, Vol. 1 (Westport, CT: Greenwood, 2008)

Cronin, Stephanie. *The Army and the Creation of the Pahlavi State in Iran, 1910–1926* (London and New York: I.B. Tauris, 1997).

——*Soldiers, Shahs and Subalterns in Iran: Opposition, Protest and Revolt, 1921–1941* (Basingstoke: Palgrave Macmillan, 2010).

Darnton, Robert. *The Great Cat Massacre and Other Episodes in French Cultural History* (New York: Vintage Books, 1985).

——"An Early Information Society: News and Media in Eighteenth-Century Paris," *American Historical Review*, CV, No. 1, Feb., 2000.

Dave, Bhava. *Kazakhstan: Ethnicity, Language, and Power* (London: Routledge, 2007).

270 Bibliography

de Grazia, Victoria. "Introduction," in Victoria de Grazia and Ellen Furlough (eds.), *The Sex of Things: Gender and Consumption in Historical Perspective* (Berkeley: University of California Press, 1996).

Devos, Bianca. *Kleidungspolitik in Iran: Die Durchsetzung der Kleidungsvorschriften für Männer unter Riżā Šāh* (Wurtzburg: Ergon, 2006).

Donia, Robert J. *Sarajevo – A Biography* (London: University of Michigan Press, 2006).

Dupree, N.H. "Behind the Veil in Afghanistan", *Asia* (July/August 1978).

——"A Building Boom in the Hindukush. Afghanistan 1921–28," *Lotus International*, No. 26 (1980).

——"Revolutionary Rhetoric and Afghan Women" *Afghanistan Council Occasional Paper* No. 23 (New York City: The Asia Society, 1981).

——"Victoriana comes to the Haremserai in Afghanistan" in Paul Bucherer-Dietschi (ed.), *Bauen und Wohnen am Hindukush* (Liestal: Stiftung Bibliotheca Afghanica, 1988).

Edgar, Adrienne. *Tribal Nation: The Making of Soviet Turkmenistan* (Princeton, NJ: Princeton University Press, 2004).

——"Bolshevism, Patriarchy, and the Nation: the Soviet Emancipation of Muslim Women in Pan-Islamic Perspective," *Slavic Review*, 2006, Vol. 65, No. 2, pp. 252–72.

Edip Adıvar, Halide. *Turkey Faces West* (New York: Arno Press, 1973 reprint edition).

Edwards, David B. *Before Taliban: Genealogies of the Afghan Jihad* (Berkeley: University of California Press, 2001).

Edwards, Holly. "Unruly Images: Photography In and Out of Afghanistan," *Artibus Asiae*, Vol. 66, No. 2, 2006.

Ekrem, Selma. *Turkey, Old and New* (New York: C. Scribner's Sons, 1947).

El Guindi, Fadwa. *Veil: Modesty, Privacy and Resistance* (Oxford and New York: Berg, 1999).

Emin (Yalman), Ahmed. *Turkey in the World War* (New Haven, CT: Yale University Press, 1930).

Ettehadieh, Mansoureh. "The Origins and Development of the Women's Movement in Iran, 1906–41," in Lois Beck and Guity Nashat (eds.), *Women in Iran from 1800 to the Islamic Republic* (Urbana and Chicago: University of Illinois Press, 2004).

Farge, Arlette and Revel, Jacques. *The Vanishing Children of Paris: Rumor and Politics before the French Revolution* (Cambridge, MA: Harvard University Press, 1991).

Farman Farmaian, Sattareh and Munker, Dona. *Daughter of Persia: A Woman's Journey from Her Father's Harem through the Islamic Revolution* (London: Broadway Books, 1992)

Fischer, Bernard. *King Zog and the Struggle for Stability in Albania* (New York: Columbia University Press, 1984).

Fleischman, Ellen L. "The Other 'Awakening': The Emergence of Women's Movements in the Modern Middle East, 1900–1940," in Margaret L. Meriwether and Judith E. Tucker (eds.), *A Social History of Women and Gender in the Modern Middle East* (Boulder, CO: Perseus, 1999).

Fleming, J. "Clouds Above Festival Kabul," *Asia*, Vol. 29, No. 4, 1929.

——"The Troubles of an Afghan King," *Asia*, May 1929, pp. 402–14.

Floor, Willem. *The Persian Textile Industry in Historical Perspective, 1500–1925* (Moyen Orient & Ocean Indien XVIe-XIXe s) (Paris: L'Harmattan, 1999).

——*Textile Imports into Qajar Iran: Russia Versus Great Britain, The Battle for Market Domination* (Costa Mesa: Mazda, 2009).

Bibliography 271

Foucault, Michel. *History of Sexuality*, Vol. 1 (London: Penguin, 1990).

Fraser-Tytler, William Kerr. *Afghanistan: A Study of Political Developments in Central Asia* (London: Oxford University Press, 1950).

Frierson, Elizabeth. "Cheap and Easy: The Creation of Consumer Culture in Late Ottoman Society," in Donald Quataert (ed.), *Consumption Studies and the History of the Ottoman Empire, 1550–1922: An Introduction* (Binghampton, NY: SUNY Press, 2000), pp. 243–61.

Gökalp, Ziya. *Principles of Turkism*, trans. Robert Devereux (Leiden, ND: E. J. Brill, 1968).

Goldberg Ruthchild, Rochelle. *Equality & Revolution: Women's Rights in the Russian Empire, 1905–1917* (Pittsburgh: University of Pittsburgh Press 2010).

Göle, Nilüfer. *The Forbidden Modern: Civilization and Veiling* (Ann Arbor: University of Michigan Press, 1996).

——"The Civilizational, Spatial, and Sexual Powers of the Secular," in Michael Warner, Jonathan Van Antwerpen, and Craig Calhoun (eds.), *Varieties of Secularism in a Secular Age* (Cambridge, MA: Harvard University Press, 2010).

Goswami, Manu. "Rethinking the Modular Nation Form: Toward a Sociohistorical Conception of Nationalism," *Comparative Studies in Society and History*, Vol. 44 (2002), pp. 770–99.

Grant, A.H. "A Winter at the Court of an Absolute Monarch," *Blackwood's Magazine*, Vol. 180, No. 1093, Nov., 1906.

Green, Nile. "The Trans-Border Traffic of Afghan Modernism: Afghanistan and the Indian 'Urdusphere'," *Comparative Studies in Society and History*, Vol. 53, No. 3, 2011.

——"The Afghan Afterlife of Phileas Fogg: Space and Time in the Literature of Afghan Travel" in Nile Green and Nushin Arbabzadeh (eds.), *Afghanistan Into Ink* (London: Hurst, 2012).

——"The Road to Kabul: Automobiles and Afghan Internationalism, 1900–1940," in Magnus Marsden and Benjamin Hopkins (eds.), *Beyond Swat: History, Society and Economy along the Afghanistan–Pakistan Frontier* (New York: Columbia University Press, 2012).

Gregorian, Vartan. *The Emergence of Modern Afghanistan* (Stanford, CA: Stanford University Press, 1969).

Grima, Benedicte. *The Performance of Emotion among Paxtun Women* (Austin: University of Texas Press, 1992).

Guha, Amalendu. "The Economy of Afghanistan During Amanullah's Reign, 1919–29," *International Studies*, Vol. 9, 1967–68.

Hamilton, Angus. *Afghanistan* (London: W. Heinemann, 1906).

Hanifi, Shah Mahmoud. *Connecting Histories in Afghanistan: Market Relations and State Formation on a Colonial Frontier* (New York: Columbia University Press, 2008).

Hanley, Will. "Grieving Cosmopolitanism in Middle East Studies," *History Compass*, Vol. 6, No. 5, 2008, pp. 1346–67.

Hegland, Mary Elaine. "The Power Paradox in Muslim Women's Majales: North-West Pakistani Mourning Rituals as Sites of Contestation over Religious Politics, Ethnicity, and Gender" in Therese Saliba, Carolyn Allen, Judith A. Howard (eds.), *Gender, Politics and Islam* (Chicago, IL: The University of Chicago Press, 2002), pp. 117–19.

Heper, Metin. *The State Tradition in Turkey* (Walkington: The Eothen Press, 1985).

272 Bibliography

Heyat, Farideh. *Azeri Women in Transition: Women in Soviet and Post-Soviet Azerbaijan* (London: Routledge, 2002).

Hopkins, B.D. *The Making of Modern Afghanistan* (London: Palgrave Macmillan, 2008).

Jacob, Wilson Chacko. *Working Out Egypt: Effendi Masculinity and Subject Formation in Colonial Modernity, 1870–1940* (Durham, NC: Duke University Press, 2011).

Kadioglu, Ayse. "Women's Subordination in Turkey: Is Islam Really the Villain?" *Middle East Journal*, Vol. 48, No. 4, 1994, pp. 645–60.

Kakar, Hasan Kawun. *Government and Society in Afghanistan: The Reign of Amir Abd al-Rahman Khan* (Austin: University of Texas Press, 1979).

Kamp, Marianne. "Unveiling Uzbek Women: Liberation, Representation, and Discourse, 1906 to 1929," PhD dissertation, University of Chicago, 1998.

——*The New Woman in Uzbekistan: Islam, Modernity and Unveiling under Communism* (Seattle: University of Washington Press, 2006).

——"Femicide as Terrorism: The Case of Uzbekistan's Unveiling Murders," in Elizabeth Heineman (ed.), *Sexual Violence in Conflict Zones: from the Ancient World to the Era of Human Rights* (Philadelphia: University of Pennsylvania Press, 2011), 56–70.

Kandiyoti, Deniz. "Emancipated but Unliberated? Reflections on the Turkish Case," *Feminist Studies*, Vol. 13, No. 2, Summer 1987.

——"Gendering the Modern: On Missing Dimensions in the Study of Turkish Modernity," in Sibel Bozdoğan and Reşat Kasaba (eds.), *Rethinking Modernity and National Identity in Turkey* (Seattle, WA: University of Washington Press, 1997), 113–32.

——"Women, Islam, and the State," in Joel Beinin and Joe Stork (eds.), *Political Islam: Essays from Middle East Report* (New York: I. B. Tauris, 1997).

Karabuda, Barbro. *Goodbye to the Fez: A Portrait of Modern Turkey*, trans. from Swedish by Maurice Michael (London: Denis Dobson Books, 1959).

Karpat, Kemal. "Bulgaria's Methods of Nation Building—The Anihilation of Minorities," *International Journal of Turkish Studies*, Vol. 4, No. 2, Fall/Winter 1989, pp. 1–23.

——(ed.). *The Turks of Bulgaria: The History, Culture, and Political Fate of a Minority* (Istanbul: The ISIS Press, 1990).

Kashani Sabet, Firoozeh. *Frontier Fictions: Shaping the Iranian Nation, 1804–1946* (Princeton, NJ: Princeton University Press, 1999).

——"Hallmarks of Humanism: Hygiene and Love of Homeland in Qajar Iran," *The American Historical Review*, Vol. 105, No. 4 (2000), pp. 1171–1203.

——"Cultures of Iranianness: The Evolving Polemic of Iranian Nationalism," in Nikki R. Keddie and Rudolph P. Matthee (eds.), *Iran and the Surrounding World: Interactions in Culture and Cultural Politics* (Seattle: University of Washington Press, 2002), 162–81.

——"Patriotic Womanhood: The Culture of Feminism in Modern Iran, 1900–1941," *British Journal of Middle Eastern Studies*, Vol. 32, No. 1, 2005, pp. 29–46.

——"The Politics of Reproduction: Maternalism and Women's Hygiene in Iran, 1896–1941," *International Journal of Middle Eastern Studies*, Vol. 38, 2006, pp. 1–29.

——*Conceiving Citizens: Women and the Politics of Motherhood in Iran* (New York: Oxford University Press, 2011).

Katouzian, Homa. "State and Society under Reza Shah," in Touraj Atabaki and Erik Jan Zürcher (eds.), *Men of Order: Authoritarian Modernization under Atatürk and Reza Shah* (London: I. B. Tauris, 2004).

Katrak, Sohrab. *Through Amanullah's Afghanistan* (Karachi: 'Sind Observer' & Mercantile Steam Press Limited, 1929).

Keddie, Nikki R. "Problems in the Study of Middle Eastern Women," *International Journal of Middle East Studies*, Vol. 10, 1979, pp. 225–40.

——*Women in the Middle East: Past and Present* (Princeton, NJ: Princeton University Press, 2007).

Khalid, Adeeb. *The Politics of Muslim Cultural Reform: Jadidism in Central Asia* (Berkeley, CA and Los Angeles, CA: 1998).

——"Introduction: Locating the (Post)-Colonial in Soviet History," *Central Asian Survey*, Vol. 26, No. 4, 2007, pp 465–73.

Kotkin, Stephen. "Modern Times: The Soviet Union and the Interwar Conjuncture," in *Kritika: Explorations in Russian and Eurasian History*, Vol. 2, No. 1, Winter 2001.

Küçük, Hülya. "Sufi Reactions against the Reforms after Turkey's National Struggle: How a Nightingale Turned into a Crow," in Touraj Atabaki (ed.), *The State and The Subaltern: Modernization, Society and the State in Turkey and Iran* (New York: I.B. Tauris, 2007), pp. 123–42.

Kumar, Arun. "Beyond Muffled Murmurs of Dissent? Kisan Rumour in Colonial Bihar," *The Journal of Peasant Studies*, Vol. 27, No. 1, Oct., 2000.

Kuru, Ahmet. *Secularism and State Policies toward Religion: The United States, France, and Turkey* (New York: Cambridge University Press, 2009).

Lamprou, Alexandros. "Between Central State and Local Society. The People's Houses Institution and the Domestication of Reform in Turkey (1932–51)," unpublished PhD dissertation, Leiden University, 2009.

Lazzerini, Edward. *Ismail Bey Gaprinskii and Muslim Modernism in Russia, 1878–1914* (Seattle: University of Washington, 1974).

Lewis, Bernard. *The Emergence of Modern Turkey* (London and New York: Oxford University Press, 1961).

Lewis, Reina. *Rethinking Orientalism: Women, Travel and the Ottoman Harem* (London: Rutgers University Press, 2004).

Libal, Kathryn. "Realizing Modernity through the Robust Turkish Child, 1923–38," in Daniel Thomas Cook (ed.), *Symbolic Childhood* (New York: Peter Lang, 2002), pp. 109–30.

——"Staging Turkish Women's Emancipation: Istanbul, 1935," *Journal for Middle East Women's Studies*, Vol. 4, No. 1, 2008, pp. 31–52.

——"Specifying Turkish Modernity: Gender, Family, and Nation-state Making in the Early Turkish Republic," in G. Brockett (ed.), *Towards a Social History of Modern Turkey: Essays in Theory and Practice* (Istanbul: Libra Kitap, 2011) pp. 81–96.

Lindisfarne-Tapper, Nancy and Ingham, Bruce. "Approaches to the Study of Dress in the Middle East" in *Languages of Dress in the Middle East* (Richmond: Curzon Press 1997), pp. 1–39.

——(eds.). *Languages of Dress in the Middle East* (Richmond: Curzon Press, 1997).

Linke, Lilo. *Allah Dethroned: A Journey Through Modern Turkey* (New York: Alfred Knopf, 1937).

Mackie, Gerry. "Ending Footbinding and Infibulation: A Convention Account," *American Sociological Review*, Vol. 61, No. 6, (December, 1996).

Macmunn, George. *Afghanistan From Darius to Amanullah* (London: G. Bell and Sons, 1929).

Mahdavi, Shireen. "Reza Shah Pahlavi and Women: A Re-evaluation" in Stephanie Cronin (ed.), *The Making of Modern Iran: State and Society under Riza Shah, 1921–1941* (London: Routledge, 2003).

274 Bibliography

Mahir-Metinsoy, İkbal Elif. "Fashion and Women in the İstanbul of the Armistice Period, 1918–23" (MA thesis, Boğaziçi University, İstanbul, 2005).

——"Poor Ottoman Turkish Women during World War I: Women's Experiences and Politics in Everyday Life, 1914–23" (PhD dissertation, Université de Strasbourg and Boğaziçi University, 2012).

Malcolm, Sir John. *The History of Persia, from the Most Early Period to the Present Time*, Vol. 2, (1815).

Marashi, Afshin. "Performing the Nation: The Shah's official state visit to Kemalist Turkey, June to July 1934" in S. Cronin (ed.), *The Making of Modern Iran: State and Society Under Riza Shah 1921–41* (London: Routledge, 2003).

Marcus, Julie. *A World of Difference: Islam and Gender Hierarchy in Turkey* (London: Allen and Unwin, 1992).

Mardin, Şerif. "Religion and Secularism in Turkey," in Ali Kazancıgil and Ergun Özbudun (eds.), *Atatürk: Founder of a Modern State* (London: C. Hurts, 1981).

Masson, Charles. *Narrative of Various Journeys in Balochistan, Afghanistan, the Panjab and Kalat* (London, Richard Bentley, 1844).

Matthee, Rudi. *The Politics of Trade in Safavid Iran: Silk for Silver, 1600–1730* (Cambridge: Cambridge University Press, 1999).

Mayeur-Jaouen, Catherine and Dupont, Anne-Laure (eds.). "Débats intellectuels au Moyen-Orient dans l'entre-deux-guerres," *REMMM*, Nos. 95, 96, 97, 98, 2002.

Metinsoy, Murat. "Fragile Hegemony, Flexible Authoritarianism, and Governing from Below: Politicians' Reports in Early Republican Turkey," *International Journal of Middle East Studies*, Vol. 43, No. 4 (Nov. 2011), pp. 699–719.

Micklewright, Nancy. "Women's Dress in 19th Century Istanbul: Mirror of a Changing Society," PhD dissertation, University of Pennsylvania, 1986).

Migdal, Joel. "Finding the Meeting Ground of Fact and Fiction: Some Reflections on Turkish Modernization," in Sibel Bozdoğan and Reşat Kasaba (eds.), *Rethinking Modernity and National Identity in Turkey* (Seattle: Washington University Press, 1997), pp. 252–60.

Molloy, Maureen. "Imagining (the) Difference: Gender, Ethnicity and Metaphors of Nation," *Feminist Review*, No. 51, 1995, pp. 94–112.

Morier, James Justinian. *A Journey Through Persia, Armenia, and Asia Minor to Constantinople, in the Years 1808 and 1809* (1816).

Mosse, George. *Nationalism and Sexuality: Middle Class Morality and Sexual Norms in Modern Europe* (Madison, WI: University of Wisconsin Press, 1985).

Mott-Smith, May. "Behind the Purdah in Afghanistan," *Asia*, No. 54, 16th Dec., 1929.

——"On through the Khyber to Kabul", *Asia*, No.29 (1929), pp.396–401.

Najmabadi, Afsaneh. "Women or Wives of the Nation?" *Iranian Studies*, Vol. 26, 1993.

——"Veiled Discourse-Unveiled Bodies," *Feminist Studies*, Vol. 19, No. 3, (Autumn, 1993), pp. 510–11.

——"Crafting an Educated Housewife in Iran," in Lila Abu-Lughod (ed.), *Remaking Women: Feminism and Modernity in the Middle East*, (Princeton, NJ: Princeton University Press, 1998), pp. 91–125.

——*Women with Mustaches and Men without Beards: Gender and Sexual Anxieties of Iranian Modernity* (Berkeley, CA: University of California Press, 2005).

Nawid, Senzil. "The Feminine and Feminism in Tarzi's Work," *Annali*, Vol. 55, No. 3, 1995, pp. 358–66.

Bibliography 275

——*Religious Response to Social Change, 1919–1929: King Aman-Allah and the Afghan Ulama* (Costa Mesa, CA: Mazda Publishers, 1999).

Neuburger, Mary. *The Orient Within: Muslim Minorities and the Negotiation of Nationhood in Modern Bulgaria* (New York: Cornell University Press, 2004).

Newman, Bernard. *Turkish Crossroads* (London: Robert Hale Ltd., 1951)

Northrop, Douglas. "Languages of Loyalty: Gender, Politics, and Party Supervision in Uzbekistan, 1927–41," *Russian Review*, Vol. 59, No. 2, 2000, pp 179–299.

——*Veiled Empire: Gender and Power in Stalinist Central Asia* (Ithaca: Cornell University Press, 2004).

Norton, John. "Faith and Fashion in Turkey," in Nancy Lindisfarne-Tapper and Bruce Ingham (eds.), *Languages of Dress in the Middle East* (Richmond: Curzon Press, 1997).

O'Hanlon, Rosalind. "Manliness and Imperial Service in Mughal North India," *Journal of the Economic and Social History of the Orient*, Vol. 42, No. 1, 1999, pp. 47–93.

Olivier, Guillaume-Antoine. *Voyage dans l'Empire Othoman, l'Egypte et la Perse, fait par ordre du gouvernement, pendant les six premières années de la République* (1807).

Olson, Emilie A. "Muslim Identity and Secularism in Contemporary Turkey: 'The Headscarf Dispute'," *Anthropological Quarterly*, Vol. 58, No. 4, Oct., 1985.

O'Neill Borbieva, Noor. "Empowering Muslim Women: Independent Religious Fellowships in the Kyrgyz Republic," *Slavic Review*, Vol. 71, No. 2, 2012, pp 288–307.

Özdalga, Elisabeth. *The Veiling Issue: Official Secularism and Popular Islam in Turkey* (Richmond: Curzon Press, 1998).

Paidar, Parvin. *Women and the Political Process in Twentieth-Century Iran* (Cambridge: Cambridge University Press, 1995).

Parla, Taha and Davison, Andrew. "Secularism and Laicism in Turkey," in Janet J. Jakobsen and Ann Pellegrini (eds.), *Secularisms* (Durham, NC: Duke University Press, 2008), pp. 58–75.

Peirce, Leslie P. *The Imperial Harem: Women and Sovereignty in the Ottoman Empire* (New York: Oxford University Press, 1993).

Pennell, T.L. *Among the Wild Tribes of the Afghan Frontier* (London: Seeley and Co., 1909).

Phillip, Thomas. "Isfahan 1881–91: A Close-up View of Guilds and Production," *Iranian Studies*, Vol. 17, No. 4, Autumn, 1984.

Popovic, Alexandre. *L'islam balkanique* (Berlin: Otto Harrassowitz, 1986).

Poullada, Leon. *Reform and Rebellion in Afghanistan, 1919–1929* (Ithaca, NY: Cornell University Press, 1973).

Quataert, Donald. "Clothing Laws, State and Society in the Ottoman Empire, 1720–1829," *International Journal of Middle East Studies*, Vol. 29, No. 3, Aug., 1997, p. 405.

Raskolnikov, F. "Civil War in Afghanistan," *The Living Age*, May 1929.

Reynolds, Nancy. *A City Consumed: Urban Commerce, the Cairo Fire, and the Politics of Decolonization in Egypt* (Palo Alto, CA: Stanford University Press, 2012).

Roberts, Mary Louise. "Gender, Consumption, and Commodity Culture," *American Historical Review*, Vol. 103, No. 3 (June 1998).

Rorlich, Azade Ayşe. *The Volga Tatars: A Profile in National Resilience* (Stanford: Hoover Institution Press, 1986).

——"The Äli Bayrmov Club, the Journal Shärg Gadïnï and the Socialization of Azeri women 1920–30," *Central Asian Survey*, Vol. 3–4, 1986, pp. 221–39.

276 Bibliography

Rostam-Kolayi, Jasamin. "Expanding Agendas for the 'New' Iranian Woman: Family Law, Work and Unveiling," in Stephanie Cronin (ed.), *The Making of Modern Iran: State and Society under Riza Shah, 1921–1941* (London and New York: Routledge, 2003).

——"Origins of Iran's Modern Girls' Schools: From Private/National to Public/State," *Journal of Middle East Women's Studies*, Vol. 4, No. 3, Fall, 2008.

Russell, Mona. *Creating the New Egyptian Woman: Consumerism, Education, and National Identity, 1863–1922* (New York: Palgrave Macmillan, 2004).

Ryzova, Lucie. "Efendification: The Rise of the Middle Class Culture in Modern Egypt," DPhil dissertation, Oxford University, 2009.

Said, Edward. *Orientalism* (New York: Pantheon Books, 1978).

Saise, Walter. "A Visit to Afghanistan," *Proceedings of the Central Asian Society*, 12 April, 1911.

Saliba, Therese, Allen, Carolyn, and Howard, Judith A. (eds.). *Gender, Politics, and Islam* (Chicago, IL: The University of Chicago Press, 2002).

Sanasarian, Eliz. *The Women's Rights Movement in Iran* (New York: Praeger, 1982).

Scarce, Jennifer. *Women's Costume of the Near and Middle East* (London: Routledge, 2003).

Schick, Irvin C. *The Erotic Margin: Sexuality and Spatiality in Alterist Discourse* (New York: Verso Press, 1999).

Schinasi, May. *Afghanistan at the Beginning of the Twentieth Century* (Naples: Istituto Universitario Orientale, 1979).

——"La Photographie en Afghanistan", *Annali*, Vol. 56, Fascicolo 2 (1996).

——"Femmes afghans: instruction et activités publiques pendant le règne amâniya (1919–29)," *Annali dell'Istituto Universitario Orientale di Napoli* 55/4, 1995, pp. 446–62.

——*Kaboul 1773–1948* (Naples : Universita? degli Studi di Napoli L'Orientale, Dipartimento di Studi Asiatici, 2008).

Schmidt-Neke, Michael. *Entstehung und Ausbau der Königsdiktatur in Albanien (1912–1939)* (Munich: Oldenbourg, 1987).

Sedghi, Hamideh.*Veiling, Unveiling, and Reveiling* (Cambridge: Cambridge University Press, 2006).

Şeni, Nora. "Fashion and Women's Clothing in the Satirical Press of Istanbul at the End of the 19th Century," in Şirin Tekeli (ed.), *Women in Modern Turkish Society* (London: Zed Books, 1995), pp. 25–45.

Shaw, Stanford and Kural Shaw, Ezel. *History of the Ottoman Empire and Modern Turkey* (Cambridge: Cambridge University Press, 1977).

Shissler, A. Holly. "Beauty is Nothing to be Ashamed of: Beauty Contests as Tools of Women's Liberation in Early Republican Turkey," *Comparative Studies of South Asia, Africa and the Middle East*, Vol. 24, No. 1, 2004, pp. 109–26.

Simpich, Frederick and "Haji Mirza Hussein" (a.k.a. Von Niedermayer, Oscar). "Every-Day Life in Afghanistan," *National Geographic*, June, 1921.

Slavs and Tartars (eds.). *Molla Nasreddin: The Magazine that Would've, Could've, Should've* (Zürich, 2011).

Slezkine, Yuri. "The USSR as a Communal Apartment, or How a Socialist State Promoted Ethnic Particularism," *Slavic Review*, Vol. 53, No. 2, 1994, pp. 414–55.

Speer, Robert Elliott and Carter, Russell. *Report on India and Persia of the Deputation: Sent by the Board of Foreign Missions of the Presbyterian Church in the U.S.A. to Visit These Fields in 1921–22* (1922).

Bibliography 277

Szamuely, Tibor. *The Russian Tradition* (New York: McGraw Hill, 1974).

Taj al-Saltana. *Crowning Anguish: Memoirs of a Persian Princess from the Harem to Modernity, 1884–1914*, ed. Abbas Amanat (Washington, DC: Mage, 2003).

Tavakoli-Targhi, Mohamad. "Women of the West Imagined: The *Farangi* Other and the Emergence of the Woman Question in Iran," in Valentine M. Moghadam (ed.), *Identity Politics and Women: Cultural Reassertions and Feminisms in International Perspective* (Boulder, CO and Oxford: Westview, 1993).

——*Refashioning Iran* (New York: Palgrave, 2001).

Thompson, Elizabeth. *Colonial Citizens : republican rights, paternal privilege, and gender in French Syria and Lebanon* (New York: Columbia University Press, 2000).

Thorburn, S.S. *Bannu: Or Our Afghan Frontier* (London: Trubner, 1876).

Todorova, Maria. "The Balkans: From Discovery to Invention," *Slavic Review*, Vol. 52, No. 2, 1992, pp. 453–82.

Tohidi, Nayereh. "Soviet in Public, Azeri in Private: Gender, Islam, and Nationality in Soviet and Post-Soviet Azerbaijan," *Women's Studies International Forum*, Vol. 19, Nos 1/2, 1996, pp. 111–23.

Toktaş, Şule. "Nationalism, Modernization, and the Military in Turkey: Women Officers in the Turkish Armed Forces," *Quaderni di Oriente Moderno*, Vol. 28, No. 84, 2004.

Toprak, Binnaz. "Women and Fundamentalism: The case of Turkey," in Valentine M. Moghadam (ed.), *Identity Politics and Women: Cultural Reassertions and Feminisms in International Perspective* (Boulder, CO: Westview, 1993), pp. 298–99.

Trud Nereid, Camilla. "Domesticating Modernity: The Turkish Magazine *Yedigün*, 1933–39," *Journal of Contemporary History*, Vol. 47, No. 3, 2012, pp. 483–504.

Ülger, S. Eriş. *Mustafa Kemal Atatürk I* (Ankara: Verlag Anadolu, 1994).

Veblen, Thorsten. *A Theory of the Leisure Class: An Economic Study of Institutions* (New York: Macmillan,1899).

von Kotzebue, Moritz. *Narrative of a Journey into Persia, in the Suite of the Imperial Russian Embassy, in the Year 1817* (1819).

Waring, Edward Scott. *A Tour to Sheeraz, by the Route of Kazroon and Feerozabad* (1807).

Weber, Charlotte. "Between Nationalism and Feminism: The Eastern Women's Congresses of 1930 and 1932," *Journal of Middle East Women's Studies*, Vol. 4, No. 1, Winter, 2008.

White, Luise. *Speaking with Vampires: Rumor and History in Colonial Africa* (Berkeley: University of California Press, 2000).

Wide, T.N.B. "Demarcating Pashto," in Nile Green and Nushin Arbabzadeh (eds.), *Afghanistan Into Ink* (London: Hurst, 2012).

——"Around the World in 29 Days: The Travels, Translations, and Temptations of an Afghan Dragoman" in Roberta Micallef and Sunil Sharma (eds.), *On the Wonders of Land and Sea* (London: Ilex, forthcoming).

Wild, Roland. "Amanullah's Fairy-Tale City," *Daily Mail* (28 September 1928).

Wills, Charles. *Persia as It Is* (1886).

Wilson, Francesca. *Muscovy: Russia Through Foreign Eyes 1553–1900* (London: Allen and Unwin, 1970).

Woodsmall, Ruth Frances. *Moslem Women Enter a New World* (New York: Round Table Press, Inc., 1936).

——*Women and the New East* (Washington, DC: The Middle East Institute, 1960).

Yeganeh, Nahid. "Women, Nationalism, and Islam in Contemporary Political Discourse in Iran," *Feminist Review*, Vol. 44, 1993, pp. 3–18.

278 *Bibliography*

Yılmaz, Hale. "Reform, Social Change and State-Society Encounters in Early Republican Turkey," unpublished PhD dissertation, The University of Utah, 2006.

Yohannan, Jacob Baba. *Woman in the Orient* (1901).

Zahedi, Ashraf. "Concealing and Revealing Female Hair: Veiling Dynamics in Contemporary Iran," in Jennifer Heath (ed.), *The Veil: Women Writers on Its History, Lore, and Politics* (Berkeley and Los Angeles: University of California Press, 2008), pp. 254–55.

Zia-Ebrahimi, Reza. "Self-Orientalization and Dislocation: The Uses and Abuses of the 'Aryan' Discourse in Iran," *Iranian Studies*, Vol. 44, No. 4, (June 2011).

Zilfi, Madeline C. *Women and Slavery in the Late Ottoman Empire* (Cambridge: Cambridge University Press, 2010).

Zürcher, Erik Jan. *Turkey: A Modern History* (London and New York: I. B. Tauris, 2004).

Index

Abduh, Muhammad 1, 238
Abdülhamid II 45
Abdülkadir Hoca 93
Abdur Rahman Khan, Amir of
  Afghanistan 166–69, 173, 174, 177,
  178, 187
Abortion 52
Activism 18–19, 20, 23, 25, 27, 30,
  40–41, 126, 151, 205–7, 212–15,
  216–23
Adatepe, Ülkü 49
Adib, Khalida 173
advertising 50, 53, 152–53, 156–58
Afet İnan, Ayşe 49
afetar 231
Ahvaz 126
Ajaria 222
Akbaba (magazine) 46–47
Akhunzadeh, Mirza Fath Ali 9
Akseki 76
al-Ayn, Qurrat 10
al-Khawatin, Seraj 166, 192
al-Lataif al-Musawara (newspaper) 181
al-Seraj, Okht 178
Alâiye 107
Alanya 73, 91, 98
Alap, Cevdet 76
Albanian Women's Association 235
Algeria 28–29
Ali, Syed Mujtaba 183, 187, 190
Amanullah Khan (King of Afghanistan,
  1919–29) 3, 13, 15, 19–20, 87–88, 163,
  165, 166, 173, 176–78, 180–83, 184–90
Amasya 92
American Girls' School (Tehran) 154
American Presbyterian Missions
  (Tehran) 150, 153
Ankara 47, 52, 53, 59–60, 62, 63–63, 67,
  69, 73–75, 77, 91, 97, 104

Antalya 61, 63, 67–70, 71, 73, 76, 97,
  98, 108
anti-clericalism 1, 10
Antifascist Women's Front of
  Bosnia-Herzegovina 21
Arak 127
Arambagh 169
Arat, Sakine 105
architecture 169
Arifiye 50
Armand, Inessa 18
Armenians 208, 213, 253
Armstrong, Harold 90
army 12, 14, 15, 22, 27, 46, 48, 88, 124,
  127, 131, 148, 154, 155, 163, 168, 170,
  174–75, 182, 184, 186, 190, 212
Art Institute of Weaving (Tehran)
  157
Artiukhina, Aleksandra 217
Arts Institute (Tehran) 157
Ashura 227
authenticity 8, 9, 14, 22, 28, 29
authoritarianism 3, 4, 16, 25–26, 61, 86,
  88, 110, 124, 125
Aydın 60, 63, 74, 92, 96, 100
Ayvalık 92

Babalık (newspaper) 76
Babism 10
Badakhshi, Makhfi 167
Bagh-e Babur 181
Baku 212, 214, 215, 219
Balıkesir 99
Balkan, Arif 91
Balkhi, Rabe'a 167
bans 1, 20; Albania 233–39, 241–46;
  Azerbaijan 218–19; Iran 110, 131,
  132, 135; Turkey 43, 54, 63, 66,
  68–69, 71–76, 92, 96, 97, 100, 104,

280 *Index*

105, 108; Uzbekistan 216–17, 221;
  see also legislation
Basra 151
Baştuğ, Türkân 71
beauty contests 24, 50–51, 54
beauty conventions 21, 24
Beg, Fuad 178
Bektashiyya 17, 231, 232, 237, 243
Benares 175
Berlin 239, 246
Beşe, Enver 92
Beyanülhak (journal) 241
Beyşehir 93
Binyazar, Adnan 98, 102
Bolshevik Revolution 212, 214
Bolshevism 210, 212, 214, 232, 243
Bolu 104
Bombay 151, 170, 171, 172, 174, 175
Bompas, Katherine 52
borqa' (burqu') 11, 20, 165, 176, 189
Borujerdi, Ayatollah Hossayn 135
Bukhara 175, 208, 209, 212
Bülbül, Nuriye 73
bureaucracy 22, 23, 27, 107, 108, 128,
  130, 256
Bursa 53, 63, 69, 95

Çakmak, Mustafa Fevzi 48
caliphate 14, 246
Çankırı 63, 70, 100
çarşaf 11, 20, 41–43, 46, 48, 50, 52, 54,
  59–77, 89, 90–92, 96–97, 100, 101,
  103–7, 108, 110, 135, 183
Caucasus 3, 7, 9, 13, 14, 16, 22, 23, 28,
  150, 206, 208, 212, 214, 215, 218,
  222
Central Asia 3, 4, 7, 9–16, 22, 23, 25,
  27, 28, 31, 175, 206, 208, 212, 213,
  215, 254
Central Asian Bureau (Communist
  Party) 215
ceremonies 20, 21, 22, 88, 124, 133,
  148, 153, 154, 155, 156, 168–71, 179,
  190
chachvon 11, 21, 24, 140, 208, 209, 214,
  222
chador (chadar, chadari) 11, 18, 19, 21,
  30, 112, 121–25, 129, 131, 132, 133,
  134, 135, 136, 138, 139, 146, 152, 153,
  165, 167, 176, 182, 186, 208, 214, 215,
  218–20, 222
Chamber of Commerce (Turkey) 70
Chernik 262
child labour 95–96

cinema 43, 99–100, 154, 178
citizenship 42, 51, 154
Civil and Military Gazette
  (Afghanistan) 187
Civil Code (Albania) 20, 233, 235, 237,
  241, 244
Civil Code (Turkey) 42, 46, 94
class 5, 6, 10–12, 15–17, 22–24, 28–29,
  31; Afghanistan 166, 168, 177–79,
  180–84, 190; Iran 122–23, 128, 129;
  Ottoman Empire 11; Soviet Union 27,
  205, 213, 221; Turkey 39–40, 46–47,
  48, 50, 54–55, 72, 88, 90, 99, 103, 107,
  109; Uzbekistan 208–9;
  see also elites, intelligentsia, wealth
clergy 1, 10; Albania 231, 232, 235,
  236, 238, 241, 243, 244; Iran 12,
  13, 17, 22, 23, 121, 125, 127, 128,
  135, 136; Soviet Union 27, 214,
  222; Turkey 15, 89, 93, 94;
  see also Islam, religion, secularism,
  ulama (ulema)
clothing, male 3, 5, 12–17, 19, 20, 24,
  25, 27, 31–32, 45, 46, 186–88, 190;
  see also hat
clubs 66, 74, 206, 213–15
coercion 1, 4, 54, 86, 133–34
Çolak, Ibrahim Bey 50
colonialism 6, 7, 11–12, 28, 29, 31, 42,
  176, 188, 205, 206, 208, 209, 210, 252,
  253, 254, 255
Commissariat of Enlightenment 219,
  222
Commissariat of Justice 218
Communist Party 16, 18, 23, 25, 27,
  205, 206, 207, 213, 215, 221;
  Azerbaijan 207, 213, 215, 218, 221,
  222, 223; Bulgaria 28, 258–60, 263;
  Turkey 99; Uzbekistan 206, 207,
  215–16, 221, 222, 223
conscription 15, 133
constitutionalism 10, 26, 28, 151, 152,
  153
consumerism 24, 39, 50, 53, 96, 149,
  151–52, 156, 157–58, 159, 164, 174,
  175, 183
controversy 1, 2, 4, 6, 12, 13, 17, 24, 28,
  59, 149, 155, 164, 169, 184
Çoruh 104
Çorum 70, 71, 96
courts 46, 68, 89, 103, 106, 207, 233,
  238, 239, 241, 242, 257
Cultural Revolution (Bulgaria) 28, 260,
  261, 262

Index 281

culture 2, 3, 6, 9, 11–16, 19–20, 22, 28–30; Turkey 40, 49, 53, 61, 66, 86, 89, 99, 100, 102, 109; Iran 149, 153–56, 158–59; Afghanistan 164–65, 169, 170, 173, 175, 177, 179–81, 183, 190, 191; Soviet Union 205–6, 208, 209, 220, 238; Albania 240, 242, 244, 246; 252–53; Bulgaria 257, 259–63; *see also* modernity, symbolism
Cumhuriyet (newspaper) 52, 53
Curzon, George Nathaniel (1st Marquess Curzon of Kedleston) 170

Dajti 249n40
Damascus 172
Darab, Mohammad 158
Daralaman 178, 179, 180
Dari 168
Darvish, Khanbaba Khan 158
Dehra Dun 170, 172
delegatka 213, 215
Delvina, Namik 236
Denizli 69, 105
Derviş, Suad 52, 54
Dibra, Hafiz Ismet 244, 245
discontent 19, 87, 96, 103, 106, 108, 109, 185
divorce 26, 210, 218, 220, 233, 242
Diyarbakır 63, 102
Dobrich 259
Dokumacı, Ahmet Şevki 74
Duma 210
Durrani, Ayesha 167
Durrës 234

economy 2–3, 5, 6, 12, 15, 19; Afghanistan 164–69, 174–78, 182, 183, 187, 190–91; Albania 232, 234, 235, 237, 240, 242, 244; Bulgaria 252, 259, 260; Turkey 42, 45, 55, 87, 89, 94, 95, 96, 99, 109; Iran 122, 149, 151, 153, 156, 158, 159; Soviet Union 205, 206
education 2–6, 8, 10, 14, 16–18, 19, 25, 30; Afghanistan 163, 167, 180, 182, 183, 186, 189; Albania 236, 238, 240, 242, 243, 244, 259; Iran 124, 126, 127–30, 131, 133, 152, 154–57; Soviet Union 207, 209–11, 215, 220, 221–23; Turkey 39–43, 46, 49, 52, 54, 94; *see also* schools
Efendieva, Shafiga 214
Egypt 6, 8, 10, 11, 18, 28, 29, 123, 142, 180, 181, 183, 184, 185, 206, 209, 246, 254

Elazığ 92, 104
Elbasan 234
elections 61, 92, 213, 259
elites 2, 3, 5–6, 9, 10–13, 15–17, 18, 21, 22, 25, 26–29, 31; Afghanistan 167, 168, 171, 173–74, 175, 180, 184, 190; Albania 231, 236, 246–47; Bulgaria 253, 255; Iran 122, 125, 151; Soviet Union 206, 214; Turkey 39–40, 42–45, 50, 53, 54, 59–60, 62, 63, 64, 66–67, 69–71, 72–73, 75–77, 86–88, 90, 99, 101–2, 109; *see also* class, intelligentsia, wealth
emancipation 1, 17, 18, 26, 40, 47, 49, 51, 61, 221, 223, 254
embassies 48, 75, 180
Enayatullah Khan (Afghanistan) 169, 170, 173, 179
enforcement 1, 2, 4, 15, 20, 23, 27, 41, 42, 45, 64, 68, 74, 124, 154, 166, 178, 189, 190, 216, 217, 235
equality 45, 89, 94, 209, 210, 213, 242, 254; *see also* marriage
Ershad al-Neswan (newspaper) 178, 181
Erzincan 63
Erzurum 104
Esenel, Mediha 98
Eskişehir 60, 98, 104
Estur Palace 186
Ethem Hoca 93
ethnicity 13, 14, 29, 31, 74, 122, 165, 176, 221
etiquette 21, 129, 155, 158, 170
Ettela'at (newspaper) 20, 125

Fanon, Frantz 28
fashion 3, 4, 11, 12, 13, 15, 16, 21, 24, 29; Afghanistan 165, 167–68, 170, 171, 172–74, 175, 178, 179, 180, 181, 182, 184, 190; Bulgaria 255, 262; Iran 123, 124, 146, 149–50, 151–52, 153–55, 156–59; Turkey 40, 46, 50, 52, 89, 90, 96, 101, 144
fatwas 121, 135, 234, 240, 241
February Revolution (1917) 210
Fehim, Münif 46
fereje 208, 233, 234, 236, 241, 257, 258, 259, 262, 263
fez 12, 14, 15–16, 17, 27, 32, 45, 46, 171, 172
film *see* cinema
fiqh (Islamic jurisprudence) 136, 239
Fiske Seminary 153
fitna (turmoil) 8, 211, 212

282   *Index*

foot binding 4, 31
footwear 48, 153, 157, 180
France 1, 2, 4, 7, 30, 150, 242, 246
Frashëri, Mehdi 17, 234, 237–38, 242,
  243, 244, 245
Free Officers (Egypt) 28

Gagauz 253
Garrus 127
Gaziantep 92, 99, 103, 106, 107
Gebze 99
gender relations 2, 6, 21, 41, 47, 69, 89,
  93, 94–95, 107, 109, 110, 178, 180
General Bureau of the Police (Iran)
  131
General Directorate of Security (Turkey)
  98
Geneva Congress of European Muslims
  (1935) 246
Georgia 208, 218, 222
Germany 246
Gholam 'Ali Khan 166
Giresun 99, 104
Gjirokastër 234, 236
Gökalp, Ziya 9, 44, 45
Gökçen, Sabiha 48, 49, 54
Golpaygan 127
Gowharshad Mosque 127
Grand National Assembly (Turkey) 48,
  105
Great Leap Forward (Bulgaria) 28, 261
Grew, Joseph 90
guidelines 69, 127, 129, 135

habara 11
Habibia College 170
Habibullah Khan (Amir of Afghanistan)
  163, 166, 169–74, 176–77, 178, 179,
  187, 188
Hadim 73
Hakkı, Tarık Us 65
Halis (Ece), Keriman 50–51
Hamidan 127
Hamilton, Angus 174
harassment 27, 67, 69, 95, 101, 190,
  223
haremseray 178
Haskovo 259, 261
hat 13–15, 16, 17, 19, 20, 42, 46, 48, 50,
  53, 54, 60, 72, 93, 104, 137, 155, 156,
  157, 171, 183, 185, 186, 187, 189;
  see also clothing, male
Hat Law (1925) Turkey 14, 19, 42, 60
  see also Uniform Dress Law Iran

headscarf 1, 4, 24, 46, 54, 59, 77, 90, 92,
  96, 105, 106, 107, 110, 123, 124, 134,
  135, 137, 165, 167, 176, 241
health 2, 6, 8, 17, 52, 55, 126, 129, 163,
  169, 177, 182, 211, 255
Herat 166
Herawi, Mahjuba 167, 171
High Council of the Sharia (Albania)
  239
Hikmat, Ali-Asghar 127, 132, 133, 134
Hindus 176
Hınıs 103
homogenization 12, 13, 17, 66, 154, 253,
  256, 259
honour 8, 17, 23, 31, 45, 52, 69, 182,
  237, 239, 245
hujum (attack) 14, 16, 18, 21, 23–28, 30,
  206, 215–18, 220, 221, 223
hygiene 24, 128, 263

identity 1, 2, 4, 5, 9, 11–13, 24, 28, 29,
  65, 93, 109, 231, 252, 253, 258
ideology 2, 5, 6, 8–9, 11, 16, 18, 19, 22,
  26, 27, 45, 51, 55, 87. 94, 95, 164, 165,
  172, 173, 174, 175, 176, 178, 178, 182,
  184, 242, 256, 259
Ikramov, Akmal 222
imports 9, 11, 150–51, 153, 158, 168,
  169–72, 174, 175, 179, 182–83, 187
Independence Day (Afghanistan) 179
Independence Tribunals (Turkey) 15
India 151, 165–72, 174, 175, 179, 180,
  181, 184, 187, 189, 190, 240, 245, 246
indoctrination 154, 156
industry 24, 94, 95, 149–51, 153,
  156–59, 166, 168, 170, 171, 174, 255
intelligentsia 5, 6, 16, 17, 208, 214, 215;
  see also class, elites
International Alliance of Women for
  Suffrage and Equal Citizenship (IAW)
  51
internationalism 171, 172, 175, 182, 183,
  184
Iraj Mirza 17
Isfahan 126, 151, 153, 157
Ishig (women's journal) 214
Ishkova, K 215, 218
Islam 1–4, 6, 7–11, 14, 16–17, 22–23,
  27–30, 32, 43, 44, 49, 86, 87, 88, 93,
  107, 109, 121, 123–27, 129–31,
  135–37, 149, 153, 183–86, 207, 210,
  214, 217, 220, 231–47, 252–64; *see
  also* clergy, religion, secularism
Islamic Association of Physicians 136

Islamic Community (Albania) 232–34, 236, 238–41, 243–46
Islamic Congress (Albania) 231, 233, 238
Islamic modernism 8, 27
Islamic Republic of Iran 1, 30, 121, 125–27, 136–37
Isparta 104
Istanbul 7, 10, 11, 39, 41, 46–47, 51–53, 60, 63, 91, 92, 93, 98, 100, 102, 104, 107, 150, 172, 180, 183, 209, 236
Italy 180, 234
Izmir 50, 69, 70, 76, 95, 97, 99, 102, 104, 144
Izmit 50

Jadidism 23, 27, 209–10, 222
Jalalabad 171, 190, 221
Jam, Mahmud 127
Janab, Olya 172
Jerusalem Congress 246
Jews 176, 208, 253
June Revolution (Albania) 233

Kabul 15, 165, 166, 168–73, 175–91
Kabuli, Gowhar 167
Kagan 208
Kalakani, Habibullah 163, 187
Kalmyks 221
Kanibadom 221
Karachi 172, 175
Kashani, Ayatollah Abol-Ghasem 135
kashf-i hijab 20, 21, 121, 123–36,
Kastamonu 69, 100
Kateb, Fayz Mohammad 170
Kavajë 234–35
Kaya, Şükrü 43, 45, 51, 65, 108
Kayseri 90, 95, 107
Kazakhs 208, 209–10, 221
Kazan 208–10
Këlcyra, Ali 236–37
Kemal, Kâmil 73
Kemal, Mustafa (Atatürk) 13, 14, 26, 39, 41–52, 63, 74, 88, 96, 104, 122, 223, 135, 177, 186, 206, 237, 238, 245, 254, 257
Kemalism 24, 28, 257
Kerim-ogly, Mir Mamed 214
Kerman 126, 151, 153
Kirmani, Mirza Aqa Khan 9
Khan-i Khanan 151
Khanom Jan 166
Khiva 208, 212
Khojayev, Fayzulla 222

Khorasan 130, 151
Khost 184
Khouri, Hanifa 181
Khujand 221
Khunsari, Ayatollah Mohammad-Taqi 135
Kirdjali 262
Kirmanshah 22
Kılıç, Ali 101
Kırklareli 71, 104
Koç, Mustafa 46
Kolarovgrad 260
Kommunistka (women's journal) 206, 218
Komsomol (Communist Youth League) 21, 216, 217, 220
Konya 67, 70, 73–74, 75, 76, 98, 103, 104
Korkuteli 98
kuchi 176
Kurds 15, 48, 122
Kütahya 92

Lab-e Darya 180
Ladies' Center (kanun-i banuvan) 25, 126–27, 132
Lahore 172, 240, 241, 246
Lahori Ahmadiyya 239, 240, 241, 246 247
land reform 217
Learning Institute for Dyeing (Tehran) 157
legislation 12, 13, 15, 16, 19, 20, 23, 49, 65, 88, 121, 123–24, 125, 127, 135, 238, 242; see also bans
legitimacy 8, 22, 27, 40–42, 49, 55, 86, 110, 243
Linke, Lilo 91
literacy 6, 42, 133, 167, 188, 213, 258, 259
London 48, 51, 169, 246
luxury 24, 171, 239, 245

madrasas 232, 233, 238, 239, 241, 244
magazines 10, 43, 44–45, 46, 53, 181
Majlis (Iran) 15, 20, 127
Maktab-e Masturat 178
Malatya 104
Malayir 127
Malcolm, Sir John 149–50
Manisa 100
manto 40, 50, 54
Maraş 72, 73, 96, 104
Mardin 104
Marriage Law (Iran, 1931) 125

284   *Index*

marriage 2, 18, 31, 41, 46, 125, 152, 157, 163, 210, 212, 215, 217, 221, 233; *see also* equality
Mashhad 15, 126, 127, 133, 134, 185
media 7, 39, 43, 45, 49, 54, 157
medicine 17, 46, 155
Menderes, Adnan 71, 98
Mersin 71, 73, 91, 93, 103, 104
Ministry of Education (Iran) 124, 126–30, 132
Ministry of Interior (Iran) 126, 127, 133, 135
Ministry of Interior (Turkey) 59, 60, 68, 69, 74
Ministry of Justice (Albania) 233
Ministry of Justice (Turkey) 102
minorities 9, 16, 18, 27, 30, 41, 102, 231, 254, 259, 263, 264
mobilization 1, 3, 14, 17, 20–22, 25, 27, 29, 30, 62, 63, 67, 69, 70, 74, 99, 100, 223, 259
modernism 2–13, 15, 16, 17, 22, 23, 24, 25, 27, 28, 30–31, 44, 65, 125, 164, 254
modernity 3, 13–14, 16, 20, 29, 30, 41, 42, 51, 53, 54, 77, 87, 109, 130, 149, 151–52, 159, 171, 172, 222, 246, 254, 255, 258; *see also* culture, symbolism
Mohammed Alim Khan (Amir of Bukhara) 200n199
mosques 46–47, 93, 104, 127, 184, 232, 239, 243, 244, 262
Motahhari, Ayatollah Mortiza 136
Mouamer Hanoum 48
Movement for Rights and Freedoms (MRF) 263
Muğla 60, 61, 64, 104
Mujahidin-i Khalq 30
Mulla Nasr-al-Din (journal) 10
Municipal Law (Turkey, 1930) 62
mursak 12
Muslim Confessional Organization (Smolyan) 258
Muslim Women's Association 210
Mussolini, Benito 185

Namayeshat-e Erfani 178
Nasrullah Khan (Afghanistan) 166, 169
National Security Service (Turkey) 104
nationalism 2–4, 8–9, 13–17, 22, 26–29, 42, 43, 49, 86–87, 126, 175, 182–84, 212, 232, 258, 263
nationalization 29, 231, 246
nationhood 41, 44, 45
New York Times 47, 48

newspapers 7, 10, 20–21, 22, 24; Afghanistan 171–73, 178, 181–83, 185, 188, 189; Albania 233–34, 236–37, 239, 241; Bulgaria 263; Iran 125, 152–53, 155–56; Soviet Union 206–7, 209, 213–14, 218, 220–21; Turkey 43, 44, 47–49, 51–53, 55, 60–63, 66, 67, 69–71, 74, 76, 88, 90, 92, 95–97, 100, 107
niqab 1, 2, 4, 11, 123, 132–33
Nishapur 130
Nives, Donna 180
No'mani, Shebli 172
Noli, Fan 233

officials 6, 12, 14, 22, 28, 39–41, 43, 45, 49, 65, 66, 67, 68–71, 76, 100, 104, 124, 128–31, 133–35, 154, 168, 186, 188, 233, 235, 237, 243, 257, 258
Okhunboboyev, Yoldash 222
opposition 2–4, 7–9, 15, 23, 25, 29, 30, 62, 64, 71–74, 92, 94, 99, 135, 156, 163, 165, 176, 184, 187, 191, 219, 234, 236, 241, 244, 245, 250
Ordu 68, 92, 104, 105, 107
Orekhalashvili, Mamia 222
Örrik, Nahid Sırrı 107
Osh 221
Otechestven Front (Fatherland Front) 259
Ottoman Empire 7, 9, 11, 13–16, 27, 39–49, 52, 53, 59, 61, 93, 152, 164, 171, 172, 174, 207, 208, 212, 231, 232, 236, 243, 254–57
overcoats 54, 63, 70–72, 77, 96–97, 103, 105–7, 135–36, 189

Paghman 171, 178, 183, 186–89
Pahlavi cap 15, 20, 155–56
Pahlavi, Muhammad Reza Shah 131
Pahlavi, Reza Shah 3, 13, 15, 19–21, 25, 26, 86–88, 93, 110, 121–27, 131–33, 135–37, 186
Pahlavi, Shams 126
Pakistan 97
Palestine 29
paranji / parandja 11, 22, 23, 24, 140, 208–9, 213–18, 220–22, 255
Paris 158, 179, 185, 244
Pashto 167
patriarchy 4, 14, 18, 28, 30, 94, 97, 206, 255
peçe / picheh 11, 20, 40–44, 46–48, 50, 52, 54, 59, 60, 61, 62–77, 123, 124, 125

Pekolcay, Necla 107
Peshawar 171, 175
peştamal 60, 63, 68, 70, 74
photography 20, 40, 48, 50, 52, 124, 167, 171–73, 179–81, 188, 240
piety 4, 8, 30, 93, 97, 211, 252
pirahan-tomban 182, 190
poetry 17, 24, 129, 167, 171, 172, 181
police 19, 23, 31, 43, 60, 62, 64–65, 68–69, 74, 75, 88–90, 92, 96, 98, 100–109, 127–28, 130–31, 133–34, 154–55, 165, 187, 188, 233–35
polygamy 94, 163, 171, 189, 237, 241
polygyny 2, 12, 209, 220
Pomaks 15–16, 253–60
Principles of Turkism 44
professionals 43, 53, 66, 176, 179, 213
propaganda 4, 20–21, 23–24, 42–43, 60, 62–68, 73, 74, 76, 86, 108, 132, 221, 233, 234, 261
prostitution 52, 69, 93, 95, 98, 99, 128
protest 86–87, 89, 101, 126–27, 156, 165, 183, 237, 261, 262
protocol 136, 170
psychological effects 5, 6, 12, 25, 29, 87, 89, 106, 109
public opinion 20, 24, 27, 102, 105, 132, 240
purdah 165, 172, 176, 178–80, 188–89

Qadiriyya 232
Qandahar 181, 186
Qasim Amin 6, 10, 123
Qom 125, 127, 134
Qulanqi, Qayum 209
Qur'an 8, 93, 209–10, 211, 239, 240, 244, 247, 262

radio 43, 45, 53
Rahmatullah Khan 181
Rasht 134, 153
Rasmiya, Asma 173, 178
Razgrad 260, 261, 262
Red Army 212
Red Crescent 70
religion 1, 3, 8, 12–16, 22–23; Afghanistan 32, 166, 176, 177, 183, 184, 185, 191; Albania 231–47; Iran 9, 122, 123, 131, 133, 149, 153, 156; Soviet Union 27, 207, 211, 216–17, 219; Turkey 14, 15, 42, 44, 47, 59, 72–73, 74, 75, 86–87, 88, 89, 92–93, 99–100, 106, 109; *see also* clergy, Islam, secularism

Republic Day (Turkey) 71
Republican People's Party (RPP, Turkey) 42, 43, 50, 59, 88
resistance 13, 16, 26, 28, 30, 31, 64, 76, 86–89, 92–93, 96, 101, 102–4, 105, 108, 109, 135, 164, 177, 189, 217, 221, 234, 253, 254, 259, 262, 264
Rida, Rashid 185
Rifaiyya 232
rights, political 19, 39–40, 52, 61–62, 64, 183, 184, 186, 212
Rize 60, 63
Rıfkı Atay, Falih 43, 54
Rodina 257, 258
ruband / *rubandeh* 11, 122, 123, 132, 185
rumours 15, 39, 54, 63, 74, 102–4, 188–89
Russia 7, 12, 13, 18, 28, 104, 150, 151, 153, 174, 175, 190, 205–15, 222, 223, 252–53, 254, 256
Russification 216, 222

Sadiyya 232
Safranbolu 63, 92
Sakariya 50
Samarkand 172, 209
Sami, Mahmud 170
Samsun 91
Sanandaj 127
sarık 43
Sart 209, 210
Saudi Arabia 4
Saydam, Refik 108
Schain, Josephine 53
schools 17, 19; Afghanistan 172, 173, 178, 179, 180, 181, 182, 185; Albania 232, 236, 243, 245; Iran 124, 127–30, 132–33, 146, 152, 154, 155, 156, 157, 158; Turkey 43–45, 49–50, 98, 104; Soviet Union 210, 212–16, 218–19, 222; *see also* education
scouts 46, 48, 131, 155
Sebilürreşad (journal) 241
seclusion 1–2, 5, 6, 10, 12, 17, 22, 23, 30, 31, 44, 75, 97, 99, 165, 168, 179, 180, 205, 208–13, 219, 236, 253
Second Eastern Women's Congress 125
secularism 1–3, 9, 13–16, 22, 27, 29, 30, 39, 43, 59, 86–88, 92–94, 99, 101–3, 109, 110, 122, 136, 149, 154, 184, 191, 231, 235–36, 237, 240, 242–47, 263; *see also* clergy, Islam, religion
Seferhisar 50
Serik 98

286   *Index*

Şevki, Ahmet 74, 96
sewing 70, 96, 150–52, 154, 156–57, 158, 172, 175, 261, 262
sexuality 17, 18, 31, 93–95, 97, 99, 109, 136
Seyhan 104
Shakhtakhtinskaia, Adilia 214
Shapati, Behxhet 233, 234, 239
shari'a 8, 41, 121, 123, 125, 130, 134, 135, 210, 211, 233, 238, 239, 241, 242, 244
Sha'rawi, Huda 18, 21
Sherkat-e Semin 181
Shərq Qadını 214
Shiraz 126
Shkodër 232, 234–35, 244
Shoppes 262
Shpuza, Selim 236
Shymkent 221
Sinop 66, 92
Siraj al-akhbar (newspaper) 173
Sivas 64, 91, 101, 105
sıkmabaş 107
Smolyan 257–58
socialism 213, 217, 232, 253, 259, 260, 263
Soviet Union 3, 13, 14, 16, 18, 20–28, 31, 205–7, 209, 213, 215, 220, 221, 223, 253–55, 258
sport 17, 49, 50, 66, 74, 99, 126, 133, 157, 170, 179, 239
Sufism 17, 232; see also individual brotherhoods
Sultanova, Ayna 214, 219
Sunnism 17, 136, 231, 237, 243
Suyum Bike (journal) 209–11
symbolism 164, backwardness 2, 5, 14,16, 70, 186; modernity 16, 40–41, 48, 49, 50, 51, 53, 54, 62, 89, 131, 185, 186, 190, 221, 234, 242, 254; revolution 21; segregation 10, 61, 167; religion 12, 13, 93, 97, 106, 253; class 24; resistance 28, 29, 101, 107, 187, 188, 191, 223, 264; tradition 30; *see also* culture, modernity
Syria 30, 173, 185, 189

Tabriz 126
Tagiyev, Zaynalabdin 214
Tahrir al-Mar'a (The Liberation of Women) 6
tailoring 70, 96, 150, 154, 156–58, 168, 171–72, 174, 175

Taliban 1, 30, 32, 163
Tan (newspaper) 53
Tanzimat 88
Tarbiyat, Hajar 133
Tarsus 91
Tarzi, Khayriya 173, 178
Tarzi, Mahmud 172–74, 178, 180
Tarzi, Soraya (Queen of Afghanistan) 18, 20, 173, 178, 180–82, 185–86, 189, 191
Tashkent 19, 20, 208, 209, 212, 215
Tatars 7, 10, 207–8, 209, 210, 211, 221, 254
Teachers' Training Colleges 21, 126, 133, 170
Tehran 10, 15, 19, 21, 122, 123, 126, 127, 133, 153, 154, 155, 157, 172
textiles 91, 94–96, 149, 153, 156, 157, 166, 175 183
The Times (of London) 48, 51
Tijaniyya 232
Tirana 234, 238, 239, 244
Tosya 69, 100
tourism 180, 237, 240
Trabzon 60, 61, 67, 70, 74, 75, 76, 93, 104
trade 89, 96, 149, 151, 168, 170, 174, 175, 184, 185, 239
transport 100, 169, 171, 174, 175, 179–80, 184
tribes 15, 30, 122–23, 150, 164, 166, 177, 188, 189, 191
Tulu'-e Afghan 181
Tunisia 1, 30
turban 16, 45, 46, 49, 50, 93, 150, 175, 176, 182, 184, 189, 190, 222, 238
Turkestan 11, 12, 21, 208, 209, 210, 212
Turkish Hearth (Türk Ocağı) 60
Turkish Village Publications 46
Turkistan (city) 221
Türkoğlu, Pakize 91, 98

ulama (ulema) 13, 23, 27, 183
Ulus (newspaper) 43, 53
umbrellas 24, 63, 72, 91, 92, 106, 107
unemployment 94, 95, 232
Uniform Dress Law Iran 15
uniforms 14, 48, 50, 97, 129, 134, 154, 168, 170, 174–75, 178
Urfa 92
Urumieh 126, 153
Uşşaki, Latife 50

Uzbekistan 26, 28, 205–6, 212, 213, 214, 215–18, 220–23
Uzer, Tahsin 75

Van 104
Vaqayi' Ittifaqiyah (magazine) 152
Varna 261
Vatan (factory) 157
Vienna 246
violence 4, 23, 25, 26, 28, 75, 121, 134, 215, 217, 220, 223, 252
Vlachs 253
Vlorë 241
Vrioni, Ilyas 244

wealth 5, 12, 47, 72, 91, 97, 102, 150, 175, 176, 178, 209, 214, 217, 221, 232; *see also* class, elites
westernization 15, 42, 47, 124, 164, 191, 234, 236, 245, 254
Westoxication 24, 30
Woodsmall, Ruth 39, 41, 50
workforce 3, 55, 94, 95, 218, 219
workplace 39, 40, 44
World War I 2, 13, 17, 94, 256
World War II 16, 27, 258

xhari 235
Xhelo, Halim 236

yashmak 11, 144, 208, 221
Yazdi, Ayatollah Abdolkarim Ha'eri 127
Yedigün (magazine) 44, 45, 53
Yeni Isik (newspaper) 262
Yeni Mersin (newapaper) 71
Yeniköy 91
Yesari, Mahmut 45
Young Women's Christian Association (Turkey) 39
Yozgat 93, 104

Zayandeh Rud (factory) 157
Zekeriya Sertel, Sabiha 54
Zëmblaku, Hafiz Abdullah 241, 243, 244, 245
Zhenotdel (Communist Party Women's Division) 18, 21, 25, 27, 206, 254, 255, 259, 261
Zile 102
Zlatovgrad 262
Zog I 235
Zonguldak 62

CPSIA information can be obtained
at www.ICGtesting.com
Printed in the USA
BVHW04*1808130418
513253BV00006B/78/P